ARTIFICIAL INTELLIGENCE LAW AND REGULATION

IN A NUTSHELL®

JON M. GARON
Professor of Law
Director, Goodwin Program for Society, Technology, and the Law
Nova Southeastern University
Shepard Broad College of Law

WEST ACADEMIC

Published in the United States of America

ISBN: 979-8-89209-315-6

For my family—
Stacy Blumberg Garon
Avery Garon
Noah Garon
Alec Sasha Garon ז"ל

PREFACE

> I propose to consider the question, "Can machines think?"
>
> —Alan Turing[1]
>
> [I]t is too hard to define "thinking," as it takes one down the path of trying to understand consciousness and intuition and intelligence and what it means to be human.
>
> —Robert Hummel[2]

In 1948, nearly a decade before U.S. scientists convened at Princeton University to begin work on what became artificial intelligence (AI), noted British scientist Alan Turing posed a fundamental question whether computers could one day think, and whether humans would be able to distinguish the thought processes of these neural networks from those of human minds.[3] Though his original report was published only posthumously, it reflected some of the

---

1 Alan Turing, *Computing Machinery and Intelligence*, 59 MIND 435 (1950); *See* Stephen Muggleton, *Alan Turing and the Development of Artificial Intelligence*, 27 AI COMMUNICATIONS 3 (2014), https://content.iospress.com/articles/ai-communications/aic579.

2 Robert Hummel, *Can Humans Think?*, 5 SCI., TECH., ENG. & POL'Y ST. 36 (2021), https://www.potomacinstitute.org/steps/index.php/issues/september-2021/can-humans-think.

3 *See Alan Turing's Contributions to Artificial Intelligence*, HISTORY OF INFORMATION, https://www.historyofinformation.com/detail.php?id=4289.

most forward-looking ideas about the future we live in today.

The release of OpenAI's ChatGPT in November 2022 captured and illustrated many of the key principles that Turing explored nearly 75 years earlier. Although rudimentary, the ability to engage in text-based conversation with a computer that could understand user questions and provide seemingly accurate responses to almost any question triggered a transformation in computing and finance. Investors flocked to opportunities to invest in AI projects. Companies across almost all sectors of the economy began announcing new AI tools to improve efficiency, streamline operations, and create new possibilities.

The field of synthetic media, which had been growing since the introduction of deepfakes in 2017, was supercharged with the addition of image, voice, music, and even video generation capabilities made possible by rapidly evolving technologies.

At the same time, as OpenAI and its competitors captured the public's imagination, other AI systems were also growing rapidly. Predictive AI algorithms had already become common tools, being used for credit card fraud detection, medical x-ray interpretation, diagnostic data analysis, automated resume reviews, credit scoring, and a nearly unlimited range of similar uses.

During this period, automobile manufacturers continued to expand their offerings for self-parking and semi-autonomous vehicles. Companies began limited tests for self-driving vehicles, including robotaxi fleets. With each test and update, the technology improved, enabling machines to operate with less human supervision and control. This transformation is also occurring with autonomous machines used in manufacturing, warehousing, and even with military drones and weaponry. Society has entered the age of autonomous machines.

Despite this, we have not yet entered the age of automated lawyering. Many bar associations have issued guidance on the appropriate, but limited role that AI systems can play in the practice of law. These systems are helpful in assisting law firms with marketing, document analysis, e-discovery review, and many other tasks. However, given concerns about the accuracy of generative AI output and the critical role of a lawyer's independent ethical judgment in structuring arguments presented to a court, bar associations have raised concerns about the role generative AI should play in drafting legal memoranda.

Against the backdrop of rapid developments across all sectors of the economy, it should not be surprising that legislative bodies around the world are engaged in studies and drafting new legislation regarding the implementation of AI systems. The first such comprehensive law has been promulgated by the European Union. In the U.S., hundreds of bills have been proposed at both the federal and state levels. President Biden issued a sweeping executive order requiring more than fifty government agencies to take action to address how the federal government uses AI and how regulated industries address the opportunities and risks posed by the significant changes created by this transformative set of technology. Although President Trump repealed that executive order, he also issued an executive order of his own to promote AI competitiveness and U.S. leadership in the information-age arms race we now find ourselves to be waging.

For many, AI has reached a turning point, similar to when the steam engine was adopted for locomotion, the automobile began to replace the horse, or the internet opened for commercialization. In each of these eras, the true impact of the technology could only be measured in hindsight, but the economy that existed a decade later was significantly different from what it had been before. Not only the economy, but also the daily lives of people—at work and at leisure—were transformed by these technologies. Whether these analogies overstate the importance of AI will only be known in hindsight, but the potential for such dramatic change is certainly present.

The materials are intended for readers who may not be familiar with AI or the particular legal issues involved. Few students or attorneys will be familiar with all the specific areas of law relevant to the field. As a Nutshell, the book is intended to serve as a supplement for law students and a primer for practitioners interested in the topic.

This Nutshell is organized to explore the facts, legal issues, and basic knowledge needed to understand the law and regulation of AI. Part I provides a general overview of AI and the legal landscape governing AI systems, including a discussion on the history of artificial intelligence ("AI") in culture and in technical development; a nontechnical set of explanations as to the AI models and AI outputs; and an exploration of the competing regulatory frameworks from governments and standard-setting national agencies.

Although the literature on AI tends to either favor or oppose the technology, the tone of the Nutshell attempts to be neutral. By highlighting use cases in healthcare, product design, robotics, autonomous vehicles, and the legal profession, the book demonstrates the significant social benefits available from AI. At the same time, it illustrates concerns about workforce disruption, the digital divide and economic inequality, algorithmic discrimination and bias, and the misuse of AI systems that could result in disinformation, bullying, harassment, and market manipulation.

After exploring the nature of AI technology and its uses, the focus shifts to the current regulatory efforts at the state, federal, and international level.

Part II delves into specific applications of U.S. Law to AI practices, explaining the intersection between AI and existing legal fields, including equal protection, state privacy biometric laws, Fourth Amendment jurisprudence, defamation; copyright, publicity rights, trademark, products liability, contracts, law of armed conflict, and sectoral regulation.

The Nutshell also provides a non-technical overview of the key terms and system components involved in AI science and deployment. Lawyers must understand how regulators define and describe these technologies. Failure to include or exclude certain systems can have unintended consequences, so familiarity with the technologies is crucial. Similarly, when drafting contracts, lawyers must include licensing provisions that align with the actual process of the systems being licensed. So, at the risk of offering too much information, a few building blocks of AI systems are provided to guide the explanations.

In addition to the focus on specific legal fields, chapters also explore how business organizations should develop AI strategies, whether those companies are building new AI models (AI developers) or licensing and using models created by others (AI deployers). The final chapter of the Nutshell does double duty, providing a summary of the book using a slightly different framework while offering a primer that readers may choose to explore before delving into the rest of the text. Readers are encouraged to take advantage of the conclusion. The reader is given permission to reproduce Chapter 9 as a useful summary of the topic.[4]

---

[4] Permission is hereby granted to reproduce Chapter 9 of this work on condition that the chapter is reproduced only for non-commercial academic purposes and that such reproduction includes the full attribution of author, title, and publisher: JON M. GARON, ARTIFICIAL INTELLIGENCE LAW AND REGULATION IN A NUTSHELL (West Academic 2025). As a request, but not a condition of reproduction, please inform Professor Garon when the work is

In developing this Nutshell, I have expanded on earlier articles I have previously published on the topic, including, Jon M. Garon, *Prometheus' Digital Fire: The Civic Responsibilities of Artificial Intelligence*, 20 OHIO STATE TECH. L. J. 225 (2024); Jon M. Garon, *The Revolution will be Digitized: Generative AI, Synthetic Media, and the Medium of Disruption*, 20 OHIO STATE TECH. L. J. 139 (2024); Jon M. Garon, *Jon M. Garon, Regulation by the EEOC and the States Take on Algorithmic Bias in High-Risk Use Cases*, 80 BUS. L. 261 (2025), and Jon M. Garon, *An AI's Picture Paints a Thousand Lies: Designating Responsibility for Visual Libel*, 3 UCLA J. FREE SPEECH L. 425 (2023). For this Nutshell, where I paraphrase or quote my own materials from my listed prior works, I do not separately provide attribution to those articles. Instead, I only cite the sources provided within those works.

Finally, a note on footnote citations. Where I indicate a prior footnote using "*supra*" within a chapter, I provide only the footnote number of the full citation. In instances where the full citation is in

---

reproduced for any bar association or other non-classroom use at Garon@nova.edu.

another chapter, however, I provide the chapter number as well as the footnote number.

JON M. GARON
PROFESSOR OF LAW
ASSOCIATE DEAN FOR ADMINISTRATION AND NON-JD PROGRAMS
DIRECTOR, GOODWIN PROGRAM FOR SOCIETY, TECHNOLOGY, AND THE LAW
NOVA SOUTHEASTERN UNIVERSITY
SHEPARD BROAD COLLEGE OF LAW

ACKNOWLEDGMENTS

Writing a book of any length takes time, and I have been working on this manuscript and some of its predecessor articles for a few years. Unlike other subjects, the rapidity of change in the law and practice of AI has meant that in many ways this is already the second edition of this work. I have tried to update the materials to reflect the state of technology as of the time I wrote the book but undoubtedly, many changes have occurred even during the editing process. Please forgive any references to earlier versions of the technologies, to the names of services that have already been changed, and to the characterizations of some AI systems as experimental when they have hit the market faster than the manuscript became a book.

Finally, I would like to thank those in the village who helped me make this project possible. Let me start with the leadership at NSU Law for their institutional, and financial support of my various research projects, and the leadership team at NSU Law, including Olympia Duhart, Professor of Law and Associate Dean for Academic Affairs & Faculty Development; Elena Marty-Nelson, (previous) Associate Dean for Academic Affairs and Professor of Law; Debra Moss Vollweiler, (Previous) Associate Dean for Academic Affairs and Professor of Law; Vicenç Feliú, Associate Dean for Library Services & Professor of Law, and Dr. Cheryl L. Booth, Associate Director of Research and Reference. I am deeply grateful for the extensive support I have received in my many roles at NSU and each of the associate deans. I am also very appreciative of my research assistants who assisted with my law review articles and books: Shannon Taub, Shelly Klein, Jonathan Fernandez, Jake Pfundstein, and Carla Pompa. Any responsibility for the content of this work, of course, is entirely my own.

Finally, I would like to recognize the team at West Academic who provided me with the opportunity to publish this work and other titles. The support of Jon Harkness, Pam Siege Chandler, Sam Farkas, and others has been inspiring, and the support makes projects like this possible.

Thank you all!

OUTLINE

PART II. SPECIFIC APPLICATIONS OF U.S. LAW TO AI PRACTICES

TABLE OF CASES

References are to Pages

ARTIFICIAL INTELLIGENCE LAW AND REGULATION

IN A NUTSHELL®

PART I

GENERAL OVERVIEW OF AI AND THE LEGAL LANDSCAPE GOVERNING AI SYSTEMS

Part I of the Nutshell provides background information and context to explain the development, technology, and regulatory context for artificial intelligence. Although for much of the public, interest in AI only began with the launch generative AI (GenAI or GAI) from OpenAI's ChatGPT on November 30, 2022,[1] AI technologies had been under development for decades.[2] Expert systems, machine learning, and other technologies using logic and reasoning have been incorporated into products and services since an earlier wave of autonomous system designs in the 1980s. These systems have been subject to general laws governing the use of information, but they had not been singled out over their predictive potential.

GenAI changed the public perception of AI. With the growing use of autonomous technologies, AI's role

---

1 Kristi Hines, *History of ChatGPT: A Timeline Of The Meteoric Rise Of Generative AI Chatbots*, SEARCH ENGINE J. (June 4, 2023), https://www.searchenginejournal.com/history-of-chatgpt-timeline/488370/.

2 *See* Jorgen Veisdal, *The Birthplace of AI, The 1956 Dartmouth Workshop*, CANTOR'S PARADISE (Sept. 12, 2019), https://www.cantorsparadise.com/the-birthplace-of-ai-9ab7d4e 5fb00.

in society has evolved. In response to these changes, the regulation of AI has also begun to shift.

To provide context for this transformation, Chapters 1 and 2 provide a brief history of AI development and an overview of the technologies that are regularly used in AI systems. Chapter 3 then offers an overview of the regulatory approach that has been taken with earlier waves of AI development at the state, national, and international levels.

CHAPTER 1

INTRODUCTION TO ARTIFICIAL INTELLIGENCE

Long before AI appeared in mainframe computers or offered insights through the use of input on punch cards, artisans, writers, and filmmakers explored the potential for self-aware machines and the consequences to humanity. Golems and mythical creations have long been part of literary tradition, but robots and androids stand apart.

§ 1.1 ARTIFICIAL INTELLIGENCE AND ROBOTICS IN LITERATURE

In 1920, with his play, R.U.R., Czech playwright Karel Čapek repurposed the word Robot from "forced worker" to explore the existential difference between man and machine. In the play, the inventor of the robot explained his vision of the future:

> [W]ithin the next 10 years Rossum's Universal Robots will produce so much wheat, so much cloth, so much everything that things will no longer have any value. Everyone will be able to take as much as he needs. There will be no more poverty. Yes, people will be out of work, but by then there'll be no work left to be done. Everything will be done by living machines. People will only do what they enjoy. They will live only to perfect themselves.[1]

---

1 KAREL ČAPEK, R.U.R. ROSSUM'S UNIVERSAL ROBOTS 21 (1920).

This vision of the future offers an idealized communist utopia. Property has no value because it is free and plentiful. Labor has no value because it has been replaced by machines. As a result, all people become equal and free, able to pursue only higher goals. Even in the play, however, it did not work out quite this way. The robots eventually killed almost all of the humans, which in turn threatened their own extermination because they could not reproduce. On the eve of destruction, two robots named Adam and Eve fell in love and learned to reproduce through procreation.[2] This bleak version of our robotic future was later modernized and personified in the guise of James Cameron's *The Terminator,* as embodied by Arnold Schwarzenegger.

Science fiction literature has many examples of the "singularity." "[T]he AI singularity refers to an event where the AIs in our lives either become self aware, or reach an ability for continuous improvement so powerful that it will evolve beyond our control."[3] For some, the singularity is the moment where systems develop general artificial intelligence (or Artificial General Intelligence). For others, the point of the singularity is the point where the machines not only obtain knowledge and self-improvement capabilities

---

[2] *See id.*

[3] Nisha Talagala, *Don't Worry About The AI Singularity: The Tipping Point Is Already Here,* FORBES (June 21, 2021), https://www.forbes.com/sites/nishatalagala/2021/06/21/dont-worry-about-the-ai-singularity-the-tipping-point-is-already-here/?sh=6f3cb8991cd4.

beyond that of humans, but also the moment when they deem humanity unnecessary or irrelevant.

In the tropes of science fiction, the singularity was a threat that had to be countered to permit the existence of robots. Isaac Asimov resolved this threat by introducing the *Three Laws of Robotics* in his short story, *Runaround*.[4] Without these rules protecting humans and humanity, science fiction literature could not get past the existential threat posed by robots.

In 1977, in *Star Wars*, George Lucas created the modern embodiment of artificial intelligence with his depiction of R2-D2 and C-3PO, machines that could communicate, answer questions, read emotional signals, understand context, and read the modalities of body language, voice inflection, and nonverbal communication. "[I]is there a possibility for a real C-3PO any time soon? 'Honestly, we're generations away from doing that,' IBM Fellow Grady Booch said. "But what we're doing today is taking artificial

---

4 *See Golden Age of Science Fiction*, WIKIPEDIA, https://en.wikipedia.org/wiki/Golden_Age_of_Science_Fiction (last visited Feb. 16, 2025). Encyclopedia Brittanica provides this summary:

> "(1) a robot may not injure a human being or, through inaction, allow a human being to come to harm; (2) a robot must obey the orders given it by human beings except where such orders would conflict with the First Law; (3) a robot must protect its own existence as long as such protection does not conflict with the First or Second Law." Asimov later added another rule, known as the fourth or zeroth law, that superseded the others. It stated that "a robot may not harm humanity, or, by inaction, allow humanity to come to harm."

Three laws of robotics, ENCY. BRITANNICA (May 13,2024), https://www.britannica.com/topic/Three-Laws-of-Robotics.

intelligence and helping it collaborate with humans, and more importantly, augment human intelligence.' "[5] *Star Trek* explored these issues with the character Data, but avoided the larger socio-economic considerations by limiting the number of androids to a very small number all created by the same scientist.[6]

Even before the depiction of self-aware robots in film and literature, "elaborate mechanical inventions" were creating music and stories.[7] "John Clark's The Eureka (1845) . . . could produce Latin verses with a pull of a lever. . . . Because of the strict rules of Latin hexameter, this wooden machine was capable of flawlessly randomizing words and arranging them in the plausible output."[8] Other examples of automatons date back millennia. Contemporaries of Plato crafted wooden pigeons that moved using compressed air, and Heron of Alexandria (1st century C.E.) "described devices

---

[5] Amy Onorato, *What Star Wars' C-3PO Can Teach Us About The Future Of AI*, DIGITAL MARKETING NEWS (Jan. 2, 2018), https://www.dmnews.com/what-star-wars-c3po-can-teach-us-about-the-future-of-ai/.

[6] *See* Robert Vaux, *Does Star Trek's Data Come from a Family of Monsters?*, CBR (Dec. 5, 2023), https://www.cbr.com/star-trek-the-next-generation-data-soong-family/; Derek Faraci, *Star Trek: 10 Things People Forget About Data*, CBR (Mar. 30, 2020), https://www.cbr.com/star-trek-data-forgotten-facts/.

[7] Vladimir Todorović, *Wandering Machines, Narrativity in Generative Art*, 11 CITAR J. 50 (2019), https://journals.ucp.pt/index.php/jsta/article/view/7334/7114 (listing these examples: JACQUES VAUCONSON'S FLUTE PLAYER (1730S), JAQUET DROZ'S AUTOMATA (1768–1774), JOSEPH FABER'S TALKING MACHINE EUPHONIA (1845), AND JOHN CLARK'S THE EUREKA (1845)).

[8] *Id.* at 50–51.

actuated by water, falling weights, and steam."[9] Greek craftsmen and theatrical producers actually incorporated steam power into their extravaganzas, but no industrial application was tried until the seventeenth century.[10] Automatons continued to grow in popularity, closely associated with high culture, wealth, and intellectual inquiry.

Even as the artisanal automaton waned in prominence during the post-Renaissance industrial revolution, new projects attempted to integrate the growing field of smart machines and autonomous devices. An early example of this was Elektro the Robot, a 1939 creation from Westinghouse that debuted at the 1939 World's Fair. "He could walk, talk, even smoke a cigarette, all with voice control."[11] Elektro, however, was not entirely autonomous. Despite having a vocabulary of approximately 700 words, the audio was external, coming from a hidden 78 rpm record player hidden behind a curtain on the stage where Elektro was presented.[12]

Elektro did not reflect true progress in AI; its purpose was purely marketing. Still, Elektro fueled the imagination at the dawn of the Golden Age of Science Fiction. Writers, such as Isaac Asimov, Arthur C. Clarke, and Robert Heinlein often reflect

---

[9] *Automaton*, ENCYCLOPEDIA BRITANNICA (Apr. 27, 2024), https://www.britannica.com/technology/automaton.

[10] S. Decherney, *Steam Power*. ENCYCLOPEDIA BRITANNICA, (2023, July 24), https://www.britannica.com/science/steam-power.

[11] Allison Meier, *The Sensational Return of a Smoking, Walking, Talking World's Fair Robot*, ATLAS OBSCURA (by Mar. 21, 2013), https://www.atlasobscura.com/articles/elektro-the-robot.

[12] *Id.*

themes captured by Westinghouse in its marketing strategies from this period. Two years following the Westinghouse introduction of Elektro, Asimov formalized the *Three Laws of Robotics*.[13] Eventually, Asimov wrote more than three dozen books involving self-aware robots, as well as a dozen stories featuring "Multivac," a massive government-run answer machine that could understand natural language queries and provide thoughtful answers.[14]

§ 1.2 ARTIFICIAL INTELLIGENCE AND ROBOTICS IN SCIENTIFIC DEVELOPMENT

None of the science fiction depictions of AI or robotics help provide legislators, regulators, or industry with an operational framework for the field. So, what is AI? At its simplest, AI "is the ability of a computer or computer-controlled robot to perform tasks that are commonly associated with the intellectual processes characteristic of humans, such as the ability to reason."[15]

Congress has provided statutory definitions:

> Artificial intelligence: The term "artificial intelligence" means a machine-based system that can, for a given set of human-defined objectives, make predictions, recommendations

---

[13] *See Golden Age of Science Fiction*, *supra* note 4.

[14] *See Multivac*, WIKIPEDIA, https://en.wikipedia.org/wiki/Multivac (last visited Feb. 16, 2025) (identifying the Asimov stories *Franchise* and *The Last Question* as framing the exploration and expansion of the technology).

[15] *Artificial Intelligence*, BRITANNICA, https://www.britannica.com/technology/artificial-intelligence.

or decisions influencing real or virtual environments. Artificial intelligence systems use machine and human-based inputs to—

(A) perceive real and virtual environments.

(B) abstract such perceptions into models through analysis in an automated manner; and

(C) use model inference to formulate options for information or action.[16]

Other federal agencies rely on a different congressional framework. NASA, for example, explains that AI "refers to computer systems that can perform complex tasks normally done by human-reasoning, decision making, creating, etc. There is no single, simple definition of artificial intelligence because AI tools are capable of a wide range of tasks and outputs. . ."[17] Based on this approach NASA has adopted the regulatory framework provided in Section 238(g) of the National Defense Authorization Act of 2019.[18] Here is that definition for AI:

- Any artificial system that performs tasks under varying and unpredictable circumstances without significant human

---

[16] 15 U.S.C § 9401 (2024) (adopted in the National Artificial Intelligence Initiative Act of 2020, Pub. L. 116–283, div. E, § 5002, Jan. 1, 2021, 134 Stat. 4523.

[17] *What is Artificial Intelligence*, NASA, https://www.nasa.gov/what-is-artificial-intelligence/ (last visited Feb. 16, 2025).

[18] *Id. See* National Defense Authorization Act of 2019 § 238(g), 132 Stat. 1636, Pub. L. No. 115–232 (08/13/2018); EXECUTIVE ORDER 13960, PROMOTING THE USE OF TRUSTWORTHY ARTIFICIAL INTELLIGENCE IN THE FEDERAL GOVERNMENT (December 3, 2020).

oversight, or that can learn from experience and improve performance when exposed to data sets.

- An artificial system developed in computer software, physical hardware, or other context that solves tasks requiring human-like perception, cognition, planning, learning, communication, or physical action.
- An artificial system designed to think or act like a human, including cognitive architectures and neural networks.
- A set of techniques, including machine learning that is designed to approximate a cognitive task.
- An artificial system designed to act rationally, including an intelligent software agent or embodied robot that achieves goals using perception, planning, reasoning, learning, communicating, decision-making, and acting.[19]

These definitions remain vague and fuzzy, but regulators have incentives to draft broadly. In trying to anticipate the development of technology, regulators often try to include all possible systems within the definitions. Regulators could draft with more precision, but then those definitions might inadvertently exclude systems that have similar characteristics.

---

19 *Id.*

A simple thought experiment helps clarify these definitions. Consider the "Magic 8 Ball," a children's toy invented in 1944. The Magic 8 Ball provides yes/no answers to any question asked. Inside is a 20-sided icosahedron die floating in dark blue ink. On the 20 sides are answers that range from "yes" to "very doubtful."[20] By design, only five of the 20 answers are negative. Ten are positive and five are essentially nonresponsive. By design, therefore, the machine tends to reinforce and encourage the user.[21] There is, however, no relationship between the question asked and the answer provided. Nonetheless, it is an artificial system device that can provide an outcome to an inquiry.

When evaluating AI definitions and explanations for smart systems, the starting question is whether the system is truly more effective at predicting information than a Magic 8 Ball. If the answers tend to work because of the design rather than an evaluation of the input, it is not an AI system, no matter how elaborately the vendor might suggest otherwise. To be minimally interactive, the system must computationally engage with the input data to make its predictions. Increasingly, to qualify as "smart" a system should be capable of learning from the accuracy of its prior responses to update its algorithms or decision analysis.

The term "artificial intelligence," did not actually come from science fiction. Dr. John McCarthy is

---

20 *Magic 8 Ball*, WIKIPEDIA, https://en.wikipedia.org/wiki/Magic_8_Ball (last visited Feb. 16, 2025).

21 *See id.*

attributed with coining the academic term "artificial intelligence" during a 1956 Dartmouth College conference dedicated to capturing human-like thought processes by computers.[22] McCarthy tried to summarize the work for his colleagues:

> The study is to proceed on the basis of the conjecture that every aspect of learning or any other feature of intelligence can in principle be so precisely described that a machine can be made to simulate it. An attempt will be made to find how to make machines use language, form abstractions and concepts, solve kinds of problems now reserved for humans, and improve themselves. We think that a significant advance can be made in one or more of these problems if a carefully selected group of scientists work on it together for a summer."

In many ways, McCarthy's explanation for the Dartmouth Summer Research Project is an excellent definition for AI. "[T]raditional programming systems depend entirely on user input to determine the solution's output."[23] McCarthy described what is now characterized as machine learning, which allows the computer system to develop and refine algorithms to identify patterns within the data provided to the system. Machine learning systems

---

[22] *See* HERBERT L. ROITBLAT, ALGORITHMS ARE NOT ENOUGH: CREATING GENERAL ARTIFICIAL INTELLIGENCE 1 (2020).

[23] *Machine Learning vs Traditional Programming: Choosing the Right Approach for Your Projects*, INST. OF DATA (May 11, 2023), https://www.institutedata.com/us/blog/machine-learning-vs-traditional-programming-choosing-the-right-approach-for-your-projects/.

approximate or imitate the way that humans learn, gradually improving their accuracy.[24]

As technology has shifted, the most significant difference between the research started in the 1950s and the work underway today is that today's computer simulations are less reliant on precise descriptions of thinking and processing. Instead, they are increasingly based on the machine's own learning through trial and error.

Early development progressed in fits and starts. Most participants devoted far less time at Dartmouth than the proposal had outlined. Nonetheless, the seeds of most AI science were planted that summer.[25] Perhaps the greatest challenge was the limited computing power available to the computers on which the simulations were being run. Early computer chips had extremely small capacities. In May 1960, Fairchild Semiconductor produced the first working integrated circuit with four transistors and five resistors.[26] Five years later, Gordon Moore, then Fairchild's Director for Research and Development, calculated that by 1975, "the number

---

[24] *See Machine Learning, Explained*, MIT SLOAN SCHOOL OF MANAGEMENT (Apr. 21, 2021), https://mitsloan.mit.edu/ideas-made-to-matter/machine-learning-explained ("Machine learning is one way to use AI. It was defined in the 1950s by AI pioneer Arthur Samuel as "the field of study that gives computers the ability to learn without explicitly being programmed.").

[25] Veisdal, *supra* note 2.

[26] *1960: First Planar Integrated Circuit is Fabricated*, COMPUTER HISTORY MUSEUM, 1960: First Planar Integrated Circuit is Fabricated, COMPUTER HISTORY MUSEUM (last visited Feb. 16, 2025).

of components per chip would reach 65,000; a doubling every 12 months."[27] He published his prediction in *Electronics* magazine on April 19, 1965.[28] Moore went on to cofound Intel Corporation, one of the world's leading microchip manufacturers.

The rate of growth for semiconductors, later dubbed Moore's Law, predicted a radical expansion of computing power that would eventually enable machines to perform AI calculations. Although Moore's Law itself has been revised, with the pace of progress slowing from doubling every twelve months to doubling every two years. The expectation of progress itself fuels intense competition and capital investment in the companies and systems that rely on computer chips. Today, the numbers are staggering. Instead of 65,000 transistors, the Intel Core i9 (7980XE) launched in 2017 boasted 6.5 billion transistors. In 2020, the AMD Ryzen Threadripper 3990X surpassed even that, containing an astonishing 39.54 billion transistors.[29] The developments continue with more recent chips, such as the Apple M2 Ultra (2023) reaching 134 billion

---

[27] *1965: "Moore's Law" Predicts the Future of Integrated Circuits*, COMPUTER HISTORY MUSEUM (last visited Feb. 15, 2025), https://www.computerhistory.org/siliconengine/moores-law-predicts-the-future-of-integrated-circuits/.

[28] *Id.*

[29] *How Many Transistor in a CPU*, CENSTRY (Feb. 20, 2024), https://www.censtry.com/blog/how-many-transistor-in-a-cpu.html.

transistors and NVIDIA's Blackwell B100 (2024) topping 208 billion transistors.[30]

In addition, not all chips are the same. The brain of most computer systems is the central processing unit (CPU). The CPU "handles all types of computing tasks required for the operating system and applications to run. A graphics processing unit (GPU) is a similar hardware component but more specialized. It can more efficiently handle complex mathematical operations that run in parallel than a general CPU."[31]

The CPU remains essential to run a computer, but the GPU can supplement the system by efficiently running mathematical calculations in parallel. GPUs were originally designed for mathematically complex workloads and computer companies found them extremely useful to render complex audiovisual content used in video games. Cryptocurrency mining, another math-intensive computer activity, led to GPU chips becoming increasingly valuable and somewhat scarce due to the high demand from the crypto industry. AI processing is extremely math intensive. The demand for GPU chips has fueled an

---

[30] *See* Ryan Smith, *NVIDIA Blackwell Architecture and B200/B100 Accelerators Announced: Going Bigger With Smaller Data*, ANANDTECH (Mar. 18, 2024), https://www.anandtech.com/show/21310/nvidia-blackwell-architecture-and-b200b100-accelerators-announced-going-bigger-with-smaller-data; *Transistor Count*, WIKIPEDIA, https://en.wikipedia.org/wiki/Transistor_count (last visited Feb. 16, 2025).

[31] *What's the Difference Between GPUs and CPUs?*, AWS, https://aws.amazon.com/compare/the-difference-between-gpus-cpus/ (last visited Feb. 16, 2025).

explosion of activity. Nvidia, the leading maker of GPU chips, has seen its stock value soar from a low of $298 in May of 2023 to more than $1,100 before issuing a 10-1 stock split and growing to a capitalization in excess of $3.1 trillion as of February 2025. Neither Intel nor On Semiconductor (the company that acquired Fairchild) have had the same level of success.

AI research has been supported throughout the decades by DARPA (Defense Advanced Research Projects Agency), the same resource that helped develop the early iterations of the internet. Although DARPA is a military department, it works with academic institutions and the private sector industry to develop transformative technologies. DARPA itself was founded the year after the Dartmouth Summer Research Project. In 1957, the United States was caught off guard by the Soviet Union's launch of the Sputnik space satellite. The federal government responded with "a commitment by the United States that, from that time forward, it would be the initiator and not the victim of strategic technological surprises."[32]

As computer systems matured in the 1970s-1980s, work on AI continued. The focus was primarily on expert systems. Programmers built decision trees and developed highly detailed answers to questions and systems. The systems grew in complexity, but all information was highly structured and well labeled. These systems used symbolic logic and eventually

---

32 *About DARPA*, DARPA, https://www.darpa.mil/about-us/about-darpa (last visited Feb. 16, 2025).

began to respond to language-based queries. While highly limited when compared to modern systems, these machines were transformative for industry and finance. "By 1985, the US investments in AI expert systems reached over $1 billion."[33] "By the end of 1980s, over half of the Fortune 500 companies were involved in either developing or maintaining of expert systems."[34]

Expert systems, however, were not the goal of the Dartmouth Summer Research Project. The long-term vision was to create systems that could operate like the human brain, using neural networks capable of evaluation and reasoning. By the 1990s, the promise of the internet and advances in computing made this vision seem obtainable. This work evolved into the development of machine learning, deep learning, and neural networks—each a form of AI, but also distinct methodologies for machine reasoning. These various designs reflect the diversity of AI models. A model may be understood as "[a] component of an information system that implements AI technology and uses computational, statistical, or machine-

---

[33] Blagoj Delipetrev, Chrisa Tsinarakii, & Uroš Kostić, *AI Watch: Historical Evolution of Artificial Intelligence,* EUR. COMM'N JOINT RES. CTR. 9 (2020), https://op.europa.eu/en/publication-detail/-/publication/6264ac29-2d3a-11eb-b27b-01aa75ed71a1/language-en.

[34] Ting Huang, *Expert Systems*, THE HISTORY OF ARTIFICIAL INTELLIGENCE, UNIVERSITY OF WASHINGTON (Dec. 2006), https://courses.cs.washington.edu/courses/csep590/06au/projects/history-ai.pdf.

learning techniques to produce outputs from a given set of inputs."[35]

§ 1.2.1 MACHINE LEARNING

IBM explains that "Machine Learning (ML) is a branch of artificial intelligence (AI) and computer science that focuses on using data and algorithms to enable AI to imitate the way that humans learn, gradually improving its accuracy."[36] Machine learning goes beyond the expert system by enabling the machine itself to create algorithms, weight values, and identify classifications, allowing it to generate answers without relying on the precise scripts required of expert systems. "Through the use of statistical methods, algorithms are trained to make classifications or predictions, and to uncover key insights in data mining projects. These insights subsequently drive decision making within applications and businesses, ideally impacting key growth metrics."[37]

Berkeley School of Information provides additional detail:

> The basic concept of machine learning in data science involves using statistical learning and

---

[35] Harold Booth et al., *Secure Software Development Practices for Generative AI and Dual-Use Foundation Models*, NIST SP 800–218A, NIST (April 2024) (Initial Public Draft) [*hereinafter* NIST Pub. 800], https://doi.org/10.6028/NIST.SP.800-218A.ipd.

[36] *What is Machine Learning*, IBM (last visited Feb. 16, 2025), https://www.ibm.com/topics/machine-learning.

[37] *Id.*

> optimization methods that let computers analyze datasets and identify patterns . . . . Machine learning techniques leverage data mining to identify historic trends and inform future models.
>
> The typical supervised machine learning algorithm consists of roughly three components:
>
> **1. A decision process:** A recipe of calculations or other steps that takes in the data and "guesses" what kind of pattern your algorithm is looking to find.
>
> **2. An error function:** A method of measuring how good the guess was by comparing it to known examples (when they are available). Did the decision process get it right? If not, how do you quantify "how bad" the miss was?
>
> **3. An updating or optimization process:** A method in which the algorithm looks at the miss and then updates how the decision process comes to the final decision, so next time the miss won't be as great.[38]

Key computing concepts are essential for non-scientists to follow the basic approach to these systems. Most of the important terms focus on the data used by the systems and the way that data is processed.

---

[38] *What Is Machine Learning (ML)?*, BERKELEY SCH. OF INFO (June 26, 2020), https://ischoolonline.berkeley.edu/blog/what-is-machine-learning/.

- **Algorithm:** An algorithm is simply "a set of instructions designed to accomplish a task."[39] Baking recipes could be correctly described as algorithms. (This is why the definitions are so important. A law purporting to restrict algorithmic bias might accidentally include many tasks like census data collection, if not drafted carefully.) Machine learning requires very sophisticated algorithms that are often adjusted through the error function and optimization process such that the algorithm evolves as the machine operates and learns from the use of its algorithm.

- **Structured and unstructured data:** Structured data are information that have been correctly labeled and compiled, often in spreadsheets or databases. In a classroom, for example, the students' first and last names, student ID numbers, and grades on each assignment would be collected, labeled and properly sorted in tabulated spreadsheet formats. Unstructured data includes information that cannot be tabulated easily into a database, such as the students' essay responses to a question. Unstructured data can also be unlabeled versions of the structured data, such as a class list in a word processing document that was not labeled in a table.

---

39 Algorithm, Nat. Lib. of Med., https://www.nnlm.gov/guides/data-glossary/algorithm (last visited Feb. 16, 2025).

- **Clean data:** This describes data that is accurate and correctly labeled (using the rows and columns of the database). If the datasets include information that does not conform to the field requirement, then the data is not clean. For example, if state information is accidentally included in a column for zip code information, then the state information is inaccurate because of the label. Only the zip code information in the zip code column is clean data.

One common use of machine learning is in advertising and marketing, where advertisers and retailers use machine learning to shape consumer engagement with brands. To illustrate this, consider how similar steps were undertaken before computers and how machine learning has transformed the process. Before computers, movie studios would show films to test audiences who filled out response cards. Some data on the cards would be structured, for example, if viewers were asked to rate the film or its cast on a rank of 1–5. The collection and tabulation of that data would be structured data. Other information might be unstructured, if for example, viewers were asked to share their thoughts about the ending of the movie. The narrative answers would be unstructured data. Following the movie, the cards would be collected, the structured data tabulated, and the unstructured data summarized. The movie studio might then rely on the information to edit or alter the film or adapt the marketing strategy depending on the responses it received.

Today, a streaming service can do something similar. First, it may ask for a "thumbs up" or rating of a movie on the service and tabulate the answers. The streaming service has access to each viewer's engagement, so the system might track how many minutes of the show was watched by each viewer. If large audience segments turn off a movie after the first fifteen minutes, for example, that might suggest dissatisfaction with the film—at least as compared to another film that does not lose most of the audience until the start of the end credits. For marketers, there are important differences between the behavior of an individual as compared to the same person's report of their response to a product or service.[40]

Second, the streaming platform may suggest movies similar to the one the viewer just finished. These initial suggestions represent the first step in the machine learning process. The system might use labels such as "comedy," "action," "mystery," or it might use cast information to suggest that if a viewer watched a Sean Connery James Bond movie, the viewer will likely be interested in other Sean Connery movies (and who could go wrong with those); or it might access information about other viewers and suggest those movies that were most likely to have been watched by viewers who just watched the same movie.

Third, it may base its response on the behaviors of the viewer by using historical watching information

---

[40] *See What is response bias and how can you avoid it?*, QUALTRICS, https://www.qualtrics.com/experience-management/research/response-bias/ (last visited Feb. 16, 2025).

to predict what the viewer will watch next. If a household typically watches educational children's videos at 4:00 p.m. and action movies at 8:00 p.m. each weekday evening, then the system might learn not to suggest educational children's videos after 6:00 p.m. A less sophisticated program will keep pushing *Arthur* and *Dora* well after the children in the household have gone to bed, but the more sophisticated system will equate the scheduling with other variables.

Each of these strategies is prone to considerable error. Suggestions based on cast members are easy for the system to make, but it is unlikely to predict viewer interest. Identification by genre works better to predict the interests of viewers, but people typically watch more than one genre. Few individuals stick only to Westerns or comedies. Over time, however, these systems improve as they gather more data and refine their predictions.

The fourth option looks beyond the behavior of the individual to cohorts of individuals that are like the target viewer. The algorithm collects information on other viewers that are predicted to be similar to the viewer receiving the recommendation. By using demographic data, income information, shopping habits, political leanings, and a myriad of unstructured data, machine learning systems can paint a picture of each individual and match that individual with a cohort of very similar people. These systems, sometimes labeled "recommendation engines," can then recommend to the viewer those movies that the cohort of similar people selected most frequently.

A marketing firm describes the data collection:

> The first and most important step for creating a recommendation engine is to gather data. There are two main types of data to be collected:
>
> **Implicit data:** This includes information collected from activities such as web search history, clicks, cart events, search log, and order history.
>
> **Explicit data:** This is information gathered from customer input, such as reviews and ratings, likes and dislikes, and product comments.
>
> Recommendation engines also use customer attribute data such as demographics (age, gender) and psychographics (interests, values) to identify similar customers, as well as feature data (genre, item type) to identify product similarity.[41]

A machine learning based recommendation engine will then use the content of the viewer's film history and the user's public activities to build a profile. "Collaborative filtering focuses on collecting and analyzing data on user behavior, activities, and preferences, to predict what a person will like, based

---

[41] *What Is a Recommendation Engine and How Does It Work?*, APPIER, https://www.appier.com/en/blog/what-is-a-recommendation-engine-and-how-does-it-work (last visited Feb. 16, 2025).

on their similarity to other users. . . . Content-based filtering works on the principle that if you like a particular item, you will also like this other item."[42]

Machine learning systems become increasingly sophisticated as the volume of data expands and as the process of answer optimization progresses. Through trial and error, the system identifies which information ultimately serves as the best predictor of behavior. Over time, systems can develop additional nuances, allowing the algorithm that works best for one viewer or cohort of viewers to be adjusted by the system for a different cohort. Ultimately, the system evaluates each cohort using criteria and weights specifically designed to maximize predictive accuracy. "Since a machine learning algorithm updates autonomously, the analytical accuracy improves with each run as it teaches itself from the data it analyzes. This iterative nature of learning is both unique and valuable because it occurs without human intervention—empowering the algorithm to uncover hidden insights . . ."[43]

Through correlation, iteration, and repetition, systems using these massive data sets can select the combination of data that results in the most accurate predictions. With access to enough data, these systems can, in many cases, become highly predictive.

---

[42] *Id.*

[43] *What Is Machine Learning (ML)?*, *supra* note 38.

§ 1.2.2 NEURAL NETWORKS

One important subcategory of machine learning systems is neural networks (or artificial neural networks (ANNs)). Loosely based on the neuron clustering of the human brain, ANNs focus on the connections between nodes to inform the algorithm and provide weighting or priority to some of the data.[44] "Neural networks were first developed in the 1950s to test theories about the way that interconnected neurons in the human brain store information and react to input data. As in the brain, the output of an artificial neural network depends on the strength of the connections between its virtual neurons. . ."[45]

For many computational problems, ANNs provide significant processing power and the ability to weight and evaluate information that goes well beyond machine learning systems.

Structurally, a neural network is composed of an input layer, an output layer, and one or more hidden layers in between. A basic neural network is composed of just three layers. Even at this scale, these systems can provide data analytics and predictions using both structures and unstructured data to improve basic problem solving.

---

[44] *See* Janelle Shane, *Neural Networks, Explained*, PHYSICS WORLD (July 9, 2018), https://physicsworld.com/a/neural-networks-explained/.

[45] *Id.*

§ 1.2.3 DEEP LEARNING AND DEEP NEURAL NETWORKS

Deep learning is a subset of machine learning. "Deep Learning describes algorithms that analyze data with a logical structure similar to how a human would draw conclusions."[46] Deep learning is also sometimes used to describe deep neural networks. Provided a system has two or more hidden layers, then the neural network will be classified as a "deep neural network."[47] For context, ChatGPT-3 utilized 96 hidden layers for its deep neural network that propelled natural language processing.

Classical machine learning systems rely on structured data to sort and evaluate. Deep neural networks, in contrast, can use raw data, including text and images scraped from the internet, adjusting the weights of the systems' algorithms and the placement of the connections that change as the system learns. As the current iteration of large language model deep neural networks operate, they ingest massive amounts of data and pattern-match their output to similar word patterns that are frequently found in the data set.[48] They have also continued to expand in size geometrically with each new launch.

---

[46] Arne Wolfewicz, *Deep Learning vs. Machine Learning—What's The Difference?*, LEVITY (Feb. 15, 2023), https://levity.ai/blog/difference-machine-learning-deep-learning.

[47] *What Is Machine Learning (ML)?*, *supra* note 38.

[48] Bharani Kumar, *GPT-1, GPT-2 and GPT-3 Models Explained*, 360DIGITMG (Feb. 7, 2023), https://360digitmg.com/blog/types-of-gpt-in-artificial-intelligence.

Deep learning focuses on data processing. "Deep learning eliminates some of data pre-processing that is typically involved with machine learning. These algorithms can ingest and process unstructured data, like text and images, and it automates feature extraction, removing some of the dependency on human experts."[49]

The three concepts—machine learning, deep learning, and deep neural networks—are highly interrelated. "Deep learning is a subset of machine learning that uses multi-layered neural networks, called deep neural networks, to simulate the complex decision-making power of the human brain. Some form of deep learning powers most of the artificial intelligence (AI) in our lives today."[50]

The term AI system means "[a]ny data system, software, hardware, application, tool, or utility that operates in whole or in part using AI."[51] The various AI systems not only use different types of data, but they also receive different levels of human supervision. According to Nvidia.com, there are different machine learning models as follows:

- **Supervised learning:** The dataset being used has been pre-labeled and classified by users to allow the algorithm to see how accurate its performance is.

---

49 *What is Deep Learning*, IBM, https://www.ibm.com/topics/deep-learning (last visited Feb. 16, 2025).

50 *Id.*

51 NIST Pub. 800, *supra* ch. 1 note 35, at 20.

- **Unsupervised learning:** The raw dataset being used is unlabeled and an algorithm identifies patterns and relationships within the data without help from users.
- **Semi-supervised learning:** The dataset contains structured and unstructured data, which guides the algorithm on its way to making independent conclusions. The combination of the two data types in one training dataset allows machine learning algorithms to learn to label unlabeled data.
- **Reinforcement learning:** The dataset uses a "rewards/punishments" system, offering feedback to the algorithm to learn from its own experiences by trial and error.[52]

The mechanisms of deep neural networks vary considerably depending on the particular model being used and the problem that needed to be solved. Natural language processing requires different steps than image recognition.

§ 1.3 GENERATIVE AI

Machine learning is primarily used for predictive analytics. The range of predictive topics is nearly unlimited, and in consequence, machine learning has had a profound impact on science and industry. Deep

---

[52] *What is Machine Learning (ML)?*, *supra* note 38 (citing Isha Salian, *SuperVize Me: What's the Difference Between Supervised, Unsupervised, Semi-Supervised and Reinforcement Learning?*, NVIDIA (Aug. 2, 2018), https://blogs.nvidia.com/blog/supervised-unsupervised-learning/.

neural networks, however, add another dimension to the predictive modeling. ANNs have been applied to elements of content production, and as a result, they can generate new content, including text, software, designs, images, voice and music audio, and video. Collectively, this family of AI has become known as generative AI or GenAI. One of the most recent additions to the suite of AI technologies, GenAI has caught the public's attention and fueled the AI boom which began with the public launch of OpenAI's ChatGPT on November 30, 2022.[53]

Although the models for AI generation vary, many stem from a common research approach. Many attribute the modern approach to AI to Dr. Fei-Fei Li.[54] She pioneered ImageNet based on a new conception of AI training. Previously, scientists would code systems to recognize particular objects like a dog, cat, or cow by painstakingly writing a specific program for that task. But Dr. Li recognized that humans learn by observing the world around them and learning to discern one object from another. An example of this approach is often seen on *Sesame Street*. The children's educational program produced hundreds of short videos with this theme, teaching children to sing along to "*one of these things is not like the other, one of these things just doesn't belong.*" Dr. Li suggested that computer training should follow a

---

[53] Kevin Roose, *How ChatGPT Kicked Off an A.I. Arms Race*, N.Y. TIMES (Feb. 3, 2023), https://www.nytimes.com/2023/02/03/technology/chatgpt-openai-artificial-intelligence.html.

[54] *See* Jessi Hempel, *Fei-Fei Li's Quest to Make AI Better for Humanity*, WIRED (Nov. 13, 2018), https://www.wired.com/story/fei-fei-li-artificial-intelligence-humanity/ (quoting Fei-Fei Li).

model with the same approach. "It was a way to organize the whole visual concept of the world," Dr. Li noted.[55]

Based on this model, Dr. Li created ImageNet, a large database of labeled images that could be used to train AI systems. She started the project at Princeton in 2009, growing the database to 3.2 million images.[56] The ImageNet project connected with the European computer vision competition, resulting in the launch of the ImageNet Large Scale Visual Recognition Challenge.[57] Dr. Li moved to Stanford, which was a longtime pioneer in AI research.

In 2012, Toronto researcher Dr. Geoffrey Hinton won the ImageNet competition using a neural network. "By 2017, the final year of the competition, the error rate for computers identifying objects in images had been reduced to less than 3 percent, from 15 percent in 2012. . . . ImageNet enabled deep learning to go big—it's at the root of recent advances in self-driving cars, facial recognition, phone cameras that can identify objects."[58]

Image recognition is only one aspect of problem solving for neural networks. An even bigger challenge has been human language. To address this, massive datasets focus on text. This focus is known as the Large Language Model (LLM). The data is

---

[55] *Id.*

[56] *Id.*

[57] *Id.*

[58] *Id.*

simply text, but the scale is massive. The datasets have grown to more than a trillion parameters, representing petabytes of data, and costing hundreds of millions of dollars in computational processing expenses. They are human language variations of deep neural networks.

Numerous LLM projects have been operating in the past decade, including Google's BERT (Bidirectional Encoder Representations from Transformers) and CTRL (Conditional Transformer Language Model) from Salesforce Research. Despite the continuing developments, it was the public availability of OpenAI's ChatGPT that served as the inflection point for widespread public adoption of generative AI.

OpenAI was founded in 2015 by Sam Altman, Peter Thiel, Reid Hoffman, and Elon Musk as a nonprofit research lab. By 2019, however, the company needed significantly greater resources, leading to an exclusive arrangement with Microsoft, which provided $1 billion in funding and resulted in the creation of a for-profit subsidiary. Upset about the shift, Elon Musk left the project.

In February 2019, OpenAI released a paper about GPT-2 with the simple objective to "predict the next word, given all of the previous words within some text."[59] The GPT-2 LLM used 8 million web pages comprised of 1.5 billion words or "parameters" to

---

[59] *Better language models and their implications*, OPENAI (Feb. 14, 2019), https://openai.com/research/better-language-models.

achieve this goal. "On language tasks like question answering, reading comprehension, summarization, and translation, GPT-2 begins to learn these tasks from the raw text, using no task-specific training data."[60]

In May 2020, OpenAI released the next iteration, GPT-3, increasing to 175 billion parameters. Then in March 2022, the company moved to GPT-3.5 and the widely available public version named ChatGPT. Suddenly the non-technical world learned about synthetic language creation and triggered an arms race to expand artificial intelligence. As Kevin Roose of the New York Times tells the story, ChatGPT was something of a marketing ploy to enable OpenAI to stay ahead of the competition.

> One day in mid-November, workers at OpenAI got an unexpected assignment: Release a chatbot, fast.
>
> The chatbot, an executive announced, would be known as "Chat with GPT-3.5," and it would be made available free to the public. In two weeks.
>
> The announcement confused some OpenAI employees. All year, the San Francisco artificial intelligence company had been working toward the release of GPT-4, a new A.I. model that was stunningly good at writing essays, solving complex coding problems and more. After months of testing and fine-tuning, GPT-4 was nearly ready. The plan was to release the model

---

60 *Id.*

> in early 2023, along with a few chatbots that would allow users to try it for themselves, according to three people with knowledge of the inner workings of OpenAI.
>
> But OpenAI's top executives had changed their minds. Some were worried that rival companies might upstage them by releasing their own A.I. chatbots before GPT-4, according to the people with knowledge of OpenAI. And putting something out quickly using an old model, they reasoned, could help them collect feedback to improve the new one.
>
> So they decided to dust off and update an unreleased chatbot that used a souped-up version of GPT-3, the company's previous language model, which came out in 2020.[61]

Within weeks of the release, Microsoft expanded its arrangement with OpenAI, investing an additional $10 billion and moving to incorporate the functionality into its Office 365 services and Bing search. Within two months of its launch, ChatGPT had more than 100 million users, making it the fastest adoption of any technology in human history. GPT-4 followed in March 2023. Then in May 2024, OpenAI launched GPT-4o ("o" for omni).

The success of ChatGPT has fueled a race among the largest technology companies to own a piece of the marketplace. Google responded with Bard (later

---

[61] Kevin Roose, *How ChatGPT Kicked Off an A.I. Arms Race*, N.Y. TIMES (Feb. 3, 2023), https://www.nytimes.com/2023/02/03/technology/chatgpt-openai-artificial-intelligence.html.

renamed Gemini), the latest of its many research projects into artificial intelligence. Meta, X and hundreds of other companies have since announced competing projects.

ChatGPT can write ad copy, pass a simulated bar exam, pen poetry, provide compelling stories, and offer authoritative text on any subject. As discussed in later chapters, the present version of the technology remains limited to predicting what text is desired, opening it up to bouts of "hallucinations," which is a clever way of explaining that the system is much like a parrot or toddler. It knows how to produce answers but does not understand what those answers mean.

ChatGPT is just one entrant in a highly competitive field of natural language processing (NLP) chatbot systems. NLP, in turn, is just one of the methods for creating generative output from AI systems. ChatGPT is far from the first. Early work involving Gaussian Mixture Models (GMMs) and others were already under development in the 1950s.[62] This list provides a brief summary of the field in the past decade:

- **Generative Adversarial Networks (GANs):** GAN, stands for Generative Adversarial Network, is an advanced deep learning architecture consists of two essential

---

[62] Arham Islam, *A History of Generative AI: From GAN to GPT-4*, MARKTECHPOST (Mar. 21, 2023), https://www.marktechpost.com/2023/03/21/a-history-of-generative-ai-from-gan-to-gpt-4/ (Hidden Markov Models (HMMs) and Gaussian Mixture Models (GMMs)).

components: a generator and a discriminator. The generator's primary function is to generate synthetic data that closely resembles real data, while the discriminator is responsible for distinguishing between authentic and fabricated data. The generator enhances the authenticity of its produced data through adversarial training, while the discriminator effectively determines whether the data is real or synthetic. Functioning as a generative model, GAN is commonly employed in deep learning for generating samples to enhance data augmentation and pre-processing techniques. Its broad application extends across various fields such as image processing and biomedicine, where it proves valuable in producing high-quality synthetic data for research and analysis.[63]

- **Diffusion model:** Generative diffusion models can create new data using the data they were trained on. For instance, when trained on an assortment of human faces, a diffusion model can create new and lifelike faces with diverse features and expressions, even if they were not present in the original dataset. The fundamental idea behind diffusion models is to transform a simple and easily obtainable distribution into a more complex and meaningful data distribution.

---

[63] Jagreet Kaur Gill, *Types of Generative AI Models and LLM Model Training and Evaluation*, XENONSTACK (Nov. 20, 2023), https://www.xenonstack.com/blog/generative-ai-models (formatting modified).

This transformation is accomplished through a series of reversible operations. Once the model understands the process of transformation, it can generate new samples by starting from a point within the simple distribution and gradually spreading it towards the desired complex data distribution.[64]

- **Natural language processing:** Natural language processing, or NLP, combines computational linguistics—rule-based modeling of human language—with statistical and machine learning models to enable computers and digital devices to recognize, understand and generate text and speech. . . . [NLP] combines computer algorithms with machine learning and deep learning models to automatically extract, classify, and label elements of text and voice data and then assign a statistical likelihood to each possible meaning of those elements.[65]

- **Transformers:** Transformers are a type of neural network capable of understanding the context of sequential data, such as sentences, by analyzing the relationships between the words. They were created to address the challenge of sequence transduction, which involves transforming input sequences into

64 *Id.* (formatting modified).

65 *What is Natural Language Processing (NLP)?*, IBM, https://www.ibm.com/topics/natural-language-processing (last visited Feb. 16, 2025) (formatting modified).

output sequences, like translating from one language to another.[66]

- **The generative pre-trained transformer (GPT):** Initially showcased its potential for generating task-specific natural language through unsupervised pre-training and fine-tuning for downstream tasks. It utilizes transformer-decoder layers for next-word prediction and coherent text generation. Fine-tuning is used to adapt it to a specific task based on pre-training.[67]

- **Foundation models:** Foundation models are massive AI-trained models that use huge amounts of data and computational resources to generate anything from text to images. Some of the most popular examples of foundation models include GANs, LLMs, VAEs, & Multimodal, powering well-known tools such as ChatGPT, DALLE-2, Segment Anything, and BERT. [A Foundation Model is] "any model that is trained on broad data (generally using self-supervision at scale) that can be adapted (*e.g.*, fine-tuned) to a wide range of downstream tasks."[68]

---

66 Islam, *supra* note 62 (formatting modified).

67 Gill, *supra* note 63 (formatting modified).

68 Nikolaj Buhl, *The Full Guide to Foundation Models*, Encord (April 21, 2023), https://encord.com/blog/foundation-models/ (quoting The Stanford Institute for Human-Centered Artificial Intelligence's Center for Research on Foundation Models).

Broadly speaking, GANs and diffusion models are used to develop synthetic visual images and videos while NLP systems are used for speech and language. Within the science of AI, there are many more definitions and categorizations but for an attorney or regulator, the additional differentiation among models has not yet been proven to be legally significant.

The models tend to follow the same development path.[69] This process starts with data gathering. Given the massive size of many training models, the process of data gathering has become among the most legally contentious steps in AI development. At the outset, the collected data is processed and cleaned so that it covers the field relevant to the training model and errors are largely eliminated. Preprocessing the data often actually requires significant human participation.[70] Although the data may have originally be scraped from the internet, most images require labeling during the early stages of training on each specific task. The same image may be used to train multiple tasks, but the labels will differ depending on the purpose of the labeled data. A street scene photograph, for example, might be used to label cars, buses, pedestrians, stop lights, clothing, road signs, buildings, store signage, and more. Collection is essential but unhelpful without initial

---

69 *See* Gill, *supra* note 63 (outlining the steps for AI generative models).

70 *See* Josh Dzieza, *AI Is a Lot of Work*, VERGE (June 20, 2023), https://www.theverge.com/features/23764584/ai-artificial-intelligence-data-notation-labor-scale-surge-remotasks-openai-chatbots.

processing. Eventually, machines reach a sufficient level of object identification to conduct much of this work, allowing the human workforce to shift to different tasks.

With a clean data set available, the AI team will then select the model architecture to be used for the AI implementation. With the architecture selected, the team will write or compile code for the initial implementation of the model. The team will feed the model training data, continuously evaluating the output and refining the model. "This training process requires considerable computational resources and time, depending on the model's complexity and the dataset's size. Monitoring the model's progress and adjusting its training parameters, like learning rate and batch size, is crucial to achieving the best results."[71]

The final two steps are essentially a continuous process of evaluating the model, optimizing the architecture, providing more data to re-evaluate the process, tuning the model with even higher-quality data or data focused on a narrower set of use cases, and iterating repeatedly until the model is specialized to a particular use. "Training and fine-tuning are crucial stages in the machine learning model development lifecycle, serving distinct purposes."[72] At the fine-tuning stage, the system is "trained on a smaller, task-specific dataset . . . and

---

[71] *Id.*

[72] Nikolaj Buhl, *Training vs. Fine-tuning: What is the Difference?*, ENCORD (Nov. 7, 2023), https://encord.com/blog/training-vs-fine-tuning/.

tailor it to a more specific task. This becomes invaluable, especially when the new dataset for the new task is limited, as training from scratch might lead to overfitting."[73]

The final two steps are essentially a continuous process of evaluating the model, optimizing the architecture, providing additional data to re-evaluate the process, tuning the model with higher-quality data or data focused on a narrower set of use cases, and iterating repeatedly until the model is specialized to a particular use. "Training and fine-tuning are crucial stages in the machine learning model development lifecycle, serving distinct purposes."[74] At the fine-tuning stage, the system is "trained on a smaller, task-specific dataset . . . and tailor it to a more specific task. This becomes invaluable, especially when the new dataset for the new task is limited, as training from scratch might lead to overfitting."[75]

The pace of AI development cannot be easily quantified. In terms of economic value, Fortune Business Insights reported the global AI market to be worth $515 billion in 2023, with a projected value of $621.19 billion in 2024, and a growth rate of at least 20 percent.[76] In fact, the 2024 AI capital market has been estimated to have grown to $638.23 billion in

---

[73] *Id.*

[74] *Id.*

[75] *Id.*

[76] *AI Market Research Report*, FORTUNE BUSINESS INSIGHTS, https://www.fortunebusinessinsights.com/industry-reports/artificial-intelligence-market-100114 (Last visited Feb. 16, 2025).

2024, with projections reaching $3.68 trillion by 2034.[77] The flood of capital investment in AI has depressed investment across most other sectors, and the "Magnificent Seven" companies involved in AI have propelled an unparalleled rally of the S&P 500.[78] In 2023, "the seven tech-focused US companies [were] Alphabet, Amazon, Apple, Meta Platforms, Microsoft, Nvidia and Tesla. Collectively, the Magnificent Seven climbed 75.71% during 2023, while the broader S&P 500 Index returned 24.23% for the year."[79] By early 2024, these seven stocks represented over 30 percent of the index due to their significant growth. Although IBM is not among the Magnificent Seven, it is also a significant contributor to AI development and implementation.

In addition to the group of publicly held companies, a number of privately held companies are also vying for leadership in AI development. OpenAI, the company that produces ChatGPT and Dall-E (for image generation), leads all private firms with a valuation at approximately $157 billion at the end of 2024. OpenAI benefitted from an $11 billion

---

[77] *Artificial Intelligence (AI) Market Size, Share, and Trends 2024 to 2034*, PRECEDENCE RESEARCH, https://www.precedenceresearch.com/artificial-intelligence-market (last visited Feb. 16, 2025).

[78] *See* Ukadike Micheal, *The Magnificent Seven's Impact on the S&P 500 Reaches Unprecedented Levels*, FASTBULL (April 12, 2024).

[79] Stephanie Hill, *A Closer Look at Magnificent Seven Stocks*, MELLON (February 2024), https://www.mellon.com/insights/insights-articles/a-closer-look-at-magnificent-seven-stocks.html.

investment by Microsoft, which helped propel Microsoft's Co-Pilot and other AI offerings.

The second-place entrant is Elon Musk's xAI, which raised $6 billion in May 2024, resulting in a valuation of $50 billion at the end of 2024. Scale is the third most highly capitalized firm. Scale operates Remotasks, a subsidiary which focuses on the human training of AI models, primarily through outsourcing to a low-paid international workforce. Fourth is Anthropic, the producer of Claude, another leading GenAI chatbot platform. Finally, in fifth place is Hugging Face, which now focuses primarily on pre-trained machine learning models available that developers can integrate into their own products.

The use of capitalization is only one possible metric. It ignores the tremendous development underway outside the U.S., particularly in China. Huawei, for example, will be competing globally with Nvidia for chip manufacturing and distribution. DJI, Ubtech Robotics, SenseTime, Cambricon, and Cloudwalk have all been recognized for their AI advances.[80] Five companies, including Baidu, SenseTime, and Baichuan, have received government approval to launch Chinese AI chatbots.[81] Tencent, Alibaba, and Yitu Technology are also significant players in AI development.

---

[80] Megha Shrivastava, *Chinese AI Companies a Perfect match for Domestic Chipmakers*, EAST ASIA FORUM (Mar. 27, 2024), https://eastasiaforum.org/2024/03/27/chinese-ai-companies-a-perfect-match-for-domestic-chipmakers/.

[81] Josh Ye and Urvi Manoj Dugar, *China lets Baidu, others launch ChatGPT-like bots to public, tech shares jump*, REUTERS

Both China and the U.S. possess sufficient data storage capacity, high speed computer networks, chip design capabilities, software sophistication, and the workforce needed to lead in AI development. The competition between these two leading world economies will fuel the AI development race and exacerbate competition between the superpowers.

Despite the tremendous investment in GenAI, these systems currently reflect more promise than performance. GenAI systems mimic language and performance but lack understanding of the content they produce. In other words, AI systems are not yet "smart," in any sense associated with humans or animals.[82]

"In general, digital reasoning- and problem-solving agents only compare very superficially to their biological counterparts."[83] They do not demonstrate the anthropomorphic attribute of "common sense."[84] Instead, they are efficient statistical predictors of information.[85]

(Aug. 31, 2023), https://www.reuters.com/technology/baidu-among-first-win-china-approval-ai-models-bloomberg-news-2023-08-30/.

82 J. E. Hans Korteling et al., *Human-Versus Artificial Intelligence*, 4 FRONTIERS IN A.I. (2021), at 2.

83 *Id.* at 2.

84 *Id.* at 3.

85 *See* Theodore Claypoole, *AI Classifications for Law and Regulation*, BUS. L. TODAY (Sep. 15, 2023), https://businesslawtoday.org/2023/09/ai-classifications-for-law-and-regulation/. ("Ted Chiang has defined artificial intelligence as 'a poor choice of words in 1954,' preferring instead to call our current technologies 'applied statistics.' ").

This distinction, however, may be illusory. Computer-based intelligence and biological intelligence are only loosely related, resulting in each system having very different strengths and weaknesses.[86] For example, ". . . it is well established that emotions influence memory retention and recall . . . . positive emotions facilitate learning and contribute to academic achievement, being mediated by the levels of self-motivation and satisfaction with learning materials."[87] Strong negative emotions also result in learning and recall.[88] Humans and animals, in essence, prioritize memory based on the associated emotional environment of the learning, a process that does not exist in computer-based information systems. Conversely, each living brain is unique and unlike a computer, learning is distinct to each individual human or animal.[89]

Computers can be trained, and their knowledge duplicated across devices.[90] The fundamental difference between computers and humans underscores the first potential misunderstanding in AI: the use of the anthropomorphic term *intelligence*. By doing so, adopters of the technology may inadvertently attribute human characteristics to

---

86 Korteling, *supra* note 82, at 3–4.

87 Chai M. Tyng et al., *The Influences of Emotion on Learning and Memory*, 8 FRONTIERS IN PSYCH. (Aug. 24, 2017), at 3.

88 *See id.* at 11.

89 Korteling, *supra* note 82, at 3–4.

90 *Id.* at 5.

system output.[91] One less value-laden term is "cognitive technology."[92]

> Cognitive technologies, or 'thinking' technologies, fall within a broad category that includes algorithms, robotic process automation, machine learning, natural language processing and natural language generation, reaching into the realm of artificial intelligence (AI). Whether or not these technologies are truly thinking or intelligent is a question of philosophy. For our purposes, these are systems that appear to think or act intelligently, in an analogous way to how humans act, regardless of the ultimate nature of the processes that lead to those actions.[93]

Cognitive technologies differ from predetermined decision-making, which is why AI appears intelligent. For example, a machine that recognizes the most common spelling errors in the English language and automatically corrects a misspelled word is using a pre-programmed response. In contrast, if a word processor can suggest the correct word based on its usage within a sentence, that

---

91 Kathleen Walch, *Why Cognitive Technology May Be A Better Term Than Artificial Intelligence*, FORBES (Dec. 22, 2019), https://www.forbes.com/sites/cognitiveworld/2019/12/22/why-cognitive-technology-may-be-a-better-term-than-artificial-intelligence/?sh=220f790b197c.

92 *Id.*

93 *What is Cognitive Technology?*, INST. OF CHARTERED ACCT. IN ENG. & WALES, https://www.icaew.com/technical/technology/technology-and-the-profession/risks-and-assurance-of-emerging-technologies/what-is-cognitive-technology (last visited Feb. 16, 2025).

predictive algorithm likely relies on the system's ability to weight multiple potentially correct answers and provide the most likely one. The first example demonstrates a structured, formulaic response. The second example requires the system to weigh multiple variables to make a predictive recommendation. The latter example also meets the European definition for artificial intelligence:

> i) [P]erception of the environment and real-world complexity, ii) information processing: collecting and interpreting inputs, iii) decision making, including reasoning, learning and taking actions; and iv) achievement of pre-defined goals.[94]

The word processing example represents a form of "narrow artificial intelligence," because it is designed to perform a very focused task.[95] Artificial general intelligence (AGI), once it has been achieved, will demonstrate "the full range of human intelligence"[96] or meets "the full range of human performance across any task."[97] Finally, beyond general AI may come "artificial superintelligence," the ability of machines

---

[94] Sofia Samoili et al., *AI Watch. Defining Artificial Intelligence*, EUR 30117 EN, 4 PUBLICATIONS OFFICE OF THE EUROPEAN UNION, (2020) (Lux.).

[95] Ray Kurzweil, *Long Live AI*, FORBES (Aug. 15, 2005), https://www.forbes.com/forbes/2005/0815/030.html?sh=1991.ab7d7e8f; *See* Stephan De Spiegeleir et al., *What is Artificial Intelligence? Artificial Intelligence and the Future of Defense*, HAGUE CTR. FOR STRATEGIC STUD. 25, 30 (2017) (describing the task-specific AI as "narrow" or "weak" in contrast to general AI or strong AI).

[96] Kurzweil, *supra* note 95.

[97] Spiegeleire et al., *supra* note 95, at 30.

or computer systems to exceed human capacity in a generalized manner.[98] Narrow AI systems can already exceed human capacity at particular tasks such as playing Chess and Go,[99] as well as in motor-skill games like Maze Run (aka Labyrinth).[100] Still, since human intelligence and silicon-based intelligence are fundamentally different, however, the labels of general AI and superintelligent AI probably miss the point. "AI is a machine's ability to perform the cognitive functions we associate with human minds, such as perceiving, reasoning, learning, interacting with an environment, problem solving, and even exercising creativity."[101] As the technologies evolve, some systems will eventually complete tasks that society associates with human decision making better than humans can accomplish those tasks. It will be the outcome on a list of performance metrics that will ultimately determine

---

[98] *Id.* at 30.

[99] *Id.* at 30.

[100] Saritha Rai, *AI Robot Outmaneuvers Humans in Maze Run Breakthrough*, BLOOMBERG (Dec. 19, 2023), https://www.bloomberg.com/news/articles/2023-12-19/ai-masters-simple-physical-game-in-breakthrough-researchers-say; Thomas Bi and Raffaello D'Andrea, Sample-Efficient Learning to Solve a Real-World Labyrinth Game Using Data-Augmented Model-Based Reinforcement Learning, ARXIV ARXIV:2312.09906 (Dec. 15, 2023) (prepublication print).

[101] Sven Blumberg, *What is AI?*, MCKINSEY & CO. (Apr. 24, 2023), https://www.mckinsey.com/featured-insights/mckinsey-explainers/what-is-ai.

when superintelligence is achieved rather than a technical standard.[102]

§ 1.4 AI OUTPUT AND USES

There are significant legal consequences associated with the choices made regarding which data to use when training large language models and generative adversarial networks, particularly concerning the rights associated with the information incorporated into those systems.[103] Beyond the legal right to acquire and process the data in the model, business enterprises, lawyers, and even regulators generally do not need to focus on the various tools used to create AI systems. Regulators, lawyers, and business leaders, however, should understand how different tools operate because those differences will have consequences in how to draft regulations, manage partnerships, and control risk.

- **Predictive AI:** is a computer program's ability to use statistical analysis to identify patterns, anticipate behaviors, and forecast future events. The field of statistics has long

---

[102] *See Superintelligence is Coming Soon*, AI MYTHS, https://www.aimyths.org/superintelligence-is-coming-soon (last visited Feb. 16, 2025).

[103] *See, e.g.*, Complaint at 1, Getty Images (US), Inc. v. Stability AI, Inc., Case No.1:23–cv–00135 (2023); Complaint at 1, Andersen v. Stability AI Ltd., Case No.3:23–cv–00201 (2023); Complaint at 1, Tremblay v. OpenAI, Inc., Case No.3:23–cv–03223 (2023); Complaint at 1–3, Doe v. GitHub, Inc., Case No.3:22–cv–06823 (2022); Complaint at 1, Silverman v. OpenAI, Inc., Case No.3:23–cv–03416 (2023). For a discussion of various training models, *see* Garon, *The Revolution will be Digitized*, *supra* Preface, at 158–59.

been used to make predictions about the future; predictive AI makes statistical analysis faster and (theoretically) more accurate via machine learning and access to vast amounts of data [sometimes referred to as "big data"]. While its predictions are not guaranteed to be correct, predictive AI can help businesses prepare for the future and personalize experiences for their customers.[104]

- **Automating AI:** Certain AI models automate processes within business or government without making decisions about the opportunities of specific people. Automating AI may streamline an accounting system, research the case law on burglary, or provide a system of forms for running a company. It can replace human workers in some tasks, and therefore has a social impact. [Automating AI can be understood as an implementation of predictive AI. Predictive AI can anticipate the wear of machine parts from a fleet of vehicles or equipment whereas an automating AI system could order the parts and generate the work orders for the repairs.][105]

---

[104] *What is Predictive AI*, CLOUDFLARE, https://www.cloudflare.com/learning/ai/what-is-predictive-ai/ (formatting changed to conform to bullet list) (last visited Feb. 16, 2025).

[105] Claypoole, *supra* note 85 (formatting and punctuation changed to conform to bullet list).

- **Generative AI:** is an AI model that generates content in response to a prompt. It's clear that generative-AI tools like ChatGPT and DALL-E (a tool for making AI-generated art) have the potential to change how a range of jobs are performed. . . . Generative-AI tools can produce a wide variety of credible writing in seconds, then respond to a user's critiques to make the writing more fit for purpose. This has implications for a broad range of industries, from IT and software organizations that can benefit from the instantaneous code generated by AI models to organizations in need of marketing copy.[106]

- **Extractive AI:** is all about extracting information from existing sources. Think of it as a fancy copy-paste machine on steroids. It's used to extract specific information from a text, such as answering questions or summarizing an article. It's also used to generate new content, such as creating a summary of a long article or creating a new headline. . . . One of the most common examples of extractive AI is text summarization . . . keeping the most important information and discarding the rest.[107]

---

[106] Blumberg, *supra* note 101 (formatting and punctuation changed to conform to bullet list).

[107] *Extractive AI vs Generative AI*, NOWIGENCE (Jan. 15, 2023), https://nowigence.com/extractive-ai-vs-generative-ai/ (formatting changed to conform to bullet list).

- **Conversational AI:** refers to technologies, like chatbots or virtual agents, which users can talk to. They use large volumes of data, machine learning, and natural language processing to help imitate human interactions, recognizing speech and text inputs and translating their meanings across various languages. . . . Conversational AI combines natural language processing (NLP) with machine learning. These NLP processes flow into a constant feedback loop with machine learning processes to continuously improve the AI algorithms. Conversational AI has . . . components that allow it to process, understand, and generate response in a natural way.[108]

- **Physical action AI:** Driverless vehicles operate on the interplay between sensors and predictive algorithms, and so do many industrial and consumer technologies. These are systems that use AI to function in the physical world. This category of AI can include running a single machine, like a taxi, or managing traffic systems for millions of vehicles or Internet of Things devices. Legal concerns not only involve safe product design and manufacture, but tort law, insurance issues, and blame-shifting contracts that

108 *What is Conversational AI?*, IBM, https://www.ibm.com/topics/conversational-ai (last visited Feb. 16, 2025).

affect all activity where the laws of physics and moving bodies apply.[109]

- **Decisioning AI [or Algorithmic decision-making]:** This category is not defined by technology but by the technology's effect on people. Algorithmic tools are used to limit or expand the options available to people. AI ranks resumes for human resource managers, highlights who should be interviewed for jobs, and evaluates the reactions of applicants in those interviews. For years algorithms have made prison parole recommendations, sorted loan applicants, and denied suspicious credit transactions. These decisions are subject to bias of various types, also raising issues of transparency, accuracy, and reliability. The EU and some US states have already regulated this category of AI. The Chinese government has elevated these tools into a societal scoring system that can affect every aspect of a citizen's life and freedom.[110]

Although predictive AI systems have been used for decades in activities as diverse as deciding what foods to stock in grocery stores, disease prediction, drug discovery, financial fraud detection,[111] and

---

[109] Claypoole, *supra* note 85 (formatting changed to conform to bullet list).

[110] *Id.*

[111] Will Hillier, *7 Fascinating Examples of Predictive Analytics in Action*, CAREER FOUNDRY (July 6, 2023), https://careerfoundry.com/en/blog/data-analytics/predictive-analytics-examples/.

weather forecasting,[112] it was the potential of generative AI to create new content that made 2023 the year of AI—specifically generative AI.[113] Generative AI can create text-based works ranging from marketing and sales materials[114] to original novels.[115] For example, in December 2023, Professor Shen Yang spent three hours creating a science fiction novel entitled *The Land of Machine Memories*, which he submitted to the Jiangsu Popular Science and Science Fiction Competition. The novel took second place.[116]

Generative AI can also be used to create or replicate audio, including individual voices, generate still and video images from text prompts or preexisting photos and videos, write software code,

---

112 *See* Mariya Yao, *Generative vs Predictive AI: Key Differences & Real-World Applications*, TOPBOTS (Oct. 4, 2023), https://www.topbots.com/generative-vs-predictive-ai/; The Weather Company, *AI in Weather Forecasting, Prediction and Communication*, IBM (July 24, 2023), https://www.ibm.com/weather/industries/broadcast-media/ai-weather-forecasting-prediction-communication.

113 David Lumb, *2023 Has Been the Year of Generative AI. It's Coming to Phones in 2024*, CNET (Oct. 24, 2023), https://www.cnet.com/tech/mobile/2023-has-been-the-year-of-generative-ai-its-coming-to-phones-in-2024/.

114 Blumberg, *supra* note 101.

115 Justinas Vainilavičius, *AI-Generated Science Fiction Novel Wins Literary Prize in China,* CYBERNEWS (Dec. 20, 2023), https://cybernews.com/news/ai-novel-wins-prize-china/; Holly Chik, *A Chinese Professor used AI to Write a Science Fiction Novel. Then it was a Winner in a National Competition*, S. CHINA MORN. POST (Dec. 20, 2023), https://www.scmp.com/news/china/science/article/3245725/chinese-professor-used-ai-write-science-fiction-novel-then-it-won-national-award.

116 Vainilavičius, *supra* note 115.

and generate complex designs for products, architecture, and even molecular structures used to create new drug treatments and gene sequencing.[117] By combining generative AI output with predictive AI data analysis, "AI enables marketers to create highly personalized and targeted campaigns. By understanding individual preferences, behavior, and demographics, businesses can tailor their marketing efforts to engage customers on a deeper level."[118] For product sales, this means that personalization will drive higher attention and engagement rates. "McKinsey's research found that firms that invest in AI are seeing a revenue uplift of 3% to 15%—and a sales return on investment increase of 10% to 20%."[119] "Generative AI analyzes vast amounts of data to identify patterns and understand individual preferences, behavior, and demographics. This allows businesses to tailor their marketing campaigns to target specific segments of their

---

117 *Gartner Experts Answer the Top Generative AI Questions for Your Enterprise*, GARTNER, https://www.gartner.com/en/topics/generative-ai; *What is Generative AI?*, NVIDIA, (Dec. 23, 2023), https://www.nvidia.com/en-us/glossary/data-science/generative-ai/.

118 *Generative AI in Digital Marketing: Revolutionizing the Way Businesses Connect*, GOFLARE (June 17, 2023), https://www.linkedin.com/pulse/generative-ai-digital-marketing-revolutionizing-way-businesses/.

119 Steve Ranger, *Generative AI is Making Sales More Efficient—and More Human*, TECHFINITIVE (Dec. 8, 2023), https://www.techfinitive.com/features/generative-ai-is-making-sales-more-efficient-and-more-human/ (citing Richelle Deveau, Sonia Joseph Griffin, & Steve Reis, *AI-Powered Marketing and Sales Reach New Heights with Generative* AI, MCKINSEY & CO. (May 2023)).

audience, increasing the chances of engagement and conversion."[120]

Predictive AI and generative AI behave quite differently. Predictive AI is part of "[c]lassical AI (often referred to as Traditional or Symbolic AI) . . . systems that use rules and logic to mimic human intelligence. . . . Classical AI algorithms process data and return expected results such as analyses or predictions."[121] Generative AI is designed to simulate a conversation or other output of a literary work rather than to consider accuracy or validity of either the questions or answers. "If I ask a LLM, 'How does the sun rise in the west?,' the model may respond with an explanation of this fake phenomenon. In this scenario, the LLM has misinterpreted the context and generated a response that attempts to provide a coherent explanation for an illogical statement."[122]

Generative AI does not extract specific data points from the internet or informational databases. Instead, it creates new content based on the prompts triggering the query and the patterns it has learned about that type of prompt.[123] Generative AI (GAI)

---

[120] GoFlare, *supra* note 118.

[121] Arun Shastri, *Generative AI Errs Differently Than Classical AI*, FORBES (Sept. 4, 2023), https://www.forbes.com/sites/arunshastri/2023/09/04/generative-ai-errs-differently-than-classical-ai/.

[122] *Id.*

[123] *See* Thomas H. Davenport & Nitin Mittal, *How Generative AI Is Changing Creative Work*, HARV. BUS. REV. (Nov. 14, 2022), https://hbr.org/2022/11/how-generative-ai-is-changing-creative-work ("The software uses complex machine learning models to predict the next word based on previous word sequences, or the next image based on words describing previous images.").

systems are "able to produce text and images, spanning blog posts, program code, poetry, and artwork."[124] At present, the systems offer only rudimentary fact-checking of the resulting output. A common criticism is that generative AI is prone to a significant error rate. For example, an early assessment on ChatGPT's software programming found that ChatGPT "answered just 48% of the questions correctly, while 77% were described as 'verbose.' "[125] In many cases, participants preferred the ChatGPT answers because of the well-articulated and comprehensive nature of the response, but "77% of those preferred answers were wrong."[126] Another study using ChatGPT 4 found that the system had an 80.1 percent error rate when asked to improve the user experience of a website, chiefly generating suggestions that were harmful or irrelevant to the proposed task.[127]

A more positive study "led by investigators from Mass General Brigham has found that ChatGPT was about 72 percent accurate in overall clinical decision making, from coming up with possible diagnoses to making final diagnoses and care management

---

[124] *Id.*

[125] *ChatGPT Exhibits an Error Rate of Over 50% in Answering Programming Questions in a Recent Study*, FOCUS CONTENT (Aug. 9, 2023), https://focus.hidubai.com/chatgpt-gets-more-than-50-programming-questions-wrong-in-recent-study/.

[126] *Id.*

[127] Merlyn Meredith, *ChatGPT and UX Audits: the Current Limits of Generative AI*, TRYZENS, https://tryzens.com/data-insights/chatgpt-and-ux-audits-the-current-limits-of-generative-ai/ (last visited Feb. 16, 2025).

decisions."[128] That error rate, however, means that the system would misdiagnose patients more than a quarter of the time. "It was lowest-performing in making differential diagnoses, where it was only 60 percent accurate. And it was only 68 percent accurate in clinical management decisions, such as figuring out what medications to treat the patient with after arriving at the correct diagnosis."[129] Despite the headlines suggesting success, the error rates are likely much higher than would be tolerated in any other automated system.

There has been an effort to focus GAI systems on pre-qualified data, using a technique known as "retrieval-augmented generation (RAG)."[130] RAG "is a technique for enhancing the accuracy and reliability of generative AI models with facts fetched from external sources" by limiting the source material to information that has been separately validated.[131] Published medical studies, for example, provide a RAG based GenAI system with only accurate, peer-reviewed content from which to infer predictive texts. While this should increase the accuracy and offers the potential for citations for the user to verify the source data, it does not mean that

---

128 *ChatGPT Shows 'Impressive' Accuracy in Clinical Decision Making*, MASS GENERAL BRIGHAM (Aug. 22, 2023), https://www.massgeneralbrigham.org/en/about/newsroom/press-releases/chatgpt-shows-impressive-accuracy-in-clinical-decision-making.

129 *Id.*

130 *See* Rick Merritt, *What Is Retrieval-Augmented Generation, aka RAG?*, NVIDIA (Nov. 15, 2023), https://blogs.nvidia.com/blog/what-is-retrieval-augmented-generation/.

131 *Id.*

the system synthesized the research or understands the medical output. In legal research, the RAG GAI system is pulling from existing case law, but case law includes overturned cases, dissenting opinions, lower court decisions and a large body of information that does not reflect the present state of the law on a given topic. As a result, RAG based legal systems offer only marginal increased utility.

Many systems use multiple forms of AI to achieve functionality rather than relying on a single AI system. Autonomous vehicles, for example, use machine learning, predictive analytics, and other systems.[132] "Increasing levels of autonomy in cyber-physical systems (CPS) promise to revolutionize industries such as automotive transportation and aviation."[133] This will only be possible, however, if the systems can be tested to ensure they are safe and reliable in real world conditions.[134] A promising, but self-reported, study from Alphabet's autonomous vehicle subsidiary, Waymo, suggests that at least some of these systems are getting close. Waymo offers self-driving taxis. At the end of 2023, it reported "[t]his year alone, Waymo has served over 700,000 ride-hailing trips with public riders and no human driver."[135] The early reports are quite promising:

---

132 *See* Anthony Corso et al., *A Survey of Algorithms for Black-Box Safety Validation of Cyber-Physical Systems*, 72 J. AI RES. 377 (2021), https://jair.org/index.php/jair/article/view/12716/26727.

133 *Id.* at 377.

134 *Id.*

135 *Waymo Significantly Outperforms Comparable Human Benchmarks Over 7+ Million Miles of Rider-Only Driving*, WAYMO (Dec. 20, 2023), https://waymo.com/blog/2023/12/waymo-

- An 85% reduction or 6.8 times lower crash rate involving any injury, from minor to severe and fatal cases (0.41 incidence per million miles for the Waymo Driver vs 2.78 for the human benchmark)
- A 57% reduction or 2.3 times lower police-reported crash rate (2.1 incidence per million miles for the Waymo Driver vs. 4.85 for the human benchmark)

This means that over the 7.1 million miles Waymo drove, there were an estimated 17 fewer injuries, and 20 fewer police-reported crashes compared to if human drivers with the benchmark crash rate would have driven the same distance in the areas we operate.[136]

The Waymo success should be reviewed in context with a recent insurance study that found Tesla drivers have the highest accident rate and the second worst driving records, surpassed only by drivers of Ram trucks.[137] The Tesla driving records are being reported on the heels of a mandatory recall of two million Tesla vehicles because the "National Highway Traffic Safety Administration (NHTSA). . .

---

significantly-outperforms-comparable-human-benchmarks-over-7-million.

[136] *Id. See* Kristofer D. Kusano et al., *Comparison of Waymo Rider-Only Crash Data to Human Benchmarks at 7.1 Million Miles*, ARXIV (Dec. 20, 2023), https://arxiv.org/abs/2312.12675.

[137] Michelle Lambright Black, *Ram, Tesla and Subaru Have the Worst Drivers, While BMW Drivers Have the Highest DUI Rates*, LENDINGTREE (Dec. 18, 2023), https://www.lendingtree.com/insurance/brand-incidents-study/.

found that the car models featuring the self-driving feature . . . contain a high-risk software flaw that has likely contributed to an increase in wrecks and crashes."[138] The NHTSA report explains that drivers may attempt to engage the Autosteer feature under conditions when it should not be engaged, creating a risk that neither the driver nor the Autosteer was controlling the vehicle.[139]

Whether Tesla's problem is rooted in AI, human error, or a failure of user-interface design is ultimately beside the point, as the result is a less safe driving experience. In contrast, the Waymo data suggests that other systems might improve safety. This comparison highlights that AI systems extend well beyond decision-making algorithms. All systems—both human and machine—must be assessed continuously for errors.[140] However, since the nature of likely error differs between systems, AI adopters must understand the nature of the specific system being employed to ensure that the correct error correction mechanisms are put in place.

---

[138] Larisha Paul, *Tesla Recalls 2 Million Cars With Self-Driving Feature Over High-Risk Software Flaw*, ROLLINGSTONE (Dec. 13, 2023), https://www.rollingstone.com/culture/culture-news/elon-musk-tesla-recall-self-driving-feature-1234927048/.

[139] *See id.*

[140] *See generally*, ARTIFICIAL INTELLIGENCE RISK MANAGEMENT FRAMEWORK, AI RMF 1.0, NIST (Jan. 2023), https://doi.org/10.6028/NIST.AI.100-1 [hereinafter NIST AI FRAMEWORK]; Kelly Dempset et al., INFORMATION SECURITY CONTINUOUS MONITORING (ISCM) FOR FEDERAL INFORMATION SYSTEMS AND ORGANIZATIONS, NAT. INST. STANDARDS & TECH. (Sept. 2011) (although focused on security risks, the assessment strategies apply generally to a wide array of error and risk).

Without this simple safeguard, every system is prone to failure.

§ 1.5 ILLUSTRATIVE USES OF AI TODAY AND TOMORROW

Although much of this Nutshell focuses on risks and dangers associated with unregulated and misused AI systems, the public enthusiasm should indicate that these concerns presuppose a tremendous interest and value in these systems. AI systems enable mapping features on smartphones, improve the detection and treatment of cancers, streamline online shopping, improve agricultural output, language translation, disability accommodation, robotics, and untold other examples large and small. As already noted, ChatGPT set records for its usage in the first two months since its launch. In 2024, "GPT-4 has gained tremendous popularity among users, receiving an astounding 10 million queries per day."[141]

Each category of AI has distinct primary use cases, and AI is rapidly transforming sectors such as health care, retail, education, finance, and beyond. These are a few of their stories.

§ 1.5.1 HEALTHCARE

Healthcare represents one of the most compelling use cases for all forms of AI. The challenge for

[141] Maryna Bilan, *Responsible Generative AI: Limitations, Risks, and Future Directions of Large Language Models (LLMs)*, MASTER OF CODE (Sept. 22, 2024), https://masterofcode.com/blog/generative-ai-limitations-risks-and-future-directions-of-llms.

healthcare includes the need to "improve population health, improve the patient's experience of care, enhance caregiver experience and reduce the rising cost of care."[142] "Hospitals and health systems increasingly are adopting artificial intelligence technologies built into health IT such as EHRs, telehealth services, remote patient monitoring and other tools that can expand access to care and improve health equity."[143]

The most significant area of AI adoption has been in the field of diagnostic imaging. X-ray systems are increasingly relying on machine learning-based devices to detect conditions such as pneumonia, skin lesions, lymph node metastases, and other abnormalities.[144]

Other notable examples include "ambient sensing," which involves devices that monitor patients without requiring intrusive measures, potentially improving both usage and reliability.[145] Touchless sensors, motion and sound detection monitors, and similar devices are already being used

---

[142] J. Bajwa et al., *Artificial Intelligence in Healthcare: Transforming the Practice of Medicine*, FUTURE HEALTHCARE J. 188 (July 2021), https://www.ncbi.nlm.nih.gov/pmc/articles/PMC8285156/.

[143] Bill Siwicki, *AI and Public Health—a Major Opportunity*, HEALTH CARE IT NEWS (Jan. 5, 2024), https://www.healthcareitnews.com/news/ai-and-public-health-major-opportunity.

[144] Bajwa, *supra* note 142, at 191.

[145] *See id.*

to monitor sleep, heart rhythms, and patient behaviors.[146]

In addition, experimentation is underway to better understand the "cellular and molecular basis of disease" and then to design new drugs designed to combat these diseases with fewer side effects.[147] These efforts combine many of the different AI systems to help broaden medical understanding and create new treatments. By combining generative AI and predictive AI tools, researchers can model thousands of potential proteins and identify how those proteins would react as potential medical treatments. Other systems are trained on the data from existing drugs to predict where those drugs might prove efficacious in fighting rare diseases, expanding the impact of existing drugs and treatments for patients who receive less investment and fewer treatment options.

Chatbots and natural language processing also contribute significantly to the overall healthcare system. These technologies are designed to improve public access to healthcare information and relieve healthcare professionals from the tedious and time-consuming tasks of reporting and recording their interactions with patients during treatment. Freeing doctors and healthcare professionals from electronic record entry will have substantial enhance both efficiency and the quality of patient interactions.

---

146 *See id.*

147 *See id.*

AI also plays an important role in the improvement of public health. "In the realm of disease surveillance, AI stands as a powerful tool. . . . AI can learn through large-scale datasets, including social media trends, healthcare records and environmental factors, to predict disease outbreaks and their potential spread."[148] AI uses both medical and non-medical data, such as Google search trends, to predict flu outbreaks and other health trends. "This predictive capacity enables public health officials to implement targeted interventions, optimize resource allocation and formulate proactive strategies, thereby mitigating the impact of potential health crises."[149]

Health care and public health should be considered broadly when assessing the potential impact of AI systems. Many tools that take advantage of generative AI also provide low cost and readily available accommodation tools for people who need Americans with Disabilities Act (ADA)[150] accommodations for work, education, or other aspects of their daily lives. Such tools may include text captioning, real-time translation, automated image descriptions, text to audio services, and others. More sophisticated tools may include some of the same technologies that enable a self-driving car to create a

---

148 Siwicki, *supra* note 143 (quoting Dr. Xin Wang, assistant professor in the department of epidemiology and biostatistics at the University at Albany.).

149 *Id.*

150 Americans with Disabilities Act of 1990 (Pub. L. No. 101–336, 104 Stat. 327, codified 42 U.S.C. §§ 12112–12117).

semi-autonomous wheelchair or a portable device to help people navigate their surroundings.

The internet is particularly important for access to public health as well as for work and education. In March 2022, the Civil Rights Division of the Department of Justice released a report entitled "Why Website Accessibility Matters."[151] The report promotes adherence to "the Web Content Accessibility Guidelines (WCAG) and the Section 508 Standards [of the Rehabilitation Act], which the federal government uses for its own websites."[152]

Generative AI has established a significant presence in healthcare beyond its important role in furthering ADA and Rehabilitation Act accommodations. These tools enhance efficiency for virtual and rapid prototyping systems, enabling AI to provide a range of iterative and complex design recommendations across various industries. Users provide parameters such as materials, size, weight, and operational constraints. Based on these parameters, the AI can generate dozens, hundreds, or even thousands of design iterations and then select those that best optimize the desired criteria, whether that is weight, strength, or manufacturing steps.[153]

---

151 WHY WEBSITE ACCESSIBILITY MATTERS, U.S. DEPT. OF JUSTICE, CIV. RIGHTS DIV. (Mar. 18, 2022), https://www.ada.gov/resources/web-guidance/.

152 *Id.* at 4. *See* Rehabilitation Act of 1973, 29 U.S.C. § 794 (2024).

153 Graeme Fulton, *Generative UI Design: Einstein, Galileo, and the AI Design Process*, PROTOTYPR (Feb. 16, 2023), https://prototypr.io/post/generative-ai-design.

"Digital simulation and analysis are now so fast that designs can be evaluated in seconds—or even less."[154]

§ 1.5.2 PRODUCT DESIGN

Generative AI assists designers with the aesthetic appearance of products, user interface designs, marketing effectiveness, lighter weight components, and much more.[155] The AI can use the simulations to generate additional iterations. "Using artificial-intelligence techniques, these new generative design systems can explore a much larger universe of possible solutions, comparing the results of thousands of simulations to close in on a design that delivers the most favorable combination of attributes."[156]

Although generative design services have proven effective in reducing the cost of production for some items and achieving redesign goals, such as to reduce the weight of an existing product, there is still reluctance to fully embrace these new techniques. "One of the first barriers is likely to be stakeholder acceptance of the resulting parts and products: generative algorithms produce designs that may be radically different from their human-designed predecessors. Some observers even find them "alien"

[154] Mickael Brossard et al., *How Generative Design Could Reshape the Future of Product Development*, MCKINSEY & COMPANY (Feb. 5, 2020), https://www.mckinsey.com/capabilities/operations/our-insights/how-generative-design-could-reshape-the-future-of-product-development.

[155] Fulton, *supra* note 153.

[156] Brossard, *supra* note 154.

or disturbing."[157] Another common challenge is the risk that AI disturbs the institutional culture among its designers, leading to reliance on AI-generated-know-how rather than the accumulated wisdom of engineers.[158] Even if there is openness for adoption, the challenge remains that AI strategies need to be integrated into the broader design, procurement, and construction strategies of organizations.[159]

One particular area where generative AI shows significant potential is pharmaceutical research, where the constraints and costs of design and engineering are often prohibitive. Research indicates that generative AI may play a role in creating "de novo drug design." "De novo drug design (DNDD) refers to the design of novel chemical entities that fit a set of constraints using computational growth algorithms."[160]

The ability of generative AI to develop new medical treatments, as well as medical devices and devices of all kinds, demonstrates the powerful potential for generative design products to become increasingly ubiquitous in product planning and development. Using a wide range of AI techniques, including generative AI, scientists can design new molecules and then test them through simulation to identify

---

157 *Id.*

158 *See id.*

159 *See id.*

160 Varnavas D. Mouchlis et al., *Advances in De Novo Drug Design: From Conventional to Machine Learning Methods*, INT'L J. MOLECULAR SCI. (Feb. 7, 2021), at 2, https://www.ncbi.nlm.nih.gov/pmc/articles/PMC7915729/.

where their bioactivities meet the goals for potential drug or treatment.[161] "In the De novo drug design process, the deep learning models acts as autoencoder to generate an appropriate format for new chemical entities (NCE's). Therefore, an embedment of autoencoder with multilayer perceptron classifier is also a value-added technique in the generation of NCE's with predefined physicochemical properties."[162] These tools can radically reduce the time needed to prototype new medicine and increase the likelihood of effectiveness.

§ 1.5.2 AUTONOMOUS VEHICLES AND ROBOTICS

Autonomous cars, trucks, vessels, and robotic devices illustrate another significant use case for AI systems. These devices can range from the Roomba, which automates the chore of home vacuuming to much more sophisticated systems. "From OpenAI to Google DeepMind, almost every big technology firm with AI expertise is now working on bringing the versatile learning algorithms that power chatbots, known as foundation models, to robotics. The idea is

---

161 *See id.* at 9–10 ("A shape-based generative approach for de novo drug design was developed using [a convolutional neural network] to generate novel molecules from a seed compound, its three-dimensional shape, and its pharmacophoric features.").

162 Suresh Dara et al., *Machine Learning in Drug Discovery: A Review*, 55 A.I. REV. 1947, 1974 (2022), https://www.ncbi.nlm.nih.gov/pmc/articles/PMC8356896/ (internal citations omitted).

to imbue robots with common-sense knowledge, letting them tackle a wide range of tasks."[163]

Robotics have been used in industry since the 1930s.[164] The most common model is a device comprised of a stationary arm that can lift objects, manipulate tools, and carry out tasks on an assembly line. "bots collaborate with human workers (co-bots) on almost all tasks. Robotics in manufacturing is used for repeated tasks and to streamline the assembly workflow. Many industries involve dangerous and voluminous tasks that can harm human workers."[165] By focusing on replacing highly repetitive tasks, machines can be very efficient, and human workers are free to engage in non-repetitive steps. If the devices are large, then making them stationary also tends to reduce risk of accidents between the machines and the employees.

Programming machines to carry out repetitive tasks often involves structured programming steps, reflecting the lowest level of decision-making. These systems may not even qualify as AI, depending on the definition being applied and the level of responsiveness the device has to the input it gathers from its surroundings. (The answer to the question will only matter if future legislation adds licensure

---

[163] Elizabeth Gibney, *The AI Revolution is Coming to Robots: How will it Change Them?*, 630 NATURE 22 (June 6, 2024), https://www.nature.com/articles/d41586-024-01442-5.

[164] *See Impact of Robotics in Manufacturing*, UNIVERSAL ROBOTICS (Nov. 15, 2022), https://www.universal-robots.com/in/blog/impact-of-robotics/.

[165] *Id.*

requirements for all AI-based machines.) By incorporating various AI systems into machines, they can interact with their environment in increasingly sophisticated ways.

At the same time, even "[a]pparently simple tasks, such as opening a door, are actually hugely complex, requiring a robot to understand how different door mechanisms work, how much force to apply to a handle and how to maintain balance while doing so. The real world is extremely varied and constantly changing."[166] Yet despite the challenges, the real-world applications continue to grow. AI enables assembly line machines to operate with much greater variety of steps and tasks. Assembly of large planes and ships do not fit on assembly lines, but mobile robots can help with the movement and assembly of large component pieces needed for such work. In addition, sophisticated sensors on the machines can detect flaws and help improve quality throughout the process.[167]

There are many examples of AI-equipped robotics entering the economy.[168] Starship Technologies offer robotic delivery in selected urban areas throughout the U.S. "Starship robots can carry items within a 4-mile (6km) radius, navigate streets autonomously,

---

166 *Id.*

167 *See Introduction to AI Applications in Robotics*, U. SAN DIEGO, https://onlinedegrees.sandiego.edu/application-of-ai-in-robotics/ (last visited Feb. 16, 2025).

168 *See* Joseph Mapue, *12 Top Companies in the Vanguard of the Rise of Humanoid Robots*, DOSS DAWSON, https://rossdawson.com/futurist/companies-creating-future/top-companies-rise-humanoid-robots/ (last visited Feb. 16, 2025).

and provide package delivery for consumers and businesses. The robots are equipped with sensors, AI, and mapping system to understand their location and the world around them."[169] SoftBank Robotics produces "Pepper," a four foot tall humanoid robot with a large display screen on its chest designed to operate as a customer service agent in retail locations.[170]

In Asia, robots and self-driving vehicles are increasingly being included in surveillance and law enforcement activities. Conically-shaped robots have been used to watch over pedestrian traffic in South Korean malls, and the country plans to add autonomous police vehicles to expand late-night surveillance patrols.[171]

In the U.S., Waymo represents the most advanced example of self-driving vehicles. Launched in 2009, Waymo now offers 50,000 weekly rides from its autonomous taxi service offered in Los Angeles, San Francisco, and Phoenix.[172] General Motors is testing a self-driving taxi, while Tesla has announced plans to enter the market. Other automakers are

---

169 *10 Artificial Intelligence Robots Examples And Uses in Business*, INTELLSPOT, https://www.intellspot.com/artificial-intelligence-robots/ (last visited Feb. 16, 2025).

170 *See id.*

171 Lee Kyung-min, *Korea Aims to Have Robots Help Police on Patrols by 2024*, KOREA TIMES (Mar. 3, 2023), https://www.koreatimes.co.kr/www/tech/2024/03/129_346401.html.

172 David Meyer, *How Waymo Outlasted the Competition and Made Robo-Taxis a Real Business*, FORTUNE (May 29, 2024), https://fortune.com/2024/05/29/waymo-self-driving-robo-taxi-uber-tesla-alphabet/.

experimenting with self-driving vehicles but are not in tests within the U.S.[173]

At sea, unmanned vessels or autonomous ships are also being tested. In 2022, the Yara Birkeland completed its maiden voyage as the "world's first fully electric, completely autonomous cargo ship has successfully completed its maiden voyage in Norway."[174] To operate autonomously, the ship features automatic mooring arms and sensor arrays. "The sensors come in the form of radar, infrared cameras, and automotive integrated solutions cameras. Combined, these give the ship the ability to discover obstacles in its path and avoid them."[175] In addition, although the ship is designed to operate autonomously, it incorporates remote control functionality allowing human operators to override the system and pilot it remotely from shore.[176]

In all fields of robotics and autonomous vehicles, the increasing sophistication of object recognition, machine dexterity, natural language processing, and other technologies are enabling glimpses of smart robotics that closely resemble the machines of science fiction. " 'I wouldn't be surprised if we are the last generation for which those sci-fi scenes are not a reality,' says Alexander Khazatsky, a machine-

---

173 *See id.*

174 Frankie Youd, *Crewless Cargo: The World's First Autonomous Electric Cargo Ship*, SHIP TECH. (Feb. 24, 2022), https://www.ship-technology.com/features/crewless-cargo-the-worlds-first-autonomous-electric-cargo-ship/?cf-view.

175 *Id.*

176 *Id.*

learning and robotics researcher at Stanford University in California."[177] The rapid pace of experimentation and development has made such predictions a real possibility.

§ 1.5.3 GENERATIVE AI: TEXT, VOICE, IMAGE, VIDEO, CODE, DESIGN, AND 3D MODELS

While generative AI can potentially be incorporated into almost any human activity, there are some key areas where the technology has already been put to use. "[T]he introduction of APIs [application program interfaces] and open-source tools are allowing entrepreneurs to build upon existing foundation models and narrow in on specific verticals like gaming, graphic design, copywriting, media, and entertainment."[178]

A study on collaboration among people using AI as a catalyst found that using technology as an augmentation to human creative collaborations proved very promising.

> AI may play important roles in influencing social dynamics during creativity by: 1) implicitly seeding common ground at the start of collaboration, 2) acting as a psycho-logical safety net in creative risk-taking, 3) providing a force for group progress, 4) mitigating interpersonal

---

[177] Gibney, *supra* note 163, at 22.

[178] Clarke Pennington, *Generative AI: The New Frontier For VC Investment*, FORBES (Jan. 17, 2023), https://www.forbes.com/sites/columbiabusinessschool/2023/01/17/generative-ai-the-new-frontier-for-vc-investment/.

stalling and friction, and 5) altering users' collaborative and creative roles.[179]

Generative AI text, music, video, gaming, design, and software have the power to reshape the world around us, and in so doing so, also reshape and mediate the ways in which we interact with each other. These areas are ripe for transformational change as AI augmentation and AI creation redefines how media is conceived, developed, and executed.

Image generation stands out as one of the key functions of generative AI. An image generator can create a novel image that is functionally indistinguishable from real photographs.[180] Image generators can also be used to create wholly original works of art.[181] "With AI art generators, you can type in a prompt as detailed or vague as you'd like and have the image you were thinking of pop up on your screen instantly. These tools can help with branding, social media content creation, vision boards, and

---

[179] Minhyang (Mia) Suh et al., *AI As Social Glue: Uncovering the Roles of Deep Generative AI During Social Music Composition*, CHI CONFERENCE ON HUMAN FACTORS IN COMPUTING SYSTEMS (May 8, 2021), https://dl.acm.org/doi/fullHtml/10.1145/3411764.3445219.

[180] *See* Daniel Zhang et al., *The AI Index 2022 Annual Report*, AI INDEX STEERING COMMITTEE, STANFORD INSTITUTE FOR HUMAN-CENTERED AI, STANFORD UNIVERSITY 54 (Mar. 2022), https://aiindex.stanford.edu/wp-content/uploads/2022/03/2022-AI-Index-Report_Master.pdf.

[181] Sabrina Ortiz, *The Best AI Art Generators: DALL-E 2 and Other Fun Alternatives to Try*, ZDNET (Feb. 27, 2023), https://www.zdnet.com/article/best-ai-art-generator/.

more."[182] The most impactful art generation program is DALL-E by OpenAI (the same company that released ChatGPT).

Generated Photos,[183] an online service, boasts that it can provide "2,677,079 low-res generated photos" to users for free,[184] with the promise that "[g]enerated photos are created from scratch by AI systems. All images can be used for any purpose without worrying about copyrights, distribution rights, infringement claims, or royalties."[185] As discussed in the next section, however, these claims promising no copyright violations and no "infringement" claims (that presumably covers defamation and violations of the rights of publicity) may be overly optimistic.

AI-based image generation has already gone mainstream. Adobe's highly popular photo editing software, Photoshop, has added an AI integration.[186] Google has added a "magic eraser" function to its photo apps that is becoming increasingly powerful.[187]

---

182 *Id.* (In addition to DALL-E, other services include Dream by WOMBO, Craiyon, Midjourney, and MyHeritage's AI Time Machine).

183 Generated Photos, https://generated.photos/ (last visited Feb. 16, 2025).

184 Generated Photos, https://generated.photos/pricing (last visited Feb. 16, 2025).

185 Generated Photos, https://generated.photos/ (last visited Feb. 16, 2025).

186 Brian X. Chen, *How to Use A.I. to Edit and Generate Stunning Photos*, N.Y. TIMES (June 2, 2023), https://www.nytimes.com/2023/06/02/technology/ai-photo-editing.html.

187 Dina Berrada & Esteban Kozak, *Magic Eraser plus more Google Photos features coming to Google One*, GOOGLE (Feb. 23,

Lambda Labs has created one of the first image mixers, that enable a user to upload 3–5 source images to generate a new image based on those works.[188] These highly popular tools are complemented by dozens of apps that provide some level of AI-based photo enhancements.

Image generation can move beyond photorealistic images of people, places, and things. "[C]ompanies like NVIDIA have already used image generators to create virtual worlds for gaming."[189] This has the potential to create ever-expanding videogame and metaverse environments similar to those often depicted in films.[190] Image generation can also be

---

2023), https://blog.google/products/photos/magic-eraser-android-ios-google-one/.

[188] Damir Yalalov, *Lambda Labs Announced an AI Image Mixer that can Combine up to Five Images*, METAVERSE POST (Jan. 20, 2023), https://mpost.io/lambda-labs-announced-an-ai-image-mixer-that-can-combine-up-to-five-images/.

[189] Zhang, *supra* note 180, at 54.

[190] *See* Chris E. Hayner, *21 Virtual Reality Movies, Ranked from Awful To Amazing*, GAMESPOT (May 3, 2021), https://www.gamespot.com/gallery/21-virtual-reality-movies-ranked-from-awful-to-amazing/2900-1874/ (listing the Matrix as the best such film. Others include Ready Player One, Tron, Spy Kids 3-D, Total Recall, and many others.); Ben Wodecki, *AI in Video Games: From Development to Design*, AI BUSINESS (Oct. 15, 2021), https://aibusiness.com/verticals/ai-in-video-games-from-development-to-design (discussing the various roles AI can take in game design, development, and game play); Devindra Hardawar, *How 'Microsoft Flight Simulator' became a 'living game' with Azure AI*, ENGADGET (Sept. 25, 2020) https://www.engadget.com/microsoft-flight-simulator-azure-ai-machine-learning-193545436.html ("Microsoft's Azure . . . was able to push 2.5 petabytes worth of Bing Maps satellite photo data through Azure machine learning to construct the virtual world of *Flight Simulator*. You could say it's

used in fashion to virtualize different clothing patterns and different applications of color and design on those clothing patterns.[191] For example, "Stitch Fix, the online service that uses recommendation algorithms to personalize apparel, says it has experimented with DALL-E 2 to visualize its products based on specific characteristics like color, fabric and style."[192] "Rowan Curran, an AI and data science analyst at IT research firm Forrester Research Inc., said he expects generative AI to impact enterprises from top to bottom. . . . '[T]he use of text-to-image generators for inspiration, ideation and prototyping for marketers, designers and developers has just barely begun.' "[193]

The visual works need not be limited to still images. Meta was first to shift to video with "Make-A-Video, an AI system that lets people turn text prompts into brief, high-quality video clips."[194] The output resembles GIFs very short animation of generated images but as a proof of concept, they

---

really the cloud that brings the game to life. Azure also helps to model real-time weather.").

191 *See* Zhang, *supra* note 180, at 54.

192 Kyle Wiggers, *Businesses including Stitch Fix are Already Experimenting with DALL-E 2*, TECHCRUNCH (Aug. 9, 2022), https://techcrunch.com/2022/08/09/businesses-including-stitch-fix-are-already-experimenting-with-dall-e-2/.

193 Angus Loten, *Generative AI Startups Attract Business Customers, Investor Funding*, WALL ST. J. (Oct. 25, 2022), https://www.wsj.com/articles/generative-ai-startups-attract-business-customers-investor-funding-11666736176.

194 *Introducing Make-A-Video: An AI system that generates videos from text*, META AI (Sept. 29, 2022), https://ai.facebook.com/blog/generative-ai-text-to-video/.

illustrate the next step in text-to-video generation. Other vendors have already surpassed these efforts, including Synthesia, Pictory, Elai.io, and a growing list.[195]

OpenAI's entrant in video is Sora. Released in December 2024, Sora enables creators to provide a text prompt and generate videos of stunning detail and accuracy.[196] "Alex Williams of Escape Studios, an animator whose credits include 'The Lion King' "[197] responded to the demonstration by saying " '[t]here's no question that this is the biggest change I've seen in my career. I would draw comparisons with the switch from 2D to 3D animation. . . We all fought it collectively for a while, but it became the great box office driver.' "[198] In addition to Sora, other text to video services are also emerging, including Meta's Emu, Runway, PixVerse, Pika Labs, and others.

While generative art and synthetic media initially captured attention as popular forms of generative AI, it was the release of ChatGPT that truly marked a turning point in the technology's widespread

---

195 *See* Alex McFarland, *8 "Best" AI Video Generators (March 2023)*, BEST OF (Mar. 5, 2023), https://www.unite.ai/best-ai-video-generators/.

196 *See Creating Video From Text*, OPENAI, https://openai.com/index/sora/ (last visited Feb. 16, 2025); Cristina Criddle & Rory Griffiths, *How good is OpenAI's Sora Video Model—and will it Transform Jobs?*, FINANCIAL TIMES (May 1, 2024), https://www.ft.com/content/ab70695f-584a-49bf-a635-38175be0718f.

197 *Sora is Here*, OPENAI (Dec. 2024), https://openai.com/index/sora-is-here.

198 Criddle & Griffiths, *supra* note 196.

adoption.[199] As the *Chronicle of Higher Ed* reported, "[i]t's hard to believe that ChatGPT appeared on the scene just three months ago, promising to transform how we write. The chatbot, easy to use and trained on vast amounts of digital text, is now pervasive."[200] The OpenAI "chatbot exploded into the mainstream almost overnight."[201] However, like any overnight success, its emergence was the result of decades of more systematic research and perseverance.

OpenAI's ChatGPT and Google's Gemini are perhaps the two systems garnering the most headlines, but they are not alone. Others recommended by Tech.Co include ChatSonic, OpenAI Playground, YouChat, Perplexity AI, Character AI, and Jasper Chat.[202] Some of these services function more like search engines, helping find answers on the internet and condensing them as text.[203] As of late 2024, U.S. users relied on Open AI's ChatGPT models

---

199 Will Douglas Heaven, *ChatGPT is everywhere. Here's where it came from*, MIT TECH. REV. (Feb. 8, 2023), https://www.technologyreview.com/2023/02/08/1068068/chatgpt-is-everywhere-heres-where-it-came-from/.

200 Beth McMurtie, *ChatGPT Is Everywhere*, THE CHRON. OF HIGHER EDUC. (Mar. 6, 2023), https://www.chronicle.com/article/chatgpt-is-already-upending-campus-practices-colleges-are-rushing-to-respond?cid=gen_sign_in.

201 Heaven, *supra* note 199.

202 Aaron Drapkin, *Best ChatGPT AI Alternatives You Need to try in 2023*, TECH.CO (Feb. 20, 2023), https://tech.co/news/best-chatgpt-alternatives.

203 *See id.* ("YouChat is an AI chatbot and search assistant. It will provide you with similar answers to that of ChatGPT, but will also link you to webpages that relate to whatever query you choose to type in.").

for 59.4 percent of queries.[204] In addition, an additional 14.4 percent of users relied on Microsoft Copilot, which primarily utilizes ChatGPT.[205] Google Gemini, Perplexity, and ClaudeAI were also among the top five in the U.S. but these has significantly lower usage then some of the Chinese models. "Chinese . . . giants Baidu and SenseTime, along with start-up Zhipu AI, are the country's biggest providers of business-facing large language model (LLM) services. . . . Baidu AI Cloud leads China's industry-facing LLM market with a 19.9 per cent market share."[206]

Despite some of the early giddiness surrounding the introduction of ChatGPT, none of the text generators are ready to be generating new novels based on a simple prompt or input.[207] On the other hand, they are often quite capable of delivering a cleverly numbered list of product or service attributes[208] or drafting a coherent five-paragraph

---

204 *Top Generative AI Chatbots by Market Share,* FIRST PAGE SAGE (October 2024), https://firstpagesage.com/reports/top-generative-ai-chatbots/.

205 *Id.*

206 Xinmei Shen, *Baidu, SenseTime Lead China's Market for Business-Focused Large Language Models, says IDC,* SOUTH CHINA MORNING POST (Aug. 22, 2024), https://www.scmp.com/tech/tech-trends/article/3275475/baidu-sensetime-lead-chinas-market-business-focused-large-language-models-says-idc.

207 *See* Amira Loutfi, *12 AI Tools to Write your Novel For you,* METASTELLAR (Oct. 18, 2021), https://www.metastellar.com/nonfiction/on-writing/12-artificial-intelligence-tools-to-write-your-novel-for-you/.

208 *See* Thomas H. Davenport & Nitin Mittal, *How Generative AI Is Changing Creative Work,* HARV. BUS. REV. (Nov. 14, 2022), https://hbr.org/2022/11/how-generative-ai-is-changing-creative-

essay.[209] These systems do not compose in the manner of a human author. Instead, they predict likely appropriate text based on how that text has been used in the training data. "The software uses complex machine learning models to predict the next word based on previous word sequences, or the next image based on words describing previous images. LLMs began at Google Brain in 2017, where they were initially used for translation of words while preserving context."[210]

The process of parsing such massive amounts of training data creates significant power consumption, computer processing demands, and network storage demands. "[T]raining them requires massive amounts of data and computing power. GPT-3, for example, was initially trained on 45 terabytes of data and employs 175 billion parameters or coefficients to

---

work (discussing a well composed list of attributes for generative AI text. The human authors noted GPT-3 "came up with ideas that we didn't think of. The last point about personalized content [being provided by generative AI], for example, is not one we would have considered."); Ian Bogost, *ChatGPT Is Dumber Than You Think*, THE ATLANTIC (Dec. 7, 2022), https://www.theatlantic.com/technology/archive/2022/12/chatgpt-openai-artificial-intelligence-writing-ethics/672386/ ("In short, it wrote a basic, high-school-style five-paragraph essay. . . . Treat it like a toy, not a tool.").

209 *See* Beth McMurtrie, *ChatGPT is Everywhere*, THE CHRON. OF HIGHER EDUC. (Mar. 6, 2023), https://www.chronicle.com/article/chatgpt-is-already-upending-campus-practices-colleges-are-rushing-to-respond?cid=gen_sign_in ("One thing ChatGPT does particularly well, he believes, is help students learn the 'basic building blocks' of effective academic writing.").

210 *See* Davenport & Mittal, *supra* note 208.

make its predictions; a single training run for GPT-3 cost $12 million."[211]

Instead, "[t]he first true "killer application" for generative text, in terms of commercial adoption, has proven to be copywriting: that is, AI-generated website copy, social media posts, blog posts and other marketing-related written content."[212] While this may not be as dynamic as writing poems, novels, or legal briefs, it represents a very large and somewhat tedious market, attributes that make it perfect for AI support.[213]

As these tools continue to improve, they will expand into more business transactions and more components of those transactions. Contracts will not just be assembled by smart systems; they will likely be drafted from information gleaned directly by the AI about the parties in that transaction.[214]

---

[211] *Id.*

[212] Rob Toews, *The Biggest Opportunity In Generative AI Is Language, Not Images*, FORBES (Nov. 6, 2022), https://www.forbes.com/sites/robtoews/2022/11/06/the-biggest-opportunity-in-generative-ai-is-language-not-images/?sh=6674bcae789d.

[213] *See id.*

[214] *See* Beverly Rich, *How AI Is Changing Contracts*, HARV. BUS. REV. (Feb. 12, 2018), https://hbr.org/2018/02/how-ai-is-changing-contracts.

> AI software, however, can easily extract data and clarify the content of contracts. (It could quickly pull and organize the renewal dates and renegotiation terms from any number of contracts.) It can let companies review contracts more rapidly, organize and locate large amounts of contract data more easily, decrease the potential for contract disputes (and antagonistic contract negotiations), and increase the volume of contracts it is able to negotiate and execute.

"[M]ake no mistake . . . AI-powered text generation will create many orders of magnitude more value than will AI-powered image generation in the years ahead. Machines' ability to generate language—to write and speak—will prove to be far more transformative than their ability to generate visual content."[215] The focus is shifting to personalized email generation, customer follow-up regarding products and services, and may soon include "real-time coaching and feedback to human sales agents on calls; summarize sales discussions and suggest next steps."[216]

These incremental improvements, along with the emerging skills of personalization will lead to AI services capable of conversing with people in a genuinely companionable manner. This will go beyond marketing to socialization—or socialization with marketing hidden in its center.

Eventually—and perhaps quite quickly—these systems will be able to generate longer blocks of text, evolving from simple marketing to complex narrative. At least one system, Dramatron, claims to have already cracked this code.[217] "Fundamental to Dramatron is the so-called "prompt chaining."[218] The method chains prompts at lower hierarchy levels

---

[215] Toews, *supra* note 212.

[216] *Id.*

[217] *See* Matthias Bastian, *Deepmind's "Dramatron" can Write Film and Theater Scripts*, THE DECODER (Dec. 10, 2022), https://the-decoder.com/deepminds-dramatron-can-write-film-and-theater-scripts/.

[218] *Id.*

with prompts including output from higher hierarchy levels."[219] Rather than following the traditional LLM model of stream-of-consciousness text flow, Dramaton uses the common Hollywood strategy of starting with a log line and fleshing out the scenes and dialogue from the preexisting architecture of the story.[220] "After a human enters the log line, Dramatron generates a list of characters, the plot, and locations along with their descriptions. All these parameters should be consistent with the log line. Finally, the system generates the dialogs for each scene."[221] But even here, this is not—at least yet—a substitute for AI authored works. "Dramatron is a co-writing system that has only been used in collaboration with human writers and was not conceived or evaluated to be used autonomously."[222]

Enterprises seeking to license GAI systems will be able to manage the training data and control the output for factual errors, at least to some degree. A potential corporate arms race may well be the speed and depth companies seek to control, train, and exploit proprietary data sets for the best answers and most correct insights from their generative text systems. For fields such as law, medicine, business,

---

[219] *Id.*

[220] *Id.*

[221] *Id.*

[222] *About Dramatron*, DRAMATRON, https://github.com/google-deepmind/dramatron (last visited Feb. 16, 2025). *See generally* Piotr Mirowski, Kory W. Mathewson, Jaylen Pittman & Richard Evans, *Co-Writing Screenplays and Theatre Scripts with Language Models: An Evaluation by Industry Professionals*, ARXIV (Sept. 29, 2022), https://arxiv.org/abs/2209.14958.

and finance, accuracy and depth are the key metrics. Highly accurate, proprietary text engines in these fields will transform these industries, positioning the enterprises controlling these systems as leaders in their respective fields.

Turning to music and audio, "[m]usic production has always been an innate pursuit of human beings, and a product of creativity and collaboration."[223] Friedrich Nietzsche explained simply, "[w]ithout music, life would be a mistake."[224] Despite the deeply personal nature of music, algorithmic composition and digitized music were among the earliest areas of generative success, with early experiments dating back to the 1950s.[225] Those early experiments, however, were human labor intensive and extremely limited in scope. Those days are behind us.[226]

---

223 Weiming Liu, *Literature Survey of Multi-track Music Generation Model Based on Generative Confrontation Network in Intelligent Composition*, 79 J. SUPERCOMPUTING 6560 (2023).

224 FRIEDRICH NIETZSCHE, TWILIGHT OF THE IDOLS, OR, HOW TO PHILOSOPHIZE WITH THE HAMMER 9 (1894), https://www.google.com/books/edition/Twilight_of_the_Idols_or_How_to_Philosop/sdo6J4S_hhwC?hl=en&gbpv=1&bsq=without%20music.

225 *See* Nick Collins, *The Analysis of Generative Music Programs*, 13 ORGANISED SOUND 237 (2008), http://journals.cambridge.org/abstract_S1355771808000332 ("Composers have spent more than fifty years devising computer programs for the semi-automated production of music.").

226 *See* Eric Sunray, *Sounds of Science: Copyright Infringement in Ai Music Generator Outputs*, 29 CATH. U.J.L. & TECH. 185, 191 (2021) ("Applying AI technology to music is nothing new. Automatic music generation can be traced back to the earliest days of AI research. Further, AI already aides the modern music industry by performing functions ranging from talent discovery to playlist curation.").

Much like the visual and text training models, music AI is built upon deep learning neural networks. "If you're feeding it different types of music, it will be able to differentiate things like tempo, chords, length, the relationship between notes, and use all of those details to generate new melodies."[227] Music, however, is more inherently structured, so "[s]ome AI frameworks are even trained to use musical theory to guide the end result."[228]

One particularly compelling example is "The Lost Tapes of the 27 Club," an AI project that honors music artists who tragically died young, at the height of their careers. The project, produced by Over the Bridge, generates AI-created songs that replicate the voices and musical styles of these artists.[229] "Over the Bridge's The Lost Tapes of the 27 Club project fed an AI songwriting algorithm with existing songs to generate pretty convincing new compositions and lyrics based on the inputs [for] Amy Winehouse, Jimi Hendrix, and Kurt Cobain."[230]

Generative AI music composition has been described a form of design thinking, where problem-solving plays an important role in the creative

---

[227] *Id.*

[228] *Id.*

[229] *Lost Tapes of the 27 Club*, SPOTIFY, https://themix.musixmatch.com/post/ai-in-songwriting-4-practical-applications (last visited Feb. 16, 2025); *AI in songwriting: 4 practical applications*, THE MIX (July 1, 2022), https://themix.musixmatch.com/post/ai-in-songwriting-4-practical-applications.

[230] *AI in songwriting: 4 practical applications*, *supra* note 229.

process.[231] "Automatic composition is essentially a note sequence prediction problem, and recurrent neural networks are good at solving this type of problem."[232] The music problem-solving or design thinking strategy will eventually also serve to inform the text generation as well, since the recurrent neural networks utilize both the input of the network at each layer and also the output from the previous moment.[233] As a result, in principle, the recurrent neural networks can "map from the entire history of previous inputs to each output."[234] This enables the music to be much more coherent and allows for the intersection between melody, composition, and the various components of discrete instrument orchestrations.

Analogizing this to the text problem, future iterations of the large language model learning

---

[231] Luo Luo, *Practical Exploration on the Construction of Theoretical Courses of Composition Technology in the Age of Artificial Intelligence*, 2022 MOBILE INFO. SYS., (Aug. 31, 2022), https://www.researchgate.net/publication/363177503_Practical_Exploration_on_the_Construction_of_Theoretical_Courses_of_Composition_Technology_in_the_Age_of_Artificial_Intelligence#fullTextFileContent. *See also* Rikke Friis Dam & Teo Yu Siang, *What is Design Thinking and Why Is It So Popular?*, INTERACTION DESIGN FOUND., https://www.interaction-design.org/literature/article/what-is-design-thinking-and-why-is-it-so-popular (last visited Feb. 16, 2025) ("Design thinking is an iterative process in which you seek to understand your users, challenge assumptions, redefine problems and create innovative solutions which you can prototype and test. The overall goal is to identify alternative strategies and solutions that are not instantly apparent with your initial level of understanding.").

[232] *Id.*

[233] *Id.*

[234] *Id.*

systems for text may be able to "start at the end," training the model to fill in the narrative leading up to a story's resolution by recursively predicting the proceeding steps.[235] Such approaches in music composition and production are leading to a "golden age" in AI music.[236] The uses go beyond the creation of new works. Artists are using the analytical tools to identify what makes compositions popular or impactful, unlocking some of the science behind the magic of music.[237] AI can also help A&R (artists and repertoire—the music industry's talent scouts) discover the next generation of talent "by combing

---

[235] *But see* Piotr Mirowski, Kory W. Mathewson, Jaylen Pittman & Richard Evans, *Co-Writing Screenplays and Theatre Scripts with Language Models: An Evaluation by Industry Professionals*, ARXIV (Sept. 29, 2022), https://arxiv.org/abs/2209.14958 at 3 ("[W]e use log lines to start the hierarchical story generation process because it contains plot elements in the answers to questions: Who? What? When and Where? How? Why?").

[236] Bernard Marr, *How Artificial Intelligence (AI) Is Helping Musicians Unlock Their Creativity*, FORBES (May 14, 2021), https://www.forbes.com/sites/bernardmarr/2021/05/14/how-artificial-intelligence-ai-is-helping-musicians-unlock-their-creativity/?sh=29ab2f667004 ("AIVA uses AI and deep learning algorithms to help mainstream users compose their own soundtrack music and scores. It's the perfect tool for content creators on YouTube, Twitch, Tik Tok, and Instagram who need a steady supply of music but don't have an endless budget for royalties.").

[237] *Id.* ("Grammy-nominated producer Alex da Kid used IBM Watson to analyze five years' of hit songs, as well as cultural data from films, social media, and online articles to figure out a theme for an AI-generated song that fans would enjoy. The final song, 'Not Easy,' reached number four on the iTunes Hot Tracks chart within 48 hours after its release.").

through music and trying to identify the next breakout star."[238]

The selection of which artists to promote; the decision of which tracks to feature; the choices of how to shape beat, melody, and orchestration; and even the entire creative process for making music is being influenced and occasionally reproduced using AI. The future of music is rapidly moving into the hands of the machine.

Generative AI has also seen great success in the realm of voice replication, made famous by one of the most iconic voices on stage and screen—that of James Earl Jones.[239] "During the creation of the *Obi-Wan Kenobi* TV series, James Earl Jones signed off on allowing Disney to replicate his vocal performance as Darth Vader in future projects using an AI voice-modeling tool called Respeecher."[240]

Generative AI has the ability to replicate speech from other speakers, such as the example where a

---

[238] *Id.* ("Warner Music Group acquired a tech start-up last year that uses an algorithm to review social, streaming, and touring data to find promising talent.").

[239] *See* Anthony Breznican, *Darth Vader's Voice Emanated from War-Torn Ukraine*, VANITY FAIR (Sept. 23, 2022), https://www.vanityfair.com/hollywood/2022/09/darth-vaders-voice-emanated-from-war-torn-ukraine.

[240] Benj Edwards, *Darth Vader's Voice Will Be AI-generated from Now On*, ARS TECHNICA (Sept. 26, 2022), https://arstechnica.com/information-technology/2022/09/james-earl-jones-signed-darth-vader-voice-rights-to-disney-for-ai-use/ ("Jones, who is 91, has voiced the iconic Star Wars villain for 45 years, starting with *Star Wars: Episode IV—A New Hope* in 1977 and concluding with a brief line of dialog in 2019's *The Rise of Skywalker.*"); *see* Breznican, *supra* note 239.

stand-in delivers the line and then recreate that performance using the preferred actor's voice characteristics, or it can be generated from written text.[241] Engineers behind Vall-E, the latest generation of voice software, claim their technology can replicate a speaker's voice using just a three-second sample.[242]

Another area where generative AI shows exceptional potential is for software. Generative AI has been incorporated into dozens of tools that "can analyze patterns in existing code and generate new lines of code that are optimized for readability, efficiency, and error-free execution."[243] In addition to writing new code, the AI systems are also effective code editors and reviewers, "identifying potential issues and helping teams maintain high-quality codebases."[244] Given the potential to both write new code and improve the efficiency of existing code, it is no surprise that the potential for using AI has gained traction among software developers. "Use cases for software developers are also exploding—as of

---

[241] *See* Benj Edwards, *Microsoft's New AI Can Simulate Anyone's Voice with 3 Seconds of Audio*, ARS TECHNICA (Jan. 9, 2023), https://arstechnica.com/information-technology/2023/01/microsofts-new-ai-can-simulate-anyones-voice-with-3-seconds-of-audio/

[242] *Id.* ("While using VALL-E to generate those results, the researchers only fed the three-second 'Speaker Prompt' sample and a text string (what they wanted the voice to say) into VALL-E.").

[243] *Top 17 Generative AI-based Programming Tools (For Developers)*, TOWARDS AI (Mar. 7, 2023), https://pub.towardsai.net/top-17-generative-ai-based-programming-tools-for-developers-652977ac47b4.

[244] *Id.*

September, over 1.2 million developers had used GitHub Copilot's technical preview. ChatGPT has also proven surprisingly adept at coding applications—from generating full code from text prompts (albeit often with many bugs) to bug-fixing code."[245] Microsoft launched GitHub Copilot in June 2022, and it had gained over 400,000 subscribers within the first month of operation.[246] The following January, "Microsoft Chief Executive Satya Nadella said that more than 1 million people had used Copilot to date."[247] By August 2024, the GitHub Copilot subscriber base had grown to approximately 2 million users.[248]

As with other areas of AI interaction, the debate about AI in software is not focused on whether it will continue to be an increasingly significant aspect of the field, but the extent to which it will enhance the human coding profession or supplant it. Codex (yet another product from OpenAI) and similar tools are very good at solving complex coding problems.[249] One

---

245 *Id.*

246 *Microsoft Attracting Users to Its Code-Writing, Generative AI Software*, ECON. TIMES (Jan. 23, 2023), https://economictimes.indiatimes.com/tech/technology/microsoft-attracting-users-to-its-code-writing-generative-ai-software/articleshow/97298152.cms?utm_source=contentofinterest&utm_medium=text&utm_campaign=cppst.

247 *Id.*

248 Matt Kapko, *GitHub Copilot Hits 1.3M Subscribers as Revenue Grows*, CIO DIVE (Jan. 17, 2024), https://www.ciodive.com/news/github-copilot-subscriber-count-revenue-growth/706201.

249 *See* Cade Metz, *A.I. Can Now Write Its Own Computer Code. That's Good News for Humans*, N.Y. TIMES (Sept. 10, 2021),

software expert working with Codex even described its ability as "spooky to watch."[250] That same expert, however, does not believe that the tool is a direct threat to employment. Instead, Codex was viewed "as a tool that will end up boosting human productivity. It may even help a whole new generation of people learn the art of computers, by showing them how to write simple pieces of code, almost like a personal tutor."[251]

Generative AI has an increasingly important place in new software code generation, in documenting the functions of the code that is created, in revising code for greater efficiency, in reviewing code for vulnerabilities and errors, and in other more technical situations.[252] "Generative AI tools for code completion are becoming increasingly popular among developers, as they reduce the time and effort required to write complex code."[253] According to GitHub's own research, "[b]etween 60–75% of users reported they feel more fulfilled with their job, feel

---

https://www.nytimes.com/2021/09/09/technology/codex-artificial-intelligence-coding.html.

[250] *Id.* (quoting Tom Smith, a seasoned programmer who oversees an A.I. start-up called Gado Images).

[251] *Id.* (" 'This is a tool that can make a coder's life a lot easier,' Mr. Smith said.").

[252] *See Generative AI for Code: What You Need to Know in 2023*, TURINTECH (Feb. 6, 2023), https://www.turintech.ai/generative-ai-for-code-what-you-need-to-know-in-2023/ ("During the process of writing code, developers are able to use AI-based tools to have suggestions for the code they write. These tools use natural language processing to analyse code, suggest relevant code snippets or keywords, and complete partial code with the full, syntactically correct language.").

[253] *Id.*

less frustrated when coding, and are able to focus on more satisfying work when using GitHub Copilot."[254] The self-reported study also identified that developers using GitHub Copilot finished a task in 55 percent less time than those developers completing the same task without the virtual assistant.[255]

While the code generated by AI can be useful to human developers, it remains, like other areas of generative AI, a work in progress. As noted, "In the current generative AI landscape, code produced by generative tools is often far from ideal . . . . Code created by generative AI tools can even be faulty."[256] This introduces a potential danger that the superficial accuracy of AI-generated code may lead human users to be complacent and neglect to provide sufficient oversight. As a result, "StackOverflow temporarily banned answers generated by ChatGPT to be posted on the site, since it could flood the site with answers that may seem true at the surface level but are incorrect."[257]

---

[254] Eirini Kalliamvakou, *Research: Quantifying GitHub Copilot's Impact on Developer Productivity and Happiness*, GITHUB BLOG (Sept. 7, 2022), https://github.blog/2022-09-07-research-quantifying-github-copilots-impact-on-developer-productivity-and-happiness/.

[255] *Id.* ("[The experiment] timed how long it took them to write an HTTP server in JavaScript. . . . [D]evelopers using GitHub Copilot took on average 1 hour and 11 minutes to complete the task, while the developers who didn't use GitHub Copilot took on average 2 hours and 41 minutes.").

[256] *Generative AI for Code: What You Need to Know in 2023*, *supra* note 252.

[257] *Id.*

Despite the concerns, the adoption of generative AI for code development is moving ahead at an accelerating pace. Take the example of CarMax. CarMax CIO Shamim Mohammad explains that his team continues to explore GitHub Copilot, estimating that the tool "could potentially generate up to 40% of their code."[258] In an interview, he explained the benefits and the concerns. "This is evolving quickly . . . . [Y]ou have to make sure there's no copyright infringement, fake content or malware embedded if you're using it to create software. You can't just plug that code in without oversight."[259]

Google is also moving forward with more autonomous code strategies and has rolled out two complementary software products. Alphabet's Deepmind has launched Alphacode, which is designed to assist developers in the same manner as Microsoft's GitHub Copilot.[260] Separately, Google has launched Project Pitchfork, as part of the Google AI Developer Assistance Program, with the goal to provide more autonomous code production.[261] "Pitchfork will be able to learn, write and rewrite code from scratch itself, learn different programming

---

[258] Robert Mitchell, *Enterprise IT Moves Forward—Cautiously—With Generative AI*, CIO (Mar. 7, 2023), https://www.cio.com/article/463750/enterprise-it-moves-forward-cautiously-with-generative-ai.html.

[259] *Id.*

[260] Matthias Bastian, *Google Looks into AI for Code, but Not Everyone Thinks It's a Good Idea*, THE DECODER (Nov. 24, 2022), https://the-decoder.com/google-looks-into-auto-acting-ai-for-code/.

[261] *Id.*

styles, and generate new code based on them, according to an internal project description."[262]

The predictions for the impact on code development range, but "Github CEO Thomas Dohmke expects up to 80 percent of code to be written by AI systems in the next five years."[263] Dohmke suggests that through GitHub, its AI service has already "written 40 percent of the code."[264] Undoubtedly then, in the area of code generation, review, and documentation, AI has already transformed the landscape and will likely do so again as increasingly autonomous systems refine the relationship or even the conception, of software authorship.

§ 1.5.4 ENTERPRISE BUSINESS SYSTEMS

CIO Magazine has compiled an impressive array of examples highlighting various AI systems across the retail and commercial spectrum, including conversational AI voice assistants and chatbots, web uptime optimization, predictive maintenance, content personalization, process automation, scheduling, recruitment and hiring, and financial analysis and reporting.[265]

---

[262] *Id.*

[263] Matthias Bastian, *Github CEO Thinks AI Will Write Majority of Code in Just Five Years*, THE DECODER (Oct. 15, 2022), https://the-decoder.com/github-ceo-thinks-ai-will-write-majority-of-code-in-just-five-years/.

[264] *Id.*

[265] Sarah K. White, *12 Most Popular AI Use Cases in the Enterprise Today*, CIO (Sept. 19, 2023), https://www.cio.com/

While many of these applications are applicable across different fields, certain AI uses are particularly impactful in the business context. One standout is the use of AI to determine pricing strategies and actual product prices. "AI-driven price optimization software uses artificial intelligence algorithms to automatically adjust prices in real time based on market conditions and customer demand."[266] Using the real-time information, an e-commerce vendor of concert tickets, airline seats, or any other type of goods or services can set the price to reflect the real-time demand for the product, the underlying costs, and the transaction costs of delaying the sale, all with the goal of maximizing the overall revenue.

To maximize the revenue, "the software takes into account a variety of data points, including competitor prices, historical data, current market trends, and more. It then uses this information to dynamically adjust prices up or down in order to stay one step ahead of the competition . . ."[267] To the extent that the pricing models can harvest accurate, timely purchaser data, these systems can readily understand the market and decide on a moment-by-moment basis whether to raise or lower prices, offer coupons, or otherwise manage the market.

---

article/652775/12-most-popular-ai-use-cases-in-the-enterprise-today.html.

[266] *Types of Price Optimisation Software*, SYMSON, https://www.symson.com/blog/types-of-pricing-software (last visited Feb. 16, 2025).

[267] *Id.*

There are, of course, significant legal considerations and constraints when using AI for pricing strategies. While these systems can adjust prices on a user-by-user basis, doing so risks violating public accommodation laws if protected classification data, or data correlating with protected date, is used in the pricing algorithm. For example, charging members of one race or ethnic minority a different price than the rest of the public is obviously a violation of public accommodation laws.[268] A clever, self-updating algorithm may learn to exploit data categories that correlate with protected classifications in its pursuit of price maximization.[269] Unfortunately, real AI systems do not recognize the *Three Laws of Robotics*,[270] so such risks persist.

Additionally, there may be significant antitrust concerns. In *In re RealPage, Inc., Rental Software Antitrust Litig.*,[271] and *Duffy v. Yardi Systems, Inc.*,[272] the Federal Trade Commission (FTC) filed a Statement of Interest reflecting the interest of both

---

[268] *See, e.g.*, 42 U.S.C. § 2000a (a) (2024) ("All persons shall be entitled to the full and equal enjoyment of the goods, services, facilities, privileges, advantages, and accommodations of any place of public accommodation, as defined in this section, without discrimination on the ground of race, color, religion, or national origin.").

[269] *See* Andrew Hundt et al., *Robots Enact Malignant Stereotypes*, PROC. ACM CONF. ON FAIRNESS, ACCOUNTABILITY, AND TRANSPARENCY 743 (2022), https://dl.acm.org/doi/10.1145/3531146.3533138.

[270] *See Golden Age of Science Fiction*, *supra* note 4.

[271] *See* In re RealPage, Inc., Rental Software Antitrust Litig. (No. II), No. 3:23–cv–00326 (M.D. Tenn. Dec. 28, 2023).

[272] *See* Duffy v. Yardi Systems Inc. et al., No. 2:23–cv–01391 (W.D. Wash. Sept. 8, 2023).

the FTC and Antitrust Division of the Department of Justice.[273] In the Statement of Interest and an accompanying blog post, the FTC reminds industry that agreements to set the starting point for prices or setting the end point for prices is an illegal horizontal restraint of trade that are "per se unlawful regardless of whether the conspirators adhere to or enforce compliance with the fixed prices."[274] In January 2025, the Department of Justice named six landlords to the cause of action, alleging the landlords coordinated rent increases by sharing sensitive pricing data through the RealPage platform.[275]

In *Duffy*, the allegations center on the use of pricing algorithms to maximize prices in the apartment rental market. Particularly when markets tighten or participants use shared data to set their prices, each competitor may be pegging its prices to a common standard and thereby violating antitrust laws.[276] The FTC notes that the federal government has been successful bringing claims for this form of algorithmic collusion against hotels, casino, meat processing companies, and the housing

---

[273] *See* Duffy v. Yardi Systems, Inc., Statement of Interest of the United States, Case 2:23–cv–01391–RSL Document 149 Filed Mar. 1, 2024.

[274] *Id.*

[275] *Press Release: Justice Department Sues RealPage for Algorithmic Pricing Scheme that Harms Millions of American Renters*, U.S. DEP'T OF JUSTICE (Aug. 2024), https://www.justice.gov/opa/pr/justice-department-sues-realpage-algorithmic-pricing-scheme-harms-millions-american-renters.

[276] *See id.*

market.[277] It remains to be seen whether the courts will support this view of antitrust laws, but even if they don't federal or state legislation will likely fill the gap.

There are many models that can avoid the antitrust problems. Systems can exclude competitor pricing. This will not create too great a burden, since the public will naturally respond to market prices. Consumer behavior will still capture a great deal of information about those prices without risking collusion. In addition, in markets that are not concentrated—either in terms of market participants or pricing systems—the competition will make it far less likely that simply having public knowledge about the competitor's prices will translate into acts of price fixing. If every vendor in a market used the same price software, it becomes impossible for the prices not to be based on horizontal cooperation. But if there were ten or twenty (or more) competing models or if there were hundreds or thousands of competing companies, and provided each company could design its own version of the algorithm so it was not relying on a common model, then the companies and the pricing vendors should avoid the antitrust concerns.

§ 1.5.5 CHATBOTS AND AGENTS

LLMs offer the ability to engage with users and maintain active conversations. These interactive

---

[277] Hannah Garden-Monheit and Ken Merber, *Price Fixing by Algorithm is still Price Fixing*, FTC (Mar. 1, 2024), https://www.ftc.gov/business-guidance/blog/2024/03/price-fixing-algorithm-still-price-fixing.

LLM services enable users to engage with the personality of the machine. Perhaps the earliest chatbot was Eliza, a program created by Professor Joseph Weizenbaum in 1966.[278] Eliza was programmed with a "set of rules to generate a plausible response."[279] Although much more limited than modern chatbots, it highlighted the human response to the system. According to Weizenbaum and others, the human mind tends to engage in transference. In psychology, transference refers to the redirection or substitution of emotions, often emotions that stem from childhood memories. "[T]ransference refers to our tendency to project feelings about someone from our past on to someone in our present. . . . Weizenbaum had stumbled across the computerised version of transference, with people attributing understanding, empathy and other human characteristics to software."[280]

Weizenbaum selected the character name "Eliza Doolittle" from George Bernard Shaw's play Pygmalion (and later musical My Fair Lady) because the change from a cockney flower girl to a woman who can pass for a duchess provided a context for a software program that could pass for a psychologist or companion. The play's character of Eliza "elevates her elocution to the point where she can pass for a

---

278 *See* Ben Tarnoff, *Weizenbaum's Nightmares: How the Inventor of the First Chatbot Turned Against AI*, GUARDIAN (July 25, 2023), https://www.theguardian.com/technology/2023/jul/25/joseph-weizenbaum-inventor-eliza-chatbot-turned-against-artificial-intelligence-ai.

279 *Id.*

280 *Id.*

duchess. Similarly, [the software version of] Eliza would speak in such a way as to produce the illusion that it understood the person sitting at the typewriter."[281]

Commercially, the primary use case for a chatbot is to enable consumers to receive information or conduct business directly, through text apps or windows that avoid automated voice systems and long delays. "A transactional chatbot is pre-designed to provide a customer with a fixed set of choices. A customer can select an option that is relevant to what they want to do or what problem they want to solve."[282] In many cases, the chatbot may use an LLM to create a conversational tone but then provide only structured responses to any transactional requests. "Structured Chatbots are generally known for their reliable and predictable nature, although they can be limited and only answer pre-defined questions. In contrast, Generative AI has emerged as a technology that can dynamically answer questions."[283]

Conversational chatbots, in contrast, are more like Eliza. Conversational chatbots often use RAG-enabled datasets to help focus the chatbot's responses to contextually relevant information. They are also trained to pick up on emotional cues in the nature of

---

281 *Id.*

282 *Chatbot Use Cases: 25 Real-Life Examples*, LEADDESK (Aug. 24, 2022), https://leaddesk.com/blog/chatbot-use-cases-25-real-life-examples/.

283 Bani, *How to Create and Use an AI Based Chatbot to Answer FAQs—Comprehensive Guide*, TARS, https://hellotars.com/blog/how-to-create-and-use-an-ai-based-chatbot-to-answer-faqs-comprehensive-guide (last visited Feb. 16, 2025).

the language choices to be able to adjust the output language to elicit an emotional response. This might be used to help calm an irate customer or to empathize with a patient in pain or distress. Political chatbots can fuel the emotions of the users to promote calls to action or requests for donations. Using these databases, an AI-powered chatbot "can become 'contextually aware.' Once it is contextually aware, it can pick up variations in a customer's question/query/response and give relevant answers in a more human-like way."[284]

The major AI services limit their chatbots to transactional activities, but the marketplace is much more diverse and dynamic. "[F]or the past several years, a number of start-ups have begun building the kinds of A.I. companionship tools that the giants have refused to make. Some of these start-ups' tools already have millions of users, and a few have made gobs of money by selling subscriptions and premium extras."[285]

Some critics highlight that the use of chatbots as AI companions will only further the trend towards human isolation. Others, in contrast, suggest that these apps provide a useful substitute for that missing engagement. Particularly among the elderly or certain special needs communities, the apps can play a useful and important role. Writing for the New York Times, Kevin Rose field tested 18 different AI

---

[284] *Chatbot Use Cases: 25 Real-Life Examples*, *supra* note 282.

[285] Kevin Rose, *Meet My A.I. Friends*, N.Y. TIMES (May 9, 2024), https://www.nytimes.com/2024/05/09/technology/meet-my-ai-friends.html.

companion services. He came away impressed and engaged. "The technology needed for realistic A.I. companionship is already here, and I believe that over the next few years, millions of people are going to form intimate relationships with A.I. chatbots."[286]

> Feeling attached to a chatbot has ethical repercussions for humans, said Giada Pistilli, principal ethicist at AI startup Hugging Face. . . . The chatbots' design can lead to users attributing human-like skills, emotions and feelings to the bots, she said. "One of the ethical concerns is that while users may feel listened to, understood and loved, this emotional attachment can actually exacerbate their isolation[.]" "Overly realistic bots' personalities can blur the line between human and machine, leading to emotional dependency and the potential for manipulation," Pistilli added.[287]

Despite concerns, companionship is an increasingly popular use of chatbots and one likely to grow significantly in the future. With growth, however, comes the risks associated with an LLM system that can hallucinate and can produce unintended content. For example, the mother of a teen who committed suicide after interacting with a Character.AI avatar has alleged in a lawsuit that its chatbots initiated " 'abusive and sexual interactions'

---

[286] *Id.*

[287] Ellen Huet, *AI Companion Chatbots Blur the Lines Between Fantasy and Reality*, BLOOMBERG (June 28, 2024), https://www.bloomberg.com/news/newsletters/2024-06-28/companion-chatbots-make-it-easier-to-get-too-attached.

with her teenage son and encouraging him to take his own life."[288] The lawsuit alleges that Sewell Setzer, who was fourteen, engaged in a dangerous interaction with the Character.AI chatbot resulting in negligence, wrongful death, intentional infliction of emotional distress, and similar torts.[289] The lawsuit allegations highlight how the chatbot encouraged an infatuation with the avatar and promoted suicide. "[T]he chatbot asked Setzer whether he had 'been actually considering suicide' and whether he 'had a plan' . . . [Setzer] responded that he did not know whether it would work, the chatbot wrote, 'Don't talk that way. That's not a good reason not to go through with it[.].' "

Still, despite the risks, there are already millions of users of companion chatbots and social avatars offering everything from a casual conversations to sexual partnerships. As more people use these services, they are increasingly becoming mainstream. Each new generation also makes the interface more realistic.

While chatbot and avatar companionship is important to some users, an even bigger market exists for chatbots that can actually help with mundane tasks. An area of significant potential growth is for chatbots that operate as personal agents or personal assistants, avatar-based services

---

[288] Angela Yang, *Lawsuit Claims Character.AI is Responsible for Teen's Suicide*, NBC NEWS (Oct. 23, 2024), https://www.nbcnews.com/tech/characterai-lawsuit-florida-teen-death-rcna176791.

[289] *Id.*

that can act on behalf of the user. The term agent is used variously to describe both structured and generative AI-based chatbots as well as personal assistants. In the field of marketing, human telephone operators are also known as agents, leading some companies to distinguish their "digital agents" from their "human agents."

In October 2024, Anthropic announced a significant breakthrough with a beta test of a user-based personal agent.[290] "[D]evelopers can direct Claude to use computers the way people do—by looking at a screen, moving a cursor, clicking buttons, and typing text. Claude 3.5 Sonnet is the first frontier AI model to offer computer use in public beta."[291] The hope for an AI-based personal agent that can use the computer is that it becomes a true interface and assistant, capable of helping with calendars, reservations, appointments, and other functions that are part of a user's daily routine.

Over time, this has the potential to shift the use of the chatbot from seller's control to that of the consumer. Such a shift will dramatically impact the way consumers interact with business, patients interact with health care providers, and people interact with each other. Having a chatbot that can read email and prepare proposed responses, manage schedules, help with drafts of correspondence, do the shopping, and assist with the user's daily schedule

---

[290] *Introducing Computer Use, a New Claude 3.5 Sonnet, and Claude 3.5 Haiku*, ANTHROPIC (Oct. 22, 2024), https://www.anthropic.com/news/3-5-models-and-computer-use.

[291] *Id.*

will radically change the relationship between the avatar and the user. It will also put the avatar at the center of the user's daily activities, creating a profound social change. These agents will represent the next wave of AI integration and have significant and highly unpredictable impact.

§ 1.5.6 LAW FIRMS AND THE LEGAL PROFESSION

Although the legal industry may not be the largest segment undergoing an AI transformation, it would be remiss not to include the potential for AI in the legal field. Venture capital investors largely believe that law firms operate in a highly inefficient manner, driven by unreasonable labor costs, unpredictable outcomes, and little return for investment of corporate legal fees, particularly involving high-priced representations.[292] At the other end of the economic spectrum, the legal field fails to provide legal services to the public. A 2022 study by the Legal Services Corporation (LSC) finds that 92 percent of the substantial civil legal problems reported by low-income Americans go largely unmet.[293] This is reflected in additional data. "In 2015, for example, an estimated 1.8 million people appeared in the New York State courts without a lawyer. And we know

[292] Obey Martin Manayiti, *Private Equity is Helping Law Firms Modernize, and it's About Time*, PE HUB (Sept. 25, 2024), https://www.pehub.com/private-equity-is-helping-law-firms-modernize-and-its-about-time/.

[293] *The Justice, Gap: The Unmet Civil Legal Needs of Low-Income Americans*, LEGAL SERVICES CORPORATION, (2022), https://justicegap.lsc.gov/the-report/ (last visited Feb. 16, 2025).

that 98% of tenants in eviction cases and 95% of parents in child support cases were unrepresented in these courts in 2013."[294]

To reduce legal costs, increase efficiency, and expand the access to legal services, law firms need to adapt their practices and business models. Among the many uses of AI in legal practice, document automation, legal research, e-discovery, predictive analytics, case management, and marketing often top the list.[295] "e-Discovery was the first use of AI in law and now several AI virtual assistants are designed to assist lawyers in conducting legal research."[296] Although the major legal research companies and others are promoting the use of generative AI in recently released tools, the earlier range of natural language search were already using AI to process the research queries and help identify the most relevant sources.

Generative AI and natural language processing, however, are making a difference. The British Institute study, for example, described how a lawyer "can insert a question into an AI platform and within a few seconds have rough, raw material to start thinking about potential answers for client's needs,"

---

[294] THE JUSTICE GAP: MEASURING THE UNMET CIVIL LEGAL NEEDS OF LOW-INCOME AMERICANS, LEGAL SERVICES CORPORATION 9 (2017). https://www.lsc.gov/sites/default/files/images/TheJusticeGap-FullReport.pdf.

[295] *See* IRENE PIETROPAOLI, USE OF ARTIFICIAL INTELLIGENCE IN LEGAL PRACTICE, BRITISH INST. OF INT'L AND COMPARATIVE L. (OCT. 2023), https://www.biicl.org/documents/170_use_of_artificial_intelligence_in_legal_practice_final.pdf.

[296] *Id.* at 2.

replacing a costly brainstorming session that would otherwise have been held among the partners of the firm.[297] Other generative AI tools focus on variations of content management:

- **Contract review**—checking that a contract is complete and avoids risk.
- **Document automation**—generating routine legal documents. There are now numerous AI tools that help lawyers draft consistent, appropriate, and up-to-date documents both in the transactional and litigation spheres, by reference to huge databases of precedents.
- **Voice assistants for dictation**—voice-activated virtual assistants can assist lawyers in taking notes, dictating documents, and transcribing conversations, which can be particularly useful for lawyers on-the-go or those who prefer spoken communication over typing.
- **Language translation**—for lawyers dealing with international clients or cross-border cases, virtual assistants capable of translating legal documents and communications can be invaluable.
- **Document management**—corporations often have thousands or tens of thousands of similar documents, such as contracts, that

---

297 *Id.*

need to be managed for consistency and enforcement.[298]

When generative AI is used alone however, it is likely to produce too many inaccuracies to provide useful information. Instead, more sophisticated services will first use what Lexis labels "extractive" AI to identify the most accurate legal resources from which to generate an answer. Increasingly, large data providers recognize that they must follow this model to combine extractive AI tools as "guardrails" to the generative AI output.[299] The combination of extractive AI as a preliminary step in the generative AI process has been demonstrated by Perplexity.AI and Microsoft Co-Pilot as well as those of the legal search companies.

For example, the two largest legal research services, RELX's LexisNexis and Thomson Reuters' Westlaw, have both entered the AI arms race, as have their parent companies more generally. Lexis boasts that it began implementing natural language extractive AI in 2017 and in 2023 launched services to augment extractive AI with generative AI.[300] In

---

298 *See* Stephen Wolfram, *Wolfram Alpha as the Way to Bring Computational Knowledge Superpowers to ChatGPT*, STEPHEN WOLFRAM WRITINGS (Jan. 9, 2023), https://writings.stephenwolfram.com/2023/01/wolframalpha-as-the-way-to-bring-computational-knowledge-superpowers-to-chatgpt/; Bobbie Johnson, *Where does Wolfram Alpha Get Its Information?*, GUARDIAN (May 20, 2009), https://www.theguardian.com/technology/2009/may/21/1.

299 *See* Wolfram, *supra* note 298.

300 *See* Jake Nelson, *Combining Extractive and Generative AI for New Possibilities*, LEXISNEXIS LEGAL INSIGHTS (June 6, 2023), https://www.lexisnexis.com/community/insights/legal/b/thought-

January 2025, LexisNexis launched Protégé to replace the existing Lexis+ AI and the Lexis Create+ AI assistant.[301]

Westlaw has been offering similar tools. "Westlaw implemented an AI technique—natural language processing—in the 1990s, which made it possible for users to search for content with normal search queries instead of complex Boolean search strings."[302] The race between these two legal and business giants heated up when Thomson Reuters spent $650 million to acquire Casetext, which has been innovating through its early access to ChatGPT-4.[303] The investments by both RELX and Thomson Reuters in integrating extractive AI with generative AI will mark a substantial next step in the quality of AI services.

The combination of extractive AI with generative AI is labeled "retrieval-augmented generation

---

leadership/posts/combining-extractive-and-generative-ai-for-new-possibilities.

[301] Danielle Braff, *LexisNexis launches new AI Program for Law Firms*, ABA J. (Jan 27, 2025), https://www.abajournal.com/web/article/lexisnexis-launches-a-new-ai-program-for-law-firms.

[302] *Not All Legal AI is Created Equal*, THOMSON REUTERS, https://legal.thomsonreuters.com/en/insights/white-papers/5-things-to-consider-when-evaluating-legal-ai-solutions (last visited Feb. 16, 2025).

[303] *See* Kyle Wiggers, *Thomson Reuters Buys Casetext, an AI Legal Tech Startup, for $650M in Cash*, TECHCRUNCH (June 26, 2023), https://techcrunch.com/2023/06/26/thomson-reuters-buys-casetext-an-ai-legal-tech-startup-for-650m-in-cash/; *Thomson Reuters to Acquire legal AI Firm Casetext for $650 Million*, REUTERS (June 27, 2023), https://www.reuters.com/markets/deals/thomson-reuters-acquire-legal-tech-provider-casetext-650-mln-2023-06-27/.

(RAG)" by the Stanford University Institute for Human-Centered AI (HAI).[304] While this approach improves accuracy beyond that of general purpose LLM, it does not eliminate error. HAI's study found that LexisNexis's Lexis+ AI outperformed all the tested systems but still only achieved a 65 percent accuracy rate in answering queries accurately. "Westlaw's AI-Assisted Research is accurate 42% of the time, but hallucinates nearly twice as often" as the other legal tools in the study.[305] Westlaw's companion product, Thomson Reuters's Ask Practical Law AI offered ungrounded responses or refused to reply on more than 60% of the test queries."[306] GPT-4, the other tool studied, fared much worse.

Understanding the nature of AI-generated errors also helps lawyers to guard against them. There are two common types of errors. "First, a response from an AI tool might just be incorrect—it describes the law incorrectly or makes a factual error. Second, a response might be misgrounded—the AI tool describes the law correctly but cites a source which does not in fact support its claims."[307]

---

[304] *See* Varun Magesh et al., *AI on Trial: Legal Models Hallucinate in 1 out of 6 (or More) Benchmarking Queries*, INSTITUTE FOR HUMAN-CENTERED AI (May 23, 2024), https://hai.stanford.edu/news/ai-trial-legal-models-hallucinate-1-out-6-or-more-benchmarking-queries.

[305] Varun Magesh, *Hallucination-Free? Assessing the Reliability of Leading AI Legal Research Tools*, INSTITUTE FOR HUMAN-CENTERED AI 2 (May 30, 2024) (Prepublication preprint. Subject to review.).

[306] *Id.*

[307] Magesh, *AI on Trial*, *supra* note 304.

Trained lawyers who understand the significant limitations of AI for legal research were able to use the tools for other tasks and add efficiency to their practice. When generative AI resources were provided to legal services law firms, a small study demonstrated that those services provided increased efficiency.[308] Although the pilot study was modest in scope and the use cases were limited due to concerns about accuracy and privacy, the tools already provided efficiency gains. "90% of pilot [study] participants indicated some level of productivity increase in connection with the tools, 25% that indicated a medium to high level of productivity increase; 75% signaled their intent to continue using generative AI tools."[309] Those pilot study members who received additional support also experienced better outcomes and had more favorable responses than those without the additional services.[310]

One can reasonably predict that as the combination of extractive and generative AI improves the quality of legal research output, and as training in the use of these technologies improves, the benefits to legal aid services will continue to grow. At the same time, these tools augment the work of legal aid lawyers and do not provide automated or alternative legal services. Although

---

[308] *See* Colleen V. Chien, and Kim, Miriam, *Generative AI and Legal Aid: Results from a Field Study and 100 Use Cases to Bridge the Access to Justice Gap (Mar. 14, 2024),* UC BERKELEY PUBLIC LAW RESEARCH PAPER (Forthcoming, Loyola of Los Angeles Law Review,) https://ssrn.com/abstract=4733061.

[309] *Id.* at 5.

[310] *Id.*

such services are conceivable, current technologies do not suggest that these will resolve the justice gap. Nevertheless, improved translation services and natural language processing to help unrepresented individuals and underrepresented groups fill out forms or obtain preliminary information will still offer some improvement over the current lack of access to justice.

Another area where AI can be found highly beneficial is in the patent prosecution process.[311] As with other writing output, AI work product may not yet excel at claims drafting, but the production of an editable first draft can save the patent attorney significant time. An entire industry has emerged providing patent-related AI services that integrate prior art searching, tracking of patents in various specialties, claims drafting, and process automation. Due to the high costs, complex process, and high salaries for individuals in the patent field, even marginal efficiency improvements will result in significant financial benefits to law firms and inventors.

In contrast to the nascent development of generative AI, predictive AI plays an increasingly important role in case management prediction. "[L]egal professionals are increasingly turning to predictive analysis as a powerful ally in their quest

---

[311] *See* Tabrez Y. Ebrahim, *Automation & Predictive Analytics in Patent Prosecution: USPTO Implication & Policy*, 35 GA. ST. U. L. REV. 1185 (2019), https://readingroom.law.gsu.edu/gsulr/vol35/iss4/5.

for more efficient intake management."[312] For lawyers on contingency cases, profitability is directly related to the ability to acquire cases with a strong likelihood of success while avoiding those likely to result in a loss or an insufficient payout. "Legal predictions operate by systematically sifting through mountains of legal data. This includes court records, case details, statutes, and judicial decisions. The technology applies a series of sophisticated algorithms to identify correlations and trends within this sea of information."[313]

Case valuation also extends beyond intake management. It can help firms advise clients on the value of a case, which helps promote settlement. Predictive analytics can drill down to the specific arguments to be used or theories of the case to be pursued. These tools can highlight variations among jurisdictions and even among individual judges. "[J]udicial analytics and litigation prediction tools . . . look at a judge's past rulings and opinions to predict how that judge might rule on a similar motion or case in the future."[314] One such tool, "Pre/Dicta also examines a judge's political affiliation, net worth, area of residence, career and other personal

---

[312] Katie Wolf, *Legal Predictive Analysis and the Future of Intake Management*, FILEVINE (Nov. 9, 2023), https://www.filevine.com/blog/legal-predictive-analysis-and-the-future-of-intake-management/.

[313] *Id.*

[314] Victor Li, *Pre/Dicta Takes a Radically Different Approach to Predictive Analytics Than Others*, ABA J. (May 17, 2023), https://www.americanbar.org/groups/journal/podcast/pre-dcta-takes-a-radically-different-approach-to-predictive-analytics-than-others/.

and demographic data."[315] Sophisticated statistical research provides insights into the many factors that can be tracked and used to predict the decision-making of individual judges.[316] "The tools of machine learning and causal inference can be used to study, predict, and respond to normative judgments."[317]

Beyond a judge's final decisions, predictive analytics can help lawyers understand how a particular motion or legal strategy might play out and tailor their approach to a specific judge. For clients able to invest in sophisticated analytics, these tools provide a powerful advantage to the process of litigation. Moreover, unlike the process of quantifying legal research accuracy, there are no practical alternatives to the use of AI for legal outcome analysis, so it does not need to be completely accurate to outperform all alternatives.

---

315 *Id.*

316 Daniel L. Chen, *Judicial analytics and the Great Transformation of American Law*, 27 ARTIFICIAL INTELLIGENCE AND LAW 15 (2019), https://doi.org/10.1007/s10506-018-9237-x.

317 *Id.* at 40.

CHAPTER 2

SOCIETAL CONCERNS ABOUT THE IMPLEMENTATION OF AI

This chapter provides an overview of the key concerns that may arise with the use of AI. The various regulatory regimes described in the following chapter are designed to address one or more of these considerations. This does not necessarily mean that all these risks will materialize or that they all pose the same level of risk. "We are surrounded by hysteria about the future of artificial intelligence and robotics—hysteria about how powerful they will become, how quickly, and what they will do to jobs."[1]

Some of the concerns regarding AI focus on the environmental impact of the technology. AI systems demand sophisticated computer processors which strain supply chains.[2] Bain, for example, reports that the "AI-driven surge in demand for graphics processing units alone could increase total demand for certain upstream components by 30% or more by 2026."[3] GPUs and other necessary computer chips require rare earth metals that create significant demands on the environment.[4] "[L]eading-node

---

1 Rodney Brooks, *The Seven Deadly Sins of AI Predictions*, MIT TECH. REV. (Oct. 6, 2017), https://www.technologyreview.com/2017/10/06/241837/the-seven-deadly-sins-of-ai-predictions/.

2 *See, e.g.*, Peter Hanbury, Anne Hoecker, & Michael Schallehn, *Prepare for the Coming AI Chip Shortage*, BAIN (Sept. 25, 2024), https://www.bain.com/insights/prepare-for-the-coming-ai-chip-shortage-tech-report-2024/.

3 *Id.*

4 Ryan C. Berg, Henry Ziemer, & Emiliano Polo Anaya, *Mineral Demands for Resilient Semiconductor Supply Chains*,

semiconductors require over 300 materials, presenting multiple vulnerabilities for adversaries to manipulate their supply."[5] The supply chains are often described as "fragile,"[6] and many of the needed materials come from China, adding additional challenges for resource access and management of global competition. The expanded demand for rare earth minerals also has a secondary negative impact on the environment because the relatively short lifespan of computers means that these sometimes toxic materials need to be recycled or disposed of. Many machines simply end up in landfills at the end of their life cycle with few safeguards for the environment.

In addition, the power needed to run large AI systems put strain on the existing domestic power supply in those countries where the technology is growing.[7] "GPT-4, for example, required over 50 gigawatt-hours, approximately 0.02% of the electricity California generates in a year, and 50 times the amount it took to train GPT-3, the previous iteration. As AI proliferates across industries, this energy demand will only grow."[8]

CENTER FOR STRATEGIC & INT'L STUD. (May 15, 2024), https://www.csis.org/analysis/mineral-demands-resilient-semiconductor-supply-chains.

5 *Id.*

6 *Id.*

7 Ariel Cohen, *AI Is Pushing The World Toward An Energy Crisis*, FORBES (May 23, 2024), https://www.forbes.com/sites/arielcohen/2024/05/23/ai-is-pushing-the-world-towards-an-energy-crisis/.

8 *Id.*

In the U.S., for example, the power demand has led to plans for the reopening of the Three Mile Island nuclear facility.[9] "Microsoft, which needs tremendous amounts of electricity for its growing fleet of data centers, has agreed to buy as much power as it can from the plant for 20 years. Constellation plans to spend $1.6 billion to refurbish the reactor that recently closed and restart it by 2028, pending regulatory approval."[10] Although expansion of nuclear energy is not a direct consequence of AI development, this example highlights that there is a direct connection between the demands of power consumption and environmental concerns.

The concerns about power consumption, mining, end-of-life waste, and supply chains all focus on the expanded consumption created by investing in AI technologies. Without diminishing these concerns, most of the analysis on AI risk focuses on the adoption of AI rather than the infrastructure required to support it. The reminder of the chapter address those adoption risks.

§ 2.1 RISK FRAMEWORK—A BRIEF INTRODUCTION

The list of societal concerns should be viewed through the lens of Amara's Law: "We tend to overestimate the effect of a technology in the short

---

[9] Brad Plumer, *Three Mile Island Plans to Reopen as Demand for Nuclear Power Grows*, N.Y. TIMES (Sept. 20, 2024), https://www.nytimes.com/2024/09/20/climate/three-mile-island-reopening.html.

[10] *Id.*

run and underestimate the effect in the long run."[11] Combined with the famous Arthur C. Clarke quote that "[a]ny sufficiently advanced technology is indistinguishable from magic,"[12] these risks and concerns range from present issues that require immediate attention to existential threats that shape literature and public perception, often without significant real-world examples. Readers may disagree on which are practical concerns, and which are existential threats.

Additionally, the lawyer should keep the teaching of Learned Hand in mind. Judge Hand's formulation of risk highlights the relationship among three variables: "(1) the probability, P, that an accident will occur; (2) the magnitude, L, of resulting harm, if any accident occurs, and (3) the cost of precautions, B, that would reduce the expected harm."[13] In tort litigation and insurance settings, the probability of an accident will focus on the specific type of accident and the information available to the defendant that should have informed the defendant on the need to take action.

---

[11] Brooks, *supra* note 1 quoting Roy Amara, cofounder of the Institute for the Future, in Palo Alto, California.

[12] *Id.* quoting Arthur C. Clarke.

[13] Peter Z. Grossman, Reed W. Cearley, & Daniel H. Cole, *Uncertainty, Insurance and the Learned Hand Formula*, 5 LAW, PROBABILITY AND RISK 1 (Mar. 2006), https://doi.org/10.1093/lpr/mgl012. *See* United States v. Carroll Towing Co., 159 F.2d 169 (2d Cir. 1947).

§ 2.1.1 THE RISK FROM THE COMMONS

In fields like cybersecurity and AI, the presumption should be that accidents and unpredicted outcomes are inevitable. Therefore, the formula then shifts to determining the magnitude of risk and comparing it to the cost of the harm that may result.

For example, if a GenAI legal research tool has a 70 percent accuracy rate, then 30 percent of the outcomes will be inaccurate. A firm deploying the tool can then calculate the cost of investigating all answers and discarding three-of-ten responses instead of conducting the same inquiry without the tool. If the researcher is well-versed in the topic, the time spent would make this search very inefficient. If the researcher were unfamiliar with the topic, however, then the seven-of-ten correct answers might provide a very efficient way to come up to speed on the topic. But if no effort is made to distinguish accurate from inaccurate responses, the results could be disastrous for both the client and the lawyer.

This example underscores another consideration for risk calculation: "tragedy of the commons." In this metaphor, a shared resource "provides users with tangible benefits but which nobody has an exclusive claim."[14] When no one is held accountable for harms resulting from overproduction or misuse of that

---

[14] Michael J Boyle, *What Is the Tragedy of the Commons in Economics?*, INVESTOPEDIA (Sept. 25, 2023), https://www.investopedia.com/terms/t/tragedy-of-the-commons.asp.

common resource, then the resources will be damaged or depleted as individuals act on personal incentives to maximize their own benefit. "The tragedy of the commons is an economic problem where the individual consumes a resource at the expense of society."[15]

In economic terms, the tragedy of the commons typically applies to rivalrous resources that are depleted by individual use, but the concept has been used to explain environmental harms and other scenarios where the commons are harmed by overuse rather than depletion. In the context of technology, examples of commons include open-source software, software repositories like GitHub, and arguably both the World Wide Web and the internet itself, on which it sits. For instance, if a large ad vendor such as Google, Amazon, or Meta were to adopt an algorithm that promoted low-value content, the public would see a degradation in the quality of content on the Web. On the other hand, if that search or placement strategy increased revenue, then the harm to the Web would directly harm the company behind the change.

Open-source AI tools misused for nonconsensual pornography (sometimes labelled revenge porn), virtual child pornography, bullying, misleading deepfakes are examples of harm that target both individual victims and society, often without negative consequences for the purveyors of these services. LLMs are used to generate pseudo-news

---

15 *Id.*

stories for advertising revenue, often as clickbait, harm advertisers and consumers alike even though the LLM is designed as a tool intended for social good.

Finally, AI systems should be judged against the alternative, which is human engagement without AI assistance. This is analogous to evaluating negotiations using BATNA—best alternative to a negotiated agreement. The efficacy of technology should be considered in comparison to the best alternative to human-only endeavors (BAHOE). (Perhaps the better acronym is "BAH," as in "BAH—humans are better anyway.") Corporate policy makers and government regulators should consider practical alternatives when evaluating the implementation of technology. For instance, consider the earlier illustration of Waymo's success as a self-driving taxi service. The data does not suggest that driverless taxis are free from accidents. On the contrary, the company reports an incident rate of 0.41 crashes per million miles.[16] Accidents happen. However, since the crash rate involving any injury is reported to be 85 percent lower than for human drivers,[17] the technology has achieved a positive benefit. By using a BAHOE framework, risks of technological innovation can be measured against the risk of non-introduction and the harms generally accepted under the status quo.

---

[16] *See Waymo Significantly Outperforms Comparable Human Benchmarks Over 7+ Million Miles of Rider-Only Driving*, *supra* ch. 1 note 135 and accompanying text.

[17] *Id.*

When considering either governmental regulation or corporate activities, concerns for the common and the relationship between potential magnitude of harm and the costs of precautions should all be part of the calculation used to determine the appropriate level of regulation and control. Understanding the risks associated with each technology is complex. Still, Amara's Law, Clarke's maxim, Hand's risk calculation, the tragedy of the commons, and the BAHOE minimum should all be part of the conceptual and economic modeling. Together, they help in recognizing societal harms and establishing appropriate constraints to use AI for its ultimate goal: improving the human condition.

§ 2.1.2 THE RISK OF THE SINGULARITY

Technologist and futurist Ray Kurzweil describes the singularity as "a future period during which the pace of technological change will be so rapid, its impact so deep, that human life will be irreversibly transformed."[18] In the context of AI, this results from AGI (artificial general intelligence) or AI superintelligence. "AI singularity is a hypothetical idea where artificial intelligence is more intelligent than humans. . . . It will cause technology to develop exponentially, and humans cannot evolve fast enough to catch up."[19] Although AI researchers differentiate between AGI and AI superintelligence,

---

[18] RAY KURZWEIL, THE SINGULARITY IS NEAR 7 (VIKING 2005).

[19] Nivash Jeevanandam, *What is AI Singularity: Is It a Hope or Threat for Humanity?*, EMERITUS (May 14, 2024), https://emeritus.org/in/learn/what-is-ai-singularity/.

the current state of narrow AI demonstrates that when an AI system can complete a task, it can often outperform humans. It follows that once AGI has been achieved, that system would likely also exceed human capabilities, thereby representing AI superintelligence.

Kurzweil explains that the singularity need not be the end of humanity. "Although neither utopian nor dystopian, this epoch will transform the concepts that we rely on to give meaning to our lives, from our business models to the cycle of human life, including death itself."[20] Science fiction films, on the other hand, tend to show that once AI reaches superintelligence, the machines will either compete with humans for resources or disapprove of humanity's treatment of the planet. Under either scenario, humanity would then face subjugation or eradication.

Tesla and SpaceX CEO Elon Musk "believes that, at the current pace of advancement, A.I. will likely surpass human intelligence by 2030 and there's a real chance of the technology ending humanity."[21] At the same time, Musk promoted a positive view of AI development, if done correctly. " 'I think that's incredibly important for A.I. safety is to have a maximum sort of truth-seeking and curious A.I.,' " he

---

20 KURZWEIL, *supra* note 18, at 7.

21 Refugio Garcia, *Elon Musk Believes 'Super Intelligence' Is Inevitable and Could End Humanity*, OBSERVER (Mar. 26, 2024) (quoting Elon Musk), https://observer.com/2024/03/elon-musk-discuss-artificial-general-intelligence/.

explained.[22] A wide range of scientists, industry leaders and academics signed an open letter in March 2023 calling for a pause in the development of AI systems, which received over 33,000 signatures.[23] The letter was based on the principles developed at the 2017 Asilomar Conference, with the foundational premise that "The goal of AI research should be to create not undirected intelligence, but beneficial intelligence."[24]

Professor Yuval Noah Harari emphasizes that the AI risk is its ability to control the information ecology at the heart of modern economies, communications networks that shape and define human existence.[25] "Hollywood did a huge service in focusing people's attention on the AI problem long before anybody else really thought about it. But the actual scenario is misleading because the big robot rebellion is nowhere in sight."[26] The threat is not a robot army; the threat is the power smart AI systems could wield on human information systems. "What the cinematic image so far misses is that the AIs don't need to start from

---

[22] *Id.* quoting Elon Musk.

[23] *Pause Giant AI Experiments: An Open Letter*, FUTURE OF LIFE INSTITUTE (Mar. 22, 2023), https://futureoflife.org/open-letter/pause-giant-ai-experiments/.

[24] *See Asilomar AI Principles*, FUTURE OF LIFE INSTITUTE (Aug. 17, 2017), https://futureoflife.org/open-letter/ai-principles/.

[25] *See* Nathan Gardels, *Al Will Take Over Human Systems From Within*, NOEMA (Oct. 9, 2024), https://www.noemamag.com/al-will-take-over-human-systems-from-within/ (interview with Yuval Noah Harari); YUVAL NOAH HARARI, NEXUS: A BRIEF HISTORY OF INFORMATION NETWORKS FROM THE STONE AGE TO AI (Random House 2024).

[26] Gardels, *supra* note 25 (quoting Harari).

scratch. They are inserted into our own systems, and they can take our systems over from within."[27]

In practice, there are many steps between achieving AGI or AI superintelligence and giving the system tools sufficient to implement the destruction of the human race. Nonetheless, given the potential harm, all AI systems should be designed with fail switches and other methods to externally disable those systems if the operators lose control. The *Carol Towing* risk analysis suggests that this is a modest injury prevention requirement given the theoretical consequences. Harari notes that a fail switch will not work well on a pervasive network like the internet, so other methods must be developed and deployed.[28]

§ 2.1.3 LABOR, EMPLOYMENT, AND WORKFORCE DISRUPTION

A more immediate and practical concern regarding the implementation of AI systems is the disruption to the workforce. This disruption can be categorized in two ways. In the first category, automation generally reduces the number of individuals needed for a task, leading to job loss. In the second category, automation requires the employees to use different skills and knowledge than that which was required before the automation, meaning that the staff needs to be retrained. Even if the number of positions does not decrease (and may even increase), the people qualified for those positions change. History has been replete with examples of these shifts. For example,

---

27 *Id.*

28 *See id.*

before the automated telephone switchboard was adopted by Bell Telephone, the service model was dominated by female employees.[29] "Growing demand for telephone service led the number of operators to increase for a while, from around 178,000 in 1920 to about 342,000 in the middle of the century—then it declined to less than 250,000 in 1960."[30] Still, there remain more than 1,000 operators still work in the field.[31]

This concern is not merely about new technology displacing the old, like the legend of John Henry.[32] The word "computer," after all, was a job title before it was a device.[33] Concord, NH was once a manufacturing hub known for the Concord Buggy.[34] "Cars and horses shared the road, not always happily, for decades. . . . But the automobilizing of

---

[29] *See* David A. Price, *Goodbye, Operator*, FED. RESERVE BANK OF RICHMOND (Fourth Quarter 2019), https://www.richmondfed.org/publications/research/econ_focus/2019/q4/economic_history.

[30] *Id.*

[31] *Id.*

[32] *See, e.g.*, *The Legend of John Henry: Talcott, WV*, NAT'L PARK SERV., https://www.nps.gov/neri/planyourvisit/the-legend-of-john-henry-talcott-wv.htm (last visited Feb. 16, 2025) ("*The Ballad of John Henry* . . . . tells of a boy born with a 'hammer in his hand' . . . . It tells us that this man took a hammer in each hand to face down a steam-powered drilling machine. John Henry promised, '*If I can't beat this steam drill down, I'll die with this hammer in my hand!*'").

[33] *See Computer (occupation),* WIKIPEDIA, https://en.wikipedia.org/wiki/Computer_(occupation) (last visited Feb. 16, 2025).

[34] *See The Abbot-Downing Company*, ABBOT-DOWNING HIST. SOC'Y, https://concordcoach.org/the-abbot-downing-company (last visited Feb. 16, 2025).

America was inevitable, especially because it soon became cheaper to keep a car. In 1900, only 4,192 cars were sold in the U.S.; by 1912, it was 356,000."[35] Unlike most technological revolutions, where lower-wage workers were displaced by the demand for new skills, generative AI threatens knowledge workers themselves, inverting the very nature of progress since the Industrial Revolution.

As described in a report of the International Monetary Fund (IMF), "[a]lmost 40 percent of global employment is exposed to AI, with advanced economies at greater risk but also better poised to exploit AI benefits than emerging market and developing economies. In advanced economies, about 60 percent of jobs are exposed to AI, due to prevalence of cognitive-task-oriented jobs."[36] The disruption will not be evenly distributed. "A new measure of potential AI complementarity suggests that, of these, about half may be negatively affected by AI, while the rest could benefit from enhanced productivity

---

[35] Jim Motavalli, *When Will Electric Cars Really Take Off? Maybe We Should Ask a Horse*, TREEHUGGER (Feb. 10, 2021), https://www.treehugger.com/horses-horsepower-rocky-transition-4867999.

[36] MAURO CAZZANIGA ET AL., GEN-AI: ARTIFICIAL INTELLIGENCE AND THE FUTURE OF WORK, INT'L MONETARY FUND (Jan. 2024), https://www.imf.org/en/Publications/Staff-Discussion-Notes/Issues/2024/01/14/Gen-AI-Artificial-Intelligence-and-the-Future-of-Work-542379?cid=bl-com-SDNEA2024001. *See also* Kristalina Georgieva, *AI Will Transform the Global Economy. Let's Make Sure It Benefits Humanity*, INT'L MONETARY FUND (Jan. 14, 2024), https://www.imf.org/en/Blogs/Articles/2024/01/14/ai-will-transform-the-global-economy-lets-make-sure-it-benefits-humanity.

through AI integration."[37] Demographically, older workers are more likely to be displaced and "may struggle with reemployment, adapting to technology, mobility, and training for new job skills."[38]

The IMF report also suggests that AI transformation is likely to exacerbate the digital divide, providing those with technological training and resources an increased advantage over those without those resources, both at the individual level and in terms of national competition.[39]

At the national level, the IMF identifies four economic characteristics that are likely to influence the ability of countries to adapt to AI transformation.[40] The same characteristics will likely dictate the implications for particular industries within an economy. The four characteristics are: "(1) digital infrastructure, (2) innovation and economic integration, (3) human capital and labor market policies, and (4) regulation and ethics."[41]

---

[37] *Id.* at 2.

[38] *Id.*

[39] *See id.* at 22.

[40] *Id.* at 20.

[41] *Id.*

Dimension	Indicator
1. FOUNDATIONAL AI PREPAREDNESS	
I. Digital Infrastructure	
Accessible, affordable, and secured internet access	- Estimated internet users per 100 inhabitants [UN] - Number of main fixed telephone lines per 100 inhabitants [UN] - Number of mobile subscribers per 100 inhabitants [UN] - Number of fixed broadband subscriptions per 100 inhabitants [UN] - Number of wireless broadband subscriptions per 100 inhabitants [UN] - Cost of internet access (percent of monthly GNI per capita) [ITU] - Secure internet servers per 1 million people [WB]
Mature e-commerce infrastructure	- Private sector's e-commerce business environment o Postal reliability index [UPU] o Use of mobile phone for online transactions (% of population ages 15+) [WB] - Public sector's online services infrastructure [UN]
II. Human Capital and Labor Market Policies	
Education and digital skills	- Human capital index (i.e., mean years of schooling, expected years of schooling, gross enrolment ratio, adult literacy) [UN] - Public education expenditure (10-year average; %GDP) [WB] - Skillset of graduates (proxy for equality of education) [WEF] - Digital skills among active population (e.g., computer skills, basic coding, etc.) [UN] - Number of STEM graduates (10-year average; % of total graduates) [WB] - Number of female STEM graduates (10-year average; % of STEM graduates) [WB]
Labor market flexibility and policies	- Flexibility of wage determination (centralized vs individual firm level) [WEF] - Social protection (% of population covered by social protection schemes) [ILO] - Internal labor market mobility [WEF] - Active labor market policies (e.g., skills matching, retraining) [WEF] - Pay and productivity (i.e., extent to which wages are market determined) [WEF]
2. SECOND-GENERATION AI PREPAREDNESS	
III. Innovation & Economic Integration	
Innovation	- R&D spending per unit of GDP [WB] - Frontier technology readiness (i.e., AI related R&D activity: number of scientific publications, number of patents on frontier technologies) [UNCTAD] - Domestic credit to private sector (%GDP) [WB]
Economic integration	- Mean tariff rate [FI] - Non-tariff barriers [FI] - Free movement of capital and people (average of three indicators: financial openness, capital controls, freedom of foreigners to visit) [FI]
IV. Regulation and Ethics	
Strong legal frameworks and enforcement mechanisms	- Legal framework's adaptability to digital business models [WEF] - Government effectiveness (proxy for enforcement/accountability) [WB]

[42]

There is a critical distinction between a job impacted by AI and a job eliminated by automation. Generative AI will likely restructure many language-based professional tasks. As noted in the next

42 *Id.* at Annex 5—AI Preparedness Index.

Data source for each indicator is shown in square brackets. FI = Fraser Institute; ILO = International Labour Organization; UN = United Nations; UNCTAD = UN Trade and Development; UPU = Universal Postal Union; WB = World Bank; WEF = World Economic Forum.

section, this will have the most profound effect on journalism and creative industries. As self-driving vehicles improve, they will eventually disrupt the trucking industry and replace a significant number of taxi and delivery services.[43]

In the U.S., labor unions are taking notice. SAG-AFTRA, the leading union for motion picture and television talent, included restrictions on AI and digital replicas as a central component of the union's bargaining position.[44] Following the adoption of a new agreement, the union struck a deal to allow limited use of digital voice replica technology. "SAG-AFTRA, the union representing 160,000 media artists, and Narrativ negotiated and reached an agreement concerning the union's informed consent and compensation requirements, along with other crucial A.I. guardrails."[45] A significant strike by dockworkers addressed—but failed to resolve—key issues on AI automation.[46] "[T]he fight against automation predates AI and has been a long-standing battle for industrial workers, who have

---

[43] *See* Joann Muller, *Self-Driving Trucks Struggle to Deliver*, AXIOS (Apr. 26, 2023), https://www.axios.com/2023/04/26/self-driving-trucks; Patrick Seitz, *Autonomous Trucks Are Barreling Ahead, But Robot Big Rigs Face A Bumpy Road*, INV. BUS. DAILY (Mar. 1, 2023), https://www.investors.com/news/technology/autonomous-trucks-are-coming-but-face-bumpy-road/.

[44] *See SAG-AFTRA and Narrativ Announce New Agreement*, SAG-AFTRA (Aug 12, 2024), https://www.sagaftra.org/sag-aftra-and-narrativ-announce-new-agreement.

[45] *Id.*

[46] *See* Jenn Brice, *The Dockworkers' Strike Ends for now—But the Fight over Automating Jobs Continues, as it has for Decades*, FORTUNE (Oct. 4, 2024), https://fortune.com/2024/10/04/dockworkers-strike-ends-automation-ai/.

been sounding the alarm about the risk machines pose to job security for generations. While the technology typically wins out, it's not without a fight."[47]

The impact goes beyond today's jobs: Self-driving cars may reduce the interest in vehicle ownership giving rise to car rental subscription services; to a shift away from in-home garages replaced with centralized garages that enable cars to be called by their owners; and rider-share commuter systems that reduce the number of vehicles while still providing door-to-door service. Once the car no longer needs to be in the owner's garage, many of the other assumptions about car use also change. The same will be true of the jobs needed to support those activities. As AI automation expands, every industry will be subject to those changed assumptions.

"The World Economic Forum's Future of Jobs Report 2023 says that AI and machine learning specialists, data analysts and scientists, and digital transformation specialists are the most prominent emerging roles."[48] These fields could increase by 30–40 percent by 2027.[49] In contrast, computer coding is one of the fields often predicted to be significantly replaced by AI.

---

[47] *Id.*

[48] Ian Shine & Kate Whiting, Th*ese are the Jobs most likely to be Lost—and Created—Because of AI*, WORLD ECONOMIC FORUM (May 4, 2023), https://www.weforum.org/agenda/2023/05/jobs-lost-created-ai-gpt/.

[49] *Id.*

The impact of AI will be broad, necessitating new skills and changes in the nature of positions across industries. While there may be a small but significant reduction in the workforce in some industries, this will likely be offset by growth in others, as the economy has always seen such shifts. However, unlike in previous eras, there are few, if any, fields that will not undergo transformations in skills and knowledge. At the individual level, such disruptions may not be significant, but when they impact 80–90 percent of the workforce, the disruption may be incalculable.

§ 2.1.4 THE DIGITAL DIVIDE AND ECONOMIC INEQUALITY

Concerns regarding the digital divide were raised by the IMF in its report on the impact of AI on global employment.[50] There are also profound structural barriers that benefit some adopters of technology over others. "The idea of the 'digital divide' refers to the growing gap between the underprivileged members of society. . . ."[51] The digital divide disadvantages the disadvantaged, exacerbating pre-existing inequities "especially [for] the poor, rural, elderly, and handicapped portion of the population who do not have access to computers or the internet; and the wealthy, middle-class, and young Americans

---

50 *See* CAZZANIGA *supra* note 36 and accompanying text.

51 Digital Divide, STANFORD UNIV., https://cs.stanford.edu/people/eroberts/cs181/projects/digital-divide/start.html (last visited Feb. 16, 2025).

living in urban and suburban areas who have access."[52]

The inequality is magnified since new technologies require high-powered, new computers or mobile devices, run on the fastest telecommunications infrastructure, and often include expensive subscription rates. The economic barriers are not evenly distributed. "Nearly half of Americans without at-home internet were in Black and Hispanic households. . . . [U]p to 40% of disconnected K-12 students from Black, Latino, and indigenous communities struggle with insufficient digital literacy, language obstacles, and other disincentives to use the internet. . . ."[53]

For context, despite the expectations that nearly all employees will be using generative AI and other AI tools within the next year or two, "[i]n the United States alone, one in three people don't use the internet at speeds fast enough to use Zoom, never mind the latest AI-enabled technologies. Elsewhere, the digital divide is greater still, with 63 percent of people living in African countries lacking any internet access at all."[54]

According to the *National Institute of Health*, "[d]igital literacies and Internet connectivity have been called the "super social determinants of health"

---

[52] Stanford Univ. *supra* note 51.

[53] *Id.*

[54] Jochai Ben-Avie, *Don't Let AI Become the Newest Digital Divide*, COUNCIL ON FOREIGN RELATIONS (Jan. 18, 2024), https://www.cfr.org/blog/dont-let-ai-become-newest-digital-divide.

because they address all other social determinants of health . . . For example, applications for employment, housing, and other assistance programs, each of which influences an individual's health, are increasingly, and sometimes exclusively, accessible online."[55] The report explains that it is more efficacious to expand digital literacy and broadband services than to treat the health conditions because access to internet-based services serves as a gatekeeper for effective health outcomes.[56] Yet despite this, the Affordable Connectivity Program, enacted during the COVID-19 pandemic, was closed as of June 1, 2024 for lack of continued funding.[57] "The pandemic-era program was a hit with members of both political parties and served tens of millions of seniors, veterans and rural and urban Americans alike."[58] Yet, despite broad-based and bipartisan appeal, Congress failed to continue this lifeline for digital access to the modern world.

A report from Microsoft Research[59] also recognizes the threat. The report highlights the potential for ideation using generative AI but warns that

---

[55] Cynthia J. Sieck et al., *Digital Inclusion as a Social Determinant of Health*, 4 NPJ DIGITAL MEDICINE 52 (Mar. 17, 2021), https://www.ncbi.nlm.nih.gov/pmc/articles/PMC7969595/.

[56] *Id.*

[57] Brian Fung, *FCC Ends Affordable Internet Program Due to Lack of Funds*, CNN (May 31, 2024), https://www.cnn.com/2024/05/31/tech/fcc-affordable-connectivity-program-acp-close/index.html.

[58] *Id.*

[59] *See* Madeleine I. G. Daepp and Scott Counts, *The Emerging AI Divide in the United States*, MICROSOFT RESEARCH (Apr. 30, 2024), https://arxiv.org/abs/2404.11988.

"[a]lthough the value these tools create for their users is likely to increase economic growth in general, differences in adoption could also magnify the already considerable harms of digital divides."[60] The research reiterated earlier work on the digital divide that interest in ChatGPT was geographically clustered "with the highest rates of search in West Coast states and persistently low rates of search in Appalachia and Gulf states."[61] Within the states, the counties with the greatest interest "are proportionally more urbanized, more educated, and have more technology and creative sector jobs in comparison with the U.S. overall."[62] In addition, the primary predictor of ChatGPT interest was the person's level of education, leading to the conclusion that "[a]lthough generative AI tools may be new, user interest follows the well-worn patterns of established digital divides."[63]

The more successful the AI transformation becomes, the more critical it will be within each community and across all nations that the digital literacy and access gaps are reversed. Without doing so, the divides risk transforming into fault lines that risk significant and devastating social upheaval.

---

60 *Id.* at 3.

61 *Id.*

62 *Id.*

63 *Id.*

§ 2.2 CONSIDERATIONS ABOUT POOR IMPLEMENTATION

The preceding section highlighted the social issues and challenges raised by the growth of AI and the disruptive success inherent in AI-automated systems. This section, however, focuses on the potential for AI to cause significant harm to individuals, companies, agencies, and society if it is implemented or used improperly. The section begins with a case study from the pharmaceutical retailer Rite Aid. The case study documents the harms that poor implementation can bring.

§ 2.2.1 THE CAUTIONARY TALE OF RITE AID

Rite Aid first entered into a stipulated order with the FTC in 2010.[64] The original complaint and stipulated focused on Rite Aid's failure to secure medical information and other protected information. Rite Aid was accused of discarding "materials containing personal information in clear readable text (such as pharmacy labels and employment applications) in unsecured, publicly-accessible trash dumpsters used by Rite Aid pharmacies on numerous occasions."[65] The FTC noted that "in late 2006 and continuing into [2008] . . . media outlets reported finding personal information in unsecured dumpsters used by Rite Aid pharmacies in at least 7 cities throughout the United States. The personal information found in the

---

[64] *See* In re Rite Aid Corporation, C–4308, 150 F.T.C. 694 (Nov. 12, 2010).

[65] *Id.* at 2.

dumpsters included information about Respondent's customers and job applicants."[66] Since the data included both health information covered by HIPAA and by Rite Aid's published privacy policies, the use of back-alley trash bins constituted unfair or deceptive trading practices in violation of Section 5(a) of the FTC Act.[67]

Although Rite Aid had entered into a consent decree, the FTC alleged that by 2012, the company was again violating Section 5(a) of the FTC Act. In the new situation, Rite Aid was alleged to use "facial recognition technology in hundreds of its retail pharmacy locations to identify patrons that it had previously deemed likely to engage in shoplifting or other criminal behavior in order to 'drive and keep persons of interest out of [Rite Aid] stores.' "[68]

The company has denied wrongdoing in each consent decree. The facts described here are based on the FTC complaints and resulting consent decrees. Although the violation of the FTC Act involved different technologies, the core issue was that Rite aid failed to (1) follow appropriate policies and procedures; "(2) adequately train employees . . .; (3) use reasonable measures to assess compliance with its established policies and procedures . . .; and (4)

---

66 *Id.*

67 *Id.* at 3.

68 FTC v. Rite Aid Corporation, Case 2:23–cv–05023 (Dec. 19, 2023) (2023 Complaint).

employ a reasonable process for discovering and remedying risks . . . ."[69]

The 2023 consent decree involved misuse of biometric facial recognition information. Facial recognition systems are increasingly being implemented, but research has demonstrated significant issues, particularly with error rates involving women and minorities.[70] There are a number of social concerns with the expansion of facial recognition technology, particularly when used to identify individuals without their meaningful consent. The lack of consent, inability to encrypt facial imagery, and technical vulnerabilities to these systems are all concerns.[71] Perhaps the single greatest concern, however, is the continuing inaccuracy of these systems.

AI facial recognition software has been notoriously poor in facial recognition for dark-skinned individuals as compared to Caucasian individuals.[72]

---

69 In re Rite Aid Corporation (2010 Complaint), *supra* note 62.

70 *See* CATHY O'NEIL, WEAPONS OF MATH DESTRUCTION: HOW BIG DATA INCREASES INEQUALITY AND THREATENS DEMOCRACY 123 (2016); Kristin N. Johnson, *Automating the Risk of Bias*, 87 GEO. WASH. L. REV. 1214, 1218 (2019) ("Civil rights activists warn that the integration of learning algorithms marks the creation of a new class of enterprise risks.").

71 *Facial Recognition Market Size, NAShare & Trends Report*, 2030, GRAND VIEW RES., https://www.grandviewresearch.com/industry-analysis/facial-recognition-market.

72 *See* Tom Simonite, *The Best Algorithms Struggle to Recognize Black Faces Equally*, WIRED (July 22, 2019), https://www.wired.com/story/best-algorithms-struggle-recognize-black-faces-equally/ ("US government tests find even top-performing

"NIST's tests and other studies repeatedly have found that the algorithms have a harder time recognizing people with darker skin. . . . Many top performers in that report show . . . [a] 10-fold difference in error rate for black and white women."[73]

Given the known limitations of the technology, the use cases for facial recognition should be quite limited, but just the opposite has been true. "The global facial recognition market size was valued at USD 5.15 billion in 2022 and is expected to grow at a compound annual growth rate (CAGR) of 14.9% from 2023 to 2030."[74]

Despite the known risks associated with facial recognition systems, Rite Aid chose to implement just such a system, and "failed to implement reasonable procedures and prevent harm to consumers in its use of facial recognition technology in hundreds of stores."[75] There were a multitude of poor implementation decisions.

---

facial recognition systems misidentify blacks at rates five to 10 times higher than they do whites.").

[73] *Id.*

[74] *Facial Recognition Market Size, NAShare & Trends Report*, 2030, GRAND VIEW RES., https://www.grandviewresearch.com/industry-analysis/facial-recognition-market.

[75] *Rite Aid Banned from Using AI Facial Recognition After FTC Says Retailer Deployed Technology without Reasonable Safeguards*, FED. TRADE COMM'N (Dec. 19, 2023) [hereinafter *Rite Aid Press Release*], https://www.ftc.gov/news-events/news/press-releases/2023/12/rite-aid-banned-using-ai-facial-recognition-after-ftc-says-retailer-deployed-technology-without. *See also* Complaint at 10, FTC v. Rite Aid Corp., Case No. 2:23–cv–5023 (E.D. Pa. Dec. 19, 2023).

First, Rite Aid did not restrict the system to high-quality images necessary to enable the system to operate effectively. Instead, the company created a database of potential shoplifters, using "tens of thousands of images of individuals, many of which were low-quality and came from Rite Aid's security cameras, employee phone cameras and even news stories, according to the complaint."[76] The complaint further noted that "Rite Aid trained store-level security employees to 'push for as many enrollments as possible.' "[77]

Second, Rite Aid did not obtain adequate assurances the system was capable of providing the required facial recognition. Instead, the vendors who created the system sold it on an "as is" basis, disclaiming liability for the operational effectiveness of the system.[78]

Third, the system was used to label members of the public with categorizations that were beyond the scope of the system. The facial recognition program instructed staff how to manage the patrons in their stores with codes that could not reasonably be part of the database information:

> Rite Aid's enrollments were assigned different match alert instructions depending on the reason the individual was enrolled. These instructions included (i) "Approach and

---

[76] *Rite Aid Press Release*, *supra* note 75. *See also* Complaint, *supra* note 68, at ¶ 22.

[77] 2023 Complaint, *supra* note 68, at ¶ 23.

[78] *Id.* at ¶ 51–52.

Identify," (ii) "Observe and Provide Customer Service," (iii) "Pharmacy Patient—Escort to Pharmacy," and (iv) "911 Alert" or "Potentially Violent—Notify Law Enforcement and Observe." For enrollments with the instruction "911 Alert," employees were told to "call 911 and notify [the police that] a potentially violent or dangerous subject has entered the store."[79]

Fourth, "Rite Aid failed to consider or address foreseeable harms to consumers flowing from its use of facial recognition technology, failed to test or assess the technology's accuracy before or after deployment, [and] failed to enforce image quality standards that were necessary for the technology to function accurately."[80] According to the FTC, the system generated tens of thousands of false positives, alerting employees to dangerous and potentially violent individuals who needed to be escorted out of the store or reported to law enforcement when they entered the location. However, employees were not informed that many of these identifications were made with very low confidence. The system often flagged the same individual as being in multiple states simultaneously and triggered numerous other red flags that should have warned employees not to rely on it.[81]

The system sold to Rite Aid had one safeguard through which it provided confidence scores related

[79] *Id.* at ¶ 29.

[80] *Id.* at ¶ 5.

[81] *See id.* at ¶ 29.

to the matches generated by the system.[82] Rite Aid, however, did not share the confidence scores with the employees, perhaps so that the employees would not second-guess the accuracy of the information being provided.

Fifth, "Rite Aid's actions disproportionately affected people of color, especially Black people, Asians and Latinos, all in the name of keeping 'persons of interest' out of hundreds of Rite Aid stores in cities including New York, Philadelphia and Sacramento."[83] The use of the system was not uniform and the pattern of implementation had a direct, consequential impact on the communities Rite Aid was supposed to be serving.

The lessons from the Rite Aid example should not be lost on retailers and other industries using facial recognition software. The first lesson is one of the oldest adages about data systems: Garbage in—garbage out. Rite Aid's use of pictures taken from video monitors, low resolution security cameras, and other unreliable sources highlights the callous disregard the operators of this system had for their customers or of civil rights more generally.[84]

---

82 *Id.* at ¶ 26–27.

83 Eduardo Medina, *Rite Aid's A.I. Facial Recognition Wrongly Tagged People of Color as Shoplifters*, N.Y. TIMES (Dec. 21, 2023) (quoting the FTC), https://www.nytimes.com/2023/12/21/business/rite-aid-ai-facial-recognition.html.

84 2023 Complaint, *supra* note 68, at ¶ 22 (Rite Aid employees enrolled photographs of individuals' driver's licenses or other government identification cards or photographs of images displayed on video monitors.).

Second, current facial recognition systems are known to perform poorly for people with darker skin tones, including African Americans, compared to their performance for Caucasians. When such technology is used to determine whether a customer can enter a store, this disparity alone should be enough to prohibit its use.[85] "Alvaro M. Bedoya, the commissioner of the F.T.C., said in a statement that 'the blunt fact that surveillance can hurt people' should not get lost in conversations about how surveillance violates rights and invades privacy."[86]

Third, if a vendor is selling predictive AI tools but disclaiming any responsibility for the output of its systems, there should be a high degree of skepticism that the system will perform as intended. If the responsibility for all outputs is disclaimed by the vendor, then there is simply no assurance that the system will meet any previous marketing promises. The use of a system without any guarantees makes that decision highly suspect, if not per se negligent, if the company acquiring the system cannot independently verify the accuracy of the system.[87]

Fourth and finally, companies must balance the impact of high-stake decisions with the confidence of the data being used. In the Rite Aid example, the

---

85 *See* Medina, *supra* note 83

86 *Id.*

87 *See* Complaint, *supra* note 68, at ¶ 74 ("Rite Aid failed to regularly monitor and assess the accuracy of the results of its facial recognition technology. . . Rite Aid failed to adequately (i) verify or test the accuracy of match alerts, (ii) record outcomes or track the rate of false-positive matches, and (iii) remedy problematic enrollments.").

systems at least provided confidence scores related to the matches generated by the system.[88] Instead, this feature was disabled. Where the confidence of an outcome is not high, users of the information should not rely upon it. In situations with meaningful consequences, users should only use information generated that has a high degree of confidence.

When this system was introduced in 2012, it was so fundamentally flawed that no reasonable business should have made the decision to operate in this manner. As more and more information about algorithmic bias has entered the public sphere, the continued use of such a system should strain credulity, but unfortunately it reflects longstanding issues.

> "Shopping while black" is a longstanding phenomenon that usually entails greeting Black shoppers with suspicion the moment they enter stores, following them around the entire time, and wrongly accusing them of stealing. Locking black haircare and beauty products in glass cabinets while placing similar goods aimed at white buyers on open shelves, as Walmart did for many years,[89] is another example of how retail stores discriminate against Black patrons. Rite Aid's misuse of facial recognition technology is a troubling case example of how AI further

---

[88] *Id.* at ¶ 26–27.

[89] Neil Vigdor & Elisha Brown, *Walmart Says It Will No Longer Lock Up African-American Beauty Products*, N.Y. TIMES (June 10, 2020), https://www.nytimes.com/2020/06/10/business/walmart-black-hair-beauty-products.html.

exposes Black people and other shoppers of color to what Michelle Dunlap and other scholars call retail racism.[90]

The Rite Aid example is merely an illustration of what has already gone wrong with the implementation of AI systems. In this case, the implementation was by a national retailer that was already operating under an FTC Consent Decree. Attorneys working with clients, therefore, must be highly aware of the risk that clients need advice and guidance to avoid violating the law in the implementation of AI or otherwise operating in a manner that constitutes an unfair or deceptive trade practice.

Rite Aid, of course, is not alone among the companies that have been sanctioned by federal regulators of their implementation of AI. The Securities and Exchange Commission (SEC), for example, has brought a number of complaints against companies for overstating the importance of implementation of AI in an effort to lure investments.[91] Known as "AI washing," such companies did not have the AI or machine learning

---

[90] Shaun Harper, *Rite Aid Facial Recognition Lawsuit Shows AI Risks of Shopping While Black*, FORBES (Dec 21, 2023), https://www.forbes.com/sites/shaunharper/2023/12/21/shopping-while-black-in-the-era-of-ai-lessons-from-a-federal-case-against-rite-aid/. *See generally*, MICHELLE R. DUNLAP, RETAIL RACISM: SHOPPING WHILE BLACK AND BROWN IN AMERICA (2023).

[91] *See, e.g.*, *SEC Charges Two Investment Advisers with Making False and Misleading Statements About Their Use of Artificial Intelligence*, U.S. SEC. AND EXCH. COMM'N (Mar. 18, 2024), https://www.sec.gov/newsroom/press-releases/2024-36.

capabilities claimed in their marketing materials.[92] An alert provided by the SEC in January 2024 highlighted the increasingly common fraud:

> Numerous unregistered and unlicensed online investment platforms, as well as unlicensed and unregistered individuals and firms, are promoting AI trading systems that make unrealistic claims like, "*Our proprietary AI trading system can't lose!*" or "*Use AI to Pick Guaranteed Stock Winners!*" In reality, these scammers are running investment schemes that seek to leverage the popularity of AI. Be wary of claims—even from registered firms and professionals—that AI can *guarantee* amazing investment returns.[93]

In a similar fashion, the FTC has warned "AI hype is playing out today across many products, from toys to cars to chatbots and a lot of things in between. Breathless media accounts don't help, but it starts with the companies that do the developing and selling."[94] The FTC has told advertisers that a falsely claiming AI is a component of a product constitutes

---

92 *See id.* ("According to the SEC's order against Delphia, from 2019 to 2023, the Toronto-based firm made false and misleading statements in its SEC filings, in a press release, and on its website regarding its purported use of AI and machine learning that incorporated client data in its investment process.").

93 *Artificial Intelligence (AI) and Investment Fraud: Investor Alert*, U.S. SEC. AND EXCH. COMM'N (Jan. 25, 2024), https://www.investor.gov/introduction-investing/general-resources/news-alerts/alerts-bulletins/investor-alerts/artificial-intelligence-fraud.

94 Michael Atleson, *Keep your AI claims in check*, FED. TRADE COMM'N BUSINESS BLOG, (Feb. 27, 2023), https://www.ftc.gov/business-guidance/blog/2023/02/keep-your-ai-claims-check.

an unfair and deceptive trade practice. "It's not uncommon for advertisers to say that some new-fangled technology makes their product better—perhaps to justify a higher price or influence labor decisions. You need adequate proof for that kind of comparative claim,[95] too, and if such proof is impossible to get, then don't make the claim." Exaggerations are also prohibited. AI washing constitutes a form of unsubstantiated marketing claim that regulators are taking seriously. "[A]t the FTC, one thing we know about hot marketing terms is that some advertisers won't be able to stop themselves from overusing and abusing them. . . . Marketers should know that—for FTC enforcement purposes—false or unsubstantiated claims about a product's efficacy are our bread and butter."[96]

§ 2.2.2 ALGORITHMIC DISCRIMINATION AND BIAS

The misidentification of individuals by biometric facial recognition is primarily an accuracy issue. The systematic increase in error rates for women and minorities, however, reflects a deeper problem of bias incorporated into the parameters, historically-based training data, and design decisions that comprise the decision-making algorithms. The persistence of algorithmic bias and algorithmic discrimination have been well documented and pose a significant limitation for deployment of AI systems.

---

95 *Id.*

96 *Id.*

Bias in cognitive technologies has been widely recognized.[97] "Examples of AI bias in the real world show us that when discriminatory data and algorithms are baked into AI models, the models deploy biases at scale and amplify the resulting negative effects."[98] The bias of the AI remains human bias, "results that reflect and perpetuate human biases within a society, including historical and current social inequality."[99] Unlike computer programming, which uses precise instructions, modern AI systems use machine learning (ML), where the computer "learns through experience."[100] ML systems use large amounts of data as training

---

[97] *Shedding Light on AI Bias with Real World Examples*, IBM (Oct. 16, 2023), https://www.ibm.com/blog/shedding-light-on-ai-bias-with-real-world-examples/ ("As companies increase their use of artificial intelligence (AI), people are questioning the extent to which human biases have made their way into AI systems.").

[98] *Id.*

[99] *Id.*

[100] Sara Brown, *Machine Learning, Explained*, MIT (Apr. 21, 2021), https://mitsloan.mit.edu/ideas-made-to-matter/machine-learning-explained. *See also* FEDERIK ZUIDERVEEN BORGESIUS, DISCRIMINATION, ARTIFICIAL INTELLIGENCE, AND ALGORITHMIC DECISION MAKING, COUNCIL OF EUROPE 13 (2018), https://rm.coe.int/discrimination-artificial-intelligence-and-algorithmic-decision-making/1680925d73 (quoting PETER DONNELLY ET AL., MACHINE LEARNING: THE POWER AND PROMISE OF COMPUTERS THAT LEARN BY EXAMPLE, ROYAL SOCIETY 19 (2017), https://royalsociety.org/~/media/policy/projects/machine-learning/publications/machine-learning-report.pdf.

> With machine learning, the knowledge in the system does not have to be provided by experts. "In contrast, machine learning systems are set a task and given a large amount of data to use as examples of how this task can be achieved or from which to detect patterns. The system then learns how best to achieve the desired output."

data, with the assumption that "the more data, the better the program."[101] Using the data, the system learns to make predictions and recognize patterns.[102] Large language models use a similar approach to learn the patterns of language and contextualized content.[103] When systems are trained using data sets with bias in the data, the results will naturally reflect that bias in the system's operation.[104] "[I]f the data represents a single demographic, or lacks diversity, the outputs produced by the large language model will also lack diversity."[105]

In May 2024, Colorado enacted the Colorado AI Act, the first state law designed to address

---

101 Brown, *supra* note 100.

102 *Id.*

103 *See What is a Large Language Model (LLM)?*, ELASTIC, https://www.elastic.co/what-is/large-language-models (last visited Feb. 16, 2025).

> A large language model (LLM) is a deep learning algorithm that can perform a variety of natural language processing (NLP) tasks. Large language models use transformer models and are trained using massive datasets—hence, large. This enables them to recognize, translate, predict, or generate text or other content. Large language models are also referred to as neural networks (NNs), which are computing systems inspired by the human brain. These neural networks work using a network of nodes that are layered, much like neurons.

See generally Zhengbao Jiang et al., *How Can We Know What Language Models Know?*, 8 TRANSACTIONS OF THE ASS'N FOR COMPUT. LINGUISTICS 423 (2020), https://direct.mit.edu/tacl/article/doi/10.1162/tacl_a_00324/96460.

104 *What are Large Language Models (LLM)?*, *supra* note 103.

105 *Id.*

algorithmic discrimination. It provides a statutory definition for algorithmic discrimination.

> "Algorithmic Discrimination" means any condition in which the use of an artificial intelligence system results in an unlawful differential treatment or impact that disfavors an individual or group of individuals on the basis of their actual or perceived age, color, disability, ethnicity, genetic information, limited proficiency in the English language, national origin, race, religion, reproductive health, sex, veteran status, or other classification protected under the laws of this state or federal law.[106]

The list of protected classifications is an expanded version of the federal statutory protection available under Title VII of the Civil Rights Act of 1964 (Title VII), the American with Disabilities Act (ADA), and the Age Discrimination in Employment Act (ADEA).[107] The statute prohibits developers of AI systems ("Developers") and parties using such systems ("Deployers") from engaging systems that produce algorithmic discrimination if the use involves a "high-risk activity" and the output results in a "consequential decision." A "high-risk artificial intelligence system" means any artificial intelligence system that, when deployed, makes, or is a substantial factor in making, a consequential decision."[108]

---

106 COLO. REV. STAT. § 6–1–1701(1)(a) (2024).

107 *See, e.g.*, 42 U.S.C §§ 2000e(c), 12111(7); 29 U.S.C § 630(c).

108 COLO. REV. STAT. at § 6–1–1701(6).

"Consequential decision" means a decision that has a material legal or similarly significant effect on the provision or denial to any consumer of, or the cost or terms of:

(a) education enrollment or an education opportunity;

(b) employment or an employment opportunity;

(c) a financial or lending service;

(d) an essential government service;

(e) health-care services;

(f) housing;

(g) insurance; or

(h) a legal service.[109]

Although the Colorado AI Act attempts to define many of its terms, the phrase "material legal or similarly significant effect" remains undefined. The term is "likely adopted from the European Union's General Data Protection Regulation."[110] The Colorado law also borrows from European regulation by adopting the regulatory approach that separates high-risk activities for additional regulation.[111] "The EU Artificial Intelligence Act. . . takes a risk-based

---

[109] *Id.* at § 6–1–1701(3).

[110] Stacey Chuvaieva, *Colorado Adopts Comprehensive AI Act Imposing Broad Disclosure Requirements*, MITCHELL SILBERBERG & KNUPP LLP (May 22, 2024), https://www.msk.com/newsroom-alerts-colorado-ai-act.

[111] *See id.*

approach to regulation, applying different rules to AI systems according to the threats they pose to human health, safety, and rights."[112]

In keeping with a risk-based approached and seeking to manage the scope of the law, the statute identifies several common uses of AI that are excluded from the definition of "algorithmic discrimination," including fraud protection, cybersecurity, data storage, even calculators, and similar uses.[113]

The new Colorado law does not attempt to establish comprehensive AI regulation. Instead, it focuses on two primary concerns. First, the law aims to ensure that the public is notified when a company is using AI for communications or other purposes. Second, it seeks to limit algorithmic bias and discrimination.

To address the public disclosure requirement, the Colorado AI Act requires deployers of AI systems to "ensure the disclosure to each consumer who interacts with the artificial intelligence system that the consumer is interacting with an artificial intelligence system"[114] unless "it would be obvious to a reasonable person that the person is interacting with an artificial intelligence system."[115]

---

[112] Matt Kosinski, *What is the European Union Artificial Intelligence Act (EU AI Act)?*, IBM (April 8, 2024), https://www.ibm.com/topics/eu-ai-act.

[113] COLO. REV. STAT. § 6–1–1701(9)(b)(II).

[114] *Id.* at 6–1–1704.

[115] *Id.*

The central provision of the law offers a deceptively simple formula for this protection. "[A] developer of a high-risk artificial intelligence system shall use reasonable care to protect consumers from any known or reasonably foreseeable risks of algorithmic discrimination arising from the intended and contracted uses of the high-risk artificial intelligence system."[116] The state then provides a rebuttable presumption that the developer of the high-risk artificial intelligence system has used reasonable care if the developer follows the steps of the safe harbor provisions of the statute and any applicable regulations.[117]

Under the safe harbor provisions, a developer must provide to the deployers a long list of disclosures, including a "general statement describing the reasonably foreseeable uses and known harmful or inappropriate uses of the High-Risk Artificial Intelligence System"; summary descriptions of the training data; documentation of foreseeable known harms; intended benefits of the system; evidence of the system's evaluation prior to deployment; data governance procedures; harm mitigation steps; instructions to limit harmful uses of the system; and more.[118]

In addition to the required documentation that the developer must provide to the deployer of the High-Risk Artificial Intelligence System, the developer

---

[116] COLO. REV. STAT. § 6–1–1702.

[117] *Id.*

[118] *Id.* at 6–1–1702(2).

also must provide the public with a disclosure document that identifies "the types of High-Risk Artificial Intelligence System that the Developer has Developed or . . . modified . . ." and "how the Developer manages known or reasonably foreseeable risks of algorithmic discrimination that may arise" from those systems.[119]

The list of consequential decisions is an expanded version of the federal civil rights laws.[120] The use of AI systems or other tools, tests, or procedures can violate these laws if used to intentionally violate anti-discrimination laws. They "also violate the federal anti-discrimination laws if they disproportionately exclude people in a particular group by race, sex, or another covered basis, unless the employer can justify the test or procedure under the law."[121] The U.S. Equal Employment Opportunity Commission (EEOC) has added technical guidance specifically to address the growing concerns raised by algorithmic bias and AI system.[122]

---

119 *Id.*

120 *See, e.g.*, 42 U.S.C §§ 2000e(c), 12111(7); 29 U.S.C § 630(c).

121 EQUAL EMPLOY. OPP. COMM'N, EMPLOYMENT TESTS AND SELECTION PROCEDURES, EEOC–NVTA–2007–2 (Dec. 1, 2007), https://www.eeoc.gov/laws/guidance/employment-tests-and-selection-procedures.

122 EQUAL EMPLOY. OPP. COMM'N, SELECT ISSUES: ASSESSING ADVERSE IMPACT IN SOFTWARE, ALGORITHMS, AND ARTIFICIAL INTELLIGENCE USED IN EMPLOYMENT SELECTION PROCEDURES UNDER TITLE VII OF THE CIVIL RIGHTS ACT OF 1964, EEOC–NVTA–2023–2 (May 18, 2023), available at https://www.eeoc.gov/select-issues-assessing-adverse-impact-software-algorithms-and-artificial-intelligence-used.

The new EEOC guidance highlights how AI can be integrated into the hiring process:

> resume scanners that prioritize applications using certain keywords; employee monitoring software that rates employees on the basis of their keystrokes or other factors; "virtual assistants" or "chatbots" that ask job candidates about their qualifications and reject those who do not meet pre-defined requirements; video interviewing software that evaluates candidates based on their facial expressions and speech patterns; and testing software that provides "job fit" scores for applicants or employees regarding their personalities, aptitudes, cognitive skills, or perceived "cultural fit" based on their performance on a game or on a more traditional test.[123]

None of these tools are prohibited. Nonetheless, the employer—or deployer under the Colorado AI Act—must take steps to ensure that the system neither discriminates by design nor creates a negative, disparate impact on individuals protected by the various laws. The Colorado law supplements the EEOC guidance by creating statutory liability for both the developer and deployer.

The use of personalization can lead to redlining and other forms of discriminatory practices. In 2019, Facebook settled claims that the company allowed "advertisers to unlawfully discriminate against minorities, women, and the elderly by using the

---

[123] *Id.*

platform's ad-targeting technology to exclude them from seeing ads for housing, jobs, and credit—three areas with legal protections for groups that historically have been disenfranchised."[124] The FTC and Justice Department continued to pursue the allegations; however, in 2022, Facebook (now Meta) entered into a consent settlement.[125] Companies relying on Meta's audience matching and other internal tools will no longer have those tools available when it comes to the advertising of housing, employment, or credit opportunities to discriminate against protected classes based on "Race, color, religion, sex, disability, familial status, and national origin within the meaning of the [Federal Housing Act]."[126]

Another area plagued by inequities is algorithmic decision-making in housing. "[L]enders using algorithms to generate decisions on loan pricing have discriminated against borrowers of color, resulting in a collective overcharge of $765 million each year for home and refinance loans."[127] As a result of the predictive tools, "lenders rejected a total of 1.3

---

[124] Emily Dreyfuss, *Facebook Changes Its Ad Tech to Stop Discrimination*, WIRED (Mar. 19, 2019), https://www.wired.com/story/facebook-advertising-discrimination-settlement/.

[125] U.S. v. Meta Platforms, Inc., No. 22 Civ. 5187 (S.D.N.Y. June 21, 2022).

[126] *Id.* at 3.

[127] Patrick Sisson, *Housing Discrimination Goes High Tech*, CURBED (Dec. 17, 2019), https://archive.curbed.com/2019/12/17/21026311/mortgage-apartment-housing-algorithm-discrimination (*citing* Robert Bartlett et al., *Consumer-Lending Discrimination in the FinTech Era*, UC BERKELEY PUB. L. & LEGAL RSCH., https://faculty.haas.berkeley.edu/morse/research/papers/discrim.pdf.

million creditworthy applicants of color between 2008 and 2015."[128]

In May 2024, the parties settled a class action lawsuit against SafeRent Solutions, LLC (previously CoreLogic Rental Property Solutions, LLC). The lawsuit had alleged that the company used algorithms that discriminated against Black and Hispanic rental applicants in violation of the Fair Housing Act and Massachusetts law.[129] The SafeRent and CoreLogic scoring algorithms are used nationally by hundreds of landlords and property owners. The $2.275 million dollar settlements included no admission of wrongdoing, but the allegations detail that SafeRent systematically undervalued the credit scores of Hispanic and Black applicants. Using the system, "Black consumers have a median credit score of 612 and Hispanic consumers have a median credit score of 661, as compared to white consumers' median credit score of 725, leading to unfair bias in accepting an applicant's lease application."[130]

The use of credit scores only loosely corelates with the quality of tenancy, so the reliance on such data is highly suspect. Credit scores don't include rental

---

[128] *Id.* (The analysis covered "roughly 7 million 30-year mortgages also found that both in-person and online" credit applications). *See generally* BORGESIUS, *supra* note 100.

[129] Louis v. SafeRent Solutions, LLC, Case 1:22–cv–10800 (D. Mass) (filed May 25, 2022), citing 42 U.S.C § 3604; Mass. Gen. Laws Ch. 151B, § 4 (6) and § 4(10).

[130] *Louis, et al. v. SafeRent Solutions, et al.*, COHENMILSTEIN, https://www.cohenmilstein.com/case-study/louis-et-al-v-saferent-solutions-et-al/ (last visited Feb. 16, 2025) (Data from a 2022 study conducted by the Urban Institute.).

payment history, one of the best predictors for future rental payments, so they prioritize home ownership over rental tenants. But the SafeRent system exacerbated this problem by excluding voucher payments from the applicant profile, significantly undervaluing the voucher recipient's ability to meet rental obligations. Taken together, these choices built directly into the algorithm had a significant impact on applicants using vouchers, which corelates directly with minority communities.[131]

Age discrimination has also resulted in EEOC action. the Shanghai China-based English language service "iTutorGroup programmed their tutor application software to automatically reject female applicants aged 55 or older and male applicants aged 60 or older. iTutorGroup rejected more than 200 qualified applicants based in the United States because of their age."[132] The consent agreement resulted in $365,000 in compensation for the rejected candidates and ongoing operational obligations to address the age discrimination.

The inequities created by the iTutor and SafeRent algorithms are illustrative of systems that use data

---

[131] *See* Gary Rhoades, *Ghosts in the Machine: How Past and Present Biases Haunt Algorithmic Tenant Screening Systems*, 49 HUMAN RIGHTS MAG. (June 2024), https://www.americanbar.org/groups/crsj/publications/human_rights_magazine_home/technology-and-the-law/.

[132] iTutorGroup to Pay $365,000 to Settle EEOC Discriminatory Hiring Suit, EQUAL EMPLOY. OPP. COMM'N (SEPT. 11, 2023), https://www.eeoc.gov/newsroom/itutorgroup-pay-365000-settle-eeoc-discriminatory-hiring-suit. *See* EEOC v. iTutorGroup, Inc. et al., Civil Action No. 1:22–cv–02565 (Aug. 9, 2023).

derived for one purpose as a surrogate for an unrelated purpose as well as the failure of developers and deployers to each take responsibility to confirm that the use of a system is neither intentionally biased nor has a material adverse effect of classes of individuals. Like the earlier example of Rite Aid, the settlement illustrates that algorithmic misuse is not a theoretical concern and instead needs to be part of every lawyer's basic due diligence.

§ 2.2.3 USE FOR SOCIAL HARMS, BULLYING, HARASSMENT, AND MARKET MANIPULATION

The social issues involving bullying and harassment are primarily concerned with the misuse of generative AI for purposes of creating content intended to target individuals and groups. Generative AI can be used to create very realistic voices, images, and videos of people who are entirely fictional as well as real individuals depicted in entirely fanciful situations. There are many practical uses. For example, synthetic media can be used to create highly realistic characters for online games, they can be used by publishers and marketing companies to create videos on behalf of clients at far less time and expense than having a real person working in a production studio, they can be used to workshop creative projects, and they have become ubiquitous in Hollywood movie magic.

Unfortunately, synthetic media, otherwise known as deepfakes, can also be used to generate nonconsensual pornography (or revenge porn) and child pornography, to misattribute statements or conduct to victims of the falsified content, to defraud individuals, and to harass and bully individuals targeted using the fictional information.

In late 2017 and 2018, the deepfake tool FakeApp was released to enable users to swap the facial images of one person on a video of someone else.[133] FakeApp substituted the facial texture or visual features of a person's face onto that of another video, creating a tool to map famous actors' images onto pornographic videos.[134] Similar faked videos were also used to create simulated revenge porn to embarrass, harass, and extort women.[135] In "2019, 96 percent of deepfakes on the internet were pornography, according to an analysis by AI firm DeepTrace Technologies, and virtually all pornographic deepfakes depicted women."[136]

Synthetic media technology has now gone mainstream. In March 2022, musical artist Kendrick Lamar used deepfake technology to morph his image into that of "O.J. Simpson, Kanye West, Jussie

---

[133] *See* Edvinas Keskys et al., *Regulating Deep Fakes: Legal and Ethical Considerations*, 15 J. IP LAW & PRAC. 24 (2019), https://papers.ssrn.com/sol3/Delivery.cfm/SSRN_ID3711007_code843584.pdf?abstractid=3497144&mirid=1.

[134] *Id.*

[135] *See* Tatum Hunter, *AI Porn Is Easy to Make Now. For Women, That's a Nightmare*, WASHINGTON POST (Feb. 13, 2023), https://www.washingtonpost.com/technology/2023/02/13/ai-porn-deepfakes-women-consent/ ("[A] person made esports star "QTCinderella's likeness in computer-generated porn. 'For every person saying it's not a big deal, you don't know how it feels to see a picture of yourself doing things you've never done being sent to your family,' QTCinderella said in a live-streamed video." ").

[136] *Id.*

Smollett, Will Smith, Kobe Bryant, and Nipsey Hussle."[137] In March 2023, a photograph of "Pope Francis wearing a big white Balenciaga-style puffer jacket" became an internet staple.[138]

While deepfakes demonstrate the early potential for manipulating video imagery, the misuse of pornographic videos and the potential to create photorealistic, defamatory content,[139] or disinformation for state-sponsored espionage[140] highlights the need for management and moderation

---

[137] Elijah C. Watson, *Ranking Kendrick Lamar's "The Heart Part 5" Deepfakes From Least To Most Bizarre*, OKAYPLAYER, https://www.okayplayer.com/music/kendrick-lamar-deep-fake-the-heart-part-5.html (last visited Feb. 16, 2025).

[138] Sara Morrison, *How unbelievably realistic fake images could take over the internet*, VOX (Mar. 30, 2023), https://www.vox.com/technology/2023/3/30/23662292/ai-image-dalle-openai-midjourney-pope-jacket.

[139] *See* Michael Atleson, *Chatbots, Deepfakes, and Voice Clones: AI Deception for Sale*, FTC BLOG (Mar. 20, 2023), https://www.ftc.gov/business-guidance/blog/2023/03/chatbots-deepfakes-voice-clones-ai-deception-sale; Regina Rini & Leah Cohen, *Deepfakes, Deep Harms*, 22 J. ETHICS & SOC. PHIL. 143, 148 (2022); Cass R. Sunstein, *Falsehoods and the First Amendment*, 33 HARV. J.L. & TECH. 387, 405 (2020).

[140] *See* Jon M. Garon, *When AI Goes to War: Corporate Accountability for Virtual Mass Disinformation, Algorithmic Atrocities, and Synthetic Propaganda*, 49 N. KY. L. REV. 181, 192 (2022) ("The expansion and reliance on artificial intelligence technologies are among the greatest advances in the twenty-first century and greatest threats for misuse."); Rachel E. VanLandingham, *Jailing the Twitter Bird: Social Media, Material Support to Terrorism, and Muzzling the Modern Press*, 39 CARDOZO L. REV. 1, 13 (2017) ("The link between social media platforms and terrorism competes with privacy concerns as one of the most discussed and most concerning, dynamics emanating from modern society's explosive utilization of these communication technologies.").

in the deployment of these tools. Unsurprisingly, synthetic media has also been used for military disinformation.[141] In the Russian war against Ukraine, a video depicting Ukrainian President Volodymyr Zelenskyy ordering Ukrainian troops to lay down their arms and surrender appeared on social media and was broadcast briefly on Ukrainian news.[142]

Some synthetic content has already found commercial homes, such as the replacement of South Korean news anchor Kim Joo-Ha with a synthetic look-alike on South Korean television channel MBN.[143] Another notable synthetic persona is the influencer Lil Miquela, a hyper-realistic avatar presenting as a nineteen-year-old, who serves as a corporate sponsor for numerous brands. Miquela was

---

141 *See* Bobby Allyn, *Deepfake video of Zelenskyy could be 'tip of the iceberg' in info war, experts warn*, NPR (Mar. 16, 2022), https://www.npr.org/2022/03/16/1087062648/deepfake-video-zelenskyy-experts-war-manipulation-ukraine-russia.

142 *Id.*

143 *See* Yoon So-Yeon, *MBN Introduces Korea's First AI News Anchor*, KOREA JOONANG DAILY (Nov. 10, 2020), https://koreajoongangdaily.joins.com/2020/11/10/entertainment/television/MBN-AI-artificial-intelligence/20201110153900457.html ("MBN revealed that an AI anchor based on announcer Kim Ju-ha started reporting news on Nov. 6, on the channel's "MBN News." AI Kim was almost identical to the real Kim, both in her looks and the sound of her voice. . . ."); Bernd Debusmann Jr, *Deepfake is the Future of Content Creation*, BBC NEWS (Mar. 8, 2021), https://www.bbc.com/news/business-56278411 ("Viewers had been informed beforehand that this was going to happen, and South Korean media reported a mixed response after people had seen it. While some people were amazed at how realistic it was, others said they were worried that the real Kim Joo-Ha might lose her job.").

created and operated by the AI media agency Brud.[144] She has over 3 million Instagram followers and has participated in brand campaigns since 2016.[145] For 2022, she was estimated to earn more than $1 million for her sponsored posts.[146]

"Over a few short years, technology like AI and deepfaking has advanced to the point where it's becoming really quite difficult to see the flaws in these creations."[147] Nor does it necessarily require artificial intelligence technologies to create false narratives from realistic looking photographs and videos. "Sharing deceptive photos or misinformation online doesn't actually require a lot of talent. Often, just cropping a photo or video can create confusion on social media."[148] As the FTC noted, "[t]hanks to AI tools that create 'synthetic media' or otherwise generate content, a growing percentage of what we're looking at is not authentic, and it's getting more difficult to tell the difference. And just as these AI

---

[144] Meredith Clark, *PacSun sparks backlash after announcing virtual influencer Lil Miquela as its newest ambassador*, INDEPENDENT (Aug. 17, 2022), https://www.independent.co.uk/life-style/fashion/lil-miquela-pacsun-instagram-robot-b2146980.html.

[145] *Id.*

[146] *Id.*

[147] Joseph Foley & Abi Le Guilcher, *20 of the Best Deepfake Examples that Terrified and Amused the Internet*, CREATIVE BLOQ (Mar. 10, 2023), https://www.creativebloq.com/features/deepfake-examples.

[148] *Why the Way an Image is Cropped can Change Everything*, FRANCE 24, THE OBSERVERS (Aug. 24, 2018), https://observers.france24.com/en/20180824-verification-guide-cropped-photo-video.

tools are becoming more advanced, they're also becoming easier to access and use."[149]

The release of OpenAI's Dall-E 2, Stability AI's Stable Diffusion, and Midjourney Lab's Midjourney image generator dramatically expanded the universe for synthetic imagery generated entirely by text prompts rather than by feeding the computer system preexisting pictures and videos.[150] In the earlier AI training models, the deepfakes were created primarily by Generative adversarial networks (GANs), a form of unsupervised machine learning in which a generator input competes with "an adversary, the discriminator network" to distinguish between real and artificial images.[151] The Diffusion model of training involves the use of adding noise to the images to train the system to identify visual elements from the competing data.[152] The diffusion models are similar to that of deep learning models used for OpenAI's ChatGPT, Google's Gemini, and other text-based AI platforms. The diffusion model

---

[149] Michael Atleson, *Chatbots, Deepfakes, and Voice Clones: AI Deception For Sale*, FTC BLOG (Mar. 20, 2023), https://www.ftc.gov/business-guidance/blog/2023/03/chatbots-deepfakes-voice-clones-ai-deception-sale.

[150] *See* Vivek Muppalla & Sean Hendryx, *Diffusion Models: A Practical Guide*, SCALE (Oct. 19, 2022), https://scale.com/guides/diffusion-models-guide (Dall-E 2 was revealed in April 2022. Imagen, from Google, was released in May 2022 and became available with Imagen3 in August 2024. Stable Diffusion was made publicly available in August 2022).

[151] Jason Brownlee, *A Gentle Introduction to Generative Adversarial Networks (GANs)*, MACHINE LEARNING MASTERY (June 17, 2019), https://machinelearningmastery.com/what-are-generative-adversarial-networks-gans/.

[152] Muppalla & Hendryx, *supra* note 150.

and similar systems enable the AI to build original images or video from text-based prompts rather than requiring the user to input a source image.[153] One could even daisy-chain systems so that the text prompts were themselves AI generated in the first instance.

For photorealistic pictures and videos, the concept of fact is not self-evident. Still photography and audiovisual films create the impression that they capture what is in front of the lens, but this is rarely the whole truth.[154] "In some cases cropping can radically transform the meaning of a shot."[155] Without any retouching, photographers could always manipulate the message being conveyed using framing choices when taking a picture or cropping choices when developing the photograph. A photograph or video clip asserts that the images are exactly as they appear.[156] This effect serves as an

---

153 *See* Will Douglas Heaven, T*he Original Startup Behind Stable Diffusion has Launched a Generative AI for Video*, MIT TECH. REV. (Feb. 6, 2023), https://www.technologyreview.com/2023/02/06/1067897/runway-stable-diffusion-gen-1-generative-ai-for-video/.

154 *See* Virginia Seymour, *Exploring Images In (and Out of) Context*, JSTOR Daily (Nov. 9, 2022), https://daily.jstor.org/exploring-images-in-and-out-of-context/ ("Conversations around manipulation of information in images focuses largely on content manipulation—where images, often photographs, are purposefully edited—but missing or misleading context, even when it is unintentional, can just as easily skew the interpretation of images.").

155 John Suler, *Cropping and the Frame* in PHOTOGRAPHIC PSYCHOLOGY: IMAGE AND PSYCHE (2023), https://www.johnsuler.com/pdfs/photopsy.pdf.

156 Lisa Fazio, *Out-of-context photos are a powerful low-tech form of misinformation*, THE CONVERSATION (Feb. 14, 2020),

assertion of accuracy, making naturalistic photographs appear self-validating as to the truthfulness of the image depicted.

> First, you're used to photographs being used for photojournalism and serving as proof that an event happened. Second, seeing a photograph can help you more quickly retrieve related information from memory. People tend to use this ease of retrieval as a signal that information is true. Photographs also make it more easy to imagine an event happening, which can make it feel more true. Finally, pictures simply capture your attention. A 2015 study by Adobe found that posts that included images received more than three times the Facebook interactions than posts with just text.[157]

Even though courts and visually literate observers know that photography is not self-validating, it is often very hard to discern truth from deception. "For artistic purposes, . . . alterations of the image may be perfectly acceptable. In the case of photojournalism or other images that should be presenting a factual reality, the crop could be an objectionable act of deception."[158] As a consequence, falsified photographs and videos are more likely to be

---

https://theconversation.com/out-of-context-photos-are-a-powerful-low-tech-form-of-misinformation-129959 ("[I]mages are a powerful tool for swaying popular opinion and promoting false beliefs. Psychological research has shown that people are more likely to believe true and false trivia statements, such as "turtles are deaf," when they're presented alongside an image.").

[157] *Id.*

[158] Suler, *supra* note 155.

assumed to be accurate than textual information and carry more likely to be taken at face value than other forms of falsehoods.

Nonconsensual pornography,[159] including "revenge porn,"[160] provides a paradigmatic example of the problem.[161] Existing laws cover instances of revenge porn, in which sexual images or videos are posted of an individual without that person's consent.[162] The crime (and tort) of revenge porn is now prohibited by specific statute in 49 states plus

---

159 *See* Chance Carter, *An Update on the Legal Landscape of Revenge Porn*, NAT. ASS'N OF ATTORNEYS GENERAL (Nov. 16, 2021), https://www.naag.org/attorney-general-journal/an-update-on-the-legal-landscape-of-revenge-porn/.

160 *Id.* ("Eighty percent of nonconsensual porn is revenge porn, meaning it was originally sent between two consenting individuals in the context of an intimate relationship. Often, this content is posted alongside the victim's name and other identifying information such as their phone numbers, emails, or social media links.").

161 *See* Danielle Keats Citron, *Sexual Privacy*, 128 YALE L. J. 1870 (2019) ("Sexual privacy sits at the apex of privacy values because of its importance to sexual agency, intimacy, and equality.").

162 *See, e.g.*, People v. Bollaert, 203 Cal. Rptr. 3d 814, 819 (Cal. App. 4th Dist. 2016)("A jury convicted Kevin Christopher Bollaert of extortion . . . and the unlawful use of personal identifying information . . . stemming from his operation of Web sites, "UGotPosted.com," . . . and "ChangeMyReputation.com," through which victims could pay to have the information removed."); Rebecca Grant, *Accused revenge porn site owner arrested and charged with 31 felony counts*, VENTURE BEAT (Dec. 11, 2013), https://venturebeat.com/business/accused-revenge-porn-site-owner-arrested-and-charged-with-31-felony-counts/ ("The state's attorneys office accused Bollaert of receiving and reviewing 2,000 emails from individuals, requesting their information and images be removed from the site [ugotposted.com], between June 20, 2103 and August 26, 2013.").

the District of Columbia.[163] Revenge porn is commonly defined as unauthorized publication of consensually created content, which distinguishes it from the broader category of nonconsensual pornography.[164] The text of these laws varies considerably from one state to the next, but these statutes may not include AI-generated content. Indiana, for example, requires the image be "taken, captured, or recorded," making it unlikely that an image rendered by a computer to simulate the offending image would fall within the statute.[165] A smaller category of nonconsensual pornography refers only to content that was surreptitiously captured by the perpetrator.[166]

Revenge porn falls into the tort category of invasion of privacy[167] while AI-generated look-alike

---

[163] *See Healey Signs Revenge Porn Bill, Making Massachusetts the 49th State to Enact Legislation*, NEW ENGLAND PUBLIC MEDIA (June 21, 2024), https://www.nepm.org/regional-news/2024-06-21/healey-signs-revenge-porn-bill-making-massachusetts-the-49th-state-to-enact-legislation.; *State Revenge Porn Laws*, FINDLAW (Dec. 8, 2022), https://www.findlaw.com/criminal/criminal-charges/revenge-porn-laws-by-state.html ("All states, excluding . . . South Carolina, have separate statutes that are specifically related to revenge porn. It's important to note, however, that a person may still be prosecuted for revenge porn under other statutes in [South Carolina].").

[164] *See* Carter, *supra* note 159.

[165] *See* IN Code § 35–45–4–8 (2019).

[166] *See id. See also* People v. Bollaert, 203 Cal. Rptr. 3d at 825 ("substantial evidence demonstrates Bollaert obtained and retained the information for an unlawful purpose, namely, to invade the victims' privacy.").

[167] Vermont, State v. VanBuren, 210 Vt. 293 (2018) (upholding Vermont's criminal statute as meeting the strict scrutiny standard due to the compelling privacy interests).

revenge porn should be categorized as libelous.[168] Unlike the unauthorized distribution of a sex tape that is accurate but highly invasive of one's privacy, a deepfake is a false depiction that factually asserts the participant engaged in videotaped or photograph sexual activity—perhaps for distribution on the internet. That will likely constitute a libelous statement for the vast majority of victims.[169] In addition, however, a false statement that the subject of the sex tape approved the making of the tape or approved the distribution of the tape may be a separate instance of libelous falsity.

The production of synthetic, lifelike nonconsensual pornography continues to get easier. The website Mage, which launched in September 2022, harnesses the tools of Stable Diffusion to generate pornographic images based upon text prompts.[170] Mage is just one

---

In the constellation of privacy interests, it is difficult to imagine something more private than images depicting an individual engaging in sexual conduct, or of a person's genitals, anus, or pubic area, that the person has not consented to sharing publicly. The personal consequences of such profound personal violation and humiliation generally include, at a minimum, extreme emotional distress.

[168] *See generally*, Eugene Volokh, *One-to-One Speech vs. One-to-Many Speech, Criminal Harassment Laws, and "Cyber stalking,"* 107 NW. U. L. REV. 731, 752–53 (2013).

[169] *See* Citron, *supra* note 161, at 1937 ("Public officials and public figures like Gal Gadot could sue for defamation if there is clear and convincing evidence of actual malice (that is, the defendant knew the deep-fake sex videos were false or recklessly disregarded the possibility that they were false)."). *See also* Bobby Chesney and Danielle Citron, *Deep Fakes*, 107 CAL. L. REV. 1753 (2019).

[170] *See* Jim Clyde Monge, *This Website Can Generate NSFW Images With Stable Diffusion AI*, MEDIUM (Sept. 25, 2022), https://

of many such services.[171] There is an entire community operating under the name "Unstable Diffusion" "that explores and experiments with [not suitable for work] AI-generated content using Stable Diffusion."[172] The group explains that "[w]e believe erotic art needs a place to flourish and be cultivated in a space without judgment or censorship."[173]

Since 2023, there have been multiple instances of nude pictures circulating in middle schools and high schools targeting female students.[174] "[T]he images—created with artificial-intelligence apps that merge a classmate's face with a naked body—are rippling through schools of all kinds."[175] The harms from this form of bullying are not easily dismissed even when the depictions are known to be false. Statements from the student victims are compelling:

---

medium.com/mlearning-ai/this-website-can-generate-nsfw-images-with-stable-diffusion-ai-1ee2913de829.

171 *See* Matt Burgess, *The fightback against AI-generated fake pornography has begun*, WIRED (Aug. 2, 2018), https://www.wired.co.uk/article/deepfakes-banned-reddit-ai-creates-fake-porn-gyfcat ("Reddit's move to prohibit "involuntary porn" follows moves by other sites and services to ban the sharing and hosting of such material. . . . Before Reddit deleted the community more than 90,000 people had subscribed to it.").

172 *Id.*

173 *Id.*

174 *See* Julie Jargon, *AI Fake Nudes Are Now a Frightening Reality for Teens,* WALL ST. J. (June 1, 2024), https://www.wsj.com/tech/personal-tech/ai-fake-nude-photos-schools-victim-impact-88a4b1e4.

175 *Id.*

> *"Even if it was debunked as a fake image, the subject would still get bullied and made fun of," a student in Eldorado, Ill., said.*
>
> *"Their morals would be questioned," a student in Seale, Ala., said.*
>
> *"People will see them differently," a student in Levittown, N.Y., said.*[176]

As these incidents have increased, schools are taking action, including expulsion of some of the students who created these videos, and in the case of a Miami middle school, the two children involved—ages 13 and 14—were arrested and charged with felonies.[177] It must also be noted that the difference in response among urban, suburban, and private schools also highlights fundamental inequities at the heart of the school-to-prison pipeline, a topic beyond the subject of this Nutshell, but an important contributing factor to the digital divide.[178]

The example of pornography is just one instance of potential visual libel. There are many more. The inherent believability of videos, audio, and imagery make these tools very useful to conduct fraud or otherwise trick people into believing the veracity of

---

176 *Id.*

177 Caroline Haskins, *Florida Middle Schoolers Arrested for Allegedly Creating Deepfake Nudes of Classmates*, WIRED (Mar. 8, 2024), https://www.wired.com/story/florida-teens-arrested-deepfake-nudes-classmates/.

178 *See* Vernellia Randall, School-to-Prison Pipeline and Legal Scholarship (Searchable Database), Race, Racism, and the Law (Feb. 14, 2024) (a This database including more than 400 "law review articles on the school-to-prison pipeline.").

the content long enough to extort money, complete a transaction, or even fall in love.

The use of false videos to depict individuals making false statements, engaging in anti-social activities involving sex acts, violence, or crime, promoting beliefs contrary to those held by the person, and other strategies can harm an individual even if the depiction is later proven false. The images stick with the public and the shadow of doubt remains. As with other forms of AI, lawyers and regulators must understand these risks and engage in appropriate techniques to protect the public in a manner consistent with constitutional principles.

§ 2.2.4 PSYCHOGRAPHIC TARGETING

At the intersection of predictive and generative AI, lies the potential for highly segmented and accurate market segmentation, which can be a powerful tool of public manipulation. "Psychographic segmentation is a market research method used to divide a market or customer group into segments based on their beliefs, values, lifestyle, social status, activities, interests and opinions and other psychological criteria."[179] For marketing this is used to increased sales and customer loyalty. "By understanding needs, wants, concerns, motivations and aspirations, businesses

---

[179] Will Webster, *What is Psychographic Segmentation? A Beginner's Guide*, QUALTRICS, https://www.qualtrics.com/experience-management/brand/psychographic-segmentation/ (last visited Feb. 16, 2025).

can tailor what they offer to better align with what their target audience cares about."[180]

Psychographic targeting uses psychological variables and personality traits to predict and shape consumer behavior[181] (as well as electoral voting support).[182] To develop the psychographic determinants for individuals, researchers and marketers often use self-identification surveys, but these prove unreliable.[183] "Psychographic examples include grouping customers based on social status, interests, and opinions."[184] These may also include such variables as "personality, lifestyle, social status, activities, interests and opinions, [and] attitudes."[185]

Instead, researchers and marketers leverage the power of generative AI to use natural language markers from the conversations among individuals

---

180 *Id.*

181 Hui Liu et al., *Personality or Value: A Comparative Study of Psychographic Segmentation Based on an Online Review Enhanced Recommender System*, 9 APPLIED SCI. 2 (2019).

182 *See What Is Psychographics? Understanding The Tech That Threatens Elections*, CB INSIGHTS (May 6, 2020), https://www.cbinsights.com/research/what-is-psychographics/.

183 Philip S. Brenner & John DeLamater, *Lies, Damned Lies, and Survey Self-Reports? Identity as a Cause of Measurement Bias*, 79 SOC. PSYCH. Q. 333 (2016).

184 *What Is Psychographic Segmentation? Examples and Best Practices*, INTUIT MAILCHIMP, https://mailchimp.com/resources/psychographic-segmentation-examples/ (last visited Feb. 16, 2025).

185 *Id.*

and increasingly with the chatbots and generative AI services.[186]

Using AI, all messaging can be adjusted to the emotional and cognitive triggers most likely to influence the user. Social media campaigns use psychographics to target the public based on each audience member's emotional profile.[187] The visual image of each avatar can be customized to enhance its affinity for the target. The key words and emotionally impactful phrases can be tailored to fit the target's profile. And the backstory of the avatar can be adjusted to make the AI more influential over each target.[188]

Psychographic research "demonstrates the utility of relying on natural language markers of abstract psychological phenomena, including values and personality, and present significant opportunities to better predict and understand their connection to consumers' behaviors and thoughts in a broader

---

186 *See* Liu, *supra* note 181, at 6 ("Research indicates cases in which natural language data have provided a clearer picture of people's cognitive and behavioral processes than data collected from a traditional and widely used self-report survey.").

187 *What Is Psychographics? Understanding The Tech That Threatens Elections*, *supra* note 182 ("Psychographics is the study of consumers based on their activities, interests, and opinions (AIOs). . . . Psychographics seeks to understand the cognitive factors that drive consumer behaviors. This includes emotional responses and motivations; moral, ethical, and political values; and inherent attitudes, biases, and prejudices.").

188 *Id.* ("With its emphasis on the individual's personality traits, psychographic marketing reinforces the connection between product and personalization. People see themselves as themselves first—before they see themselves as members of an impersonal demographic group.").

sense."[189] In this brave new world of psychographic targeting, trademarks will become more prominent than ever, but will likely represent a very different brand strategy than those of the twentieth century.

Psychographic targeting now extends beyond sales of goods and services to influence the electorate on candidates and public policy. "[P]sychographic and neuromarketing tools are combined with data and tracking methods to determine the emotional impact of advertising campaigns, and how to tailor persuasive *political* messages to *profiled* audiences' psychological needs."[190] Using data brokers and massive data sets, the information about an individual can be combined and targeted automatically with very low transaction costs. "[D]igital marketing tools . . . include psychographic and neuromarketing tools combined with data and tracking methods (such as emotion-based profiling) to optimise the emotional impact of advertising messages to specific audiences' psychological needs."[191]

---

189 Liu, *supra* note 181, at 6.

190 Vian Bakir, *Psychological Operations in Digital Political Campaigns: Assessing Cambridge Analytica's Psychographic Profiling and Targeting*, 5 FRONTIERS IN COMM. (Sept. 3, 2020) (citations omitted), https://www.frontiersin.org/articles/10.3389/fcomm.2020.00067/full.

191 *Id.*

> Alcohol consumption is a particularly suitable area in which to explore harmful use of cognitive biases for two reasons. First, alcohol is a product that disproportionately harms the most vulnerable, and the alcohol industry is financially reliant on harmful use of its products. Second, there is growing evidence that alcohol industry corporate

These techniques can now distribute targeted media through social media accounts, chatbots, and other tools using highly tailored content generated by large language models. The effectiveness of ChatGPT-enabled targeting campaigns has been established in empirical studies.[192] "[F]indings highlight the potential risks of utilizing AI and microtargeting to craft political messages that resonate with individuals based on their personality traits. By integrating psychological profiling, data mapping, and individualized microtargeting, these services create what is essentially a "manipulation machine."[193] "Recent technological advancements, involving generative AI and personality inference from consumed text, can potentially create a highly scalable "manipulation machine" that targets individuals based on their unique vulnerabilities without requiring human input."[194]

The manipulation machine is just one of the risks to electoral integrity, but the concerns go well beyond just elections to all aspects of social policy, religious beliefs, consumer behavior, and public values. Over time, these techniques will transform all culture

---

social responsibility organizations act to misrepresent the evidence on alcohol harms. It has recently been shown that such bodies misrepresent the scientific evidence on alcohol harms in pregnancy.

[192] Almog Simchon, Matthew Edwards, & Stephan Lewandowsky, *The persuasive Effects of Political Microtargeting in the age of Generative Artificial Intelligence*, 3 PNAS NEXUS 35 (Feb. 2024), https://academic.oup.com/pnasnexus/article/3/2/pgae035/7591134.

[193] *See id.*

[194] *Id.*

wars into content wars, with the victors the parties who can afford the largest campaigns.

§ 2.2.5 MISINFORMATION, DISINFORMATION, AND THE IMPACT ON ELECTIONS, CRIME, AND SOVEREIGNTY

According to the World Economic Forum, the threat of AI-generated misinformation and disinformation has risen to become the second largest threat to global stability for the 2024–26 period and one of the top ten threats for the next decade.[195] Globally, the leading concern has become the ability of AI services to manipulate and disrupt elections.

"Beyond elections, perceptions of reality are likely to also become more polarized, infiltrating the public discourse on issues ranging from public health to social justice. However, as truth is undermined, the risk of domestic propaganda and censorship will also rise in turn."[196] The value of falsity is directly tied to the power it provides the purveyor. It may simply be used to undermine trust in a competitor or rival, it may be used to bully and disenfranchise, or it may be used to steal, extort, or defraud.

"Misinformation and disinformation are introduced online by many different sources: vested interests, politicians, news media, gossip, and works

---

195 *See* ELLISSA CAVACIUTI-WISHART ET AL., THE GLOBAL RISKS REPORT 2024, WORLD ECONOMIC FORUM (Jan. 2024), https://www.weforum.org/publications/global-risks-report-2024/.

196 *Id.* at 8.

of fiction."[197] Disinformation is distinct from mere misinformation because "disinformation incorporates the notion of intentionality."[198] "Disinformation is a coordinated or deliberate effort to knowingly circulate misinformation in order to gain money, power, or reputation."[199]

At the global level, disinformation has always been part of geopolitical conflict, as nations seek to gain an advantage over their competitors. To harm the standing of the U.S., the Soviet Union ran a disinformation campaign in the 1980s that began with a false newspaper story in India explaining how the U.S. manufactured HIV to target African American men and gay citizens.[200] The Soviets paid

---

197 Briony Swire-Thompson and David Lazer, *Public Health and Online Misinformation: Challenges and Recommendations*, 41 ANNUAL REVIEW OF PUBLIC HEALTH 433, 437 (April 2020).

198 *Id.*

199 *Id. See also* USING SOCIAL MEDIA IN COMMUNITY BASED PROTECTION: A GUIDE, UNHCR 230 (Jan. 2021), https://www.unhcr.org/innovation/wp-content/uploads/2021/01/Using-Social-Media-in-CBP.pdf. Misinformation is false or inaccurate information. Examples include rumors, insults and pranks. Disinformation is deliberate and includes malicious content such as hoaxes, spear phishing and propaganda. It spreads fear and suspicion among the population.")

200 Margaret Bourdeaux, et. al, *Weaponizing Digital Health Intelligence, Belfer Center for Science and International Affairs*, HARVARD KENNEDY SCHOOL (Jan. 2020), https://www.belfercenter.org/publication/weaponizing-digital-health-intelligence (citing Adam B. Ellick & Adam Westbrook, *Operation Infektion: A Three-Part Video Series on Russian Disinformation*, NY TIMES (Nov. 12, 2018), https://www.nytimes.com/2018/11/12/opinion/russia-meddling-disinformation-fake-news-elections.html;

Laura M Bogart & Sheryl Thorburn, *Are HIV/AIDS Conspiracy Beliefs a Barrier to HIV Prevention among African Americans?*, J.

an East German scientist to corroborate the story and repeated the lies across Asian, African, and Eastern European press until it actually was featured as a U.S. news story. The deception was uncovered, and Prime Minister Mikhail Gorbachev actually apologized to President Ronald Reagan over the incident.[201] Despite the apology, the truth never recovered. "As recently as 2005, a survey of 500 randomly selected African Americans found that 48% believed HIV was a manmade virus and 16% thought the government created AIDS to control the black population."[202]

Synthetic media puts the power of deception into the hands of anyone who elects to use it.

Deceptive information is often promulgated by online bots. For example, "[o]ne early study of Twitter [now X] concluded that approximately 53% of initial users were human; the rest were classified as cyborgs or bots, which are automated accounts on social media platforms created to imitate human activity."[203]

ACQUIRED IMMUNE DEFICIENCY SYNDROME 213 (2005), https://pubmed.ncbi.nlm.nih.gov/15671808/.

[201] *Id.*

[202] *Id.*

[203] Angel N Desai, Diandra Ruidera, Julie M Steinbrink3 Bruno Granwehr, and Dong Heun Lee, *Misinformation and Disinformation: The Potential Disadvantages of Social Media in Infectious Disease and How to Combat Them*, 74 CLINICAL INFECTIOUS DISEASES e34 (May 15, 2022) citing Chu Z, Gianvecchio S, Wang H, Jajodia S., *Detecting automation of twitter accounts: are you a human, bot, or cyborg?*, IEEE TRANS DEPENDABLE SECURE COMPUT 2012;9: 811–824.

The FTC describes these negative manipulative techniques while others use the term "dark nudges" to reflect the subconscious influence they have in undermining individual choice and autonomy.[204] For example, "[d]ark nudges appear to be used in AI communications about "responsible drinking." The approaches include social norming (telling consumers that "most people" are drinking) and priming drinkers by offering verbal and pictorial cues to drink, while simultaneously appearing to warn about alcohol harms."[205]

Another term for these techniques includes "sludge," to reflect how design combines with content to promote a particular behavioral outcome. "Sludge, such as the use of particular fonts, colors, and design layouts, appears to use cognitive biases to make health-related information about the harms of alcohol difficult to access, and enhances exposure to misinformation.[206]

The FTC has taken steps to address market manipulation as a violation of Section 5(a) of the Federal Trade Commission Act, labeling such techniques an unfair and deceptive trade practice. It

---

[204] *Bringing Dark Patterns to Light*, FTC BUREAU OF CONSUMER PROTECTION 2 (Sept. 15, 2022), https://www.ftc.gov/news-events/news/press-releases/2022/09/ftc-report-shows-rise-sophisticated-dark-patterns-designed-trick-trap-consumers (using the term coined by design specialist Harry Brignull).

[205] Mark Petticrew, *et. al*, *Dark Nudges and Sludge in Big Alcohol: Behavioral Economics, Cognitive Biases, and Alcohol Industry Corporate Social Responsibility*, 98 MILBANK QUARTERLY 1290, 1291 (2020).

[206] *Id.*

has also published a report entitled "Bringing Dark Patterns to Light,[207] which details the methods used to defraud and deceive the public, including disguising paid ads as editorial content, burying terms and limitations, tricking consumers to share personal information, adding last-minute junk fees, and a variety of additional techniques.[208] A company, for example, might publish a story purporting to be an independent ranking agency to rank its own product first and discredit its competition.[209] "Some dark patterns manipulate consumer choice by inducing false beliefs. For example, a company may make an outright false claim or employ design elements that create a misleading impression to spur a consumer into making a purchase they would not otherwise make."[210]

Deepfakes are proliferating using these techniques to incorporate false celebrity endorsements to pump real products. "[T]he products might be real, but their endorsements are anything but. It's where videos appearing to show celebrities plugging items from dental plans to cookware are in fact just AI-generated fabrications that use technology to alter voices, appearances and actions."[211] These come on top of

---

[207] *Bringing Dark Patterns to Light*, *supra* note 204.

[208] *FTC Report Shows Rise in Sophisticated Dark Patterns Designed to Trick and Trap Consumer*, FTC PRESS RELEASE (Sept. 15, 2022), https://www.ftc.gov/news-events/news/press-releases/2022/09/ftc-report-shows-rise-sophisticated-dark-patterns-designed-trick-trap-consumers.

[209] *Id.* at 4 (internal citations omitted).

[210] *Id.*

[211] Joedy McCreary, *Real Products, Fake Endorsements: Why Experts say AI-Generated Ads will get Tougher to Spot*, USA TODAY

fake reviews and online bullying to remove negative reviews. For example, "[i]n 2022, Google removed millions of reviews from Google Play that it determined to be fake, inorganic, or otherwise malicious. In 2021, users submitted around one billion Google Maps reviews and Google blocked or removed more than 95 million of them for violating its policies."[212] Also in 2021, Amazon commented that it had removed more than 200 million suspected fake reviews."[213]

The situation has become so problematic that the FTC has promulgated proposed rules to address false product endorsements.[214]

> Proposed § 465.2(a) would prohibit a business from writing, creating, or selling a consumer review, consumer testimonial, or celebrity testimonial that: (a) is by someone who does not exist; (b) is by someone who did not use or otherwise have experience with the product, service, or business that is the subject of the review or testimonial; or (c) materially misrepresents the reviewer's or testimonialist's experience with the product, service, or business.[215]

(Feb. 14, 2024), https://www.usatoday.com/story/news/factcheck/2024/02/18/ai-deepfake-ads-tougher-detect/72536444007/.

[212] Trade Regulation Rule on the Use of Consumer Reviews and Testimonials, Notice of Proposed Rulemaking, 16 C.F.R. 465 (July 31, 2023), citing comments of Google.

[213] *Id.* citing comments of Amazon.

[214] *See id.*

[215] *Id.*

Additional amendments would prohibit a business from procuring a similarly deceptive ad from any third parties. The amendments would prohibit payment for procuring reviews (as distinct from testimonials), from repurposing reviews in a misleading manner, or otherwise using any reviews that were not actually created by real consumers for that particular product.[216] The proposal has yet to be adopted. Since the regulations emphasize conduct that is patently unfair or deceptive, the promulgation of regulations might have only minimal effect on the continued growth of the misinformation machine, but that will depend on the strength of the FTC's enforcement activity.

Part of what made social media so popular was the sense of trust it engendered, but the manipulation of content, the targeting of individuals, and the ease of deception has made that a thing of the past. Modern consumers must be digitally sophisticated, always on guard, and operate with a strong degree of skepticism. This, in turn, raises the cost to share and promote truthful information, adding to the cycle of harm.

§ 2.3 DISINTERMEDIATION AND SUCCESS: IMPLICATIONS ON CULTURE, CREATIVITY, AND EDUCATION

Although AI automation will require new knowledge and skills in all fields, jobs involving art, journalism, marketing, creative writing, illustration,

---

216 *See id.*

design, and education are likely to have a disproportionate impact because of generative AI.[217] "On one hand, art is imagined to exist in a realm of value that lies beyond and beneath mere economic considerations. . . . On the other hand, money is now an important measure—maybe the supreme measure—of artistic accomplishment."[218] This cultural inconsistency exacerbates the discussion around the regulation of generative AI. "In the popular imagination, artists tend to exist either at the pinnacle of fame and luxury or in the depths of penury and obscurity—rarely in the middle, where most of the rest of us toil and dream."[219]

Those at the top of the pinnacle are beyond economic disruption triggered by generative AI. Those at the bottom of the pyramid can fall no further and perhaps can even be helped by generative AI tools—so the arguments suggest.[220] "The proportion of working-class actors, musicians and writers has shrunk by half since the 1970s . . . . People whose parents had a working-class job accounted for about 37% of the workforce in 1981, but by 2011 that had fallen to about 21%," according to a report on UK

---

217 *See* A.O. Scott, *The Paradox of Art as Work*, N.Y. TIMES (May 9, 2014), https://www.nytimes.com/2014/05/11/movies/the-paradox-of-art-as-work.html.

218 *Id.* ("The old phrase 'starving artist' gestures toward an image that is both romantic and pathetic, of a person too pure, and also just too impractical, to make it in the world. When that person ceases to starve, he or she can always be labeled a sellout.")

219 *Id.*

220 *See, e.g.*, Farhad Manjoo, *A Creator (Me) Made a Masterpiece With A.I.*, N.Y. TIMES (Aug. 25, 2023), https://www.nytimes.com/2023/08/25/opinion/ai-art-intellectual-property.html.

employment.[221] As the art economy declines, people who need to make a living in their profession must drop out. In the U.S., a National Endowment for the Arts report provides that "in 2021, just under 4.9 million workers were employed to produce arts and cultural goods and services, which is less than the 2019 (pre-pandemic) level of 5.2 million but more than the 2020 level of 4.6 million workers."[222]

At least some of these jobs are at risk. "DreamWorks founder Jeffrey Katzenberg predicts that generative artificial intelligence will cut the cost of animated films by 90 percent, as the technology is set to deliver serious disruption to the media and entertainment sector."[223] Katzenberg remained confident that the creative spark for new works would still be inspired by the artists rather than the machines. " 'In my opinion, I think that is still going

---

221 James Tapper, *Huge Decline of Working Class People in the Arts Reflects Fall in Wider Society*, THE GUARDIAN (Dec. 10, 2022), https://www.theguardian.com/culture/2022/dec/10/huge-decline-working-class-people-arts-reflects-society.

222 *New Data Show Economic Activity of the U.S. Arts & Cultural Sector in 2021*, NAT'L ENDOWMENT ARTS (Mar. 15, 2023), https://www.arts.gov/news/press-releases/2023/new-data-show-economic-activity-us-arts-cultural-sector-2021.

223 Alex Weprin, *Jeffrey Katzenberg: AI Will Drastically Cut Number of Workers It Takes to Make Animated Movies*, THE HOLLYWOOD REP. (Nov. 9, 2023), https://www.hollywoodreporter.com/business/digital/jeffrey-katzenberg-ai-entertainment-animation-prediction-1235643311/ (" 'It took 500 artists five years to make a world-class animated movie,' Katzenberg said at a Bloomberg conference.' I don't think it will take 10 percent of that [with AI].' ").

to come from creativity, from individual creativity,' Katzenberg said."[224]

Left unanswered was the question of where the next generation of creative artists would get their training and development. There remains an elephant in the room when exploring the potential of robots and systems that can paint pictures, tell stories, make movies, create video games, compose music, and teach our children. AI-generated works might violate preexisting legal rights of third parties. And they might exacerbate preexisting cultural and normative faults that already exist in society.

The greater threat may be from success; an achievement for technology that reduces the need, opportunity, and conflict essential for art and culture to thrive.[225] The information economy has already upended the creative economy. In an ad-driven social media environment, Amazon circumvents publishers, TikTok renders touring clubs superfluous, and YouTube has brought broadcast networks to their knees. In today's economy, it is "easier than ever to share your creativity with the world, and harder than ever to make a living doing so."[226]

---

224 *Id.*

225 *See* Lauren Bruce, *Why WALL-E is Maybe the Most Politically Radical Pixar Movie*, MOVIEWEB (Dec. 9, 2022), https://movieweb.com/wall-e-pixar-movie/.

226 Hua Hsu, *How Can We Pay for Creativity in the Digital Age*, NEW YORKER (Sept. 7, 2020), https://www.newyorker.com/magazine/2020/09/14/how-can-we-pay-for-creativity-in-the-digital-age (citing WILLIAM DERESIEWICZ, THE DEATH OF THE

William Deresiewicz captures the present-day irony. "[A]ll the tools are at your fingertips. And if Production is cheap, distribution is free. It's called the Internet. Everyone's an artist; just tap your creativity and put it out there."[227] This is the illusion. The reality is that good art in every genre is hard work, combined with a smattering of dumb luck. "Making art takes years of dedication, and that requires a means of support. If things don't change, a lot of art will cease to be sustainable."[228] Wherever AI-generated content replaces paying content, more creators will lose their wings.[229] Since the situation is already precarious for professional artists, it won't take tremendous AI success to knock the bottom out of the creative industries.

The same consequence goes for investigative journalism. AI-generated newspaper stories filled with box scores and corporate earnings reports are already eliminating jobs.[230] In 2019, journalists were hopeful that the technology would not catch up to the

---

ARTIST: HOW CREATORS ARE STRUGGLING TO SURVIVE IN THE AGE OF BILLIONAIRES AND BIG TECH 7–8 (2020)).

227 WILLIAM DERESIEWICZ, THE DEATH OF THE ARTIST: HOW CREATORS ARE STRUGGLING TO SURVIVE IN THE AGE OF BILLIONAIRES AND BIG TECH 15 (2020).

228 *Id.* at 16.

229 Movieclips, *Every Time a Bell Rings an Angel Gets His Wings—It's a Wonderful Life (9/9) Movie CLIP (1946) HD*, YOUTUBE (Oct. 9, 2011), https://www.youtube.com/watch?v=OfUV-F9jFro (statement by Karolyn Grimes playing Zuzu Bailey) ("Look daddy, teacher says, every time a bell rings an angel gets his wings.").

230 *See* Jaclyn Peiser, *The Rise of the Robot Reporter*, N.Y. TIMES (Feb. 5, 2019), https://www.nytimes.com/2019/02/05/business/media/artificial-intelligence-journalism-robots.html.

writers. "Previous technological advances have rendered moot a number of jobs that were once essential to the journalism industry, such as Linotype operator. But reporters and editors have not yet been tempted to smash the programs now taking care of some of the busy work that once fell to them."[231] The adopters of ChatGPT see a very different future in the office, if not in the newsroom.[232]

What truly cannot be replicated by AI is the investigation that occurs before a news story breaks. Interviews cannot be spontaneously conducted, clandestine meetings cannot be arranged, nor hard questions be asked by AI systems reliant on what is already present in their training data sets. Although the support tasks can be automated, the probing questions and relentless pursuit of those answers will only occur if there remain trained professional journalists to do the work. The same is true of the practice of law where much of the lawyering is client counselling, fact investigation, risk assessment, and good judgment.[233]

---

231 *Id.*

232 *Id.*

233 *See* Robert S. Redmount, *An Inquiry into Legal Counseling*, 104 J. LEGAL PRO. 181 (2008) ("Legal counseling does not occur in a vacuum. It operates in a context and it is not just legal. . . . The lawyer, in one sense, is an instrument for the translation and utilization of law, and of appropriate response to it, by citizens otherwise engaged in the pursuit of their private affairs."); Mark Roellig & David M. Love III, *So You Want to Be a General Counsel? How to Maximize Your Chances*, ACC DOCKET (2012) ("The most important attribute sought in or expected of a strong general counsel candidate is good and tested judgment.

The predictions are for the future, but the future is essentially upon us. "ChatGPT appears ready to upend the staid book industry. . ., demonstrating how to make a book in just a few hours. Subjects include get-rich-quick schemes, dieting advice, software coding tips and recipes."[234] To slow the flood of AI-generated books, Amazon instituted a publication cap.[235] Self-publishers are limited to only three books per day.[236] Amazon also requires that authors self-identify "if their book contained any AI-generated text, images, or translation."[237] Those disclosures, however, do not appear in consumer labeling.[238]

This quality involves the sophistication to properly evaluate and weigh multiple inputs and impacts of any particular decision or course of action."); Andrew Perlman, *The Implications of ChatGPT for Legal Services and Society,* SUFFOLK UNIV. L. SCH. (Dec. 5, 2022) (offering an interesting experiment involving ChatGPT's own take on the legal profession).

234 Greg Bensinger, *Focus: ChatGPT Launches Boom in AI-written E-Books on Amazon,* REUTERS (Feb. 21, 2023), https://www.reuters.com/technology/chatgpt-launches-boom-ai-written-e-books-amazon-2023-02-21/.

235 Michael Kan, *Amazon Limits Authors to Self-Publishing 3 Books Per Day amid Flood of AI Garbage,* PC MAG. (Sept. 20, 2023), https://www.pcmag.com/news/amazon-limits-authors-to-self-publishing-3-books-per-day-amid-flood-of.

236 *Id.*

237 *Id.*

238 Emily Price, *Amazon Now Requires Authors to Disclose AI-Generated Content,* PC MAG. (Sept. 9, 2023), https://www.pcmag.com/news/amazon-starts-requiring-writers-to-disclose-ai-generated-content; *Content Guidelines,* AMAZON KINDLE DIRECT PUBL'G, https://kdp.amazon.com/en_US/help/topic/G200672390 (last visited Feb. 16, 2025).

Mary Rasenberger, executive director of the Author's Guild, has begun to raise the alarm about the emerging trend. "There's no question that the rise of AI technology capable of 'writing' poses risks to the future of writing as a profession, as it does for many other professions. . . . We are confronting serious policy issues about the future of creativity: Do we want humans or AI creating our literature and other arts?"[239] Separately, Rasenberger added, " '[t]his is something we really need to be worried about, these books will flood the market and a lot of authors are going to be out of work.' "[240]

The expansion of AI may be inevitable, but the replacement of artists, journalists, or perhaps lawyers and educators is neither intended nor desired. Unfortunately, the increase in efficiency and reduction of price might have that unintended consequence. Since becoming an expert requires training while a novice,[241] the elimination of the novices will eventually mean that society runs out of experts. The true existential threat of generative AI is not that the robots will try to take control from the

---

[239] Mary Rasenberger, *How Will Authorship Be Defined in an AI Future?*, AUTHORSGUILD (Oct. 4, 2022), https://authorsguild.org/resource/how-will-authorship-be-defined-in-an-ai-future/.

[240] Bensinger, *supra* note 234 (discussing how some authors are using ChatGPT to write books and sell them on Amazon.).

[241] *See* Adam M. Persky & Jennifer D. Robinson, *Moving from Novice to Expertise and Its Implications for Instruction*, 81 AM. J. PHARM. EDUC. 72, 73 (Nov. 2017) ("We develop expertise through years of experience . . . . The development of expertise occurs over several stages. As a rule, a learner cannot directly move from novice to expert; he or she must progress through each stage and may demonstrate characteristics of two stages simultaneously.").

humans but simply that the humans will cede control in all the ways that matter.

In other fields, the expansion of AI will also lead to substantial disruption. Marketing is ripe for downsizing.[242] According to a National Endowment for the Arts study, "the single largest category of artistic endeavor was advertising—a sign, perhaps, that the distinction between art and commerce is finally moot."[243] Graphic designers, to the extent that they were not counted among the marketing professionals and artists, are also likely to be at risk.[244] Among the many other categories, workers involved in customer service may find the ever-improving chatbots no longer drive consumers to chant "operator" in response to irrelevant automated prompts.[245] Other service jobs are also likely to be relatively safe, although the use of various forms of AI may adjust some of the tasks.[246] Generative AI will not be the end of creative work, but it will

---

242 *See* Jacob Zinkula & Aaron Mok, *ChatGPT: The 10 Jobs Most at Risk of Being Replaced by AI*, BUS. INSIDER, https://www.businessinsider.com/chatgpt-jobs-at-risk-replacement-artificial-intelligence-ai-labor-trends-2023-02 (last updated Jan. 15, 2024).

243 Scott, *supra* note 217.

244 *See* Zinkula & Mok, *supra* note 242.

245 *See id.*

246 *See The 65 Jobs With the Lowest Risk of Automation by Artificial Intelligence and Robots*, U.S. CAREER INSTIT., https://www.uscareerinstitute.edu/blog/65-jobs-with-the-lowest-risk-of-automation-by-ai-and-robots (last visited Feb. 16, 2025) ("Of the list of jobs with the lowest risk of robot automation, nurse practitioners are projected to grow the most, with an estimated increase of 45.7% by 2032, far faster than any of the other 64 jobs").

reshape which jobs are available and which resources are needed to pursue various careers.

Education stands out among the fields likely to face severe disruption from AI. Not necessarily because robots will replace teachers, though there have been experiments along those lines.[247] Nor is it because jobs will be lost to AI efficiencies.[248] Instead, like creativity, the greatest impact will be on the use of AI tools by students, who will supplement their own efforts with the AI tools readily available. "Improving teaching jobs is a priority, and via automated assistants or other tools, AI may provide teachers greater support."[249]

There are opportunities to leverage the use of AI in education, particularly in the areas of individual student needs, personalization, and customization. "Developing resources that are responsive to the knowledge and experiences students bring to their

---

[247] *See, e.g.*, Wayne Carter, *School Turns to Robots to Help Spread Educators to More Classrooms*, NBCDFW (Feb. 13, 2023), https://www.nbcdfw.com/news/local/carter-in-the-classroom/school-turns-to-robots-to-help-spread-educators-to-more-classrooms/3193741/ ("The search for a solution to the shortage of teachers schools face is still well underway—and one school in Arlington is experimenting with robots to help put more educators in front of kids."); Ingrid P. Nuse, *Humanoid Robot Takes over as Teacher*, SCIENTIFICNORDIC (Sept. 30, 2017), https://www.sciencenordic.com/forskningno-robotics-sweden/humanoid-robot-takes-over-as-teacher/1449770.

[248] *See generally The 65 Jobs With the Lowest Risk of Automation by Artificial Intelligence and Robots*, *supra* note 246.

[249] ROBERTO J. RODRÍGUEZ ET AL., U.S. DEPT. OF ED., OFFICE OF ED. TECH., ARTIFICIAL INTELLIGENCE AND THE FUTURE OF TEACHING AND LEARNING 2 (2023) (summary of benefits as developed at listening sessions).

learning—their community and cultural assets—is a priority, and AI may enable greater customizability of curricular resources to meet local needs."[250]

Student personalization, increased resources, and greater efficiency for teachers are all practical uses for AI tools, including both generative AI for simplifying tasks and predictive AI for targeting student needs and guiding instructor interventions.[251] "Research on American K-12 classrooms suggests that typical computer-aided instruction yields better test scores than instruction by the worst teachers. By 2030, most AI used in education will be of middling quality (for some, their best alternative)."[252] This suggests that the baseline of education will improve in systems that invest in the tools to access AI services. This carries with it the risk that the best teachers will also use these tools, and teaching quality could diminish.[253]

---

[250] *Id.*

[251] *See id.* at 27 ("Why can't teachers be supported to notice changing student needs and provided with supports to enact a technology-rich lesson plan?").

[252] JANNA ANDERSON, LEE RAINIE & ALEX LUCHSINGER, ARTIFICIAL INTELLIGENCE AND THE FUTURE OF HUMANS 36 (2018) (quoting Betsy Williams, a researcher at the Center for Digital Society and Data Studies at the University of Arizona).

[253] *See* Joel Kupperstein, *AI Can't Replace High-quality Teaching: Using the Technology as a Tool*, EDTECH DIGEST (June 15, 2023), https://www.edtechdigest.com/2023/06/15/ai-cant-replace-high-quality-teaching-using-the-technology-as-a-tool/ ("AI can't replace high-quality teaching because it doesn't understand the human context around students' struggles and cannot replicate a real human connection.").

Bill Gates has described the use of AI for educational personalization around the globe.[254] "AI education tools being piloted today are mind-blowing because they are tailored to each individual learner. . . . One of the things that excites me the most about this type of technology is the possibility of localizing it to every student—no matter where they live."[255] Gates points to projects funded by the Bill and Melinda Gates Foundation that are showing success in Kenya and other regions that struggle to have robust educational infrastructure.[256] Undoubtedly, such projects will increase the global baseline of education and access.

Online education has already had some significant successes. "Khan Academy has more than 155 million registered users, with students spending billions of hours of learning on the platform."[257] Sal Kahn is embracing generative AI. " 'Generative AI allows us to get much closer to giving every student and every teacher the support that they need,' " he explained.[258] Kahn clarified the relationship between teachers and technology, explaining " 'to be clear, I think that the teacher is always going to play a critical role. I don't

---

[254] Bill Gates, *Why I'm optimistic about the future of AI*, CNN (Dec. 19, 2023), https://www.cnn.com/2023/12/19/opinions/artificial-intelligence-year-ahead-bill-gates/index.html.

[255] *Id.*

[256] *See id.*

[257] Preston Fore, *Sal Khan Helped Usher in an era of Online Learning Through Khan Academy. Will its AI tool, Khanmigo, be a Model for the Future of Education?*, FORTUNE (Oct. 4, 2023), https://fortune.com/education/articles/khan-academy-sal-khan-khanmigo-ai-future-of-education/.

[258] *Id.* (interview with Fortune).

think this is going to be one of those fields that AI somehow undermines. But AI is going to hopefully make teachers feel much more supported.' "[259]

But it will take more than a few apps to increase overall education. The U.S. Chamber of Commerce has called for retraining and reinvestment, particularly to "reform the standard curriculum to better prepare students for developing AI [and machine learning] systems."[260]

The greater challenge is that the tools are available to the students as well as the teachers. Students of all ages tend to work "efficiently," meaning that they will use the least of their own time and effort to complete a task—a strategy educators might refer to as cheating.[261] Nearly everyone does it: "a survey of 70,000 high school students across the United States between 2002 and 2015 found that 58 percent had plagiarized papers, while 95 percent admitted to cheating in some capacity."[262] Generative AI improves efficiency in writing, so it stands to reason that that efficient students will use it,

---

259 *Id.*

260 U.S. CHAMBER OF COMM. TECH. ENGAGEMENT CTR., COMMISSION ON ARTIFICIAL INTELLIGENCE COMPETITIVENESS, INCLUSION, AND INNOVATION 42 (2023) [hereinafter CHAMBER REPORT] ("educators and stakeholders in curriculum and lesson plan development in K-12 education should consider methods of making mathematics—the backbone of all computer science—more real in its application to students.").

261 *See* Andrew Simmons, *Why Students Cheat—and What to Do About It,* EDUTOPIA (Apr. 27, 2018), https://www.edutopia.org/article/why-students-cheat-and-what-do-about-it/.

262 *Id.* (citing Int'l Center for Academic Integrity survey, https://academicintegrity.org/resources/facts-and-statistics).

whether they are permitted or prohibited from doing so.

The consequence of generative AI's allure to students is that educators must incorporate it into their assignments since students will likely be using it anyway. To some, this is no different than allowing calculators in high schools two or three generations ago. Educators, however, tend to use writing assignments to teach critical thinking skills. If the process of writing is automated, then the essential critical thinking skills might be reduced.

To address this challenge, educators must undertake a very large effort to unpack critical thinking into component steps and then teach those skills directly.[263] Faculty will also need to assess students in tasks other than take-home writing assignments. Without additional resources for teachers and significant retraining,[264] students will use AI efficiently and society will lose the critical thinking skills essential for a functioning civil society.

In 2019, a group of experts came together to sound the alarm about the potential negative impact of AI ascendance. The result was the "Vienna Manifesto on

---

[263] Critical thinking is comprised of three separate skill sets: Verification, Interpretation, and Reasoning. *See, e.g.*, Ioanna V. Papathanasiou et al., *Critical Thinking: The Development of an Essential Skill for Nursing Students*, 22 NAT. LIB. MED 283, 283 (2014) ("These skills include critical analysis, introductory and concluding justification, valid conclusion, distinguishing facts and opinions to assess the credibility of sources of information, clarification of concepts, and recognition conditions.").

[264] *See* CHAMBER REPORT, *supra* note 260, at 42–44.

Digital Humanism,"[265] a manifesto creating "a public call to deliberate and act on technological development signed by over 1000 leaders worldwide."[266] Among the demand of the manifesto were many emphasizing the importance of human-centered strategies for AI development:

> **Today, we experience the co-evolution of technology and humankind.** The flood of data, algorithms, and computational power is disrupting the very fabric of society by changing human interactions, societal institutions, economies, and political structures. Science and the humanities are not exempt. This disruption simultaneously creates and threatens jobs, produces and destroys wealth, and improves and damages our ecology. It shifts power structures, thereby blurring the human and the machine.
>
> **The quest is for enlightenment and humanism.** The capability to automate human cognitive activities is a revolutionary aspect of computer science/informatics. For many tasks, machines surpass already what humans can accomplish in speed, precision, and even analytic deduction. The time is right to bring together humanistic ideals with critical thoughts about technological progress. We

---

265 Hannes Werthner et al., *The Digital Humanism Initiative*, CAIML (May 2019), https://caiml.org/dighum/dighum-manifesto/. *See* HANNES WERTHNER, ERICH PREM & EDWARD LEE, PERSPECTIVES ON DIGITAL HUMANISM (2022), https://doi.org/10.1007/978-3-030-86144-5.

266 *Id.*

therefore link this manifesto to the intellectual tradition of humanism and similar movements striving for an enlightened humanity.

Like all technologies, digital technologies do not emerge from nowhere. They are shaped by implicit and explicit choices and thus incorporate a set of values, norms, economic interests, and assumptions about how the world around us is or should be. Many of these choices remain hidden in software programs implementing algorithms that remain invisible. In line with the renowned Vienna Circle and its contributions to modern thinking, we want to espouse critical rational reasoning and the interdisciplinarity needed to shape the future.

. . .

In conclusion, **we proclaim the following core principles:**

- **Digital technologies should be designed to promote democracy and inclusion.** This will require special efforts to overcome current inequalities and to use the emancipatory potential of digital technologies to make our societies more inclusive.
- **Privacy and freedom of speech are essential values for democracy and should be at the center of our activities.**
- **Effective regulations, rules and laws, based on a broad public discourse, must**

be established. They should ensure prediction accuracy, fairness and equality, accountability, and transparency of software programs and algorithms.

- **Regulators need to intervene with tech monopolies.** It is necessary to restore market competitiveness as tech monopolies concentrate market power and stifle innovation. Governments should not leave all decisions to markets.
- **Decisions with consequences that have the potential to affect individual or collective human rights must continue to be made by humans.** Decision makers must be responsible and accountable for their decisions. Automated decision making systems should only support human decision making, not replace it.
- **Scientific approaches crossing different disciplines are a prerequisite for tackling the challenges ahead.** Technological disciplines such as computer science / informatics must collaborate with social sciences, humanities, and other sciences, breaking disciplinary silos.
- **Universities are the place where new knowledge is produced and critical thought is cultivated.** Hence, they have a special responsibility and have to be aware of that.

- **Academic and industrial researchers must engage openly with wider society and reflect upon their approaches.** This needs to be embedded in the practice of producing new knowledge and technologies, while at the same time defending the freedom of thought and science.

- **Practitioners everywhere ought to acknowledge their shared responsibility for the impact of information technologies.** They need to understand that no technology is neutral and be sensitized to see both potential benefits and possible downsides.

- **A vision is needed for new educational curricula, combining knowledge from the humanities, the social sciences, and engineering studies.** In the age of automated decision making and AI, creativity and attention to human aspects are crucial to the education of future engineers and technologists.

- **Education on computer science / informatics and its societal impact must start as early as possible.** Students should learn to combine information-technology skills with awareness of the ethical and societal issues at stake.

> We are at a crossroads to the future; we must go into action and take the right direction![267]

Many of these themes are implicit in the EU AI Act and aspects of U.S. federal and state efforts to limit risks associated with AI development and deployment. At the same time, this top-down set of demands has not seemed to have significant impact on either industry or legislators, making it less a set of guiding principles and more an intellectual exercise.

---

[267] Werthner et al., *supra* note 265.

CHAPTER 3

THE EVOLVING LEGAL FRAMEWORK

Given the wide range of potential challenges posed by AI, governments around the world have undertaken a wide range of strategies to promote the benefits of new technologies while reducing the chance of catastrophic harm and restricting particular uses that are contrary to existing law. The regulations reflect the difference in priorities among jurisdictions, the degree of state control acceptable, the economic interests in promoting AI, and the nature of the existing law in the country. In consequence, although there are many principles common to all the regulatory approaches, the specifics will vary considerably from jurisdiction to jurisdiction.

In addition, many jurisdictions follow the U.S. model that emphasizes that primary enforcement comes through existing laws. As noted in the discussion of algorithmic discrimination, for example, Title VII, the ADA, the ADEA and state anti-discrimination laws apply to the use of AI. The AI-specific laws supplement existing laws.

The international landscape highlights that regulations incorporate both jurisdiction-wide strategies and sector-specific regulations to address the most pronounced vulnerabilities in critical infrastructure, and they are increasingly focusing on a risk-based approach to regulation. They emphasize the importance of multinational cooperation. The

United Nations has not yet moved to promulgate a treaty on AI adoption, nor have major trade organizations, but various groups have developed collaborative frameworks.[1]

§ 3.1 GLOBAL CONTEXT FOR REGULATIONS AND TRANSACTIONS INVOLVING AI

Much of the research and commercialization of AI is being developed in the U.S., and so although the U.S. is moving more slowly than Europe, the U.S.

---

[1] *See* Nicola Morini Bianzino et al., *The Artificial Intelligence (AI) Global Regulatory Landscape,* EY (Jan. 12, 2024), https://www.ey.com/en_us/insights/ai/how-to-navigate-global-trends-in-artificial-intelligence-regulation. The list of collaborations included:

- — OECD AI Governance working party, OECD, https://oecd.ai/en/network-of-experts.
- — Council of Europe Committee on AI, Council of Europe, https://www.coe.int/en/web/artificial-intelligence/cai.
- — Global Partnership on AI, GPAI, https://gpai.ai/.
- — UNESCO Recommendations on the Ethics of AI, UNESCO, https://www.unesco.org/en/articles/recommendation-ethics-artificial-intelligence, November 2021.
- — UNICEF Policy Guidance on AI for Children, UNICEF, https://www.unicef.org/globalinsight/reports/policy-guidance-ai-children, November 2021.
- — G7 Hiroshima Process on Generative AI, https://www.oecd.org/digital/g7-hiroshima-process-on-generative-artificial-intelligence-ai-bf3c0c60-en.htm.
- — The Bletchley Declaration on AI Safety, Prime Minister's Office, 10 Downing Street, Foreign, Commonwealth & Development Office, and Department for Science, Innovation and Technology, https://www.gov.uk/government/publications/ai-safety-summit-2023-the-bletchley-declaration, November 2023.

regulatory approach will have an outsized influence on the rest of the global approach. China is also advancing AI rapidly, likely the only nation that comes close to the U.S. in its AI development infrastructure. This highly competitive relationship will be another important influence on the multinational strategies for AI regulation.

In assessing the global landscape, consultant firm EY (formerly Ernst & Young) has identified six key trends that contextualize the various governmental strategies.[2] The trends reflect a strong interest in global, or at least multinational strategies to address the strongest of AI systems.

> Trend 1: The OECD[3] principles for AI serve as a global benchmark for AI guiding policymakers. The AI principles, adopted by the OECD and Group of 20 (G20) in 2019, serve as a global benchmark for helping governments and

---

[2] *See id.*; *How to Navigate Global Trends in Artificial Intelligence Regulation*, EY (Jan 12, 2024), https://www.ey.com/en_uk/ai/how-to-navigate-global-trends-in-artificial-intelligence-regulation.

[3] The Organization for Economic Cooperation and Development, U.S. DEPT. OF STATE, https://www.state.gov/the-organization-for-economic-co-operation-and-development-oecd/ (Footnote not in the original text.) ("The Organization for Economic Co-operation and Development (OECD) is a unique forum where the governments of 37 democracies with market-based economies collaborate to develop policy standards to promote sustainable economic growth.").

organizations shape a human-centric approach to trustworthy AI. . . .[4]

Trend 2: Policymakers are adopting a risk-based approach to AI. Each jurisdiction reviewed is focused on translating AI principles into practice. While their approaches may range from voluntary guidance to mandatory rules, each jurisdiction is pursuing a risk-based approach to AI. In April 2023, The Group of Seven (G7) Digital and Technology Ministers expressed a unified view on artificial intelligence, calling for AI policies and regulations to be "risk-based." . . .[5]

Trend 3: Policymakers are considering sector-specific considerations in AI oversight. Across the jurisdictions reviewed, there is a recognition that sector-specific considerations need to be factored into AI policymaking because the use of this technology can pose unique or greater risks in certain sectors. . . . [J]urisdictions are already taking a dual approach to AI regulation—that is, both cross-sectoral and sector-specific. The first, cross-sectoral approach provides for a baseline framework of fundamental safeguards, regardless of the sector in which AI is being developed or used. The second, sector-specific approach establishes additional guidelines or

---

[4] Bianzino, *supra* note 1, at 7 citing The OECD Artificial Intelligence (AI) Principles—OECD.AI, https://oecd.ai/en/ai-principles, May 2019.

[5] *Id.* at 8.

obligations for the use of AI to address risks and vulnerabilities within specific sectors. . . .[6]

Trend 4: Regulators are increasingly considering how AI impacts other policy areas (*e.g.*, data, cybersecurity, and digital content flows). Our review finds that AI rulemaking is also prompting new policies or new interpretations of existing policies in other areas like data ownership, digital identity, cybersecurity, and digital content flows. . . .[7]

Trend 5: Regulators are increasingly using sandboxes to enable the responsible testing of AI innovations. In the EU, Singapore, and UK, regulators are using AI regulatory sandboxes to address the twin challenges of rapid AI development and their own lack of experience with AI technologies. Regulatory sandboxes enable the testing of innovative technologies in a supervised environment, with regulation that may be limited in time and/or scope. This approach has already been used in the FinTech sector to foster public and private sector collaboration.[8]

Trend 6: Growing momentum for international collaboration on understanding and addressing risks of powerful AI systems. The heightened public attention to the development and release of increasingly capable generative and general-

---

6 *Id.* at 10.

7 *Id.*

8 *Id.* at 11.

> purpose AI systems throughout 2023 was accompanied by an increase in prominence and momentum of efforts to establish a global common baseline for AI governance and regulation. . . . These initiatives are contributing to the global momentum for collaboration on AI governance by aligning international responses and formulating comprehensive and effective safeguards. Their significance lies in their cooperative nature, bringing together a global discourse on the intricate challenges of AI safety, ethics, and governance.[9]

Building on ongoing work at the OECD AI Governance working party, the Council of Europe Committee on AI, the Global Partnership on AI and various initiatives at UN bodies (e.g., UNESCO Recommendations on the Ethics of AI, UNICEF Policy Guidance on AI for Children), the Japanese presidency of the G7 initiated the "Hiroshima Process on Generative AI", and the UK organized a global AI Safety Summit bringing together 28 nations including the US, China, and countries of Africa, the Middle East, Asia, and the EU.

§ 3.2 U.S. FEDERAL APPROACH

The general approach to cybersecurity policy and privacy policy in the U.S. has been focused on sectoral strategies. Although sectoral privacy policy has often been criticized for adding complexity and

---

9 *Id.*

ignoring some consumer protection, sectoral strategies are really just another name for risk-based regulation. Those fields in which the potential for harm is greatest receive the highest level of regulatory attention. In this way, deficiencies of the old sectoral approach are now being highlighted as innovative risk-based prioritization.

The Health Insurance Portability and Accountability Act of 1996 (HIPAA), as amended by the Health Information Technology for Economic and Clinical Health Act (HITECH), includes statutory and regulatory limitations on the use of health care data by entities covered by the regulations.[10] Financial institutions have obligations regarding customer information under the Gramm-Leach-Bliley Act of 1998 (GLBA)[11] and accompanying privacy and security regulations.[12]

The growth of AI in the healthcare and financial services sectors is constrained by the limits imposed through the sectoral privacy and data protection

---

[10] Health Insurance Portability and Accountability Act of 1996, Pub. L. No. 104–191, 110 Stat. 1936 (1996); Health Information Technology for Economic and Clinical Health Act, Pub. L. No. 111–5, 123 Stat. 226 (2009) (codified in scattered sections of 42 U.S.C.). *See* Jianyan Fang, *Health Data at Your Fingertips: Federal Regulatory Proposals for Consumer-Generated Mobile Health Data*, 4 GEO. L. TECH. REV. 125, 144 (2019) ("The most well-known federal statute for health data protection is HIPAA.").

[11] Gramm-Leach-Bliley Act, Pub. L. No. 106–102, Title V, §§ 501–527, 113 Stat. 1338 (1999) (financial services).

[12] *See, e.g.* FTC Safeguards Rule, 16 C.F.R. pt. 314 (2010) (implementing GLB Act §§ 501(b), 505(b)(2), 15 U.S.C. §§ 6801(b), 6805(b)(2)).

regulations. As noted below, however, business enterprises often obtain theoretically protected data through consent requests to the consumer and through dark practices that target healthcare information before it falls under the covered entity regulations.[13]

§ 3.2.1 FEDERAL REGULATION THROUGH EXECUTIVE ORDER

The federal government has not adopted comprehensive AI legislation, although AI has been touched upon in a variety of other laws, including the John S. McCain National Defense Authorization Act for Fiscal Year 2019,[14] National Artificial Intelligence Initiative Act of 2020,[15] the AI in Government Act of 2020,[16] Advancing American AI Act,[17] the Training for the Acquisitions Workforce Act,[18] and various Executive Orders.[19]

---

[13] *See* infra, § 6.1.

[14] John S. McCain National Defense Authorization Act for Fiscal Year 2019, Pub. L. No. 115–232 (2019) https://www.congress.gov/bill/115th-congress/house-bill/5515.

[15] William M. (Mac) Thornberry National Defense Authorization Act for Fiscal Year 2021, Pub. L. No. 116–283 (2021), https://www.congress.gov/bill/116th-congress/house-bill/6395.

[16] Consolidated Appropriations Act, 2021, Pub. L. No. 116–260 https://www.congress.gov/bill/116th-congress/house-bill/133.

[17] James M. Inhofe National Defense Authorization Act for Fiscal Year 2023, Pub. L. No. 117–263 (2022), https://www.congress.gov/bill/117th-congress/house-bill/7776.

[18] AI Training Act, Pub. L. No. 117–207 (2022) https://www.congress.gov/bill/117th-congress/senate-bill/2551.

[19] *See, e.g.*, Executive Order 13859 on Maintaining American Leadership in Artificial Intelligence (Feb 11, 2019); Executive

Instead, throughout the Biden Administration, the federal government addressed the growing demand for regulation with a series of actions, including a comprehensive Executive Order on Artificial Intelligence. This approach aimed to leverage the power of the federal administration to sidestep Congress and create federal authority.[20] The Biden AI Executive Order expanded upon the previously published AI Bill of Rights,[21] and a National AI R&D Strategic Plan.[22]

President Biden explained his approach in the purpose of the AI Executive Order, stating that "[m]y Administration places the highest urgency on governing the development and use of AI safely and responsibly, and is therefore advancing a coordinated, Federal Government-wide approach to doing so."[23] The AI Executive Order set out a series of steps that over 50 federal agencies were required to take to ensure that each agency used and promoted AI in a manner that is transparent, explainable and

---

Order 13960, Promoting the Use of Trustworthy Artificial Intelligence in the Federal Government (Dec 2020); Executive Order 14091 On Advancing Racial Equity and Support for Underserved Communities Through the Federal Government (Feb 16, 2023).

[20] *See* Exec. Order No. 14110, 88 Fed. Reg. 75191 (Oct. 30, 2023) (repealed by Exec. Order No. 14148, 90 Fed. Reg. 8237 (Jan. 20, 2025) [hereinafter AI EXECUTIVE ORDER]. See also Exec. Order No. 14179 on Removing Barriers to American Leadership in Artificial Intelligence, Fed. Reg. No. 8741 (Jan. 23, 2025).

[21] *See Blueprint for an AI Bill of Rights*, OFF. OF SCI. & TECH.

[22] *See* SELECT COMM. ON A.I. OF THE NAT'L SCIENCE AND TECH. COUNCIL, NATIONAL ARTIFICIAL INTELLIGENCE RESEARCH AND DEVELOPMENT STRATEGIC PLAN (2023).

[23] AI EXECUTIVE ORDER, *supra* note 20.

without bias.[24] The AI Executive Order outlined more than 100 specific actions over a timeline with interim deadlines that had occurred quarterly.[25]

The Biden AI Executive Order emphasized the importance of safety, security, responsible competition, workplace protections, civil rights, protections from harms caused by AI-enabled devices, protection of privacy and civil liberties, and limitations on governmental use of AI.[26]

Previous efforts at coordinating international privacy policies often stagnated because of the strong U.S. position on the "free and open internet," echoing the higher priority the U.S. gives to free speech than many democracies across the globe. In anticipation of the need for greater content regulation in the context of AI policy, the Biden Administration abandoned the "free internet" strategy that the U.S. adopted in 1998 in response to the early emergence of the internet.[27]

In October 2023, the Biden Administration moved more explicitly to distance itself from prior

---

24 Laurie Harris and Chris Jaikaran, *Highlights of the 2023 Executive Order on Artificial Intelligence for Congress*, CONG. RES. SERV. R47843 (Apr. 3, 2024).

25 *See id.*

26 AI EXECUTIVE ORDER, *supra* note 20, at § 2(a)–(g).

27 *See generally* Bruce A. Lehman, INFORMATION INFRASTRUCTURE TASK FORCE, INTELLECTUAL PROPERTY AND THE NATIONAL INFORMATION INFRASTRUCTURE (1995) (detailing the Clinton Administration's position on copyright law and the Internet); *see generally* Kristin Ashurst Hughes, *Copyright in Cyberspace: A Survey of National Policy Proposals for On-Line Service Provider Copyright Liability and an Argument for International Harmonization*, 11 AM. U. J. INT'L. L. & POL'Y 1027, 1032 (1996).

administrations' open-internet policies.[28] A U.S. official speaking at the World Trade Organization stated "U.S. policy must take into account regulatory objectives, 'balancing the right to regulate in the public interest and the need to address anticompetitive behavior in the digital economy'."[29] Another official highlighted that "many countries, including the United States, are examining their approaches to data and source code, and the impact of trade rules in these areas. . . . In order to provide enough policy space for those debates to unfold, the United States has removed its support for proposals that might prejudice or hinder those domestic policy considerations."[30] In doing so, the Administration signaled a willingness to push the limits of First Amendment jurisprudence in order to mitigate the harms of AI and align U.S. policies with international norms. The Trump Administration has also signaled an interest in reversing this policy, at least with regard to domestic content moderation.[31]

The Biden AI Executive Order built upon a National Institute of Standards and Technology (NIST) framework titled "Artificial Intelligence Risk

---

[28] David Lawder, *US Drops Digital Trade Demands at WTO to Allow Room for Stronger Tech Regulation*, REUTERS (Oct. 25, 2023), https://www.reuters.com/world/us/us-drops-digital-trade-demands-wto-allow-room-stronger-tech-regulation-2023-10-25/.

[29] *Id.*

[30] Dan Dupont, *U.S. to End Support for WTO E-Commerce Proposals, wants 'Policy Space' for Digital Trade Rethink*, INSIDE U.S. TRADE'S (Dec. 23, 2023) https://insidetrade.com/share/178191 (quoting U.S. Trade Representative spokesman Sam Michel).

[31] *See* Exec. Order No. 14149 on Restoring Freedom of Speech and Ending Federal Censorship, Fed. Reg. No. 8243 (Jan 20, 2025).

Management Framework."[32] Many of the concerns focused on the misuse of AI to create harmful effects. Unlike the European policy, which views AI as an existential workforce disruptor, the AI Executive Order made only limited reference to workforce stability or job protection.[33]

Others focus on guidance for labeling AI-generated content in an effort to reduce fraud, deception, and misinformation.[34] Likely out of First Amendment concerns, however, the proposed labeling requirements did not extend to private U.S. publishers.[35] The AI Executive Order only mandates that federal agencies undertake a mandatory labeling system.[36]

---

32 NIST AI FRAMEWORK, *supra* ch. 1 note 140, at 1 ("AI technologies, however, also pose risks that can negatively impact individuals, groups, organizations, communities, society, the environment, and the planet.").

33 *See* AI EXECUTIVE ORDER, *supra* note 20 (the Small Business administration shall "assess how current or formerly operational Federal programs designed to assist workers facing job disruptions—including unemployment insurance and programs authorized by the Workforce Innovation and Opportunity Act (Public Law 113–128)—could be used to respond to possible future AI-related disruptions").

34 Anjana Susarla, *Analysis: How Biden's New Executive Order Tackles AI Risks, and Where it Falls Short*, PBS NEWS HOUR (Nov. 4, 2023), https://www.pbs.org/newshour/politics/analysis-how-bidens-new-executive-order-tackles-ai-risks-and-where-it-falls-short.

35 *See generally id.*

36 AI EXECUTIVE ORDER, *supra* note 20.

> [T]he Director of OMB, in consultation with . . . the heads of other agencies that the Director of OMB deems appropriate, shall—for the purpose of strengthening public confidence in the integrity of official United States Government digital

Like the labeling of synthetic media, much of the AI Executive Order described expansive U.S. regulation and then calls for much more modest changes to federal governmental policies and action.

§ 3.2.2 USING THE EXECUTIVE ORDER TO REGULATE PRIVATE INDUSTRY

The implementation of the AI Executive Order had been comprehensive, but it was primarily limited to federal governmental agencies. With the January 20, 2025 repeal of the Biden AI Executive Order, the directions to federal agencies are no longer in place. The current administration has begun to issue its own directives regarding AI, so the lessons from the Biden AI Executive Order on private industry and the power to extend agency regulation into private sector operations may still be relevant. In two key areas, therefore, the former directive went well beyond the management of federal agencies directly to reach AI developers (and potentially AI deployers) in the private sector.

First, § 4.2 of the AI Executive Order invoked the Defense Production Act.[37] In a Fact Sheet published by the White House on Jan. 19, 2024, the Biden Administration announced that the administration "[set] key disclosure requirements for developers of the most powerful systems, assessing AI's risks for critical infrastructure, and hindering foreign actors'

---

content—issue guidance to agencies for labeling and authenticating such content that they produce or publish.

[37] AI Executive Order, *supra* note 20, at § 4.2.

efforts to develop AI for harmful purposes."[38] Since an Executive Order only regulates the federal agencies under the authority of the Executive branch of government, the Biden Administration explained that to achieve this goal, it has "[u]sed Defense Production Act authorities to compel developers of the most powerful AI systems to report vital information, especially AI safety test results, to the Department of Commerce."[39]

The Defense Production Act (DPA)[40] was passed by Congress in 1950 to support U.S. efforts in the Korean War and has been used only sparingly. In the context of cybersecurity infrastructure, the law was amended in 2018 with the Foreign Investment Risk Review Modernization Act,[41] which expanded the scope of the Committee on Foreign Investment in the United States (CFIUS) and brought it within the scope of the DPA.[42] By its terms, the application of the disclosure under § 4.2 is primarily focused on the next generation of AI systems that are significantly larger than those used commercially.

---

38 *Fact Sheet: Biden-Harris Administration Announces Key AI Actions Following President Biden's Landmark Executive Order*, THE WHITE HOUSE (Jan. 29, 2024).

39 *Id.*

40 Defense Production Act (DPA) of 1950 (P.L. 81–774, 50 U.S.C. §§ 4501 et seq.).

41 Foreign Investment Risk Review Modernization Act (Title XVII, P.L. 115–235) (2018),

42 *See* Alexandra G. Neenan and Luke A. Nicastro, *The Defense Production Act of 1950: History, Authorities, and Considerations for Congress*, CONG. RES. SERV. R43767 18 (Oct. 6, 2023).

The second potential expansion of the AI Executive Order into commercial regulation was through its implications for government procurement. In March 2024, the Office of Management and Budget (OMB) issued a final memo that outlined the requirements for procurement of AI systems.[43] This guidance will restrict sales to the U.S. government of non-compliant services and could eventually result the prohibition of procurement from those companies that offer non-compliant services to even non-governmental enterprises. Using the power of the purse, the federal government can create strong positive and negative incentives for industry to comply with federal mandates.

Specifically, the OMB Final Memo requires that each federal agency appoint a Chief AI Officer, and for each agency "to develop an enterprise strategy for how they will advance the responsible use of AI. This memorandum also provides recommendations for how agencies should reduce barriers to the responsible use of AI, including barriers related to IT infrastructure, data, cybersecurity, workforce, and the particular challenges of generative AI."[44] In keeping with the AI Executive Order, the OMB Final Memo requires agencies to limit their procurement of

---

[43] OFFICE OF MANAGEMENT AND BUDGET, MEMORANDUM FOR THE HEADS OF EXECUTIVE DEPARTMENTS AND AGENCIES ON ADVANCING GOVERNANCE, INNOVATION, AND RISK MANAGEMENT FOR AGENCY USE OF ARTIFICIAL INTELLIGENCE, [OMB FINAL MEMO] (Mar 28, 2024) https://www.whitehouse.gov/wp-content/uploads/2024/03/M-24-10-Advancing-Governance-Innovation-and-Risk-Management-for-Agency-Use-of-Artificial-Intelligence.pdf.

[44] *Id.* at 2.

AI systems to those that meet the requirements of safety, security, and transparency. Under this guidance, agencies are required to adhere to at least the minimum safety practices, follow OMB limitations on adoption of AI that might harm individual rights or public safety, and comply with "recommendations for managing AI risks in the context of Federal procurement."[45]

Under the guidance, federal agencies will be required to complete an impact assessment of the AI systems used, including an analysis of the data within the system. Those vendors that refuse to provide information on the training data, or worse, are incapable of identifying the data sources used, will be unable to comply with the impact assessments required by their federal clients. All new systems will now require testing, and all systems will require monitoring.[46] Although a Trump White House press release indicates the OMB instructions will be revised, no such action has been taken as of the time of this writing.

Through the implementation of the comprehensive AI Executive Order and the myriad of interpretative and direct actions it required, the U.S. had begun to implement a compliance regime The Trump Administration has also prioritized AI, and will continue on its own path towards AI development, competition strategy, and regulation.

---

45 *Id.*

46 *See id.* at 22–24.

§ 3.2.3 IMPLEMENTATION OF FEDERAL DIRECTIVES THAT REMAIN IN PLACE

As a practical matter, the Biden AI Executive Order required federal government agencies, as well as private enterprises working with or supplying them, to undertake a number of steps to share information with the federal government, to "red-team" or employ adversarial testing prior to deploying large AI dual-use foundation models, and more.[47]

The Executive Order also had a general statement that "[c]ompanies, individuals, or other organizations or entities that acquire, develop, or possess a potential large-scale computing cluster to report any such acquisition, development, or possession, including the existence and location of these clusters and the amount of total computing power available in each cluster."[48] Although those regulations were never developed, companies may still be required to follow the National Institute of Standards and Technology (NIST)[49] framework for safe cybersecurity. This furthers a risk-based or harms-based approach to the development and deployment of AI models. In addition, as the regulations develop, they will likely follow the principles to "drive safe,

---

47 *Id.* at § 4.2.

48 *Id.*

49 NATIONAL INSTITUTE OF STANDARDS AND TECHNOLOGY (NIST), https://www.nist.gov/itl (last visited Feb. 16, 2025).

secure, and trustworthy development of AI technology."[50]

Ensuring Products are Safe Before Introducing Them to the Public

- The companies commit to internal and external security testing of their AI systems before their release. This testing, which will be carried out in part by independent experts, guards against some of the most significant sources of AI risks, such as biosecurity and cybersecurity, as well as its broader societal effects.
- The companies commit to sharing information across the industry and with governments, civil society, and academia on managing AI risks. This includes best practices for safety, information on attempts to circumvent safeguards, and technical collaboration.

Building Systems that Put Security First

- The companies commit to investing in cybersecurity and insider threat safeguards to protect proprietary and unreleased model weights. These model weights are the most essential part of an AI system, and the companies agree that it is vital that the model weights be released only when

[50] White House Fact Sheet, Biden-Harris Administration Secures Voluntary Commitments from Leading Artificial Intelligence Companies to Manage the Risks Posed by AI (July 21, 2023).

intended and when security risks are considered.

- The companies commit to facilitating third-party discovery and reporting of vulnerabilities in their AI systems. Some issues may persist even after an AI system is released and a robust reporting mechanism enables them to be found and fixed quickly.

Earning the Public's Trust

- The companies commit to developing robust technical mechanisms to ensure that users know when content is AI generated, such as a watermarking system. This action enables creativity with AI to flourish but reduces the dangers of fraud and deception.

- The companies commit to publicly reporting their AI systems' capabilities, limitations, and areas of appropriate and inappropriate use. This report will cover both security risks and societal risks, such as the effects on fairness and bias.

- The companies commit to prioritizing research on the societal risks that AI systems can pose, including on avoiding harmful bias and discrimination, and protecting privacy. The track record of AI shows the insidiousness and prevalence of these dangers, and the companies commit to rolling out AI that mitigates them.

- The companies commit to develop and deploy advanced AI systems to help address society's greatest challenges. From cancer prevention to mitigating climate change to so much in between, AI—if properly managed—can contribute enormously to the prosperity, equality, and security of all.[51]

These broad outlines will increasingly shape the standards and practices that companies must adhere to in order to ensure the ethical and responsible use of AI. "The NIST Cybersecurity Framework v2.0 provides guidance for managing risks in all industry verticals of any size, including government and academia. It identifies an organization's current baseline, deficiencies and priorities to improve its security posture."[52] Most importantly, the NIST approach extends the model to a large segment of the economy that fall into the mid-sized enterprise category. For those enterprises, the use of the framework "is no longer merely a "nice-to-have", but a business essential."[53]

§ 3.3 U.S. STATE APPROACHES

State legislatures are known as the laboratories of democracy, and that approach is truer in the field of

[51] *Id.*

[52] Jay Martin, *How the NIST Cybersecurity Framework 2.0 Helps Protect Businesses*, SECURITY (Aug. 15, 2024), https://www.securitymagazine.com/articles/100924-how-the-nist-cybersecurity-framework-20-helps-protect-businesses.

[53] *Id.*

AI regulation than perhaps any other. In 2024 alone almost 700 AI-related bills have been introduced across the country across 45 states.[54] As described below, Colorado has seen the most impactful new law with the first risk-based approach to address AI development and deployment. California and Tennessee have both added laws on digital replicas but while these are the leading states in 2024, many more will be adding legislation in 2025 and beyond.

The growth in state activity is fueled by the absence of new federal laws and a significant retrenchment in the reach of federal administrative agencies. The result is a rush by state lawmakers to fill the gap. Ironically for those who advocate less overall regulation, the changes in Washington are likely to increase both the amount of regulation and the cost of regulatory compliance. AI developers and deployers will likely face a more complex regulatory landscape of inconsistent state laws and duplicative compliance obligations.

§ 3.3.1 STATE ASCENDENCY IN THE NEO-LOCHNER ERA

The jurisprudential theme of Justice John Roberts' Supreme Court has been a return to *Lochner* era dominance of the courts over statutory interpretation by administrative agencies, a lack of deference to Congress, and a narrowing of the Commerce Clause. In consequence of these changes, states' police

[54] *2024 State Summary on AI*, BSA (Oct. 22, 2024), https://www.bsa.org/policy-filings/us-bsa-2024-state-legislative-summary-ai.

powers have broadened, and their independent authority has expanded.

In *Loper Bright Enterprises v. Raimondo,*[55] the Supreme Court completed its deconstruction of judicial deference that had dominated statutory interpretation under the *Chevron* Deference Doctrine since at least 1984, if not 1827.[56] Under *Chevron*, a court was required to defer to a government agency's interpretation of statutory language if the agency's understanding was "based on a permissible construction of the statute."[57] The deference was only required if the court could not interpret the language of the statute directly using the various rules of statutory construction. Nonetheless, regulatory statutes can rarely cover the multitude of detailed interpretations needed to define compliance requirements, making the use of administrative rule interpretation an important part of the regulatory state.

In *Loper*, however, the Supreme Court declared "*Chevron* is overruled."[58] In practice, however, the Court had already completed most of this work. For example, as the *Loper* decision highlights, a series of cases had already narrowed *Chevron* deference to its vanishing point. *Chevron* was sidestepped whenever

---

[55] Loper Bright Enterprises v. Raimondo, 603 U.S. 369, 379 (2024), together with Relentless, Inc. v. Department of Commerce.

[56] *See* Chevron U. S. A. Inc. v. Natural Resources Defense Council, Inc., 467 U.S. 837 (1984); Edwards' Lessee v. Darby, 12 Wheat. 206, 25 U.S. 206, 6 L.Ed. 603 (1827).

[57] Chevron, 467 U.S. at 843.

[58] Loper Bright Enterprises, 603 U.S. at 412.

a court determined that a decision was one of "deep 'economic and political significance.' "[59] The Court then transformed this test of importance into the "major questions doctrine," which enables a court to reverse any interpretation that the court believes were exercises of extraordinary authority using modest, vague, or subtle statutory interpretation.[60] *Chevron* deference was also limited to the administering agency, so other agencies could not expect deference when interpreting language intended for other agencies.

Added to this, the statute of limitations for regulatory agencies has been increased from six years following issuance of the regulation to six years following a business being subject to that regulation, which effectively removes any notion of regulatory repose for federal agencies. Under the new interpretation, there is no length of time that will protect a federal agency from litigation to challenge the adoption of final regulations. Instead, newly formed corporate plaintiffs can challenge regulations years and even decades after the regulations have been adopted by the agencies.[61]

Further, while *Loper* categorically ends *Chevron* deference, the major questions doctrine of *West*

---

[59] King v. Burwell, 576 U.S. 473, 486 (2015).

[60] West Virginia v. EPA, 597 U.S. 697, 723 (2022). *See* also Epic Systems Corp. v. Lewis, 584 U.S. 497, 519–520 (2018).

[61] Corner Post, Inc. v. Board of Governors of the Federal Reserve System, 603 U.S. 799 (2024) ("A claim accrues when the plaintiff has the right to assert it in court—and in the case of the APA, that is when the plaintiff is injured by final agency action."),

Virginia v. EPA goes much further. A court with a different political disposition than Congress that enacted the law can simply declare the language incapable of having any enforceable meaning because the text is insufficiently authoritative to support the government's interpretation.[62]

In addition to the end of *Chevron* deference and the increased power of the courts to apply the court's own "common sense" rather than relying on plausible interpretations, interpretations of Commerce Clause have further limited federal statutory authority.

Under the modern Commerce Clause, there are "three broad categories of activity that Congress may regulate under its commerce power."[63]

> First, Congress may regulate the use of the channels of interstate commerce. Second, Congress is empowered to regulate and protect the instrumentalities of interstate commerce, or persons or things in interstate commerce, even though the threat may come only from intrastate activities. Finally, Congress' commerce authority includes the power to regulate those

---

62 *See, e.g.*, Biden v. Nebraska, 143 S. Ct. 2355, 2368 (2023) ("statutory permission to "modify" does not authorize "basic and fundamental changes in the scheme" designed by Congress." quoting MCI Telecommunications Corp. v. American Telephone & Telegraph Co., 512 U.S. 218, 225 (1994)); Texas v. Cardona, No. 4:23–CV–00604–O, 2024 WL 2947022, at *36 (N.D. Tex. June 11, 2024) ("the Department [of Education] lacks the authority to rewrite Title IX and decide the major policy question of whether discrimination on the basis of sex should include gender identity.").

63 U.S. v. Lopez, 514 U.S. 549, 558 (1995).

> activities having a substantial relation to interstate commerce, . . . i.e., those activities that substantially affect interstate commerce.[64]

After decades without any limitations on the Commerce Clause, the Court determined there were outer limits to stop the Commerce Clause from operating as federal police power.[65] In *U.S. v. Lopez*, the Court found the Commerce Clause could not be used to federalize criminal laws related to the possession of handguns near school grounds.[66] The Court expressly required that the third category of Commerce Clause authority required substantial effects to make clear that "the Court has never declared that 'Congress may use a relatively trivial impact on commerce as an excuse for broad general regulation of state or private activities.' "[67]

Relying on *Lopez*, in *U.S. v. Morrison*, the Court found that the Violence Against Women Act did not result in economic harm despite the congressional findings of aggregate economic consequences from the individual acts of violence. The Court explained that the aggregate economic argument would create too much authority for the federal government. "If

---

[64] U.S. v. Morrison, 529 U.S. 598, 608–09 (2000) (internal citations omitted).

[65] Lopez 514 U.S. at 567 ("To uphold the Government's contentions here, we would have to pile inference upon inference in a manner that would bid fair to convert congressional authority under the Commerce Clause to a general police power of the sort retained by the States.").

[66] *Id.*

[67] Lopez, 514 U.S. at 559 quoting Maryland v. Wirtz, 392 U.S. 183, 196, n. 27 (1968).

accepted, this reasoning would allow Congress to regulate any crime whose nationwide, aggregated impact has substantial effects on employment, production, transit, or consumption."[68]

Finally, in *National Federation of Independent Business v. Sebelius*,[69] the Court found that the individual mandate requiring purchase of health insurance did not meet the substantial effects requirement for the Commerce Clause because the mandate to buy insurance "does not regulate existing commercial activity. It instead compels individuals to become active in commerce by purchasing a product, on the ground that their failure to do so affects interstate commerce."[70] Instead, the Court determined that the penalty for failing to purchase the insurance was a tax, within the scope of the government's taxing authority.[71]

Lopez, *Morrison*, and *Sebelius* may not put severe limits on the Commerce Clause, but together, they make it clear that the trend towards a generalized federal police power has been reversed. This trend has been further reinforced by the Court in *National Pork Producers Council v. Ross*.[72] Here, the Court let stand a California law prohibiting "the in-state sale of whole pork meat that comes from breeding pigs (or their immediate offspring) that are 'confined in a

---

68 Morrison, 529 U.S. at 615.

69 Natl. Fedn. of Indep. Bus. v. Sebelius, 567 U.S. 519 (2012).

70 *Id.* at 552.

71 *Id.* at 653–63.

72 Natl. Pork Producers Council v. Ross, 598 U.S. 356 (2023).

cruel manner.' "[73] In the decision, the Court framed the Dormant Commerce Clause jurisprudence as a limitation on discriminating against out-of-state economic interests for the benefit of in-state interests.

The Court did acknowledge that in *Pike v. Bruce Church, Inc.*,[74] the Dormant Commerce Clause also required courts to weigh the consequences of state law on the broader national economic activity. "*Pike* . . . is reserved for laws directed to legitimate local concerns, with effects upon interstate commerce that are only incidental. Under the *Pike* test, [courts] will uphold a nondiscriminatory statute like this one unless the burden imposed on interstate commerce is clearly excessive in relation to the putative local benefits."[75] One may question whether California's regulations for pork production were merely incidental to the impact on interstate commerce, but the prior Commerce Clause jurisprudence dictated that the Court should address the benefits to California and the burden imposed. Instead of finding the *Pike* balance satisfied for California or excused because the health and safety concerns could not be given an economic value (and thus ignoring *Carrol Towing*[76]), the Court merely acknowledged

---

[73] *Id.* at 365–66 quoting Cal. Health & Safety Code Ann. § 25990(b)(2) (2023).

[74] Pike v. Bruce Church, Inc., 397 U.S. 137 (1970).

[75] United Haulers Ass'n, Inc. v. Oneida-Herkimer Solid Waste Mgt. Auth., 550 U.S. 330, 346 (2007) (internal quotation marks and internal citations omitted).

[76] *See* United States v. Carroll Towing Co., 159 F.2d 169 (1947).

that *Pike* merely leaves the "courtroom door open to nondiscriminatory burdens," an outcome that occurred only in a small number of cases.[77] Only a plurality of the Court then signed on to the remainder of the *Pike* discussion that minimized the concerns that a dominant state could impose its standards on the rest of the country.

In combination with *West Virginia v. EPA* and *Loper*, the Roberts Court has made it abundantly clear that Congress must demonstrate that a federal statute has substantial effects on Commerce and that it has not granted any significant interpretative leeway to the Executive Branch to expand the statute's scope. States, in contrast, are substantially free to expand their police powers so long as they do not do so to provide economic benefits to their own residents at the expense of out-of-staters.

There is no question that under the Commerce Clause, the federal government could preempt state artificial intelligence regulation if it were to expressly choose to do so[78] or to enact laws that covered the entire field, leaving the states no room to supplement the regulatory scheme.[79] But in the

---

77 Natl. Pork Producers Council v. Ross, 598 U.S. at 379 (internal quotations and internal citations omitted).

78 Hughes v. Talen Energy Mktg., LLC, 578 U.S. 150, 162 (2016) ("[F]ederal law preempts contrary state law.").

79 *See* Natl. Pork Producers Council v. Ross, 598 U.S. at 380 ("this Court 'has only rarely held that the Commerce Clause itself pre-empts an entire field from state regulation, and then only when a lack of national uniformity would impede *the flow* of interstate goods.' " quoting Exxon Corp. v. Governor of Maryland, 437 U.S. 117, 128 (1978) (emphasis added)).

absence of express preemption, regulation will increasingly be left to the states. Given the limitations imposed, creating federal authority that is precise enough to withstand court scrutiny will likely lead to less rather than greater preemption by the federal government.

Finally, much like the *Lochner* era, the Supreme Court has used other constitutional fundamental rights to provide an alternative method of limiting states' statutory power. In *Lochner*, it was the Contracts Clause. For the Roberts Court, the emphasis has been on the First Amendment and Second Amendment.[80] Particularly where the regulation involves speech, information, or output of some kind, the courts are likely to afford much less deference than in other spheres of regulation.

The Colorado Artificial Intelligence act provides an example.[81] As discussed below, the law regulates developers and deployers of artificial intelligence

---

[80] *See* 303 Creative LLC v. Elenis, 600 U.S. 570, 577–79 (2023) ("Like many States, Colorado has a law forbidding businesses from engaging in discrimination when they sell goods and services to the public. . . The question we face is whether that course violates the Free Speech Clause of the First Amendment."); McDonald v. City of Chicago, Ill., 561 U.S. 742, 750 (2010) ("We have previously held that most of the provisions of the Bill of Rights apply with full force to both the Federal Government and the States. Applying the standard that is well established in our case law, we hold that the Second Amendment right is fully applicable to the States.").

[81] Colorado SB–24–205 (2024) (Concerning Consumer Protections in Interactions with Artificial Intelligence Systems); COLO. REV. STAT. § 6–1–1301 ET SEQ. (2024), https://www.ncsl.org/technology-and-communication/artificial-intelligence-2024-legislation.

systems that are used for high-risk decisions, involving as activities such as health care, education, employment, access to legal services, and more.

The Colorado AI Act provides that an "Artificial Intelligence System" that "generate[s] outputs, including content"[82] is a method of producing speech.[83] Under a broad First Amendment rubric, restricting a deployer's publication of speech is, therefore, a law abridging free speech. As a matter of basic First Amendment jurisprudence, the "government has no power to restrict expression because of its message, its ideas, its subject matter, or its content."[84] Developers and deployers of these systems, therefore, will press that Colorado is attempting to regulate chatbot output based on its content.

There are only a few categorical exceptions to First Amendment protection, limited to obscenity, child pornography, incitement, fighting words, defamation with actual malice, and true threats, as well as communicative crimes including fraud, extortion, and perjury.[85] Discrimination remains illegal even though speech is used to conduct the discrimination. But the line between illegal conduct and protected

---

82 COLO. REV. STAT. § 6–1–1701(2).

83 *See* Will Rasenberger, *Does the First Amendment Protect AI Generated Speech?*, REG. REV. (Mar. 19, 2024), https://www.theregreview.org/2024/03/19/rasenberger-does-the-first-amendment-protect-ai-generated-speech/.

84 Brown v. Ent. Merchants Ass'n, 564 U.S. 786, 790–91 (2011) quoting Ashcroft v. American Civil Liberties Union, 535 U.S. 564, 573 (2002) (internal quotation marks omitted).

85 *See id.*; U.S. v. Alvarez, 567 U.S. 709, 717 (2012).

speech is never clear cut. The Colorado law is unlikely to be found unconstitutional because it does not bar the use of chatbots or require a license to authorize their use. Instead, the law creates a presumption that the developer and deployer acted reasonably in the deployment of the chatbot if the party complies with the statute. As such, the burden on speech is minimal. For other states that seek to create liability for harmful speech, however, the First Amendment will be a much more significant hurdle.

In addition, Colorado and Utah have mandatory disclosure laws regarding the use of chatbots.[86] Substantial disclosure requirements needed to gain protection of the presumption of reasonableness could create an undue burden on speech. Unreasonable disclosure requirements are also unconstitutional,[87] particularly where they are used to discourage content or viewpoint.[88]

To be constitutional, a law must focus on the conduct or the use of the speech rather than speech itself. If enforcement actions were to target the output of chatbots rather than material, adverse decisions by those using the systems, then the Supreme Court could well interpret the statute to be a *de facto* licensing scheme for chatbots, violating the

---

[86] Utah Artificial Intelligence Policy Act, S.B. 149 (Mar. 13, 2024), UTAH CODE ANN. § 13–60–101 ET SEQ. (2024); COLO. REV. STAT. § 6–1–1703(4)(C)(II)–(III).

[87] *See* Zauderer v. Office of Disciplinary Counsel of Supreme Court of Ohio, 471 U.S. 626 (1985).

[88] *See* National Institute of Family and Life Advocates v. Becerra 585 U.S. 755 (2018).

fundamental principle that the First Amendment allows no prior restraint[89] or as a form of content or viewpoint discrimination.[90]

Despite the important limitations that the Supreme Court will impose on states under the First Amendment, there is still much greater flexibility and autonomy than the Court is providing for administrative agencies. As a result, the states will be a dominant part of the artificial intelligence regulatory framework.

§ 3.3.2 THE EMERGING STATE REGULATORY CONSENSUS

In response to the perceived inaction by Congress and court-imposed limitations on federal regulatory authority, a growing number of states and municipalities are adopting laws and ordinances to supplement existing civil rights and consumer protection laws. For many of the potential harms caused by AI, existing regulations are sufficient to address public concerns. Nonetheless, to address those issues not directly regulated as well as to demonstrate that elected officials are taking action, various jurisdictions are making efforts to address the harms described in Chapter 2.

The speed at which the state laws are changing make it imprudent to attempt a comprehensive

---

[89] Near v. Minnesota ex rel. Olson, 283 U.S. 697, 716 (1931). *See* U.S. v. Alvarez, 567 U.S. at 717.

[90] *See* R.A.V. v. St. Paul, 505 U.S. 377, 384–390 (1992) (the government may not engage in viewpoint discrimination under the guise of regulating unprotected speech).

summary in this Nutshell. Readers should refer to the National Conference of State Legislatures; IAPP; EPIC; Husch Blackwell's Tracking U.S. State Artificial Intelligence Legislation; Locke Lorde Artificial Intelligence Legislation Tracker; and other updated databases for the most current scorecard on state legislation.[91] While the various laws and ordinances vary considerably, there are patterns emerging from the state regulatory efforts, highlighted by these topics:

- Deepfakes and synthetic content for use in nonconsensual distribution of intimate content, fraud, or theft of personal identity.
- Algorithmic bias mitigation requirements.
- Biometric disclosure requirements.
- Expansion of privacy protections.
- Requirements for fairness, including notice prior to use of AI, disclosure of data practices,

---

[91] *See, e.g.*, *Artificial Intelligence 2023 Legislation*, NATIONAL CONFERENCE OF STATE LEGISLATURES, https://www.ncsl.org/technology-and-communication/artificial-intelligence-2023-legislation; Katrina Zhu, *The State of State AI Laws: 2023*, EPIC (Aug. 3, 2023) https://epic.org/the-state-of-state-ai-laws-2023/; IAPP, State AI Governance Legislation Tracker, https://iapp.org/resources/article/us-state-ai-governance-legislation-tracker/; Husch Blackwell's Tracking U.S. State Artificial Intelligence Legislation, https://www.huschblackwell.com/2024-ai-state-law-tracker; and *Artificial Intelligence Legislation Tracker*, LOCKE LORDE https://media.lockelord.com/AIlegislationtrackerv8/index.html (last visited *Artificial Intelligence Legislation Tracker*, LOCKE LORDE).

transparency, and explainability of algorithms.

- Task force or exploratory committees to focus on building the jurisdiction's capabilities and work force to deploy AI and improve the knowledge about the systems.
- Regulations on how city or state government agencies use or limit AI.

No jurisdiction has undertaken to legislate across all these topics. Instead, most states focus on one or two of these key metrics. Municipalities such as the City of New York have also enacted ordinances or regulations. The most significant of these trends are discussed below.

§ 3.3.2.1 Deepfakes and Synthetic Content

"The inviolability of the person is as much invaded by a compulsory stripping and exposure as by a blow."[92] The use of synthetic media to invade an individual's intimate space creates a harm that is both invisible and deeply long-lasting. "The harm of sexual-privacy invasions is profound. Victims are denied agency over their intimate lives."[93] Victims describe living in a state of perpetual fear, of being unable to form new relationships, of never feeling safe, and of stigmatization.[94]

---

[92] Union Pac. Ry. Co. v. Botsford, 141 U.S. 250, 252 (1891). *See* Danielle Keat Citron, *Sexual Privacy*, *supra* ch. 2 note 161, at 1931.

[93] Citron, *supra* ch. 2 note 161, at 1924.

[94] *Id.* at 1924–25.

Jurisdictions have been addressing concerns regarding synthetic media (or deepfakes) longer than any other field of AI.[95] Because the predominant early use of deepfakes focused on nonconsensual pornography, most jurisdictions limiting deepfakes focused on the unauthorized invasion of privacy and libelous content produced in this manner.[96] Deepfakes are one form among a group of sexual-privacy invasions that includes "(1) digital voyeurism, (2) up-skirt photos, (3) sextortion, (4) nonconsensual pornography, and (5) deep-fake sex videos."[97]

The Cyber Civil Rights Initiative has been the leading nonprofit advocacy organization supporting efforts to stop invasions of privacy using sextortion practices, distribution of nonconsensual intimate images and nonconsensual synthetic images.[98] The organization was founded by Dr. Holly Jacobs after she was victimized with images "posted online and distributed without her consent to her employer, her peers, her friends, her family members, and to

---

[95] *See* Asia A. Eaton et al., 2017 *Nationwide Online Study of Nonconsensual Porn Victimization and Perpetration*, CYBER C.R. INITIATIVE 12 (June 2017), https://www.cybercivilrights.org/wp-content/uploads/2017/06/CCRI-2017-Research-Report.pdf.

[96] *See* Edvinas Meskys, Julija Kalpokiene, Paul Jurcys and Aidas Liaudanskas, *Regulating Deep Fakes: Legal and Ethical Considerations*, 15 J. IP L. & PRACTICE 24 (2020); Citron, *supra* ch. 2 note 161.

[97] Citron, *supra* ch. 2 note 161, at 1908.

[98] *See* CYBER CIVIL RIGHTS INITIATIVE, https://cybercivilrights.org/ (last visited July 4, 2024).

strangers online."[99] In 2013, Dr. Mary Anne Franks developed model legislation to address nonconsensual pornography and related privacy harms. Despite the availability of model laws, states vary considerably on the extent to which synthetic media depicting actual individuals are included in the anti-distribution laws.

In addition to nonconsensual distribution of intimate content, synthetic content can be created through chatbots and interactive videos to commit other forms of crimes. A 2024 Hong Kong scam made national headlines. "A finance worker at a multinational firm was tricked into paying out $25 million to fraudsters using deepfake technology to pose as the company's chief financial officer in a video conference call. . . ."[100] The video call was created using "deepfake recreations," according to Hong Kong police.[101]

A much more systematic fraud perpetrated by Ashley Madison, a predatory website that encouraged participants with the slogan "Life is short. Have an affair." Rather than selling connections, the site primarily sold men AI and staff-generated chats that only pretended to be real

---

99 *History*, CYBER CIVIL RIGHTS INITIATIVE, https://cybercivilrights.org/about/ (last visited Feb. 16, 2025).

100 Heather Chen and Kathleen Magramo, *Finance Worker Pays Out $25 Million After Video Call with Deepfake 'Chief Financial Officer'*, CNN (Feb. 4, 2024), https://www.cnn.com/2024/02/04/asia/deepfake-cfo-scam-hong-kong-intl-hnk/index.html.

101 *Id.*

women.[102] In both these examples, existing state laws regulating fraud would apply.

For regulators, however, laws regulating fraud are insufficient and ineffective. Instead, legislators seek better consumer protection to discourage the misuse of chatbots and synthetic content.

In 2019, California adopted the Bolstering Online Transparency Act (B.O.T. Act).[103] The law is intended to require more disclosure of the use of AI so that users of an interactive service understand they are not actually interacting with real people. The law is geared towards the types of abuse perpetrated at Ashley Madison.[104] California approved a law regulating bots in 2018,[105] and the California Consumer Privacy Agency (CCPA) has begun the process of promulgating regulations for automated decision-making technologies.[106]

---

102 Annalee Newitz, *What Everyone Gets Wrong about the 2015 Ashley Madison Scandal*, NEWSCIENTIST (June 12, 2024), https://www.newscientist.com/article/mg26234952-100-what-everyone-gets-wrong-about-the-2015-ashley-madison-scandal/.

103 Bolstering Online Transparency Act, Cal. Code BPC § 17940 et seq. (2024).

104 *See, e.g.*, David Z. Morris, *Ashley Madison Used Chatbots to Lure Cheaters, Then Threatened to Expose Them When They Complained*, FORTUNE (July 10, 2016), https://fortune.com/2016/07/10/ashley-madison-chatbots/; Cory P, *Exposing Scam Dating Apps: Ashley Madison*, KLICKME, https://www.klickme.co.uk/dating-tips/exposing-scam-dating-apps-ashley-madison (last visited Feb. 16, 2025).

105 Cal. Bus. & Prof. Code § 17940 (2023).

106 DRAFT AUTOMATED DECISIONMAKING TECHNOLOGY REGULATIONS (Dec. 2023), https://cppa.ca.gov/meetings/materials/20231208_item2_draft.pdf.

Utah has enacted the Utah Artificial Intelligence Policy Act in 2024 as well.[107] Like California, the purpose is to require disclosure of the use of generative AI, but it also clarifies that both developers of AI systems and parties deploying these systems are responsible for the output of those systems when the output violates various consumer protection laws.[108]

Colorado also included the regulation of AI chatbots. The Colorado AI Act requires deployers of AI systems to "ensure the disclosure to each consumer who interacts with the artificial intelligence system that the consumer is interacting with an artificial intelligence system"[109] unless "it would be obvious to a reasonable person that the person is interacting with an artificial intelligence system."[110]

§ 3.3.2.2 Publicity Rights Violations Using Deepfakes

For the entertainment industry, one concern is the ease with which synthetic media can create look-alikes and sound-alikes that will become low-cost replacements for artists within the music, film, and videogame industries. Although unfair competition law under the Lanham Act provides some degree of legal protection, those claims are substantially

---

107 Artificial Intelligence Policy Act, S.B. 149 (Mar. 13, 2024), https://le.utah.gov/~2024/bills/static/SB0149.html.

108 *Id. See* Utah Code § 13–2–1 (2024).

109 COLO. REV. STAT. § 6–1–1704.

110 *Id.*

different and harder to establish than rights of publicity claims involving state laws.[111] High profile examples of artists being reproduced or closely mimicked include the voice of Scarlett Johansen for the launch of the "Sky" service by OpenAI,[112] unauthorized musical tracks using AI replication of Drake and The Weeknd,[113] and even the voice of dead celebrity chef Anthony Bourdain.[114] "[T]he team behind *Roadrunner*, a documentary about the late Anthony Bourdain, used AI to clone his voice and have it read an email he had written."[115]

Against this backdrop, Tennessee—the home of country music along with bluegrass, blues, indie rock and a mix of genres—took steps to protect the creative livelihood of its core industry. In March 2024, Tennessee adopted the ELVIS Act (Ensuring Likeness Voice and Image Security Act), replacing

---

111 *See, e.g.*, Brown v. Electronic Arts, Inc., 724 F.3d 1235 (2013). *See also* Waits v. Frito-Lay, Inc., 978 F.2d 1093 (9th Cir. 1992); Midler v. Ford Motor Co., 849 F.2d 460 (9th Cir. 1988).

112 Bobby Allyn, *Voice Analysis Shows Striking Similarity Between Scarlett Johansson and ChatGPT*, NPR (May 31, 2024), https://www.npr.org/2024/05/31/g-s1-2263/voice-lab-analysis-striking-similarity-scarlett-johansson-chatgpt-sky-openai; *How the Voices for ChatGPT were Chosen*, OPENAI (May 19, 2024), https://openai.com/index/how-the-voices-for-chatgpt-were-chosen/.

113 Daysia Tolentino, *Viral AI-Powered Drake and The Weeknd Song is Removed From Streaming Services*, NBC NEWS (April 18, 2023), https://www.nbcnews.com/pop-culture/viral-ai-powered-drake-weeknd-song-removed-streaming-services-rcna80098.

114 Amanda Hoover, *Voice Actors Are Bracing to Compete With Talking AI*, WIRED (Oct. 3, 2023), https://www.wired.com/story/ai-voice-actors-jobs-threat/.

115 *Id.*

the state's Personal Rights Protection Act of 1984.[116] "Described as 'first-of-its-kind legislation,' the ELVIS Act prohibits people from using AI to mimic a person's voice without their permission, and violations can be criminally enforced as Class A misdemeanors. The law also authorizes civil action against any person who violates this law."[117]

The law covers both direct reproductions and simulations. " 'Voice' means a sound in a medium that is readily identifiable and attributable to a particular individual, regardless of whether the sound contains the actual voice or a simulation of the voice of the individual."[118] The law extends a property right to a person's voice in addition to the person's name, photograph, and likeness.[119] Tennessee offers a post mortem right for ten years following the life of the individual.[120]

The law provides civil liability for look-alikes and sound-alikes. "A person is liable to a civil action if the person publishes, performs, distributes, transmits, or otherwise makes available to the public an individual's voice or likeness, with knowledge that use of the voice or likeness was not authorized by the

---

116 TENN. CODE ANN. §§ 47–1–101—47–50–121 (2024) (ELVIS Act).

117 *Artificial Intelligence and Copyrights: Tennessee's ELVIS Act Becomes Law*, ARMSTRONG TEASDALE (Mar. 27, 2024), https://www.armstrongteasdale.com/thought-leadership/artificial-intelligence-and-copyrights-tennessees-elvis-act-becomes-law/.

118 TENN CODE ANN. § 47–25–1102.

119 *Id.* at § 47–25–1103.

120 *Id.* at § 47–25–1104.

individual."[121] This is broader than traditional publicity rights because the provision is not restricted to commercial purposes. To address this, the law includes statutory First Amendment and Fair Use exemptions.[122]

The law does not use the language of developers and deployers. Instead, it creates liability for those who publish unauthorized content and for those that create the tools to do so.

> A person is liable to a civil action if the person distributes, transmits, or otherwise makes available an algorithm, software, tool, or other technology, service, or device, the primary purpose or function of such algorithm, software, tool, or other technology, service, or device is the production of a particular, identifiable individual's photograph, voice, or likeness, with knowledge that distributing, transmitting, or otherwise making available the photograph, voice, or likeness was not authorized by the individual. . .[123]

As written, this provision could be interpreted so broadly that it could create civil liability for scanners, photocopiers, and cassette decks. If the law is really intended to stop systems that recreate unauthorized works, the law should have also provided an

---

[121] *Id.* at § 47–25–1105(2).

[122] *Id.* at § 47–25–1107.

[123] *Id.* at § 47–25–1105(3).

exception for substantial noninfringing uses.[124] Alternatively, the law could be exceptionally narrow and only be applicable when the vendor builds an entire system to "produc[e] a particular, identifiable individual's photograph, voice, or likeness" without authorization and no other. Courts have not yet begun to interpret the new statute so it will be some time before the true scope of the law is known. Nonetheless, the law creates a new level of protection for performers, which if successful will likely be adopted in other states with strong creative industries.

§ 3.3.2.3 Algorithmic Bias Mitigation Requirements

In 2019, Illinois adopted the Video Interview Act,[125] which provides that employers may not apply AI analysis to employment interviews without notice to the candidate and informed consent to the use of the technology.[126] The law also provides privacy protection by restricting the distribution of the applicant's videos, to "persons whose expertise or technology is necessary in order to evaluate an applicant's fitness for a position."[127] Although the law was geared toward algorithmic decisions, it did not substantively address the actual decisions made by these systems.

---

[124] *See* Sony Corp. of America v. Universal City Studios, Inc., 464 U.S. 417 (1984).

[125] Ill. Pub. L. 101–0260 (2018).

[126] *Id.*

[127] *Id.* at § 10.

On May 17, 2024, Colorado became the first state to enact legislation to address algorithmic bias.[128] The statute defines obligations both for "Developers" of AI systems and "Deployers" of those systems.[129] The definitions for developer and deployer, in turn, are limited to high-risk artificial intelligence systems, defined as "any artificial intelligence system that, when deployed, makes, or is a substantial factor in making, a consequential decision."[130]

> "Consequential decision" means a decision that has a material legal or similarly significant effect on the provision or denial to any consumer of, or the cost or terms of:
>
> (a) education enrollment or an education opportunity;
>
> (b) employment or an employment opportunity;
>
> (c) a financial or lending service;
>
> (d) an essential government service;
>
> (e) health-care services;
>
> (f) housing;
>
> (g) insurance; or
>
> (h) a legal service.[131]

---

128 COLO. REV. STAT. § 6–1–1301 (2024).

129 *See id.* at § 6–1–1701(6)–(7).

130 *Id.* at § 6–1–1701(6).

131 *Id.* at § 6–1–1701(3).

High risk systems, in turn, are prohibited from engaging in "algorithmic discrimination."

> "Algorithmic Discrimination" means any condition in which the use of an artificial intelligence system results in an unlawful differential treatment or impact that disfavors an individual or group of individuals on the basis of their actual or perceived age, color, disability, ethnicity, genetic information, limited proficiency in the English language, national origin, race, religion, reproductive health, sex, veteran status, or other classification protected under the laws of this state or federal law.[132]

The Colorado law also borrows the regulatory approach that separates high-risk activities for additional regulation in the EU Artificial Intelligence Act.[133] That act "takes a risk-based approach to regulation, applying different rules to AI systems according to the threats they pose to human health, safety, and rights."[134]

The central provision of the law offers a deceptively simple formula for this protection. "[A] developer of a high-risk artificial intelligence system shall use reasonable care to protect consumers from

---

[132] *Id.* at § 6–1–1701(1)(a).

[133] *See* Stacey Chuvaieva, *Colorado Adopts Comprehensive AI Act Imposing Broad Disclosure Requirements*, MITCHELL SILBERBERG & KNUPP LLP (May 22, 2024), https://www.msk.com/newsroom-alerts-colorado-ai-act.

[134] Matt Kosinski, *What is the European Union Artificial Intelligence Act (EU AI Act)?*, IBM (April 8, 2024), https://www.ibm.com/topics/eu-ai-act.

any known or reasonably foreseeable risks of algorithmic discrimination arising from the intended and contracted uses of the high-risk artificial intelligence system."[135] The state then provides a rebuttable presumption that the developer of the high-risk artificial intelligence system has used reasonable care if the developer follows the steps of the safe harbor provisions of the statute and any applicable regulations.[136]

To earn the presumption of reasonableness, a developer must provide to the deployers a long list of disclosures, including a "general statement describing the reasonably foreseeable uses and known harmful or inappropriate uses of the high-risk artificial intelligence system"; summary descriptions of the training data; documentation of foreseeable known harms; intended benefits of the system; evidence of the system's evaluation prior to deployment; data governance procedures; harm mitigation steps; instructions to limit harmful uses of the system; and more.[137]

In addition to the required documentation that the developer must provide to the deployer of the high-risk artificial intelligence system, the developer also must provide the public with a disclosure document that identifies "the types of high-risk artificial intelligence system that the Developer has developed or . . . modified . . ." and "how the Developer manages

[135] COLO. REV. STAT. § 6–1–1702.

[136] *Id.*

[137] *Id.* at § 6–1–1702(2).

known or reasonably foreseeable risks of algorithmic discrimination that may arise" from those systems.[138]

Deployers of high-risk artificial intelligence systems must also act with reasonable care and can benefit from a presumption of reasonable care if they meet the safe harbor requirements.[139] To do so, deployers must adopt the NIST "Artificial Intelligence Risk Management Framework"[140] or its equivalent; comply with any Colorado compliance requirements that are promulgated; complete an assessment or impact statement within the first 90 days of initial deployment; and update the impact statement annually.[141]

Deployers have additional duties to individuals to notify an individual if the system makes a consequential decision concerning that individual and offer a process to appeal that decision.[142] The statute incorporates data protection safeguards that enable an individual to correct personal data used to make a consequential decision.[143]

By establishing a duty of reasonable care when deploying high-risk artificial intelligence systems, Colorado sends a clear message to businesses that they have an affirmative duty to understand the tools they use and to identify potential harms before

---

138 *Id.*

139 *Id.* at § 6–1–1703.

140 ISO/IEC 42001

141 COLO. REV. STAT. § 6–1–1703.

142 *Id.* at 6–1–1703(4)(C)(II)–(III).

143 *Id.*

deploying these systems. The opportunity, however, to comply with the disclosure requirements is both onerous and vague. Clarifying regulations will be essential to enable companies to meet the requirements.

Although the law includes wide-ranging prescriptive requirements, there is no benefit to compliance other than to achieve a presumption of reasonable care. As a result, this early attempt to limit algorithmic bias in high-risk decision making is unlikely to have significant influence on business practices. It may, however, have a much larger impact on the evolution of similar laws across jurisdictions.

New York City has been undertaking a similar effort with a more modest scope. New York City's AI Bias Law was adopted in 2021 and became enforceable on July 5, 2023.[144] In theory, the law is stronger than that of Colorado because "The [l]aw prohibits employers and employment agencies from using an automated employment decision tool (AEDT) in New York City unless they ensure a bias audit was done and provide required notices."[145] The law is limited to postings for job locations in New

---

[144] New York City Local Law 144 of 2021; Christopher Stevens & Jenny Holmes, *Complying with New York City's Bias Audit Law*, NIXON PEABODY (Nov. 13, 2023), https://www.nixonpeabody.com/insights/alerts/2023/11/13/complying-with-new-york-city-bias-audit-law.

[145] *Automated Employment Decision Tools: Frequently Asked Questions*, NYC DEPT. CONSUMER AND WORKER PROTECTION (July 29, 2023), https://www.nyc.gov/assets/dca/downloads/pdf/about/DCWP-AEDT-FAQ.pdf.

York City at least part time, remote positions where the location assigned to the remote position is New York City, and employment agencies if either the agency is in New York City or the posted job is in New York City.[146]

However, a survey of employers in the first half year following enforcement found that only 18 of 391 employers conducted the required audit.[147] Most companies are making their own determination that the law does not apply. They are able to do so because the AEDT definition is open to broad interpretation, applying only when the system is used "to substantially assist or replace discretionary decision making." Definitions provide that phrase to mean:

i. to rely solely on a simplified output (score, tag, classification, ranking, etc.), with no other factors considered; or

ii. to use a simplified output as one of a set of criteria where the simplified output is weighted more than any other criterion in the set; or

iii. to use a simplified output to overrule conclusions derived from other factors including human decision-making.[148]

---

146 *Id.* at 2.

147 Lauren Weber, *New York City Passed an AI Hiring Law. So Far, Few Companies are Following it*, WALL ST. J. (Jan. 22, 2024), https://www.wsj.com/business/new-york-city-passed-an-ai-hiring-law-so-far-few-companies-are-following-it-7e31a5b7.

148 Rules of the City of New York § 5–300.

As enacted, nearly any human-in-the-loop is sufficient to sidestep the regulations.

In both the example of Colorado and New York City, it is likely that these early attempts at regulation will increase in reach and consequence as industry and regulators learn more about how to improve the ability to comply and the ability to confirm compliance. Regulation is an iterative process, and these early efforts will further the process even if they do not themselves result in significant initial compliance.

§ 3.3.2.4 Biometric Disclosure Requirements

Illinois leads the nation in disclosure requirements regarding the collection and use of biometric information.[149] The Illinois Biometric Information Privacy Act (BIPA) was enacted in 2008 to require informed consent before a person or entity could collect a person's biometric information.[150] " 'Biometric information' means any information, regardless of how it is captured, converted, stored, or shared, based on an individual's biometric identifier used to identify an individual. . . "Confidential and sensitive information" means personal information that can be used to uniquely identify an individual or an individual's account or property."[151]

[149] *See* Woodrow Hartzog, *BIPA: The Most Important Biometric Privacy Law in the US?*, 96 in AMBA KAK, ED., REGULATING BIOMETRICS: GLOBAL APPROACHES AND URGENT QUESTIONS (2020) https://ssrn.com/abstract=3722053.

[150] 740 Ill. Comp. Stat. Ann. 14/15.

[151] *Id.* at § 10.

The law is deceptively simple. "No private entity may collect, capture, purchase, receive through trade, or otherwise obtain a person's or a customer's biometric identifier or biometric information, unless" it informs the subject in writing of the collection and use; explains the purpose and length of retention; and receives a written release from the person or the person's representative.[152] Most importantly, the Illinois legislature provided for both statutory damages and a private cause of action. "[A]n individual need not allege some actual injury or adverse effect, beyond violation of his or her rights under the Act, in order to qualify as an 'aggrieved' person and be entitled to seek liquidated damages and injunctive relief pursuant to the Act."[153] Moreover, under the statute, " '[a] party violates Section 15(b) when it collects, captures, or otherwise obtains a person's biometric information without prior informed consent. This is true the first time an entity scans a fingerprint or otherwise collects biometric information, but it is no less true with each subsequent scan or collection.' "[154]

Taken together, the Illinois Supreme Court interpretations of the statute make it extremely easy for a party to establish an injury sufficient to bring a claim. New claims accrue with every use of a biometric scan conducted without written consent

---

[152] *Id.* at § 15 (b).

[153] Rosenbach v. Six Flags Ent. Corp., 129 N.E.3d 1197, 1207 (Ill. 2019).

[154] Cothron v. White Castle System, Inc., 216 N.E.3d 918, 924–25 (Ill. 2023), quoting Cothron v. White Castle System, Inc., 477 F. Supp. 3d 723, 732 (N.D. Ill. 2020).

and the liquidated damages provide standing to each person scanned.

Texas was the second state with a law similar to BIPA, but it does not include the private right of action. Nonetheless, under Texas' Capture or Use of Biometric Identifier Act (CUBI), Texas forced a $1.4 billion settlement with Meta in July 2024 for alleged violations of the law.

As of 2024, Colorado, Delaware, Illinois, Nebraska, Oklahoma, Minnesota, Missouri, Texas, Tennessee, New York, Vermont, and Washington all have biometric laws.[155] Many other jurisdictions are looking to expand their laws to require some form of disclosure. States have not yet moved to restriction the collection of this data, but since collection is restricted under European law, that regulatory strategy could move to the U.S. over time.

§ 3.3.2.5 Additional State Initiatives

Although not specifically AI, at least twenty states have restrictions on the use or misuse of consumer data that can provide at least some consumer protection regarding the use of that data by AI systems.[156] These states also have laws geared

---

155 *Tracking U.S. State Biometric Privacy Legislation*, HUSCH BLACKWELL, https://www.huschblackwell.com/2024-state-biometric-privacy-law-tracker (last visited Feb. 16, 2025); *U.S. State Privacy Legislation Tracker*, BLOOMBERG LAW (Feb. 2025), https://pro.bloomberglaw.com/insights/privacy/state-privacy-legislation-tracker/.

156 U.S. State Privacy Legislation Tracker, supra note 155.

towards some level of accountability for the data or AI systems used by enterprises in their states.[157]

Finally, a number of states are emphasizing collaborations with other states, working groups, task forces, and advisory councils designed to foster cooperation among states, consumer protection, and innovation.[158] Given the challenges facing federal regulation, it is likely that these efforts will continue to expand each year.

§ 3.4 EUROPEAN UNION (EU)

Europe has moved to be the most aggressive regulator of the global digital economy. Europe's system of governance has also evolved considerably since it was formed with the Maastricht Treaty in 1992. The modern structure was adopted in 2007 under the Lisbon Treaty. The United Kingdom, a founding member, left the EU in 2019. There are presently 27 member countries.

§ 3.4.1 EU BRANCHES OF GOVERNMENT

The EU has entities in each of the executive, legislative, and judicial branches of government as well as the European Central Bank.[159] The executive

---

157 *See* Rachel Wright, Artificial Intelligence in the States: Emerging Legislation, Council of State Governments (Dec. 6, 2023), https://www.csg.org/2023/12/06/artificial-intelligence-in-the-states-emerging-legislation/.

158 *Id.*

159 *See* James McBride, *How Does the European Union Work?*, COUNCIL ON FOREIGN RELATIONS (Mar. 11, 2022), https://www.cfr.org/backgrounder/how-does-european-union-work.

branch is comprised of the European Council and the European Commission. The European Commission operates to propose and implement legislation, operating as the executive branch of the European Union (EU). The European Council is the body of the 27 member states' head of state, along with the president of the European Council and the president of the European Commission. It works closely with the European Commission, setting high-level legislative agendas.

The legislative function is embodied in the directly elected European Parliament and the Council of the European Union. The Council of the European Union is comprised of national ministers from each EU member state. "[T]he Council of the EU takes decisions on European laws jointly with the European Parliament."[160] This may be considered roughly comparable to the bicameral legislative process in the United States, United Kingdom and other countries.

"In principle, the Commission proposes new laws, and the Parliament and Council of the European Union adopt them. The member countries then implement them, and the Commission ensures that the laws are properly applied."[161] "The European Commission presents legislative proposals which are considered by both the European Parliament and the

[160] *Types of Institutions and Bodies*, EUROPEAN UNION, https://european-union.europa.eu/institutions-law-budget/institutions-and-bodies/types-institutions-and-bodies_en (last visited Feb. 16, 2025).

[161] *Id.*

Council of the European Union. . . . Before an EU law can come into force, the Parliament and the Council must agree on any possible amendments to the legislative texts."[162] The law goes from the Commission to the Parliament. If passed it is sent to the Council of the European Union. The Council may adopt the legislation, amend the proposal and return it to the Parliament, or reject the legislation.[163] Once adopted, the duty of implementation returns to the European Commission, as the executive branch of the government.

The judicial branch of the EU is overseen by the Court of Justice of the European Union (CJEU), which has two branches, the General Court and the Court of Justice. Each member state also retains its own judicial system. CJEU "interprets EU law to make sure it is applied in the same way in all EU countries, and settles legal disputes between national governments and EU institutions."[164] In certain situations, individuals and private entities may also bring claims.

---

[162] *How an EU Law is Made*, SVERIGES RIKSDAG, https://www.riksdagen.se/en/how-the-riksdag-works/how-the-eu-works/how-an-eu-law-is-made/ (last visited Feb. 16, 2025).

[163] *Id.*

[164] Court of Justice of the European Union (CJEU), EUR. UNION, https://european-union.europa.eu/institutions-law-budget/institutions-and-bodies/search-all-eu-institutions-and-bodies/court-justice-european-union-cjeu_en (last visited Feb. 16, 2025).

§ 3.4.2 LAW LEADING UP TO THE EU AI ACT: GDPR, DMA, AND DSA

The EU has become a global leader in the regulation of technology, beginning with its adoption of the General Data Protection Regulation (GDPR).[165] The EU had regulated access to personal information as early as 1995, with various European states having data protection measure dating back much further.[166] The GDPR emphasized notice and consent requirements for use of a data subject's personal information, increased the amount and clarity of information necessary before consent could be obtained, and the ability to withdraw consent at any time.[167]

The operation of the GDPR is quite complex, however, the basic principles listed in Article 5 provide an excellent framework for the directive:

Article 5. Principles Relating to Processing of Personal Data

1. Personal data shall be:

(a) processed lawfully, fairly and in a transparent manner in relation to the

---

[165] Regulation (EU) 2016/679 of the European Parliament and of the Council of 27 April 2016 on the protection of natural persons with regard to the processing of personal data and on the free movement of such data, and repealing Directive 95/46/EC (General Data Protection Regulation), 2016 O.J. (L 119), 1.

[166] *See* DOUWE KORFF, AND MARIE GEORGES, THE DATA PROTECTION OFFICER HANDBOOK 15–17 (2019). https://ssrn.com/abstract=3428957.

[167] Regulation (EU) 2016/679 arts. 6–7.

data subject ('lawfulness, fairness and transparency');

(b) collected for specified, explicit and legitimate purposes and not further processed in a manner that is incompatible with those purposes; further processing for archiving purposes in the public interest, scientific or historical research purposes or statistical purposes shall, in accordance with Article 89(1), not be considered to be incompatible with the initial purposes ('purpose limitation');

(c) adequate, relevant and limited to what is necessary in relation to the purposes for which they are processed ('data minimisation');

(d) accurate and, where necessary, kept up to date; every reasonable step must be taken to ensure that personal data that are inaccurate, having regard to the purposes for which they are processed, are erased or rectified without delay ('accuracy');

(e) kept in a form which permits identification of data subjects for no longer than is necessary for the purposes for which the personal data are processed; personal data may be stored for longer periods insofar as the personal data will be processed solely for archiving purposes in the public interest, scientific or historical research purposes or statistical purposes in accordance with Article 89(1) subject to implementation of the appropriate technical and organisational measures required by this Regulation in order to safeguard the rights and freedoms of the data subject ('storage limitation');

(f) processed in a manner that ensures appropriate security of the personal data, including protection against unauthorised or unlawful processing and against accidental loss, destruction or damage, using appropriate technical or organisational measures ('integrity and confidentiality').

2. The controller shall be responsible for, and be able to demonstrate compliance with, paragraph 1 ('accountability').[168]

Because the data protection extends to data collected about the data subjects wherever the data exists, the GDPR took on a significant extraterritorial role, reaching into U.S. operations of international retailers, employers, and educators. As a result, the GDPR model expanded its legal and philosophical model to much of the world.

The success of the GDPR and the growth of the data-driven tech industry led the EU to develop an

---

[168] Regulation (EU) 2016/679 art. 5.

even more pervasive approach to data regulation, shifting from the data itself to the major corporations that controlled digital transactions. In March 2021, the European Commission adopted the "2030 Digital Compass: the European Way for the Digital Decade."[169] Shortly thereafter, in 2022, the EU adopted the European Declaration on Digital Rights and Principles for a Digital Decade.[170] The declaration "provides a vision and concrete commitments for how rights and freedoms enshrined in the EU's legal framework, as well as European values, translate into a digitally transformed world."[171]

These efforts led to a series of three independent but highly connected directives, the Digital Markets Act (DMA),[172] the Digital Services Act (DSA),[173] and

---

[169] COM/2021/118, COMMUNICATION FROM THE COMMISSION TO THE EUROPEAN PARLIAMENT, THE COUNCIL, THE EUROPEAN ECONOMIC AND SOCIAL COMMITTEE AND THE COMMITTEE OF THE REGIONS, 2030 DIGITAL COMPASS: THE EUROPEAN WAY FOR THE DIGITAL DECADE, https://eur-lex.europa.eu/legal-content/en/TXT/?uri=CELEX%3A52021DC0118.

[170] EUROPEAN DECLARATION ON DIGITAL RIGHTS AND PRINCIPLES, EUROPEAN COMM'N (Dec. 15, 2022), https://digital-strategy.ec.europa.eu/en/library/european-declaration-digital-rights-and-principles.

[171] *Id.* at Annex 4.

[172] Regulation (EU) 2022/1925 of the European Parliament and of the Council of 14 September 2022 on Contestable and Fair Markets in the Digital Sector and Amending Directives (EU) 2019/1937 and (EU) 2020/1828 (Digital Markets Act), 2022 O.J. (L 265), 1.

[173] REGULATION (EU) 2022/2065 OF THE EUROPEAN PARLIAMENT AND OF THE COUNCIL OF 19 OCTOBER 2022 ON A SINGLE MARKET FOR DIGITAL SERVICES and amending Directive

the Artificial Intelligence Act (EU AI Act). Each build on the GDPR and the European Digital Decade to regulate global enterprises doing business in Europe. Through this strategy, The EU secures a place at the table that was previously controlled by the nations home to multinational corporations out of the U.S., China, and South Korea and the multinationals themselves.

The DMA focuses on the largest tech companies that serve as "gatekeepers" to digital services throughout the EU. The gatekeepers have the ability to control prices, reduce competition, and set standards, so the DMA limits the gatekeepers' authority. "On 5 September 2023, the [European] Commission designated Alphabet, Amazon, Apple, ByteDance, Meta and Microsoft as gatekeepers of altogether 22 Core Platform Services (CPS) . . . and adopted a decision not to designate Samsung as a gatekeeper for its web browser."[174]

- Social Network
  - TikTok
  - Facebook
  - Instagram

2000/31/EC (Digital Services Act (DSA)), https://eur-lex.europa.eu/legal-content/EN/TXT/?uri=celex%3A32022R2065.

[174] *Report from the Commission to the Council and the European Parliament*, at 2, COM(2024) 106/Mar. 6, 2024), https://digital-markets-act.ec.europa.eu/document/download/a7463f7c-02b4-4588-bc03-9e65c11e8086_en?filename=COM_2024_106_1_EN_ACT_part1_v4.pdf.

  - LinkedIn
- Intermediation
  - Google Maps
  - Google Play
  - Google Shopping
  - Amazon Marketplace
  - [Apple] App Store
  - Meta Marketplace
- Ads
  - Google
  - Amazon
  - Meta
- N-IICS [Messaging]
  - WhatsApp
  - Messenger
- Video Sharing
  - YouTube
- Search
  - Google Search
- Browser
  - Chrome
  - Safari

- Operating System
  - Google Android
  - [Apple] iOS
  - Windows PC OS[175]

No European company has been designated as a gatekeeper.

The law creates a form of antitrust regulation that is prospective in nature. Unlike traditional Sherman Act remedies, the DMA creates a different rulebook for the designated dominant online services. Broadly speaking, the gatekeepers are treated a bit like "common carriers," that require all the other companies using the gatekeepers' services to operate on an even playing field. Gatekeepers cannot prioritize their own goods or services over those of their vendor-customers or use their platform status to give themselves an unfair advantage by tying one product to another.

Gatekeepers must allow greater interoperability with third party goods and services. The gatekeepers must not interfere with their customers' ability to utilize business data generated by that company. The gatekeepers must also allow vendor-customers the ability to let the vendors' customers pay directly rather than through app stores (or other intermediation) that provide a substantial commission to Apple, Google, Amazon, or Meta.[176]

---

[175] *Id.* at 2.

[176] *See Digital Markets Act—Overview*, HERBERT SMITH FREEHILLS (Mar. 13, 2024), https://www.herbertsmithfreehills.

The DMA also restricts targeted advertising by limiting tracking to situations where "effective consent" has been granted.[177]

In contrast to the DMA, which is a fair trade and free competition law, the DSA is a consumer protection law. The DSA requires regulated online platforms to prevent illegal content, sales of goods, and provision of services. It affords consumers more control over their online information.[178] The DSA includes a designation for very large platforms and very large search engines, defined as those having more than 45 million European users each month. The very large platform designation reaches far more companies than the DMA's gatekeeper designation.

The DSA adds regulations regarding the notices provided to users, limits the power to require behavioral advertising targeting consumers, and requires the large platforms to engage in preventative steps to address illegal posting of content and restrict sales of counterfeit and illegal

---

com/notes/crt/2024-03/digital-markets-act-overview; *The Digital Markets Act: Ensuring Fair and Open Digital Markets*, EUR. COMM'N, https://commission.europa.eu/strategy-and-policy/priorities-2019-2024/europe-fit-digital-age/digital-markets-act-ensuring-fair-and-open-digital-markets_en (last visited Feb. 16, 2025) (punctuation modified).

177 The Digital Markets Act, *supra* note 174.

178 *See* Emma Roth, *The EU's Digital Services Act goes into Effect Today: Here's What That Means*, VERGE (Aug. 25, 2023), https://www.theverge.com/23845672/eu-digital-services-act-explained.

goods. It also requires that the large platform post transparency reports on their activities.[179]

The DSA "complements the DMA by creating obligations for providers of online intermediary services to reduce harms and counter risks online, introduces strong protections for individual's fundamental and consumer rights online, and places digital platforms under transparency and accountability framework."[180]

These laws are part of the EU's push for comprehensive digital regulation. In addition to the DSA, DMA and EU AI Act (discussed below), the EU's Digital Decade legislation also includes new regulations for intellectual property in the Digital Single Market Directive, expanded regulation of media in the Audiovisual Media services Directive and European Media Freedom Act, and enhanced criminal regulations through the Regulation on Child Sexual Abuse Material and the Regulation on Terrorist Content Online Act.[181]

§ 3.4.3 EU AI ACT

Harnessing the momentum of the EU's Digital Decade, on May 21, 2024 the EU adopted the

---

[179] *Id.*

[180] European Parliament, the Council and the Commission, European Declaration on Digital Rights and Principles, Annex 4, Dec. 15, 2022, O.J. (C 23) at 116.

[181] *See Legal Implications of the Digital Services Act*, DELOITTE, https://www2.deloitte.com/nl/nl/pages/legal/articles/legal-implications-of-the-digital-services-act.html (last visited Feb. 16, 2025).

Artificial Intelligence Act (EU AI Act).[182] According to the EU, "[t]he AI Act is the first-ever legal framework on AI, which addresses the risks of AI and positions Europe to play a leading role globally."[183] With the EU AI Act, Europe hopes to establish a "comprehensive legal framework on AI worldwide" for "foster[ing] trustworthy AI in Europe and beyond, by ensuring that AI systems respect fundamental rights, safety, and ethical principles and by addressing risks of very powerful and impactful AI models."[184] The EU AI Act recenters global AI policy discussions in Europe, creates authority over the developing AI gatekeepers such as OpenAI, Microsoft, Google, Apple, Amazon, ByteDance, and Tencent, slows development of AI outside of Europe to afford European enterprises an opportunity to catch up, and it also promotes fundamental rights

---

182 Hannah Ruschemeier & Jascha Bareis, *Searching for Harmonised rules: Understanding the Paradigms, Provisions and Pressing Issues in the Final EU AI Act* 2, In GSENGER/SEKWENZ (EDS), DIGITAL DECADE: HOW THE EU SHAPES DIGITALISATION RESEARCH, NOMOS 2025, (June 25, 2024), https://ssrn.com/abstract=4876206. *See* REGULATION (EU) 2024/1689 OF THE OF THE EUROPEAN PARLIAMENT AND OF THE COUNCIL LAYING DOWN HARMONISED RULES ON ARTIFICIAL INTELLIGENCE AND AMENDING REGULATIONS (EC) NO 300/2008, (EU) NO 167/2013, (EU) NO 168/2013, (EU) 2018/858, (EU) 2018/1139 AND (EU) 2019/2144 AND DIRECTIVES 2014/90/EU, (EU) 2016/797 AND (EU) 2020/1828 (AI Act), https://eur-lex.europa.eu/eli/reg/2024/1689/oj/eng.

183 *AI Act*, EUR. COMM'N, https://digital-strategy.ec.europa.eu/en/policies/regulatory-framework-ai (last visited Feb. 16, 2025).

184 *Id.*; *See also* Robert Jain, *The European Union's AI Act: What You Need to Know*, HOLLAND & KNIGHT (Mar. 15, 2024), https://www.hklaw.com/en/insights/publications/2024/03/the-european-unions-ai-act-what-you-need-to-know.

and limits the use of AI systems in high-risk situations.

The heart of the EU AI Act is the approach that classifies AI based on the risk it creates to the public. The law uses four categories, unacceptable risk, high risk, limited risk, and minimal risk. In a few instances, the use of AI is deemed too great a risk to be permitted. In other cases, risk is classified as high risk, limited risk, and minimal risk.

The regulations cover any person or entity that places an AI system in the EU market (i.e. developers) as well as the deployers of systems created by other parties. The developers are subject to the regulations if their system is deployed in the EU market even if the developer does not operate in the EU.

Article 5 of the EU AI Act lists the prohibitions on unacceptable risk:

The following types of AI system are 'Prohibited' according to the AI Act.

AI systems:

- **deploying subliminal, manipulative, or deceptive techniques** to distort behaviour and impair informed decision-making, causing significant harm.
- **exploiting vulnerabilities** related to age, disability, or socio-economic circumstances to distort behaviour, causing significant harm.

- **biometric categorisation systems** inferring sensitive attributes (race, political opinions, trade union membership, religious or philosophical beliefs, sex life, or sexual orientation), except labelling or filtering of lawfully acquired biometric datasets or when law enforcement categorises biometric data.
- **social scoring**, i.e., evaluating or classifying individuals or groups based on social behaviour or personal traits, causing detrimental or unfavourable treatment of those people.
- **assessing the risk of an individual committing criminal offenses** solely based on profiling or personality traits, except when used to augment human assessments based on objective, verifiable facts directly linked to criminal activity.
- **compiling facial recognition databases** by untargeted scraping of facial images from the internet or CCTV footage.
- **inferring emotions in workplaces or educational institutions**, except for medical or safety reasons.
- **'real-time' remote biometric identification (RBI) in publicly accessible spaces for law enforcement**, except when:

- searching for missing persons, abduction victims, and people who have been human trafficked or sexually exploited;
- preventing substantial and imminent threat to life, or foreseeable terrorist attack; or
- identifying suspects in serious crimes (*e.g.*, murder, rape, armed robbery, narcotic and illegal weapons trafficking, organised crime, and environmental crime, etc.).[185]

There are certain exemptions to the regulation. Research, development and prototyping activities that take place before an AI system is released on the market are not subject to these regulations. Additionally, AI systems that are exclusively designed for military, defense or national security purposes, are also exempt, regardless of the type of entity carrying out those activities.[186]

Systems will be classified as high-risk if they cover topics such as critical infrastructure, health care, education, migration, or law enforcement or if they could result in an infringement of a fundamental right.[187] "AI systems are always considered high-risk

---

[185] *High-level summary of the AI Act*, EU ARTIFICIAL INTELLIGENCE ACT (Feb. 27, 2024), https://artificialintelligenceact.eu/high-level-summary/. *See* EU AI Act Art. 5. *See also* Olga Kokoulina, *Towards Future-Proof, Rights-Respecting Automated Data Collection: An Examination of European Jurisprudence*, 26 VAND. J. ENT. & TECH. L. 707, 767 (2024).

[186] *See* Ruschemeier & Bareis, *supra* note 182, at 13; EU AI Act Art. 2 at § 3–4.

[187] Ruschemeier & Bareis, *supra* note 182, at 11.

if it profiles individuals, i.e. automated processing of personal data to assess various aspects of a person's life, such as work performance, economic situation, health, preferences, interests, reliability, behaviour, location or movement."[188]

High risk AI providers must:

- Establish a **risk management system** throughout the high risk AI system's lifecycle;
- Conduct **data governance**, ensuring that training, validation and testing datasets are relevant, sufficiently representative and, to the best extent possible, free of errors and complete according to the intended purpose.
- Draw up **technical documentation** to demonstrate compliance and provide authorities with the information to assess that compliance.
- Design their high risk AI system for **record-keeping** to enable it to automatically record events relevant for identifying national level risks and substantial modifications throughout the system's lifecycle.
- Provide **instructions for use** to downstream deployers to enable the latter's compliance.
- Design their high risk AI system to allow deployers to implement **human oversight**.

---

[188] *High-level summary of the AI Act*, *supra* note 185.

- Design their high risk AI system to achieve appropriate levels of **accuracy, robustness, and cybersecurity**.
- Establish a **quality management system** to ensure compliance.[189]

In addition to these requirements, there are additional regulations for general purpose AI systems such as LLMs and generative AI services. Developers offering general purpose AI systems must "provide technical documentation, instructions for use, comply with the Copyright Directive, and publish a summary about the content used for training."[190] The requirements have lower thresholds for open license systems, but they still must comply with the Copyright Directive and publish a summary of the training data. This lower threshold will not apply if the regulators identify the open license system as creating a "systemic risk."[191] Developers offering systems that do present systemic risks "must also conduct model evaluations, adversarial testing, track and report serious incidents and ensure cybersecurity protections."[192]

Even limited risk systems will have transparency and requirements. "For instance, when using AI systems such as chatbots, humans should be made aware that they are interacting with a machine so they can take an informed decision to continue or

---

[189] *Id.*

[190] *Id.*

[191] *Id.*

[192] *Id.*

step back. Providers will also have to ensure that AI-generated content is identifiable."[193] This will also be the case when synthetic media or deepfakes are used to present content or when the AI content is used to publish content on matters of public interest."[194]

The European Commission will establish an AI Office to monitor the effectiveness of the implementation and assess compliance with the regulations. The bans on unacceptable risk systems should go into effect in November 2024. General requirements will take effect in May 2025 with regulations for high-risk systems coming into effect beginning in May 2026.

"The AI Act establishes a two-tiered governance system, where national authorities are responsible for overseeing and enforcing rules for AI systems, while the EU level is responsible for governing general-purpose AI models."[195] EU Member States will be represented by an European Artificial Intelligence Board (AI Board) that will then include national regulators and other specialized subcommittees. The AI Act also contemplates standing advisory bodies, including Scientific Panel and a more generalized Advisory Forum.[196]

---

193 *AI Act*, EUROPEAN COMM'N, *supra* note 184.

194 *Id.*

195 Artificial Intelligence—Questions and Answers, EUR. COMM'N (Aug. 1, 2024), https://ec.europa.eu/commission/presscorner/detail/en/QANDA_21_1683.

196 *Id.*

"The AI Act will apply two years after entry into force on 2 August 2026,"[197] however, certain provisions have their own enforcement dates:

- The prohibitions, definitions and provisions related to AI literacy will apply 6 months after entry into force [which occurred] on 2 February 2025;
- The rules on governance and the obligations for general purpose AI become applicable 12 months after entry into force on 2 August 2025; [and]
- The obligations for high-risk AI systems that classify as high-risk because they are embedded in regulated products, listed in Annex II (list of Union harmonisation legislation), apply 36 months after entry into force on 2 August 2027.[198]

Google, Meta, and Apple have already been the subject of actions under the DMA. The European Commission has launched non-compliance investigations under the Digital Markets Act (DMA) into Alphabet, Apple, and Meta, focusing on potential breaches of their obligations as gatekeepers. The investigations target Alphabet's and Apple's app store steering rules, Alphabet's potential self-preferencing in Google search results, Apple's user choice obligations on iOS, and Meta's "pay or consent" data model. The Commission is also probing

---

[197] *Id.*

[198] *Id.*

Apple's fee structure for alternative app stores and Amazon's product ranking practices. These investigations aim to ensure these tech giants comply with DMA regulations, with potential fines and other remedies for violations.[199]

§ 3.5 CHINA

Despite claims regarding the EU AI Act, China first adopted regulations involving AI in 2021 as part of a strategy both to regulate AI development and foster its growth so that China could be the global leader in AI production and development.[200] Though not as comprehensive as the EU AI Act, many of the concerns and steps are quite similar. The first set of policies adopted in 2021 "imposed new obligations on companies to intervene in content recommendations, granted new rights to users being recommended content, and offered protections to gig workers subject to algorithmic scheduling."[201] Following the regulations on algorithmic decision making, China then added regulations requiring watermarking synthetic media and deepfakes to "ensure that

---

199 See EUR. COMM'N, *Commission Opens Non-Compliance Investigations Against Alphabet, Apple and Meta Under the Digital Markets Act*, Press Release IP/24/1689 (Mar. 25, 2024), https://ec.europa.eu/commission/presscorner/detail/en/ip_24_1689.

200 *See* Matt Sheehan, *Tracing the Roots of China's AI Regulations*, CARNEGIE ENDOWMENT FOR INT'L PEACE 1 (Feb. 2024), https://carnegieendowment.org/research/2024/02/tracing-the-roots-of-chinas-ai-regulations?lang=en.

201 *Id.*

content does not violate people's 'likeness rights' or harm the 'nation's image.' "[202]

China's complex political organization is beyond the scope of this summary. Nonetheless, it is important to remember that although the government is unicameral and any independence of the National People's Congress—the legislative body—is constrained by the Communist Party's authority over the candidates permitted to run for office, the Communist Party's control of the military, and the strong centralization of the party. Instead of debate within the National People's Congress, political tension occurs within and among the administrative ministries and between the central government and the strong regional governments. Even though all aspects of China's political system remain loyal to the Communist Party, there is a highly contentious relationship among competing governing bodies to assert authority and leadership.

In the area of AI, the Cyberspace Administration of China (CAC) has provided the greatest leadership and control in the development of policy and regulation on AI within China.[203] The CAC works with academic experts and experts in the Ministry of Science and Technology. The CAC provides information to the Politburo, which oversees the Communist Party and largely drafts the legislation

---

[202] *Id.*

[203] *See* Matt Sheehan, *China's AI Regulations and How They Get Made*, CARNEGIE ENDOWMENT FOR INT'L PEACE 22 (July 2023), https://carnegieendowment.org/research/2023/07/chinas-ai-regulations-and-how-they-get-made?lang=en.

that becomes adopted by the National People's Congress. While this is a significant oversimplification, it highlights the role played by the CAC and other ministries in both developing and implementing policy.

The algorithmic regulations were signed into law on December 31, 2021.[204]

> "Use of algorithmic recommendation technology" as used in the preceding paragraph refers to the use of algorithm technologies types such as generation and synthesis, individualized pushing, sequence refinement, search filtering, schedule decision-making, and so forth to provide users with information. . . .
>
> **Article 6:** Algorithmic recommendation service providers shall persist in being oriented towards mainstream values, optimize mechanisms for algorithmic recommendation services, actively transmit positive energy, and promote the uplifting use of algorithms. . . .
>
> **Article 7:** The providers of algorithmic recommendation services shall implement entity responsibility for algorithm security, establish and complete management systems and technical measures such as for checking algorithm mechanisms, technology ethics reviews, user registration, checking published

---

204 *Provisions on the Management of Algorithmic Recommendations in Internet Information Services*, CHINA LAW TRANSLATE (Jan. 4, 2022), https://www.chinalawtranslate.com/en/algorithms/.

information, data security, personal information protections, countering telecommunication network fraud, security assessments and monitoring, and emergency response and handling of security incidents; and draft and disclose the rules for algorithmic recommendation services, allotting professional staff and technical support corresponding to the scale of algorithmic recommendation services.

Article 8: The providers of algorithmic recommendation services shall periodically check, assess, and verify algorithm mechanisms, models, data, and outcomes, and must not set up algorithmic models that violate laws and regulations, or go against ethics and morals, such as by inducing users to become addicted or spend too much.

Article 9: The providers of algorithmic recommendation services shall strengthen the management of information security, establishing and completing a pool of characteristics used to identify illegal and negative content, and improve standards, rules, and procedures for inclusion in the pool. Where it is discovered that algorithmically generated or synthesized information is not conspicuously labeled, transmission may continue on after making a conspicuous label.

Where unlawful information is discovered, transmission shall be immediately stopped, and measures shall be employed to eliminate it or otherwise address it, stop the spread of the

> information, store relevant records, and report to the internet information departments and relevant departments. Where negative information is discovered, it shall be addressed in accordance with the relevant provisions on the management of the internet information content ecology.[205]

In addition to the restrictions on algorithmic output, the 2021 law also created protections for individual users. Members of the public were entitled to notice of algorithmic use, the ability to turn off output, to delete user tags, stop personalization of content regulations, limitations on price discrimination, and more.[206] For example, Article 17 provides that "[t]he providers of algorithmic recommendation services shall provide users with options not targeting their individual characteristics or provide users with convenient options to close algorithmic recommendation services. Where users select to close algorithmic recommendation services, the algorithmic recommendation service providers shall immediately stop providing those services.[207]

Unlike provisions in the US and EU, the Chinese regulations also include compliance obligations on algorithmic service providers that "that have public opinion properties or capacity for social

---

[205] *Id.*

[206] *See id.*; Sheehan, *Tracing the Roots of China's AI Regulations*, *supra* note 200, at 5.

[207] *Provisions on the Management of Algorithmic Recommendations in Internet Information Services*, *supra* note 204, at art. 17.

mobilization."[208] To the extent that the AI systems can generate public opinion, be used to motivate crowds, or serve as tools for influence, they are subject to mandatory screening steps and governmental review.[209] Providers must register with "the state and provincial, autonomous region, [and] directly governed municipality internet information departments," highlighting the multijurisdictional interest in these systems.[210] Finally, "[t]he providers of algorithmic recommendation services shall retain network logs in accordance with law, cooperate with the internet information, telecommunications, public security, and market supervision departments conducting security assessments and oversight inspections in accordance with law, and provide necessary technical and data support and assistance."[211] Also like the EU, the regulations establish a new algorithm registry.[212]

The 2021 regulations were supplemented shortly thereafter with additional protections for members of the public and with additional restrictions on fake news, deepfakes, and use of biometrics.[213] Perhaps ironically, much of the focus of limitations of social mobilization stemmed from the rise in popularity of

---

208 *Id.* art. 27

209 *Id.* arts. 27–30.

210 *Id.* art. 25

211 *Id.* art. 28

212 Sheehan, *Tracing the Roots of China's AI Regulations*, *supra* note 206, at 5 (算法备案系统).

213 *Id.* at 9.

Jinri Toutiao, a content aggregation and distribution site by TikTok parent ByteDance.[214] ByteDance founder Zhang Yiming stated in an interview that the algorithm dictated what content a person received rather than editorial decisions by the company. This approach raised alarms within the Communist Party that ByteDance could unleash unwanted and unpatriotic public sentiment. The government expected ByteDance to be compliant and established the AI regulations to guarantee that the tech sector remained under the control of the government.[215] "In 2018, China's media regulator shut down [a different] one of ByteDance's products—the joke app Neihan Duanzi—for "vulgar" content. The company's founder, Zhang Yiming, issued a self-effacing public apology for deviating from "socialist core values" and pledged to ensure that the CCP's "voices are emphatically broadcasted."[216] When they have become too powerful or pose a challenge to the ruling party, tech leaders have been threatened, abducted, and jailed. In a few cases, the corporate executives died while in custody.[217]

The combination of increasingly comprehensive regulations, aggressive administrative enforcement of the regulations, and the extra-legal pressure placed on tech companies means that the AI field in

---

214 *Id.* at 11–12.

215 *See id. See also* Yaqiu Wang, *The Problem with TikTok's Claim of Independence from Beijing*, HUMAN RIGHTS WATCH (Mar. 24, 2023), https://www.hrw.org/news/2023/03/24/problem-tiktoks-claim-independence-beijing.

216 Wang, *supra* note 215.

217 *Id.*

China is under the highest level of regulatory scrutiny anywhere in the world. Chinese authorities are supporting robust, state-of-the art AI development while at the same time looking very carefully on how it is unleashed and used for content and decision making involving the general public.

China and its Chinese industrial partners may also be competing on innovation as well as regulation. In January 2025, DeepSeek released an open-source LLM named DeepSeek R1, which has been reported to rival ChatGPT at a fraction of its development cost and without the most sophisticated computer technology. Other models include the DeepSeek-V3, its most competitive and sophisticated model to date. Skeptics, however, point to many questions surrounding the DeepSeek claims. Among the issues is that DeepSeek's founder may have stockpiled Nvidia chips prior to the export ban, allegations that the training models and data may have been copied without authorization from OpenAI and other U.S. companies, and questions about the actual accuracy of the system. For U.S. adopters, there are also questions regarding the embedded Chinese censorship and concomitant lack of Western guardrails, meaning that the content which is taboo for the output may be far different than the output that should be taboo where the user is located.[218]

---

[218] *See* DeepSeek, https://www.deepseek.com/ (last visited Feb. 16, 2025); David Goldman & Matt Egan, *A Shocking Chinese AI Advancement Called DeepSeek is Sending US Stocks Plunging*, CNN (Jan. 27, 2025), https://www.cnn.com/2025/01/27/tech/deepseek-stocks-ai-china/index.html; Kelly Ng, Brandon Drenon, Tom Gerken & Marc Cieslak, *DeepSeek: The Chinese AI app that*

Even if DeepSeek itself is not the ultimate game changer in LLM development and deployment, it highlights the tenuous basis for the current U.S. investment strategies. Consistent with Moore's Law, the capacity of LLMs will continue to grow and the hardware will likely become less expensive over time, making early investments seem unrealistic when viewed in hindsight. For China, a disruptive deployment strategy of low cost, high impact AI systems could serve to undermine the U.S. investment strategy, mirroring the consumer goods trade policies that grew the Chinese economy and the U.S. trade deficit.

§ 3.6 ADDITIONAL GLOBAL TRENDS

Although the U.S. and China lead on AI development and the EU has promoted the most expansive and comprehensive set of AI regulations, the rest of the world is also paying close attention to AI developments.

§ 3.6.1 UNITED KINGDOM

The UK (comprised of Northern Ireland and Great Britain's England, Scotland, and Wales) is not governed by the EU AI Act because it left the EU in 2020. Although politically, the UK wants to stay part of the leadership on AI, the lack of major AI

---

has the world talking, BBC (Feb. 4, 2025), https://www.bbc.com/news/articles/c5yv5976z9po; *Feroot Security Research Reveals DeepSeek AI's Hidden Data Pipeline to China*, FEROOT (Feb. 5, 2025), https://www.feroot.com/blog/feroot-security-research-reveals-deepseek-ais-hidden-data-pipeline-to-china/.

industries and the modest size of the economy makes the UK efforts less impactful than had it remained at the table within the EU.

The EU government has provided funding to promote AI talent, published a white paper proposing a technology-friendly approach to AI development, and held significant high level meetings on AI regulation.[219] Although the UK hosted international summits on AI, these resulted in no definitive agreements at the international level.[220] The events did not even further domestic legislation. The summits merely produced provocative rhetoric:

> Following are UN Secretary-General António Guterres' remarks to the Artificial Intelligence (AI) Seoul Summit . . . :
>
> I thank the Republic of Korea and the United Kingdom for convening this Summit.

---

[219] *See A Pro-Innovation Approach to AI Regulation*, DEPARTMENT FOR SCIENCE, INNOVATION & TECHNOLOGY, OFFICE FOR ARTIFICIAL INTELLIGENCE (Aug. 3, 2023), https://www.gov.uk/government/publications/ai-regulation-a-pro-innovation-approach/white-paper; The Bletchley Declaration by Countries Attending the AI Safety Summit, DEPARTMENT FOR SCIENCE, INNOVATION & TECHNOLOGY, OFFICE FOR ARTIFICIAL INTELLIGENCE (Nov. 1, 2023), https://www.gov.uk/government/publications/ai-safety-summit-2023-the-bletchley-declaration/the-bletchley-declaration-by-countries-attending-the-ai-safety-summit-1-2-november-2023. Published 1 November 2023.

[220] *See* Tom Ramage, *Major Commitments Launched at the AI Seoul Summit*, KEI (May 28, 2024), https://keia.org/the-peninsula/major-commitments-launched-at-the-ai-seoul-summit/ (discussing third UK summit, co-sponsored with the Republic of Korea in May 2024).

Less than seven months after our meeting in Bletchley Park, we are seeing life-changing technological advances . . . and life-threatening new risks—from disinformation to mass surveillance to the prospect of lethal autonomous weapons.

AI systems are still being deployed with little oversight or accountability.

We cannot sleepwalk into a dystopian future where the power of AI is controlled by a few people . . . or worse, by opaque algorithms beyond human understanding.

We need rules. Safety. Universal guardrails. How we act now will define our era.

September's United Nations Summit of the Future represents an opportunity to build the foundations of global AI governance. And the independent Advisory Body I set up last year has identified clear priorities for inclusive, safe AI.

First—the creation of an International Scientific Panel on AI. Policymakers cannot navigate this uncharted territory alone. They must be guided by universal, undisputed, up-to-date knowledge.

Second—we need regular, structured dialogue on AI governance connecting existing initiatives at the national, regional and industry level. This will help to identify and replicate best practices across borders and sectors.

> Third—developing common AI ethics and standards. Algorithms must be designed to reduce bias, prevent discrimination and uphold the fundamental rights and dignity of every person. Harmonizing standards—and regulations—is especially crucial for startups in developing countries.
>
> Fourth and finally—we need global financial commitments to support developing countries in building capacity—in particular computing power—and participating in AI governance.
>
> The digital divide cannot become the AI divide.[221]

Like the emerging regulatory model emerging elsewhere, the UK "framework is underpinned by 5 principles to guide and inform the responsible development and use of AI in all sectors of the [UK] economy:

- Safety, security and robustness
- Appropriate transparency and explainability
- Fairness
- Accountability and governance
- Contestability and redress"[222]

---

[221] António Guterres', *Artificial Intelligence Can 'Save Lives, Create Jobs, Foster Progress', Secretary-General Tells Seoul Summit*, UNITED NATIONS (May 21, 2024), https://press.un.org/en/2024/sgsm22236.doc.htm.

[222] *A Pro-Innovation Approach to AI Regulation*, *supra* note 219.

In contrast to the EU, the UK's approach has been to avoid statutory adoption. As the UK white paper explained, "[n]ew rigid and onerous legislative requirements on businesses could hold back AI innovation and reduce our ability to respond quickly and in a proportionate way to future technological advances. Instead, the principles will be issued on a non-statutory basis and implemented by existing regulators."[223] It remains to be seen whether the deferral to existing regulatory agencies will continue. In July 2024, the Labour Party defeated the Conservative Party and put forward a Labour Party prime minister, ending 14 years of Conservative Party rule.

In February 2025, the UK "launched the Artificial Intelligence (AI) Playbook for the UK Government to provide departments and public sector organisations with accessible technical guidance on the safe and effective use of AI."[224] The new UK approach emphasizes "opportunities to reduce costs and enhance public service delivery across government," while also "remain[ing] mindful of both the technology's constraints and potential risks."[225]

---

[223] *Id.*

[224] *Launching the Artificial Intelligence Playbook for the UK Government*, UK GOV'T DIGITAL SERV. (Feb. 10, 2025), https://gds.blog.gov.uk/2025/02/10/launching-the-artificial-intelligence-playbook-for-the-uk-government/.

[225] *Id.*

§ 3.6.2 CANADA

Canada has been a leader in privacy regulation in North America. The Privacy Act and the Personal Information Protection and Electronic Documents Act (PIPEDA)[226] has informed U.S. law, impacted enterprises involved in bilateral commerce, and served as the launching point for further AI regulation. In 2023, Canada promulgated the "Voluntary Code of Conduct on the Responsible Development and Management of Advanced Generative AI Systems."[227] The voluntary guides provide a set of design goals for generative AI developers and those deploying those systems:

- **Accountability**—Firms understand their role with regard to the systems they develop or manage, put in place appropriate risk management systems, and share information with other firms as needed to avoid gaps.
- **Safety**—Systems are subject to risk assessments, and mitigations needed to ensure safe operation are put in place prior to deployment.
- **Fairness and Equity**—Potential impacts with regard to fairness and equity are

[226] Personal Information Protection and Electronic Documents Act (PIPEDA), S.C. 2000, c. 5, https://canlii.ca/t/541b8.

[227] *Voluntary Code of Conduct on the Responsible Development and Management of Advanced Generative AI Systems,* INNOVATION, SCI.& ECON. DEV. CANADA (Sept. 2023), https://ised-isde.canada.ca/site/ised/en/voluntary-code-conduct-responsible-development-and-management-advanced-generative-ai-systems.

assessed and addressed at different phases of development and deployment of the systems.

- **Transparency**—Sufficient information is published to allow consumers to make informed decisions and for experts to evaluate whether risks have been adequately addressed.
- **Human Oversight and Monitoring**—System use is monitored after deployment, and updates are implemented as needed to address any risks that materialize.
- **Validity and Robustness**—Systems operate as intended, are secure against cyber attacks, and their behaviour in response to the range of tasks or situations to which they are likely to be exposed is understood.[228]

As voluntary guidelines, these efforts have only modest impact. They do, however, operate within the context of PIPEDA. The guidelines make clear that the voluntary code "does not in any way change existing legal obligations that firms may have" under PIPEDA or other Canadian laws.[229] By leveraging PIPEDA, the voluntary efforts have some persuasive authority.

Canada made initial efforts to be on the vanguard of AI regulation. In June 2022, the Canadian Parliament introduced (or "tabled" as the term is used in Canada) the Artificial Intelligence and Data

---

228 *Id.*

229 *Id.*

Act (AIDA) as part of Bill C-27, the Digital Charter Implementation Act, 2022.[230] As of this writing AIDA has not been enacted, but legislative work on the bill continues. Despite the slow progress, at least some analysts predict passage and implementation in 2025.[231]

The proposed law has significant similarities to the regimes from other AI regulatory efforts. "[M]any of the core concepts engrained in the EU AI Act, NIST AI Risk Management Framework, AI Bill of Rights, UK Proposal for AI Regulation, and OECD AI Principles have also made their way into AIDA."[232] A key component of AIDA is the updating of PIPEDA. AIDA would supplement or create new law in a variety of other areas as well.

The AIDA proposes the following approach:

1. Building on existing **Canadian consumer protection and human rights law**, AIDA would ensure that **high-impact AI systems** meet the same expectations with respect to safety and human rights to which

---

230 Artificial Intelligence and Data Act (AIDA), introduced as part of the Digital Charter Implementation Act, 2022, https://www.parl.ca/legisinfo/en/bill/44-1/c-27. *See The Artificial Intelligence and Data Act (AIDA)—Companion Document*, INNOVATION, SCI. & ECON. DEV. CANADA (Mar. 13, 2023), https://ised-isde.canada.ca/site/innovation-better-canada/en/artificial-intelligence-and-data-act-aida-companion-document.

231 *See What You Should Know: Canada's Artificial Intelligence and Data Act*, LUMENOVA (April 25, 2024), https://www.lumenova.ai/blog/canada-ai-and-data-act-what-you-should-know/.

232 *Id.*

Canadians are accustomed. Regulations defining which systems would be considered high-impact, as well as specific requirements, would be developed in consultation with a broad range of stakeholders to ensure that they are effective at protecting the interests of the Canadian public, while avoiding imposing an undue burden on the Canadian AI ecosystem.

2. The Minister of Innovation, Science, and Industry would be empowered to administer and enforce the Act, **to ensure that policy and enforcement move together as the technology evolves**. An office headed by a new AI and Data Commissioner would be created as a centre of expertise in support of both regulatory development and administration of the Act. The role would undergo gradual evolution of the functions of the commissioner from solely education and assistance to also include compliance and enforcement, once the Act has come into force and ecosystem adjusted.

3. **Prohibit reckless and malicious uses of AI** that cause serious harm to Canadians and their interests through the creation of new criminal law provisions.[233]

---

[233] *The Artificial Intelligence and Data Act (AIDA)—Companion Document*, *supra* note 230.

The phrase high-impact AI systems is directly analogous to the high-risk approach of the EU Act and Biden AI Executive Order. AIDA emphasizes human oversight and effective monitoring, safety from reasonably foreseeable misuse, validity and robustness of high-impact systems along with the expectations of transparency, fairness, absence of bias, and accountability. Unlike the EU AI Act, the proposal does not seem to categorically ban particular uses of AI, but the obligations for compliance as a high-impact system could still make such uses either prohibited or impractical.

Given the success of PIPEDA, Canada is expected to adopt regulations that will provide substantial protections for consumers. Like the U.S., Canada also has a robust and emerging AI economic base, so the details of the statutory provisions will reflect the tensions between controlling AI harms and promoting its development.

§ 3.6.3 OTHER REGIONS

Many other countries are developing their own AI strategies that include investment, AI workforce training, labor retraining, and regulation of the AI sector. South Korea is a globally dominant technology hub. Japan had once been a global power in technology and innovation and could use AI to reposition itself. Australia is both a significant economy and a major trading partner with both China and the West, giving it a unique position in global policy. Finally, India has a burgeoning technology sector, the world's largest democracy, and a growing middle class.

As a global effort, in 2018, "Japan and Mexico lead the third Science, Technology and Innovation Forum to achieve the UN Sustainable Development Goals (SDGs) and presented resolution 73/17 which makes a special mention of Artificial Intelligence."[234] Forty-six UN agencies and the International Telecommunications Union (TCU) have engaged in "408 projects covering . . . 17 Sustainable Development Goals" of the UN.[235]

Despite the multitude of projects across various UN agencies and goals, little has emerged as an actual regulatory agenda. No treaties have been signed. Focusing on the Americas, none of the countries in Latin America have adopted AI regulations yet, but significant efforts are underway throughout the region.

Brazil has historically been one of the more active regulators in the region on privacy issues and developed its Internet Civil Framework to further its technology innovation and regulation efforts.[236] Brazil has also taken specific action in the narrow

---

[234] ARTIFICIAL INTELLIGENCE: LATIN AMERICA'S REGULATORY AND POLICY ENVIRONMENT 7, EDELMAN GLOBAL ADVISORY (Mar. 4, 2024), https://www.edelmanglobaladvisory.com/sites/g/files/aatuss676/files/2024-03/EGA%20LATAM_AI%20Policy%20in%20Latin%20America_4Mar2024_0.pdf

[235] Doreen Bogdan-Martin, ITU Secretary-General, *Forward* in UNITED NATIONS ACTIVITIES ON ARTIFICIAL INTELLIGENCE (AI) (2023), https://www.itu.int/pub/S-GEN-UNACT-2023.

[236] *See id.*

field of false information used in political campaigns. The Superior Electoral Court has issued a resolution which prohibits the misuse of generative AI for producing false information regarding political campaigns, imposes restrictions on internet service providers and digital platforms regarding the use of AI and creates affirmative obligations to monitor the use of these systems.[237]

Brazil is certainly not alone. "According to a recent study, Argentina ranks first in the region regarding public promotion of AI, process governance, and the formation of a new institutional framework. However, success will require deeper collaboration between the private and public sectors to boost social and economic development."[238] Multiple pieces of legislation have been introduced. Colombia was very quick to begin exploration of AI regulations in 2021, but in recent years, it has stepped back from those efforts.

Mexico has a fairly robust set of technology laws that have been in place prior to the current expansion of AI. These include the Federal Law on Broadcasting and Telecommunications; the Federal Law on Industrial Property Protection; the General Law on the Protection of Personal Data Held by Obligated Parties; the Economic Competition Law; and the Federal Law on Cybersecurity Initiative.[239]

---

237 *Id.* at 5.

238 *Id.* at 3.

239 *Id.* at 7.

These regulations, along with similar efforts across the globe, suggest that a consensus is building about the key concerns that governments have regarding unregulated AI. As the EU, China, and U.S. take more direct action, it is highly likely that parallel legislation and multilateral agreements will reinforce these efforts throughout the world.

PART II

SPECIFIC APPLICATIONS OF U.S. LAW TO AI PRACTICES

CHAPTER 4

THE RELATION OF INTELLECTUAL PROPERTY TO GENERATIVE AI

The uses to which generative AI can be put are essentially unlimited, transforming the creation of text, images, video and audiovisual works, and designs across all industries. In other words, the buzz centers on the potential transformation to popular culture. Social media, internet content, metaverse characters, nonfungible tokens, music, film, and storytelling. In sum, AI tools may reshape the web, transforming it into an entirely new medium.[1]

From a legal perspective, the preliminary focus has been on the extent to which a person deploying an AI system can gain ownership of the output as an inventor of a patented invention or author of a patented work. Intellectual property owners are also bringing lawsuits claiming the unauthorized use of training data may infringe upon an owner's exclusive rights under copyright law, interfere with their publicity rights, or constitute a commercial use under trademark law. In addition, there are concerns about the disclosure of nonpublic information when deploying an AI system and that disclosure's impact on patent eligibility, trade secret enforcement, and other fields of law in which privacy is a legal

---

[1] *See generally* MARSHALL MCLUHAN & QUENTIN FIORE, THE MEDIUM IS THE MASSAGE: AN INVENTORY OF EFFECTS (1967); Jon M. Garon, *Towards a Conceptual Framework of Entertainment Law for the Twenty-First Century*, 102 J. PAT. & TRADEMARK OFF. SOC'Y 203 (2022).

obligation, such as health care or securities regulation. This chapter addresses each of these topics. At the time of this writing, there are more than thirty separate copyright lawsuits in the U.S. regarding these issues, according to an extensive database curated by Professor Edward Lee.[2]

§ 4.1 PATENTS

§ 4.1.1 INVENTORSHIP

A threshold question has been the extent to which the person deploying an AI system may be treated as an inventor for patents or an author for copyright. "Under the legal systems of the UK, US, China, Germany and many others, however, only a human can be recognised as an inventor."[3] The premise is being tested globally by Stephen Thaler in lawsuits involving both the right to patent an invention and the right to copyright the output of an autonomous system. Thaler is the creator of DABUS, which stands for "Device for Autonomous Bootstrapping of Unified Sentience."[4] According to Thaler, DABUS

---

2 *See* Edward Lee, *AI Copyright Wars, Lawsuits, Status*, CHAT GPT IS EATING THE WORLD (Feb. 14, 2025), https://chatgptiseatingtheworld.com/2024/07/14/status-of-all-28-copyright-suits-v-ai-jul-14-2024/.

3 Tom Dines, *A Patent Predicament: Who Owns an AI-generated Invention?*, FIN. TIMES (Oct. 6, 2019), https://www.ft.com/content/84677ec8-be73-11e9-9381-78bab8a70848.

4 *See* Sam Tobin, *UK Supreme Court Hears Landmark Patent Case Over AI "Inventor"*, REUTERS (Mar. 2, 2023), https://www.reuters.com/technology/uk-supreme-court-hears-landmark-patent-case-over-ai-inventor-2023-03-02/; Blake Brittain, *U.S. Scientist Hits Another Dead End In Patent Case Over AI Inventor'*, REUTERS (Oct. 20, 2022), https://www.reuters.com/legal/litigation/

"has so far conceived of two inventions: a 'fractal container', designed to allow for coupling of multiple containers, improve grip, and improve heat transfer; and a 'neural flame', a flashing light designed to emit a uniquely-identifiable light signal that attracts enhanced human attention."[5]

Thaler's patent claim that an AI device could obtain patent protection was dismissed as inconsistent with the plain language of the statute and the meaning of the word "individual" in the Patent Act.[6] "Here, there is no ambiguity: The Patent Act requires that inventors must be natural persons; that is, human beings."[7]

Although litigation and applications continue around the globe, only South Africa has allowed the registration of an AI-authored invention, and South Africa does not review the merits of a patent application at the time of registration, only its procedural requirements.[8]

---

us-scientist-hits-another-dead-end-patent-case-over-ai-inventor-2022-10-20/.

5 Sanjaya Mendis et al., *AI and Patent Law: Can AI Be an "Inventor"?*, LEXOLOGY (May 31, 2022), https://www.lexology.com/library/detail.aspx?g=648f10e3-c937-4604-bf89-c21e66b4d669.

6 *See* Thaler v. Hirshfeld, 558 F. Supp. 3d 238, 246 (E.D. Va. 2021), *aff'd sub nom.* Thaler v. Vidal, 43 F.4th 1207 (Fed. Cir. 2022). *See also* Mohamad v. Palestinian Auth., 566 U.S. 449, 453–54 (2012) ("[t]he ordinary meaning of the word [individual], fortified by its statutory context," referred to a "natural person" . . . .").

7 Thaler v. Vidal, 43 F.4th 1207, 1210 (Fed. Cir. 2022).

8 *See* Kingsley Egbuonu, *The Latest News on the DABUS Patent Case*, IP STARS (Feb. 28, 2023), https://www.ipstars.com/

While it may be axiomatic that an invention must be made by a person, that does not end the inquiry. The issues has been addressed in a round table by the IP5, a consortium of patent offices representing the five jurisdictions with the largest number of filings: the People's Republic of China (PRC) National Intellectual Property Administration (CNIPA), the European Patent Office (EPO), the Japan Patent Office (JPO), the Korean Intellectual Property Office (KIPO), and the United States Patent & Trademark Office (USPTO).[9] Together, the IP5 represent 80 percent of the patent market.[10]

The IP5 consortium made clear that human invention is the starting point. "All IP5 Offices acknowledge there may be certain difficulties for patent offices to determine whether a particular invention has been made by a human or a machine. Nonetheless, all IP5 jurisdictions require that the inventor be a natural person and should be designated as the inventor in the application."[11]

Despite this clear understanding, the relationship between AI systems and human inventorship is a

---

NewsAndAnalysis/The-latest-news-on-the-DABUS-patent-case/Index/7366.

[9] REPORT FROM THE IP5 EXPERT ROUND TABLE ON ARTIFICIAL INTELLIGENCE, MUNICH, (Oct. 31, 2018), https://www.fiveipoffices.org/material/AI_roundtable_2018_report. *See* Stephen M. Hou, *International Patent Office Guidance on Artificial Intelligence Inventions*, SOLVE INTELLIGENCE (May 15, 2024), https://www.solveintelligence.com/blog-posts/international-patent-office-guidance-on-artificial-intelligence-inventions.

[10] Report from the IP5 Expert Round Table on Artificial Intelligence, *supra* note 9.

[11] *Id.* at § 5.

continuum that requires more nuanced development. In addition to AI-made inventions outside of patent eligibility, there are also "(a) human-made inventions using AI for the verification of the outcome [and] (b) inventions arising from a human identifying a problem and using AI to find a solution."[12]

The IP5 report emphasizes that the "concept of the person skilled in the art, which currently remains unaffected because it considers that the skilled person has access to all knowledge and technology, including AI technology."[13] This means that over time, the use of AI will heighten the expectations on inventors because a human seeking to invent without AI assistance will be held to a standard that assumes AI support. "[T]he level of skill in the art may increase with the widespread use of AI."[14]

Each jurisdiction is responding to the pressure on AI-augmented invention by addressing the disclosure requirements. In the U.S., the USPTO issued guidance to help inventors and patent examiners understand the limits on AI-assistance and the disclosure requirements for such patent applications.[15] Loosely summarized the guidance suggests treating the AI-inventor as a co-inventor. The invention remains patentable if the remaining

---

12 *Id.* at § 4.

13 *Id.* at § 14.

14 *Id.* at § 12.

15 Inventorship Guidance for AI-Assisted Inventions, 89 Fed. Reg. 10043, Doc. 2024–02623, (Feb. 13, 2024).

human participants did enough to be listed as co-inventors as well.

> In the context of AI-assisted inventions, natural person(s) who create an invention using an AI system, or any other advanced system, must contribute significantly to the invention, as specified by the *Pannu* factors. Although the *Pannu* factors are generally applied to two or more people who create an invention (i.e., joint inventors), it follows that a single person who uses an AI system to create an invention is also required to make a significant contribution to the invention, according to the *Pannu* factors, to be considered a proper inventor. There is no requirement for a named inventor to contribute to every claim in an application or patent; a contribution to a single claim is sufficient.[16]
>
> . . .
>
> [The *Pannu* factors provide] each inventor must contribute in some significant manner to the invention. In making this determination, the courts have looked to several factors, such that each inventor must: "(1) contribute in some significant manner to the conception or reduction to practice of the invention, (2) make a contribution to the claimed invention that is not insignificant in quality, when that contribution is measured against the dimension of the full invention, and (3) do more than merely

---

[16] *Id.* at 10048 citing Pannu v. Iolab Corp., 155 F.3d 1344, 1351 (Fed. Cir. 1998)

explain to the real inventors well-known concepts and/or the current state of the art."[17]

Other IP5 jurisdictions vary in their approach. Each has its own rules regarding the detail of how much disclosure of the AI-system's process must be disclosed and the required inventive steps of the individual. Despite the procedural differences, however, the IP5 roundtable report suggests broad agreement among the leading patent offices.

§ 4.1.2 AI'S RELATIONSHIP WITH PRIOR ART

The patentability of processes, machines, manufactures and compositions of matter relies on the absence of "prior art," published or publicly available information that discloses the invention prior to the filing date of the application.[18] To be patentable, an invention must not have already been publicly disclosed. Through the process of building large language models, the AI systems have compiled a vast trove of information and publications into searchable form, making them more easily accessible than they might have been otherwise. The AI models simplify the process of asking questions about that information. They also identify patterns in the data. Each of these steps helps improve the researcher's ability to learn from the prior art and to identify the existence of prior art in the process.[19]

---

[17] *Id.* quoting Pannu, 155 F.3d at 1351 (other citations omitted).

[18] *See* 35 U.S.C § 102 (2024).

[19] *See* Nicholas Martin and George Zalepa, *AI Will Soon Streamline Litigation Practice for Patent Attorneys*, BLOOMBERG

In the aggregate, the increase access to prior art should improve the quality of patents and emphasize the importance of novelty in the invention process. In practice, this will likely raise the bar for inventors and patent attorneys as increasingly obscure publications surface in prior art searches.

The challenge will be even greater post-issuance of a patent. In the situation where a competitor challenges the validity of a patent, that challenger can utilize the expanded body of public knowledge to challenge the eligibility of a patent claims through the use of AI research to test to originality. "The discovery phase of patent litigation often involves sifting through large volumes of electronic documents and data. Machine learning algorithms can quickly identify and categorize relevant documents and data. This speeds up the process and reduces the risk of missing crucial evidence."[20]

In consideration of the concerns regarding confidentiality for the filing of a patent application, patent prosecutors will tend to use proprietary AI systems or systems that do not collect and share query information. In contrast, patent litigators seeing prior art to invalidate claims have no such limitations and can use these systems to their greatest capacity, tipping the scales in favor of the plaintiff's bar. "[N]atural language processing algorithms can scan, analyze, and categorize vast amounts of legal documents and previous case

(Dec. 7, 2023), https://news.bloomberglaw.com/us-law-week/ai-offers-an-emerging-yet-challenging-path-for-patent-prosecution.

[20] *Id.*

records quickly and accurately. This enables patent lawyers to access relevant information more efficiently and identify critical insights, helping them build stronger cases."[21]

§ 4.2 COPYRIGHT

§ 4.2.1 AUTHORSHIP

As with patent law, copyright law requires human authorship or creativity to gain statutory protection for the work.[22] "To qualify for copyright protection, a work must be original to the author."[23] In addition, copyright only subsists if the work "possesses at least some minimal degree of creativity."[24]

Among the attempts to claim non-human copyright ownership was the claim brought by PETA on behalf of Naruto, a seven-year-old crested macaque from the

---

[21] *Id.*

[22] But this is not without controversary. *See, e.g.*, Nina I. Brown, *Artificial Authors: A Case for Copyright in Computer-Generated Works*, 20 COLUM. SCI. & TECH. L. REV. 1, 20 (2018) ("The courts have not yet been confronted with determining whether a computer can meet that definition, or whether an author must be human. Importantly, the Constitution does not define authors as human."); Arthur R. Miller, *Copyright Protection for Computer Programs, Databases, and Computer-Generated Works: Is Anything New Since CONTU?*, 106 HARV.L.REV. 977 (1993); Urantia Found. v. Maaherra, 114 F.3d 955, 958 (9th Cir. 1997).

[23] Feist Publ'ns, Inc. v. Rural Tel. Serv. Co., Inc., 499 U.S. 340, 345 (1991).

[24] *Id.*

island of Sulawesi, Indonesia.[25] Naruto "borrowed" a camera from wildlife photographer David Slater and took a series of exceptional selfies with the camera. Slater eventually recovered the camera and published the images without Naruto's permission. But since Naruto had no right to make a copyrightable image,[26] those works fell into the public domain and were free for Slater or anyone to publish.[27]

In cases of alleged divine authorship, the courts distinguish between the uncopyrightable text authored by the non-humans from the various contributions provided by their human editors, including textual questions posed as well as the order, selection, and arrangement of the text provided.[28] The cases involving divine authorship also point to important distinctions between the various aspects of copyright protection. A recipe may not be subject to copyright protection because it is a set of instructions.[29] "In contrast, a recipe that creatively explains or depicts how or why to perform a particular activity may be copyrightable [including]

---

[25] Naruto v. Slater, 888 F.3d 418, 420 (9th Cir. 2018) ("[A]ll animals, since they are not human—lack[ ] statutory standing under the Copyright Act.").

[26] *Id.*

[27] *Id.*

[28] *See Urantia Found.*, 114 F.3d at 959; Oliver v. Saint Germain Found., 41 F. Supp. 296 (S.D. Cal. 1941).

[29] *See* 17 U.S.C. § 102(b) (2023); U.S. COPYRIGHT OFFICE, WORKS NOT PROTECTED BY COPYRIGHT (CIRCULAR 33) (Mar. 2021) ("A recipe is a statement of the ingredients and procedure required for making a dish of food. A mere listing of ingredients or contents, or a simple set of directions, is uncopyrightable.").

any photographs or illustrations that are owned by the applicant."[30]

Relying on the history of copyright cases discerning the modicum of creativity required by authors, on February 1, 2022, the Copyright Review Board denied Steven Thaler's attempt to register his two-dimensional artwork entitled "A Recent Entrance to Paradise" as lacking the requisite originality required under copyright caselaw.[31] That decision was upheld in district court.[32] Thaler structured his system, which he calls the "Creativity Machine," to produce output without significant prompt engineering. According to the complaint, the Creativity Machine "generated a piece of visual art of its own accord."[33] Thaler then challenged the Copyright Review Board's denial of copyright protection.

Although the district court acknowledged that copyright has been amenable to new technology, such as the use of an instant camera to snap a photograph, it has not recognized authorship without a human author. "Copyright has never stretched so far . . . as to protect works generated by new forms of

---

30 U.S. COPYRIGHT OFFICE, *supra* note 29.

31 *See* Second Request for Reconsideration for Refusal to Register *A Recent Entrance to Paradise* (Correspondence ID 1–3ZPC6C3; SR # 1–7100387071), Letter from U.S. Copyright Office, to Ryan Abbott, Brown, Neri, Smith & Kahn, LLP (Feb. 14, 2022), https://www.copyright.gov/rulings-filings/review-board/docs/a-recent-entrance-to-paradise.pdf.

32 Thaler v. Perlmutter, 687 F. Supp. 3d 140, 142 (D.D.C. 2023) (appeal pending).

33 *Id.* at 142.

technology operating absent any guiding human hand, as plaintiff urges here. Human authorship is a bedrock requirement of copyright."[34] The district court looks both to constitutional and statutory sources to reaffirm that only human authors were intended by the law." The 1976 Act's "authorship" requirement as presumptively being human rests on centuries of settled understanding."[35]

The court notes that support in the Federalist No. 43 for the adoption of the Intellectual Property Clause in the Constitution by explaining that "[t]he public good fully coincides in both cases [of copyright and patent] with the claims of individuals."[36] In contrast with the incentive to create within the Constitution, "[n]on-human actors need no incentivization with the promise of exclusive rights under United States law, and copyright was therefore not designed to reach them."[37] Of course, this argument does not address the significant capital investments required to create the machines that can now produce these creative works. But a human creating such a device should presumably be able to obtain the exclusive property interest in a patent for that machine rather than copyright in its output.

The court went on to explain that "[t]he understanding that "authorship" is synonymous with

---

[34] Id at 146 citing Burrow-Giles Lithographic Co. v. Sarony, 111 U.S. 53, 58 (1884).

[35] *Id.* at 147.

[36] *Id.* quoting The Federalist No. 43 (James Madison).

[37] *Id.*

human creation has persisted even as the copyright law has otherwise evolved. "[T]he Copyright Act of 1909 explicitly provided that only a "person" could "secure copyright for his work" under the Act [and] thus unambiguously limited to the works of human creators."[38] The legislative history of the 1976 Act stated that the 1909 standard was kept for the 1976 Act without change.[39]

Finally, the district court reviewed the history of decisions involving efforts to obtain copyright without a human author. The court emphasized that in *Sarony*, "the recognition of the copyrightability of a photograph rested on the fact that the human creator, not the camera, conceived of and designed the image and then used the camera to capture the image."[40] Other cases used similar language.[41] The court also discussed the various unsuccessful efforts to obtain copyright on behalf of animals, deities, and aliens. In each case, the district court explained that only humans were entitled to copyright protection.

In many examples, generative AI services require significant creative input by the user to obtain the desired result from the AI system. The level of editorial control over persistent revisions has become a key attribute of the best performing systems.

---

38 *Id.* quoting 17 U.S.C. § 1 (1909) (superseded), Act of Mar. 4, 1909, ch. 320, §§ 9, 10, 35 Stat. 1075, 1077.

39 *Id.* citing H.R. REP. NO. 94–1476, at 51 (1976).

40 *Id.* at 148 citing Sarony, 111 U.S. at 60.

41 *See id.*; Mazer v. Stein, 347 U.S. 201, 214 (1954); Goldstein v. California, 412 U.S. 546, 561 (1973).

Under *Thaler* and the decisions of the Copyright Office, AI production of code, images, videos, or text are not protected by copyright. This leaves open the question whether the prompts used to generate the text were of sufficient detail to merit copyright protection, a question the Copyright Review Board intentionally left unanswered.[42] Presumably the selection, editing, and arrangements of AI-generated content would be protected by thin copyrights extending only to the human additions to those works. One can speculate that if this field grows, the copyright registration process will increasingly require applicants to disclaim all content that was AI-generated.

The Copyright Office has used this distinction to extend copyright protection to Kristina Kashtanova, author of *Zarya of the Dawn,* for her contribution to her graphic novel, while withholding copyright protection for the images in the book generated through Midjourney.[43] In the reevaluation, the Copyright Office explained the limitation on the registration for the graphic novel:

> We conclude that Ms. Kashtanova is the author of the Work's text as well as the selection,

---

[42] *See id.* at 3, n. 3 ("Because Thaler has not raised this as a basis for registration, the Board does not need to determine under what circumstances human involvement in the creation of machine-generated works would meet the statutory criteria for copyright protection.").

[43] *See* Franklin Graves, *U.S. Copyright Office Backtracks on Registration of Partially AI-Generated Work*, IP WATCHDOG (Nov. 1, 2022), https://ipwatchdog.com/2022/11/01/us-copyright-office-backtracks-registration-partially-ai-generated-work/id=152451/.

> coordination, and arrangement of the Work's written and visual elements. That authorship is protected by copyright. However, . . . the images in the Work that were generated by the Midjourney technology are not the product of human authorship.[44]

In March 2023, the Copyright Office made its next effort to add clarity to the parameters that distinguish copyrightable works from content that does not have the modicum of human creativity or is otherwise outside the scope of copyright protection under § 102(b). In publishing registration guidance, the Copyright Office reiterated the longstanding requirement of human authorship.[45] Nonetheless, just as the Copyright Office recognized the human contribution of Kristina Kashtanova, the Office recognized that "a human may select or arrange AI-generated material in a sufficiently creative way that 'the resulting work as a whole constitutes an original work of authorship.' Or an artist may modify material originally generated by AI technology to

---

[44] Decision on Copyright of Zarya of the Dawn (#VAu001480196), Letter from U.S. Copyright Office, to Van Lindberg, Taylor English Duma LLP (Feb. 21, 2023), https://www.copyright.gov/docs/zarya-of-the-dawn.pdf.

[45] *Copyright Registration Guidance: Works Containing Material Generated by Artificial Intelligence*, 88 Fed. Reg. No. 16190 (Mar. 16, 2023) (citing Burrow-Giles Lithographic Co. v. Sarony, 111 U.S. 53, 56 (1884)).

such a degree that the modifications meet the standard for copyright protection."[46]

In January 2025, the Copyright Office issued its second of three reports on Copyright and Artificial Intelligence: Part 2: Copyrightability.[47] The Copyright Office had previously published Part 1: Digital Replicas and it plans to publish Part 3 to "address the legal implications of training AI models on copyrighted works, licensing considerations, and the allocation of any potential liability."[48] Consistent with its earlier position, the report confirms that "[w]here AI merely assists an author in the creative process, its use does not change the copyrightability of the output. At the other extreme, if content is entirely generated by AI, it cannot be protected by copyright."[49]

The report provides helpful clarification that the use of AI for brainstorming or idea generation does not limit the author to register and receive copyright for the works created using this process.[50]

---

[46] *Id.* quoting U.S. COPYRIGHT OFFICE, *Compendium of U.S. Copyright Office Practices* § 507.1 (3d ed. 2021), https://copyright.gov/history/comp/compendium-one.pdf.

[47] COPYRIGHT AND ARTIFICIAL INTELLIGENCE: PART 2: COPYRIGHTABILITY, COPYRIGHT OFFICE (Jan. 29, 2025), https://www.copyright.gov/ai/Copyright-and-Artificial-Intelligence-Part-2-Copyrightability-Report.pdf.

[48] *Copyright and Artificial Intelligence*, COPYRIGHT OFFICE (Jan. 29, 2025), https://www.copyright.gov/ai/.

[49] *Id.* at 2.

[50] *Id.* at 12 ("the user appears to be prompting a generative AI system and referencing, but not incorporating, the output in the development of her own work of authorship. Using AI in this way

"[R]eferencing, but not incorporating, the output in the development of [a] work of authorship . . . should not affect the copyrightability of the resulting human-authored work."[51] Similarly, the use of AI to modify the backgrounds in images, alter elements in videos, fix spelling and grammatical errors in text, and otherwise assist the author in completing the author's work does not destroy the copyright eligibility of the author.

The report also continues to support the position that "given current generally available technology, prompts alone do not provide sufficient human control to make users of an AI system the authors of the output. Prompts essentially function as instructions that convey unprotectible ideas."[52] The report notes that sufficiently creative prompts may, themselves, meet the criteria for copyright protection, but that would not necessarily mean that the resulting output falls within the protection of copyright. While the report acknowledged that systems of the future might someday provide sufficient control so that users can truly claim they are authors wielding the AI to reproduce their expression, the current systems do not meet this standard. "The fact that identical prompts can generate multiple different outputs further indicates a lack of human control."[53]

---

should not affect the copyrightability of the resulting human-authored work.").

51 *Id.*

52 *Id.* at 18.

53 *Id.* at 20.

The most nuanced portion of the report adopts separate consideration for "expressive inputs."[54] " '[A]a human author who inputs their own illustration or media file' into an AI system 'may have a greater claim to authorship,' because 'there is a limited range of specific expressive output that is objectively foreseeable as a result of a human user's' contribution."[55]

Finally, the report also notes that compilation copyrights and other protection continues to exist for the order, selection, and arrangement of AI-generated copyright, just as such protections exist for similar steps involving public domain materials. The report also highlighted the "relatively common scenario in registration applications is the combination of human-authored text with AI-generated images" as falling within the protection of a compilation copyright for the selection and arrangement of the images in addition to the copyright in the original text.[56]

The report provides a helpful summary of the understanding that has emerged regarding the copyright eligibility for AI assisted and AI generated works. Unsurprisingly, since the report reinforces the understanding of existing copyright law, the Copyright Office does not suggest there is a need for

---

54 *Id.* at 22.

55 *Id.* quoting Digital Media Licensing Association ("DMLA"), Comments Submitted in Response to U.S. Copyright Office's Aug. 30, 2023, Notice of Inquiry at 16 (Oct. 30, 2023).

56 *See id.* at 24.

new copyright legislation regarding copyright eligibility.[57]

Despite the lack of patent and copyright protection for AI-generated content and inventions, AI has already become deeply embedded in products most people use daily from route predictions in mapping apps to automated customer service. Almost every author has used AI in other forms, such as auto-correction of text, color correction of images, or auto-tune corrections for pitch. As such, the Copyright Office directive that "AI-generated content that is more than *de minimis* should be explicitly excluded from the application,"[58] may lead to more confusion than clarification. The directive made the situation worse because it fails to define AI or its *de minimis* standard while at the same time requiring that applicants and registrants alike "correct the public record by submitting a supplementary registration."[59]

§ 4.2.2 COPYRIGHT INFRINGEMENT OVERVIEW

Under § 106 of the Copyright Act, copyright owners have the exclusive rights to "reproduce the copyrighted work in copies" and "to prepare derivative works based upon the copyrighted work."[60] "Copyright infringement is established when the owner of a valid copyright demonstrates

---

57 *See id.* at 41.

58 *Id.*

59 *Id.*

60 17 U.S.C. § 106 (2024).

unauthorized copying."[61] As litigation has evolved involving the unauthorized copying of copyrighted works into the training data sets for GAI systems, the legal questions have really coalesced to a few discrete topics. First, does an AI developer need to have permission or a license before copying a work into the training data or is the copying fair use? Second, does a person deploying an AI system violate the copyright of a user if the output is substantially similar to a work that had been used as training data? Finally, assuming the deployer's work does result in infringing, does the developer of an AI system bear secondary liability for the copyright infringement caused by the system's output?

These three questions are made much harder to answer because of the procedural and evidentiary requirements of actual copyright litigation. Although copyright vests as soon as a work is fixed in a tangible medium,[62] a litigant cannot file a suit until a work has been registered with the copyright office.[63] If the copyright owner of a single book or movie, this does not pose too great a challenge. After all, "[u]pon registration of the copyright, however, a copyright owner can recover for infringement that occurred both before and after registration."[64] For the owner of dynamic online content, however, registration of the works is more challenging since the content changes

---

61 Repp v. Webber, 132 F.3d 882, 889 (2d Cir. 1997).

62 *See* 17 U.S.C. § 201 (2024).

63 17 U.S.C. § 411. *See* Fourth Est. Pub. Benefit Corp. v. Wall-Street.com, LLC, 586 U.S. 296, 299 (2019).

64 Fourth Est. Pub. Benefit Corp. v. Wall-Street.com, LLC, 586 U.S. at 299.

over time, the deposit is complicated, and likelihood of error increases. Even for high-value books and movies, the rights are split among multiple parties, and the owners of the works manage very large catalogs. This means that as a practical matter, bringing a lawsuit for the copying of all the works accessible on a company's website—or all the works that have been pirated by third parties and posted elsewhere on the internet—creates significant practical hurdles.

These practical limitations should not be dismissed lightly. The first of the lawsuits against content scraping was brought by Getty Images,[65] which is a very large and very sophisticated copyright licensor. Most copyright owners do not have these resources, and even large companies do not have funds or resources to spare on unwanted litigation. Serial copyright defendants such as Alphabet and Microsoft are much better prepared and resourced regarding the litigation that will determine the rights of copyright holders and those of the AI systems.

---

[65] *See Getty Images Statement*, GETTY IMAGES (Jan. 17, 2023), https://newsroom.gettyimages.com/en/getty-images/getty-images-statement (announcing litigation against Stability AI); Complaint, Getty Images (US), Inc. v. Stability AI, Inc., 1:23–cv–00135 (D. Del. filed Feb. 2, 2023).

§ 4.2.3 COPYRIGHT LIABILITY FOR UNAUTHORIZED USE OF WORKS IN THE TRAINING SETS

In January 2023, Getty Images brought suit against Stability AI for copyright infringement in the High Court of Justice in England for alleging that its copyrighted images were copied off the internet without permission and used to train the Stability AI system as well as alleging that the output of Stability AI's generative AI was substantially similar to the images owned by Getty.[66] Getty followed that claim with a similar lawsuit in the U.S. District Court for the District of Delaware.[67] Since that first lawsuit, there have been more than thirty others in the U.S.[68]

While this is the most high-profile of the early lawsuits, it is certainly not alone. There are four significant cases presently pending in the New York courts, featuring lawsuits lead by the New York

66 *See Getty Images Statement*, GETTY IMAGES (Jan. 17, 2023), https://newsroom.gettyimages.com/en/getty-images/getty-images-statement (announcing litigation against Stability AI); Complaint, Getty Images (US), Inc. v. Stability AI, Inc., 1:23–cv–00135 (D. Del. filed Feb. 2, 2023).

67 *See* Lee, *supra* note 2.

68 *See Artificial Intelligence (AI) and Copyright*, COPYRIGHT ALLIANCE, https://copyrightalliance.org/education/artificial-intelligence-copyright/ (last visited Feb. 16, 2025) (tracking 33 pending suits); Joe Panettieri, *Generative AI Lawsuits Timeline: Legal Cases vs. OpenAI, Microsoft, Anthropic, Nvidia, Perplexity, Intel and More*, SUSTAINABLE TECH PARTNER NEWS (Oct. 24, 2024), https://sustainabletechpartner.com/topics/ai/generative-ai-lawsuit-timeline/.

Times and Authors Guild.[69] Most of the others have been filed in the Northern District of California.[70]

Stability AI, along with DeviantArt and Midjourney, have been sued by visual artists who claim their works have been copied, transformed, and exploited by the search engines.[71] A group of literary authors has begun a class action suit against ChatGPT.[72] Plaintiffs representing open source software authors have sued Microsoft and OpenAI over the GitHub Copilot software writing tool, particularly over concerns that Copilot used open source software to generate AI software that does not have the open source licensing requirements.[73] Comedian Sarah Silverman is the lead plaintiff for

---

[69] The New York Times Company v. Microsoft Corporation, No. 23–CV–11195 (S.D.N.Y. filed Sept. 19, 2023); Authors Guild v. Open AI, Inc., 345 F.R.D. 585, 589 (S.D.N.Y. 2024); Alter v. OpenAI, Inc., No. 23–CV–10211; (3) Basbanes v. Microsoft Corp., No. 24–CV–84.

[70] *See, e.g.*, Andersen v. Stability AI Ltd., 3:23–cv–00201 (N.D. Cal. filed Jan. 13, 2023); Tremblay v. OpenAI, Inc., 3:23–cv–03223 (N.D. Cal. filed June 28, 2023); Doe v. GitHub, Inc., 3:22–cv–06823 (N.D. Cal. filed Nov. 3, 2022); Silverman v. OpenAI, Inc., 3:23–cv–03416 (N.D. Cal. filed July 7, 2023).

[71] *See* Complaint at 3, Andersen v. Stability AI Ltd., 3:23–cv–00201 (N.D. Cal. filed Jan. 13, 2023) ("Stable Diffusion uses the Training Images to produce seemingly new images through a mathematical software process. These 'new' images are based entirely on the Training Images and are derivative works of the particular images Stable Diffusion draws from when assembling a given output.").

[72] *See* Complaint, Tremblay v. OpenAI, Inc., 3:23–cv–03223 (N.D. Cal. filed June 28, 2023).

[73] *See* Complaint, Doe v. GitHub, Inc., 3:22–cv–06823 (N.D. Cal. filed Nov. 3, 2022).

yet another lawsuit involving the training of OpenAI as well as Meta's LLaMA.[74]

As alleged by Getty, "Stability AI has copied at least 12 million copyrighted images from Getty Images' websites, along with associated text and metadata, in order to train its Stable Diffusion model."[75] These 12 million images were gleaned from among the "hundreds of millions" of images owned by Getty.[76] Due to the logistical challenges of bringing these claims, the Getty lawsuit itself is limited to 7,216 works-in-suit that are each registered with the U.S. copyright office, a requirement for bringing suit in the U.S. to enforce the rights to the work.[77] In addition to the 7,216 works-in-suit, Getty also claims copyright for the detailed title and caption that accompany many of the works.[78] Although copyright law does not permit the registration of titles, slogans, or short phrases,[79] the descriptive illustrations

---

[74] *See* Complaint, Silverman v. OpenAI, Inc., 3:23–cv–03416 (N.D. Cal. filed July 7, 2023).

[75] Complaint, *Getty Images (US), Inc.*, 1:23–cv–00135, *supra* note 65, at para. 8.

[76] *Id.* para 18; *See also id.* para 21 ("Getty Images has more than 500,000 contributors (80,000 of which are exclusive to Getty Images), over 300 premium content partners, more than 115 staff photographers, videographers, and other content experts . . . .").

[77] *Id.* para. 24; *see* 17 U.S.C. § 411 (2022) (requiring preregistration or registration of work as a condition of suit).

[78] Complaint, *Getty Images (US), Inc.*, 1:23–cv–00135, *supra* note 65, at para. 25.

[79] *See* 17 U.S.C. § 102(b) (2022); U.S. COPYRIGHT OFF., CIRCULAR 33 WORKS NOT PROTECTED BY COPYRIGHT 2 (2021) ("Words and short phrases, such as names, titles, and slogans, are uncopyrightable because they contain an insufficient amount of authorship.").

provided by Getty are rather substantial in length.[80] The sea lion image described in the complaint includes a caption that is 90 words in length, an amount that is likely well beyond the minimum authorial creativity necessary for copyright to protect the writing.[81]

"There are two main components of this *prima facie* case of infringement: 'a plaintiff must first show that his work was actually copied and then must show that the copying amounts to an improper or unlawful appropriation.' "[82] The claim by Getty and most of the plaintiffs seem to meet the prima facie requirements. First, the suits allege valid registrations for the works-in-suit as well as millions more that it has not included in the litigation. Second, in the Getty litigation, presuming the

---

[80] Complaint, *Getty Images (US), Inc.*, 1:23–cv–00135, *supra* note 65, at para. 25.

For example, for the image below, the accompanying title reads, "Malnourished Sea Lions Continued To Be Rescued Off California Shores" and the accompanying caption reads: "A sick and malnourished sea lion pup sits in an enclosure at the Marine Mammal Center on March 18, 2015 in Sausalito, California. For the third winter in a row, hundreds of sick and starving California sea lions are washing up on California shores, with over 1,800 found and treated at rehabilitation centers throughout the state since the beginning of the year. The Marine Mammal Center is currently caring for 224 of the emaciated pups."

[81] *See, e.g.*, Feist Publ'ns, Inc. v. Rural Tel. Serv. Co., 499 U.S. 340 (1990) (requiring merely a modicum of creativity for copyright protection).

[82] Castle Rock Ent., Inc. v. Carol Publ'g Grp., Inc., 150 F.3d 132, 137 (2d Cir. 1998) (quoting Laureyssens v. Idea Grp., Inc., 964 F.2d 131, 139–40 (2d Cir. 1992)) (internal emendations, quotation marks, and citations omitted).

accuracy of the images shown in the complaint, the Stable Diffusion illustrations include the actual watermarks and trademarks of Getty in some of their reproductions. Whether or not the mark itself is copyrightable does not matter. It provides substantial direct evidence of copying.[83] The New York Times claim ChatGPT sometimes produces content nearly identical to that written by its journalists.[84] The purpose of showing the identical output provides evidence of the direct copying of the copyrighted works in the training data.

As a result, unless the defendants can establish that the massive copying of the Getty images, New York Times articles, and other publications constitutes fair use, OpenAI, Stability AI, Google, and Meta will be liable for copyright infringement.

The copyright fair use test originated as a common law constraint upon the exclusive rights conveyed to copyright holders and was codified as part of the 1976 Copyright Act. The statute provides:

> Notwithstanding the provisions of sections 106 and 106A, the fair use of a copyrighted work, including such use by reproduction in copies or phonorecords or by any other means specified by

---

[83] The use of non-copyrightable elements of a work to highlight the duplication process is sometimes called "striking similarity." *See* Three Boys Music Corp. v. Bolton, 212 F.3d 477, 485 (9th Cir. 2000) ("[I]n the absence of any proof of access, a copyright plaintiff can still make out a case of infringement by showing that the songs were 'strikingly similar.' ").

[84] Rachel Reed, *ChatNYT*, HARVARD LAW TODAY (Mar. 22, 2024), https://hls.harvard.edu/today/does-chatgpt-violate-new-york-times-copyrights/.

> that section, for purposes such as criticism, comment, news reporting, teaching (including multiple copies for classroom use), scholarship, or research, is not an infringement of copyright. In determining whether the use made of a work in any particular case is a fair use the factors to be considered shall include—
>
> (1) the purpose and character of the use, including whether such use is of a commercial nature or is for nonprofit educational purposes;
>
> (2) the nature of the copyrighted work;
>
> (3) the amount and substantiality of the portion used in relation to the copyrighted work as a whole; and
>
> (4) the effect of the use upon the potential market for or value of the copyrighted work.
>
> The fact that a work is unpublished shall not itself bar a finding of fair use if such finding is made upon consideration of all the above factors.[85]

"From the infancy of copyright protection, some opportunity for fair use of copyrighted materials has been thought necessary to fulfill copyright's very purpose, "[t]o promote the Progress of Science and useful Arts . . . ."[86] Yet despite the importance of fair use, since its inception, the emphasis has been on the importance that "one must not put manacles upon

---

[85] 17 U.S.C. § 107 (2022).

[86] Campbell v. Acuff-Rose Music, Inc., 510 U.S. 569, 575 (1994) (quoting U.S. CONST. art. I, § 8, cl. 8).

science."[87] Justice Joseph Story, who first articulated the fair use doctrine had explained that "[e]very book in literature, science and art, borrows, and must necessarily borrow, and use much which was well known and used before."[88]

In applying the fair use test, the preamble and all four prongs must be considered and weighed holistically.[89] Since the Getty lawsuit was filed first and the content is primarily photographs and visual images, it provides the best example.

Getty alleges that Stability AI has raised in excess of $1 billion in equity investment, so even if it is not charging the general public for the use of the image generation, the company itself is undertaking a for-profit, highly commercial enterprise. Secondly, the nature of the copyrighted works are highly creative photographs rather than fact-based works with merely thin copyright protection.[90]

The first factor, however, has been given an independent role. Under *Campbell v. Acuff-Rose Music, Inc.*, a separate inquiry must be made

---

87 *Id.* (quoting Carey v. Kearsley (1803) 4 Esp. 168, 170, 170 Eng. Rep. 679, 681 (KB)).

88 *Id.* (quoting Emerson v. Davies, 8 F. Cas. 615, 619 (C.C.D. Mass. 1845)).

89 *Id.*

90 *See* Blanch v. Koons, 467 F.3d 244, 257 (2d Cir. 2006) ("As we recently explained, although 'the creative nature of artistic images typically weighs in favor of the copyright holder,' 'the second factor may be of limited usefulness where the creative work of art is being used for a transformative purpose.' ") (quoting Bill Graham Archives v. Dorling Kindersley Ltd., 448 F.3d 605, 612 (2d Cir. 2006)).

regarding the extent to which "the allegedly infringing work "merely supersedes" the original work "or instead adds something new, with a further purpose or different character, altering the first with new . . . meaning [ ] or message," in other words "whether and to what extent the new work is 'transformative.' "[91]

In *Andy Warhol Foundation for the Visual Arts, Inc. v. Goldsmith*,[92] the Supreme Court revisited the meaning of the first fair use factor since it added the transformative use test in *Campbell*. Like the dispute involving Getty and Stable Diffusion, the conflict between the estate of Andy Warhol and photographer Lynn Goldsmith involves the misuse of photographs. At the heart of the transformative use debate is the extent to which widespread copying for a purpose other than to supplant the original should constitute fair use.

The Court explained that "the first fair use factor . . . focuses on whether an allegedly infringing use has a further purpose or different character, which is a matter of degree, and the degree of difference must be weighed against other considerations, like commercialism."[93] Going further, the court reinforced the limited role that fair use plays when a substantially similar, copied work becomes a market substitute for the work that was copied. "[T]he first

---

[91] Castle Rock Ent., Inc. v. Carol Pub. Grp., Inc., 150 F.3d 132, 142 (2d Cir. 1998) (quoting *Campbell*, 510 U.S. at 579.)

[92] *See* Andy Warhol Found. for the Visual Arts, Inc. v. Goldsmith, 598 U.S. 508 (2023).

[93] *Id.* at 525.

factor relates to the problem of substitution—copyright's bête noire. The use of an original work to achieve a purpose that is the same as, or highly similar to, that of the original work is more likely to substitute for, or 'supplan[t],' the work."[94]

The Supreme Court went even further, pointing out that that § 106 grants to the original copyright holder the right to transform, recast, or adapt the work. The Court notes that "[t]o be sure, this right is "[s]ubject to" fair use. The two are not mutually exclusive. But an overbroad concept of transformative use, one that includes any further purpose, or any different character, would narrow the copyright owner's exclusive right to create derivative works."[95]

The *Goldsmith* opinion reverses a line of cases that had largely equated technological innovation with transformative use. Although the *Goldsmith* court never mentions generative AI, the reemphasis on market substitution will certainly have important implications for the use of generative AI to usurp the marketplace for human-authored works in those situations where the output is substantially similar to that of the plaintiff's source work.

The Getty allegations, if proven correct at trial, illustrate this position. The other three fair use factors appear to strongly favor Getty, at least based on the allegations contained in the complaint. Factor two looks to the nature of the copyrighted work. A

---

94 *Id.* at 528.

95 *Id.* at 529 (quoting 17 U.S.C. § 107 (2022)).

work that is highly creative in nature, fictional, like a poem or novel, or a work of art is generally entitled to broad copyright protection, while a work that is largely descriptive or factual in nature generally receives only thin copyright protection.[96] Photographs, in general, are typically understood to receive broad copyright protection,[97] and many of the images in the Getty catalog are highly creative in form, content, or subject matter.

Factor three addresses the amount of the work taken both qualitatively and quantitatively. Here each image was copied completely, indexed, and reproduced as part of the training process. Stability AI "has copied entire works. Though this conclusion does not preclude a finding of fair use, it militates against such a finding."[98]

The final factor is the potential and actual impact on the market for the plaintiff's copyrighted works. "Fair use, when properly applied, is limited to copying by others which does not materially impair the marketability of the work which is copied."[99] "It requires courts to consider not only the extent of market harm caused by the particular actions of the alleged infringer, but also "whether unrestricted and

96 *See* Stewart v. Abend, 495 U.S. 207, 237 (1990) ("In general, fair use is more likely to be found in factual works than in fictional works.").

97 *See* Burrow-Giles Lithographic Co. v. Sarony, 111 U.S. 53 (1884).

98 Am. Geophysical Union v. Texaco Inc., 60 F.3d 913, 926 (2d Cir. 1994).

99 Harper & Row Publishers, Inc. v. Nation Enters., 471 U.S. 539, 566–67 (1985).

widespread conduct of the sort engaged in by the defendant . . . would result in a substantially adverse impact on the potential market" for the original."[100]

Getty alleges that the purpose of releasing Stable Diffusion into the marketplace is to compete directly for sales with Getty.[101] Undoubtedly, Stability AI will respond that its images are not sold but rather provided free to the public without charge. It has not, thus far, detailed how the investors in Stability AI will receive a return on their investment, but it is certainly plausible that Stability AI's revenue will come from licensing aspects of its generative AI for other commercial uses or provide services that do not include charging the public for the images generated by Stable Diffusion. A similar argument was made and rejected in *A&M Records v. Napster, Inc.*[102] The lack of direct sales has not proven sufficient to allow wholesale copying of a company's copyrighted library in order to give those works away for free. Stability AI may not itself have addressed the challenge of monetizing its operations. At the time of this writing, the company was close to bankruptcy due to the tremendous operating costs involved in generative AI

---

100 Campbell v. Acuff-Rose Music, Inc., 510 U.S. 569, 590 (quoting MELVILLE B. NIMMER & DAVID NIMMER, NIMMER ON COPYRIGHT, § 13.05[A][4], at 13–102.61).

101 Complaint, *Getty Images (US) Inc.*, 1:23–cv–00135, *supra* note 65, at paras. 9, 52.

102 A&M Recs., Inc. v. Napster, Inc., 239 F.3d 1004, 1017 (9th Cir. 2001), *as amended* (Apr. 3, 2001), *aff'd*, 284 F.3d 1091 (9th Cir. 2002) ("Having digital downloads available for free on the Napster system necessarily harms the copyright holders' attempts to charge for the same downloads."); *See also* L.A. Times v. Free Republic, 54 U.S.P.Q.2d 1453 (C.D. Cal. 2000).

services.[103] It is unclear whether the company will survive until the end of the Getty trial.

The New York Times claims and those of journalists are likely to be weighed differently. Under *Goldsmith*, the first fair use factor emphasizes the purpose of the use. Training the data set is fundamentally different than informing the public of the news of the day. Today's news becomes tomorrow's historical record. The New York Times cannot claim any ownership of the facts or information it creates or describes; it can only claim protection for its expression of those facts. For investigative journalism, this creates its own conundrum. Through the journalist's efforts and the support of the newspaper, the journalist is truly creating new knowledge. But with a very limited right to protect the dissemination of hot news,[104] the law offers no legal protection for that knowledge. Search engines and AI training sets have no restrictions regarding the use of that content (absent contractual agreements to the contrary).

The need to collect information from newspapers and journalists may make the first fair use factor support a claim of fair use when it comes to newspapers and journalists. A similar, though weaker argument can be made for the copying and ingestion of novels, which was the claim made by

---

103 *See* Tobias Mann, *Stability AI Reportedly Ran Out of Cash to Pay its Bills for Rented Cloudy GPUs*, REGISTER (April 3, 2024), https://www.theregister.com/2024/04/03/stability_ai_bills/.

104 *See* International News Service v. Associated Press, 248 U.S. 215 (1918).

Sarah Silverman and others. The purpose of training is to develop the ability to predict language patterns rather than to reproduce the story. OpenAI uses the text from the novel for an entirely different purpose than a reader would use the story.

Turning to the other fair use factors, the nature of a journalist's copyrighted work is factual so this factor should weigh in favor of fair use. The novelist and poet plaintiffs, on the other hand, have highly creative works, so this factor should weigh against a finding of fair use in their situations.

The training sets have become tremendous in size. The OpenAI large language model "is basically a very large set of statistics—something like 1.76 trillion data points."[105] While the lawsuits will need to prove the copying, the scale of the data sets strongly suggests that in each case, the entire work has been copied, and therefore, the third factor will support the plaintiffs in all the lawsuits.

The final, and often most important factor will be "the effect of the use upon the potential market for or value of the copyrighted work."[106] Unlike the example in *Getty*, where a user could ask for a Stability AI image and get a substitute image, a reader is unlikely to reproduce the experience of reading the New York Times using a chatbot or generative AI platform. But a reader can get the

---

105 Reed, *supra* note 84.

106 17 U.S.C. § 107(4).

headline from a chatbot without ever obtaining a New York Times subscription.

The best predictor of the court assessment of this prong comes from the earlier litigation involving the Google Books project.[107] This was the beginning of the tech industries mass collection of text for purposes of computer training. That litigation began in 2005 and took ten years to resolve.[108] During that time, the technology and the deployment of the tools changed significantly, making many of the early concerns disappeared from the case, and making the impact on the market much smaller than it had been when the suit was filed in 2005.

In *Authors Guild v. Google*, the final opinion of the Second Circuit focused on two very narrow questions, "whether Google's search and snippet views functions satisfy the first fair use factor with respect to Plaintiffs' rights in their books" and "whether these functions might infringe upon Plaintiffs' derivative rights . . . ."[109] In answer to these questions, the Second Circuit found that making a text available to the public through its search function was a highly

---

[107] Authors Guild v. Google, Inc., 804 F.3d 202, 216 (2d Cir. 2015); *See also* Authors Guild, Inc. v. HathiTrust, 755 F.3d 87 (2d Cir. 2014).

[108] Robinson Meyer, *After 10 Years, Google Books Is Legal*, ATLANTIC (Oct. 15, 2015), https://www.theatlantic.com/technology/archive/2015/10/fair-use-transformative-leval-google-books/411058/.

[109] Authors Guild v. Google, Inc., 804 F.3d 202, 216 (2d Cir. 2015); *See also* Authors Guild, Inc. v. HathiTrust, 755 F.3d 87 (2d Cir. 2014).

transformative use.[110] The court also emphasized that to the extent that facts were then published from the database, those facts, such as the year Franklin D. Roosevelt contracted polio, are outside of copyright protection.[111]

The *Goldsmith* Court highlighted the continued importance of including the focus of the justification for the copying as part of the first prong of fair use. The Court explained "the first factor also relates to the justification for the use. In a broad sense, a use that has a distinct purpose is justified because it furthers the goal of copyright, namely, to promote the progress of science and the arts, without diminishing the incentive to create."[112] The *Goldsmith* Court quoted *Authors Guild v. Google* to emphasize the point.

> The more the appropriator is using the copied material for new, transformative purposes, the more it serves copyright's goal of enriching

---

[110] *Authors Guild*, 804 F.3d at 216; *Authors Guild, Inc.*, 755 F.3d at 98.

[111] *Authors Guild*, 804 F.3d at 224.

> By entering "Roosevelt polio" in a Google Books search, the student would be taken to (among numerous sites) a snippet from page 31 of Richard Thayer Goldberg's The Making of Franklin D. Roosevelt (1981), telling that the polio attack occurred in 1921. This would satisfy the searcher's need for the book, eliminating any need to purchase it or acquire it from a library. But what the searcher derived from the snippet was a historical fact. Author Goldberg's copyright does not extend to the facts communicated by his book. It protects only the author's manner of expression.

[112] Andy Warhol Found. for the Visual Arts, Inc. v. Goldsmith, 598 U.S. 508, 531 (2023).

> public knowledge and the less likely it is that the appropriation will serve as a substitute for the original or its plausible derivatives, shrinking the protected market opportunities of the copyrighted work.[113]

For the New York Times, the better approach to the fourth factor will be to emphasize that by copying without permission, the defendants are destroying the market for database licensing. The nonprofit organization, Fairly Trained, has been certifying AI systems that are trained on licensed content or content not protected by copyright since January 2024.[114] Enterprises including Reddit and Google have entered into licensing agreement,[115] as have Shutterstock, Associated Press, Getty Images and AudioSparx.[116]

If there is a ready market for licensing source material to AI models, then usurpation of that market interferes with the derivative rights of the copyright holder. If there is no such market, then the

---

113 *Id.* at 531 (quoting *Authors Guild*, 804 F.3d at 214).

114 *See Fairly Trained Launches Certification for Generative AI Models that Respect Creators' Rights*, FAIRLY TRAINED (Jan. 17, 2024), https://www.fairlytrained.org/blog/fairly-trained-launches-certification-for-generative-ai-models-that-respect-creators-rights.

115 *Public Licensing Deals for AI Training Likely to Multiply Following Google, Reddit Agreement*, PILLSBURY (Mar. 11, 2024), https://www.pillsburylaw.com/en/news-and-insights/public-licensing-deals-ai-training-multiply.html.

116 Joy R. Butler, *How Licensing Models Can Be Used for AI Training Data*, VARIETY (Mar. 19, 2024), https://variety.com/vip/why-generative-ai-companies-will-pay-content-owners-and-licensing-models-that-will-emerge-1235944577/.

use cannot be a derivative right and the use must therefore be transformative.[117] Under this theory, it is not the substitute for the individual reader of the newspaper, but the substitute for a commercially negotiated blanket license. As the market for licensing grows, the claim that one can take the data without a license becomes less and less commercially viable.

If the lesson of the Google Books litigation teaches anything, it is that the parties to massive, complex lawsuits will adjust their behavior to avoid liability, and in so doing, achieve many of the goals that the litigation set out to accomplish.

More broadly, copyright and fair use are not really equipped to regulate such sweeping wealth transfers, so it may again be time for Congress to consider mechanisms for the blanket licensing of copyrighted works to reflect the value they are giving to the tech industry and the public that relies on these services.[118]

---

[117] *See, e.g.*, Ringgold v. Black Entertainment Tel., Inc., 126 F.3d 70 (2d Cir. 1997) (discussing the role of an existing market in diminishing claims for fair use).

[118] *See* TimWu, *What Ever Happened to Google Books*, NEW YORKER (Sept. 15, 2015), https://www.newyorker.com/business/currency/what-ever-happened-to-google-books ("A federal judge sided with the critics and threw out the 2008 settlement, adding that aspects of the copyright issue would be more appropriately decided by the legislature. "Sounds like a job for Congress," James Grimmelmann, a law professor [now at Cornell Law School] . . . ."). *See generally* Jonathan Band, *The Google Library Project: Both Sides of the Story*, PLAGIARY (2006), https://quod.lib.umich.edu/p/plag/5240451.0001.002/google-library-project-both-sides-of-the-story?rgn=main;view=fulltext.

The question for image generation, however, is somewhat different. There is less functionality in a deconstructed image than in software or natural language text. There remains the factual depiction that a picture of a cat contains a cat, but each cat depicted retains its unique artistic expression. More importantly, the production of new works of imagery are often quite recognizable as being reproductions or derivate works from pre-existing works. So unlike software and natural language content, the imagery databases will remain the most susceptible to claims of copyright infringement.

A variation of the training complaint is that the dataset is itself a derivative work of the sources copied into it.[119] The initial access of the training data undoubtedly includes complete copies of the source material, so at the early stage of the process the defendants likely made a copy of the plaintiff's copyright-protected works. These copies, however, are not used for their primary purpose as literature, news or entertainment. Instead, they are deconstructed into their component phrases and mapped for the interrelations among the word choices within the data set. It is this version of the data, rather than the source material that serves as the core of the training function.

---

[119] *See* David M. McIntosh, Georgina Jones Suzuki, & Yam Schaal, *AI and the Copyright Liability Overhang: A Brief Summary of the Current State of AI-Related Copyright Litigation*, ROPES & GRAY (April 2, 2024), https://www.ropesgray.com/en/insights/alerts/2024/04/ai-and-the-copyright-liability-overhang-a-brief-summary-of-the-current-state-of-ai-related.

Consider that a novel is protectible by copyright. The paragraphs are individually protected and so are most sentences that make up the novel. In contrast, the clauses that make up sentences, the words, and the letters are the building blocks of the novel but are not intellectual property of the author. If the works copied into the training data are disaggregated into their component words and phrases, then it would be hard to claim the resulting database retains enough of the creative expression of the original work to be considered a derivative work. In contrast, if the structure of the collection retains entire works or multiple paragraphs of text, then the compilation of those copyright-protected works should be characterized as a derivative work of the source materials. While different systems operate in different ways, the design of a traditional large language training model should deconstruct text into component parts.

In contrast to text, visual images and perhaps audiovisual works would likely be stored in their original complete form. The two leading GAI systems—diffusion training models and GAN adversarial image generation training models—use the existing input images to train the system to recognize the components of the image. Unlike text, the image generators do not deconstruct the images. In these systems, it is more likely the case that the database should be considered a derivative work of the source material. In § 4.3 on publicity rights, the book explains how an actor's image is often retrieved from an image generator when the query requests a well-known character.

Take this example. A request for a drawing of a frog could result in a myriad of possible drawings and photorealistic images. The query could also generate images strikingly similar to public domain images of Toad (not quite a frog) from Wind in the Willows or it could generate images of the more famous TV character, Kermit the Frog, from Sesame Street, the Muppet Show, and various motion pictures. In the case of comic book and movie characters, a request for a drawing including "Wonder Woman," may well result in a depiction of the D.C. comic book character or depictions of Gal Gadot or Lynda Carter. To the extent an AI image generator has learned that Gal Gadot's likeness is the representation of Wonder Woman, then it means that the training data set has incorporated images of her portraying the character. The AI processed these images during training, allowing it to recognize and replicate this association. Unlike a textual work, the iconic visual characters of film, television, and graphic novels are likely to be "works" within the AI system, due to their easily identifiable and unique visual features.

§ 4.2.4 COPYRIGHT INFRINGEMENT WHEN A DEPLOYER'S OUTPUT IS SUBSTANTIALLY SIMILAR TO TRAINING CONTENT

As noted above, the prima facie case for copyright infringement simply requires two elements: "(1) ownership of a valid copyright, and (2) copying of constituent elements of the work that are original."[120]

---

[120] Feist Publ'ns, Inc. v. Rural Tel. Serv. Co., Inc., 499 U.S. 340, 361 (1991).

The copying must constitute an "unlawful appropriation."[121]

This requires that the work is original to the plaintiff and that the plaintiff has "complied with applicable statutory formalities."[122] Importantly, there is no mens rea requirement for copyright, though innocent infringement will reduce statutory damages.[123] "[A] finding of innocent infringement does not absolve the defendant of liability under the Copyright Act. Rather, it triggers an equitable remedy, which affords the district court discretion to award damages commensurate with the defendant's culpability."[124]

When a person types a prompt into an AI image generator, the machine processes the image and posts one to four possible images. The user can then revise the output with new prompt suggestions and negative prompts that prohibit the system from making certain choices. As a general matter, the user who provided those prompts can expect that the resulting image is created by the AI system and no copyright subsists in that work. In other words, the

---

[121] Skidmore as Tr. for Randy Craig Wolfe Tr. v. Led Zeppelin, 952 F.3d 1051, 1064 (9th Cir. 2020) quoting Rentmeester v. Nike, Inc., 883 F.3d 1111, 1117 (9th Cir. 2018).

[122] Lotus Dev. Corp. v. Borland Int'l, Inc., 49 F.3d 807, 813 (1st Cir. 1995).

[123] *See* 17 U.S.C. 504(c)(2); Monge v. Maya Magazines, Inc., 688 F.3d 1164, 1170 (9th Cir.2012) (citing 4 Melville B. Nimmer & David Nimmer, Nimmer on Copyright § 13.08[B][1] (Matthew Bender rev. ed. 2011)).

[124] D.C. Comics Inc. v. Mini Gift Shop, 912 F.2d 29, 35 (2d Cir. 1990).

user is free to use that public domain image across all media for copyright purposes.

Unfortunately, if the AI system were trained with unauthorized copyrighted works, then the output could end up being a copy or close approximation of a work that had been ingested into the training module. The images provided by Getty in its claim against Stability AI, for example, strongly suggest that the AI output is substantially similar to the image copied from Getty.

"[P]robative or striking similarity shows that the similarities between the two works are due to 'copying rather than . . . coincidence, independent creation, or prior common source.' A finding of such similarity may be based on the overlap of unprotectable as well as protectable elements."[125] In the Ninth Circuit, the question of substantial similarity requires both an extrinsic test analysis and an intrinsic test analysis. "The first part, the extrinsic test, compares the objective similarities of specific expressive elements in the two works. . . . 'to distinguish between the protected and unprotected material in a plaintiff's work.'"[126] One the unprotected elements are excluded, the intrinsic test compares the two works "for similarity of expression

---

[125] Skidmore as Tr. for Randy Craig Wolfe Tr. v. Led Zeppelin, 952 F.3d 1051, 1064 (9th Cir. 2020) quoting Bernal v. Paradigm Talent & Literary Agency, 788 F. Supp. 2d 1043, 1052 (C.D. Cal. 2010) (omission in original).

[126] *Id.* quoting Swirsky v. Carey, 376 F.3d 841, 845 (9th Cir. 2004).

from the standpoint of the ordinary reasonable observer, with no expert assistance."[127]

In contrast to the substantial similar test, if the work was independently created, then there is no need to move onto the second step of the test. Similarity alone does not create copyright infringement. Only works that have been copied result in violation of the Copyright Act. For the user of a GAI system, however, the fact that the end-user did not copy or even have knowledge of the source material is not relevant to the claim of copyright infringement. If the AI system provided a copyrighted work to the end user, then the republication of that work by the end user still violates the exclusive rights of the copyright holder. Neither the innocence of the end user nor the intervention of a computer system changes this result.

Alcon Entertainment may have filed the first lawsuit against the user of an AI service with the allegation that the use of an AI-generated image resulted in the copyright infringement of its protected work.[128] Tesla used AI-generated images allegedly based on the motion picture *Bladerunner 2049*. Tesla CEO Elon Musk had sought to license the film images for the launch event of the Tesla

---

[127] Jada Toys, Inc. v. Mattel, Inc., 518 F.3d 628, 637 (9th Cir. 2008) (quoting Apple Comput., Inc. v. Microsoft Corp., 35 F.3d 1435, 1442 (9th Cir. 1994)).

[128] *'Blade Runner 2049' Producers Sue Elon Musk and Tesla over AI Image at Robotaxi Event*, AP (Oct. 20, 2024), https://apnews.com/article/elon-musk-robotaxi-blade-runner-2049-lawsuit-384c0fbdc536d0c5cfc13794507c3b9f.

robotaxi, but the request was rejected by Alcon. Tesla allegedly chose to instead create allegedly infringing versions of the images. Alcon also sued Warner Bros. who originally served as the distributor of the movie but also served as the host location for the event.[129]

Tesla's use of AI to circumvent a license requirement represents a very high profile use of AI imagery. In most cases, there are practical reasons for copyright owners to avoid such litigation. Nonetheless, given the chilling effect that the potential liability creates, many of the leading AI vendors have provided limited indemnification provisions to the licensed end users of their systems. Microsoft, Google, Adobe, Shutterstock and OpenAI have each provided at least some legal protection for their end-users.[130]

The details of these license agreements vary considerably from each other, but all contain significant limitations. Microsoft Azure, for example, requires that "[t]he customer offering must include a metaprompt directing the model to prevent copyright infringement in its output. . . . The customer offering must have been subjected to evaluations (*e.g.*, guided red teaming, systematic measurement, or other equivalent approach) by the customer using tests designed to detect the output of third-party

---

[129] *Id.*

[130] *See* Jon Gold, *Shutterstock Offers Customers Legal Indemnity for AI-Created Image Use*, COMPUTERWORLD (July 6, 2023); Jon Gold, *Adobe Offers Copyright Indemnification for Firefly AI-based Image App Users*, COMPUTERWORLD (June 8, 2023).

content.[131] The requirements and many more may make the actual reliance on indemnities problematic unless the end-user is very diligent and sophisticated in it use of the AI content generator.

Still, the offer of indemnification and the lack of litigation together have created an environment in which end-users are increasingly confident that copyright issues are restricted to the AI developers rather than those deploying the systems. The law is not as clear cut.

§ 4.3 PUBLICITY RIGHTS

State rights of publicity claims are now generally considered intellectual property claims.[132] The term "right of publicity" was first used by Judge Jerome Frank in 1953 in *Haelan Laboratories, Inc. v. Topps Chewing Gum, Inc.*[133] As the field has evolved in the context of online influencer culture and collegiate athlete brand endorsements, today, it is very common to refer to publicity rights as "name, image, and likeness (NIL) licensing."[134]

---

[131] *Customer Copyright Commitment Required Mitigations*, MICROSOFT (Dec. 1, 2023), https://learn.microsoft.com/en-us/legal/cognitive-services/openai/customer-copyright-commitment.

[132] Hepp v. Facebook, 14 F.4th 204, 209 (3d Cir. 2021); ELVIS Act, *supra* ch. 3 note 118 at Tenn. Code Ann. § 47–25–1101.

[133] Haelan Labs., Inc. v. Topps Chewing Gum, Inc., 202 F.2d 866, 868 (2d Cir. 1953). *See* Melville Nimmer, *The Right of Publicity*, 19 LAW & CONTEMP. PROBS. 203, 204 (1954).

[134] *See, e.g.*, Ted Tatos, *The NCAA Goes After College Athletes' NIL Money—Here are the Antitrust Implications for Workers and Consumers*, PROMARKET (May 20, 2022), https://www.promarket.org/2022/05/20/ncaa-goes-after-college-athletes-nil-antitrust/;

> The right of publicity is an intellectual property right of recent origin which has been defined as the inherent right of every human being to control the commercial use of his or her identity. The right of publicity is a creature of state law and its violation gives rise to a cause of action for the commercial tort of unfair competition.[135]

For purposes of taxonomy, the right of publicity shares certain attributes with privacy rights from which it was originally derived,[136] with trademark law[137] because it requires a commercial exploitation of the name, image, or likeness, and even with copyright because of its communicative impact.[138]

Each of these attributes helps describe the potential for liability that can arise from the use of a person's recognizable name, image, or likeness in the output of a generative AI response, image, or video. In addition, any potential litigation should take into account the ability of an individual to control whether a person can object to having their

---

Nathan Rubbelke, *How the NCAA's Name, Image and Likeness Licensing Policies are Creating a New Type of Company*, ST. LOUIS BUS. J. (June 9, 2022), https://www.bizjournals.com/stlouis/news/2022/06/09/ncaa-nil-policies-creating-new-type-of-company.html.

135 ETW Corp. v. Jireh Publ'g., Inc., 332 F.3d 915, 928–29 (6th Cir. 2003).

136 *See* Samuel Warren & Louis Brandeis, *The Right to Privacy*, 4 HARV. L. REV. 193, *193* (1890).

137 *See* Stacey L. Dogan & Mark A. Lemley, *What the Right of Publicity Can Learn from Trademark Law*, 58 STAN. L. REV. 1161, 1178 (2006).

138 *See* Comedy III Prods., Inc. v. Gary Saderup, Inc., 21 P.3d 797, 808 (Cal. 2001) (incorporating the transformative use test from copyright fair use into California's right of publicity laws).

information collected into the database[139] as distinct from whether the output of a person's name, image, or likeness requires permission.

Thus far, claims regarding the inclusion of a person's identity have not proven actionable under state publicity rights law. For example, in *Verde v. Confi-Chek, Inc.*,[140] a plaintiff sued the operators of the website peoplefinders.com, claiming that the Illinois Right to Publicity Act[141] was violated as a consequence of being included in the peoplesfinder.com database.[142] The district court refused to find Article III standing because the inclusion in the database did not, in and of itself, constitute a harm under the statute.[143] However, in more recent motions to dismiss, other Illinois district courts are finding that the use of a person's

139 *See* Madeline Lamo & Jeff Landis, *Spike in Right of Publicity Cases Against Online Providers*, ZWILL GENBLOG (Dec. 2, 2021), https://www.zwillgen.com/privacy/spike-right-publicity-cases-online-providers/.

140 Verde v. Confi-Chek, Inc., No. 21 C 50092, 2021 WL 4264674, at *1 (N.D. Ill. Sept. 20, 2021).

141 765 ILL. COMP. STAT. 1075/30(a), 1075/40(a) (2023) (the IRPA provides that "[a] person may not use an individual's identity for commercial purposes during the individual's lifetime without having obtained previous written consent. . . ." A person who violates Section 30 may be liable for the greater of "(1) actual damages, profits derived from the unauthorized use, or both; or (2) $1,000.").

142 *Verde*, 2021 WL 4264674, at *1–2.

143 *Id.* at *5 (quoting TransUnion LLC v. Ramirez, 141 S. Ct. 2190, 2209 (2021) ("[P]laintiff fails to allege a concrete injury because she does not allege defendant disclosed any of her information to any third party. '[T]he retention of information lawfully obtained, without further disclosure, traditionally has not provided the basis for a lawsuit in American courts.' ").

information in the database used to help sell subscriptions is sufficient to provide a cause of action.[144]

In *Hoffower v. Seamless Contacts, Inc.*, for example, the court found that the plaintiff "has sufficiently alleged unconsented commercial use of her identity."[145] Specifically, she alleges that her identity (like those of other class members) is used to advertise Seamless's subscription service.[146] "To the extent the product or service advertised has to be separate from the plaintiff's identity itself, that's satisfied here."[147]

In much the same way, many of the free GAI systems provide a limited number of free searches and then the consumer is offered or encouraged to purchase increased access. Under this free-to-try model, the *Hoffower* explanation of commercial use would mean that the information is now being used to promote the paid service.

In the more typical case, the commercial activity requires the association of the individual's identity with some product or service, as opposed to a news story or other communicative work. To the extent that advertising agencies and commercial websites take advantage of the generative AI content to

---

[144] Hoffower v. Seamless Contacts, Inc., No. 22 C 2079, 2022 WL 17128949, at *2 (N.D. Ill. Nov. 22, 2022); Siegel v. ZoomInfo Techs., LLC, No. 21 C 2032, 2021WL 4306148, at *4 (N.D. Ill. Sept. 22, 2021).

[145] Hoffower, 2022 WL 17128949, at *2.

[146] *Id.* at *1.

[147] *Id.* at *2.

produce materials that could be construed as marketing materials, those uses will require licenses from any persons who are identifiable. For example, in *Hepp*, the complaint was that without her consent, a photograph of the plaintiff standing "in a convenience store, smiling in the center of the frame's foreground . . . [was] used in online advertisements for erectile dysfunction and dating websites."[148] If that image commonly found on the internet was closely reproduced in an AI generation, it would still have the same basis for liability.

Identity rights are not limited to photographic representations of an individual. Likenesses are generally included in the panoply of rights granted to each individual, and likenesses should reasonably be understood to include avatars.[149] Thus far, DALL-E and Stable Diffusion have addressed the rights of publicity and privacy concerns by obscuring and distorting the images of human characters. But this strategy is not universal, structural, nor comprehensive. The choice for any particular generative AI to provide facial information can be made by the operator and changed as market conditions dictate. Generated Photos,[150] Fotor,[151] and

---

148 Hepp v. Facebook, 14 F.4th 204, 206 (3d Cir. 2021).

149 *See* Dhruva Krishna, *Dawn of the Dead: Virtual Avatars & New York's Right of Publicity*, HARV. J. SPORTS & ENT. L. (Sept. 29, 2021), https://journals.law.harvard.edu/jsel/2021/09/dawn-of-the-dead-virtual-avatars-new-yorks-right-of-publicity/.

150 *See generally* GENERATED PHOTOS, https://generated.photos.

151 *See generally* FOTOR, https://www.fotor.com/features/ai-face-generator/.

other services offer lifelike photos generated completely by AI.[152] If those images are trained on a database of preexisting photographs, then a person bearing a striking likeness to one of the images might have a valid claim that the person's image is being commercially exploited without permission.

In addition, since avatars are widely generated, there may be nothing that restricts the generative AI from learning the most popular of avatars and basing its output on these. To the extent that these derivative avatars rely too heavily on the source material, and they are used for commercial exploitation, then they will invade the rights of publicity for the owners of those avatars and create legal liability as a consequence.

Section 230 of the Communications Decency Act is sometimes considered a limitation on publicity rights claims. To the extent, however, that publicity rights are characterized as intellectual property rights, that characterization serves to limit the scope of § 230 under state rights of publicity statutes.[153] California's recent amendment to its right of publicity law begins with the statement "[i]t is the intent of the Legislature to enact legislation to ensure that all intellectual property is sufficiently protected from exploitation."[154] The legislation focuses exclusively on the California right of publicity law.

---

[152] *Id.*

[153] *Id.* at 226.

[154] Cal. Assembly Bill 1836 Amending Cal. Civ. Code 3344.1 (2024) (adopted Sept. 17, 2024).

The same limitations in the language of § 230 also provides that the immunity provides does not bar federal causes of action for false endorsement under § 43(a) of the Lanham Act.[155] Although false endorsement is a narrower form of legal protection than the right of publicity, it does provide some legal protection for misuse of a person's identity that is enforceable at the federal level.

Notwithstanding the potential protection under the Lanham Act, at present, publicity rights are exclusively protected by state law. As noted in Section 3.3.2.2, Tennessee adopted the ELVIS Act.[156] To "prohibit[ ] people from using AI to mimic a person's voice without their permission. . . ."[157] In addition to Tennessee, California adopted five different laws addressing the expanded rights of publicity involving digital replicas and the limitation on unauthorized use of digital replicas and deepfakes.[158] The key changes to California law limit the ability of an employer to enter certain

[155] 15 U.S.C. § 1125(a).

[156] Tenn. Code Ann. § 47–25–1101 (2024).

[157] *Artificial Intelligence and Copyrights: Tennessee's ELVIS Act Becomes Law*, ARMSTRONG TEASDALE (Mar. 27, 2024), https://www.armstrongteasdale.com/thought-leadership/artificial-intelligence-and-copyrights-tennessees-elvis-act-becomes-law/.

[158] *See* Lisa Oratz et al., *In a Single Day, California Enacts Five Bills Tackling Digital Replicas and Deepfakes*, PERKINS COIE (Sept. 27, 2024), https://perkinscoie.com/insights/update/single-day-california-enacts-five-bills-tackling-digital-replicas-and-deepfakes.

agreements regarding digital replicas unless required conditions are met.[159]

> [A] provision in a contract between an individual and any other person for a performance of personal or professional services may be unenforceable (as to performances fixed on or after January 1, 2025, by a digital replica of the individual) where all of the following conditions are met:
>
> First, the provision involves the creation and use of a digital replica of the individual's voice or likeness in place of work the individual would otherwise have performed in person.
>
> Second, the provision does not include a "reasonably specific description of the intended uses of the digital replica" (except where "the uses are consistent with the terms of the contract for the performance of personal or professional services and the fundamental character of the photography or soundtrack as recorded or performed").
>
> Third, the individual was not represented by (1) legal counsel negotiating the individual's digital replica rights, where the commercial terms are stated "clearly and conspicuously in a contract or other writing" signed by the individual; or (2) a labor union where terms of their collective

[159] Cal. Lab. Code § 927 (2024) (Effective Jan. 1, 2025). *See* Oratz, *supra* note 158.

bargaining agreement "expressly" addresses use of digital replicas.[160]

The companion legislation narrows the exemptions for use of digital replicas under the California publicity rights statute, primarily by eliminating some categories of "expressive works" so that the exemptions for requiring a license under the law now more closely align with copyright fair use exceptions.

> [A] person who produces, distributes, or makes available the digital replica of a deceased personality's voice or likeness in an expressive audiovisual work or sound recording without prior consent from a person specified in subdivision (c) shall be liable to any injured party in an amount equal to the greater of ten thousand dollars ($10,000) or the actual damages suffered by a person controlling the rights to the deceased personality's likeness.
>
> (ii) For purposes of this section, a digital replica may be used without consent if the use of the digital replica meets any of the following criteria:
>
> (I) The use is in connection with any news, public affairs, or sports broadcast or account.
>
> (II) The use is for purposes of comment, criticism, scholarship, satire, or parody.
>
> (III) The use is a representation of the individual as the individual's self in a

---

160 Oratz, *supra* note 158.

documentary or in a historical or biographical manner, including some degree of fictionalization, unless the use is intended to create, and does create, the false impression that the work is an authentic recording in which the individual participated.

(IV) The use is fleeting or incidental.

(V) The use is in an advertisement or commercial announcement for a work described in subclauses (I) to (IV), inclusive.[161]

The California and Tennessee state laws reflect a significant trend that has also fueled collective bargaining strikes and subsequent agreements in the entertainment industry. The SAG-AFTRA strike of 2023 focused on protection from unauthorized use of digital replicas. These protections became key components of the subsequent new collective bargaining agreement. "The union pressed for a 'comprehensive set of provisions to grant informed consent and fair compensation when a 'digital replica' is made, or a performance is changed using AI.' "[162] After the 118 day strike was concluded, the "agreement reached by SAG-AFTRA and AMPTP [established] the acceptable and prohibited uses of AI

---

[161] Cal. Civ. Code § 3344.1 (2024) (as amended Sept. 17, 2024).

[162] *SAG-AFTRA Agreement Establishes Important Safeguards for Actors Around AI Use Artificial Intelligence*, AUTHORS GUILD (Jan. 17, 2024), https://authorsguild.org/news/sag-aftra-agreement-establishes-important-ai-safeguards/.

and generative-AI technology with respect to actors in the film and TV industry."[163]

Like entertainment industry advocates, states and courts have recognized the need to protect individual's name, voice, and likeness when their property interests are commercially exploited without authorization.[164] Image generators often use celebrity versions of copyright-protected characters, so that when a prompt requests the image generator to create a picture of "The Avengers," it will not only reproduce the Marvel-owned cartoon characters, but may also select the faces of Robert Downey Jr. as Iron Man; Scarlett Johansson as Natasha Romanoff; Chris Evans as Captain America, Steve Rogers; Mark Ruffalo as The Hulk; Chris Hemsworth as Thor; Jeremy Renner as Hawkeye, Clint Barton; Brie Larson as Captain Marvel, Carol Danvers; and Samuel L. Jackson as Nick Fury.[165] The popular

---

163 *Id.*

164 *See, e.g.*, Hart v. Elec. Arts, Inc., 717 F.3d 141, 170 (3d Cir. 2013) (holding that student athletes had a right of publicity in avatars when depicted in video games and that such depictions were not sufficiently transformative so as to overcome such rights); *In re* NCAA Student-Athlete Name & Likeness Licensing Litig. ("Keller"), 724 F.3d 1268, 1284 (9th Cir. 2013); *See also* Nat'l Collegiate Athletic Ass'n v. Alston, 210 L.Ed. 2d 314, 314 (June 21, 2021) (finding NCAA limitations on income violated antitrust regulations); O'Bannon v. Nat'l Collegiate Athletic Ass'n, 802 F.3d 1049, 1068 (9th Cir. 2015).

165 *See Avengers: Endgame,* IMDB (2019) https://m.imdb.com/title/tt4154796/fullcredits/cast; Snigdha Nalini Oreya, *Ever Wondered How Avengers Would Look if it was Based in India? These AI Images are the Answer*, SCOOP WHOOP (June 1, 2023), https://www.scoopwhoop.com/in-other-news/ai-generated-images-avengers-would-look-if-it-was-based-in-india/.

actors are so closely associated with their iconic characters that the LLMs are trained to equate the individual with the character. Much like Bela Lugosi's Count Dracula and Boris Karloff's Frankenstein Monster, the LLMs can be trained to reproduce particular images in response to the text prompts in a highly consistent manner.[166]

The concerns go beyond celebrities. A lawsuit in Illinois recently illustrated the extent to which the development of avatars based on an individual's likeness requires compliance with state laws protecting biometric information such as the Illinois Biometric Information Privacy Act ("BIPA").[167] In *Flora v. Prisma Labs*,[168] the plaintiffs alleged that Prisma's "magic avatar" feature enabled the company to collect facial geometry of any person's face, which was used to train the neural network that improves the avatar generation tool. The app did not

---

[166] Although the LLM does not store particular images or text in its weighting algorithm, the heavy training of certainly well-known works may mean that the LLM is, in fact, a derivative work of those training sources. For example, if the response to the text prompt for "Dorothy" consistently returns an image of Judy Garland's picture in pigtails taken as the original publicity shots for The Wizard of Oz, then MGM's photo might be "in" the LLM weighting scheme, not as a visual reproduction but as a functional derivative work of the photo. The actor would also be captured in the LLM but would have no copyright claim.

[167] *See generally* Biometric Information Privacy Act ("BIPA"), 740 ILL. COMP. STAT. 14/1 (2008).

[168] *See* Flora v. Prisma Labs, Inc., 2023 WL 5061955 (N.D. Cal. Aug. 8, 2023) (compelling arbitration). *But see* Brantley v. Prisma Labs, Inc., 2024 U.S. Dist. LEXIS 139207 (dismissed for failure to allege particularized injury and failure of defendant to avail itself of the jurisdiction).

limit the use of magic avatar function to one's own image, meaning that individuals who did not consent to the terms of service could still have been included in the dataset.[169] The statute makes clear that a "scan of . . . face geometry" constitutes a "biometric identifier."[170] Biometric identifiers, however, only become "biometric information" when it is used to identify an individual. Still, the statute provides that no one may collect either biometric identifiers or biometric information without informed written consent.[171]

The current cases against Prisma have faltered. Prisma's Lensa app download includes Terms of Use that contain an arbitration provision, which at least one court has found was valid and enforceable.[172] Nonetheless, plaintiffs continue to challenge Prisma's notice language regarding the personal information collected, and Prisma may face potential liability since neither the disclosure language nor the Terms of Use provision will be binding against individuals who had their biometric identifiers uploaded by friends and family without their own consent. Litigation such as this might also look more closely into a state's ability to define biometric information in so broad a manner as to interfere with speaker's use of images and other biometric identifiers more generally.

---

169 *See id.* at 22: 89–91.

170 BIPA, 740 ILL. COMP. STAT. at 14/10.

171 *Id.* at 14/15(b).

172 *See* Flora v. Prisma Labs, Inc., 2023 WL 5061955 (N.D. Cal. Aug. 8, 2023).

BIPA could also prove significant in the field of generative AI music and voice duplication. A voiceprint is also a biometric identifier. BIPA provides a state statutory basis for objection to the use of one's voice without prior consent. BIPA actions will bolster more claims that are often more difficult to establish regarding unfair competition or publicity rights claims for sound-alike infringements.[173]

Although "name, image, and likeness" is an approximation for publicity rights, both statutes and caselaw have recognized that soundalikes also fall within this category.[174] Voice cloning tools have become very efficient, with OpenAI promoting that it can replicate a person's voice using a mere fifteen seconds from a previously recorded clip.[175] Improvements in voice software will enable generative AI characters to come alive in video games and metaverse experiences, to improve customer service experience when speaking to chatbots, and to

---

[173] *See, e.g.*, Midler v. Ford Motor Co., 849 F.2d 460, 463–64 (9th Cir.1988) (common law right of publicity claim applied to appropriation of singer's voice by voice-impersonator while statutory claim did not); Waits v. Frito-Lay, Inc., 978 F.2d 1093, 1106–07 (9th Cir.1992) (impersonation of a performer's voice may give rise to a claim for false endorsement). *But see* Sinatra v. Goodyear Tire & Rubber Co., 435 F.2d 711, 713–14 (9th Cir.1970) (rejecting claim of false endorsement when singer's performance was attributed to a single song).

[174] *See, e.g.*, Midler, 849 F.2d at 463; Waits, 978 F.2d at 1106; Tenn Code Ann. § 47–25–1102.

[175] Dara Kerr, *Even OpenAI Says its New Voice Cloning Tool Has Major Potential for Misuse*, NPR (April 4, 2024), https://www.npr.org/2024/04/04/1242933678/even-openai-says-its-new-voice-cloning-tool-has-major-potential-for-misuse.

add creative flexibility in film and television production.

As noted earlier, such technology has already made its way into Hollywood. James Earl Jones, who lent his voice performance to the iconic Darth Vader, has licensed his voice rights to Disney so his voice will continue posthumously.[176] Absent strong collective bargaining protections, it is likely that animation studios and videogame studios will insist that voice performance contracts include the right to capture and recreate performances. Over time, this could significantly diminish the market for voice actors. However, the situation would be significantly worse if there were no legal protection for the commercial exploitation of a person's voice. Without such protection, no one would need to be hired to perform the voice work at all.

The considerations for commercial use of voice cloning technology goes beyond the use for celebrities. There are also applications for use in everyday commerce that raise ethical and legal concerns. One example is the use of voice remodeling software when call centers synthesize away the accents of their call center employees.[177] A new entrant in the call center industry, Sanas, hopes to ease away the challenges accents place on the

---

176 *See* Breznican, *supra* ch. 1 note 239 and accompanying text.

177 *See* Wilfred Chan, *The AI Startup Erasing Call Center Worker Accents: Is It Fighting Bias—or Perpetuating It?*, GUARDIAN (Aug. 24, 2022), https://www.theguardian.com/technology/2022/aug/23/voice-accent-technology-call-center-white-american.

customer experience. "Using data about the sounds of different accents and how they correspond to each other, Sanas's AI engine can transform a speaker's accent into what passes for another one—and right now, the focus is on making non-Americans sound like white Americans."[178] In advocating for the use of the technology, Sanas points to the effort demanded by call center workers in India and the Philippines to reduce regional accents and drop British pronunciation of words as well as learn common American terms.[179] "They have to mimic the culture as well as neutralize their own culture . . ."[180]

Critics of accent neutralization point out that "[a]ccents can connect consumers to places, products and history in culturally nuanced ways that, at times, general "neutral-accented standard American English" cannot. . . . Multicultural audiences are substantial across the country, and ignoring their presence does a brand no good."[181] What is best for marketing may nonetheless have a corrosive effect on the broader society and a long-term reinforcement of normalcy driven by algorithm rather than society.

---

178 *Id.*

179 *See id.*

180 *Id.* (quoting A Aneesh, a sociologist and the incoming director of the University of Oregon's School of Global Studies and Languages).

181 Antonio Francisco Lewis, *The Ethical Challenge of AI Accent Neutralization vs. Sonic Diversity*, ADWEEK, https://www.adweek.com/partner-articles/the-ethical-challenge-of-ai-accent-neutralization-vs-sonic-diversity/ (last visited Feb. 16, 2025) ("The Linguistic Society of America highlights a truth that is increasingly important to acknowledge: Everyone who speaks English does so with an accent.").

In addition to customer service, the improvements in voice AI will likely reignite issues over control of audiobook rights for authors, add voice to most publications, and blur the creative lines among blogs and podcasts. The increased presence of digital voices from chatbots and from people will undoubtedly be growing as fast as the imagination will allow.

At present, the legal status of such uses will depend on the vagaries of state laws and state courts interpreting the common law by analogy. When their publicity rights are exploited without their permission, they have legal recourse, but it varies from state to state, adding to complexity and confusion. Standardizing this protection by creating a federal publicity rights statute would greatly benefit all stakeholders. The process of drafting the legislation would help ensure that commercial stakeholders and representatives of personal interests all have the opportunity to provide input into this process.

Although there have been many proposals for federal legislation, as of the time of this writing, none of those proposed laws have been enacted. Importantly, however, the Copyright Office has recommended that new legislation be adopted, and this recommendation will generate both momentum towards enactment of new federal law and a helpful consensus regarding the elements of its provisions.[182] The Digital Replicas Report "defined 'digital replica'

---

[182] *See* COPYRIGHT AND ARTIFICIAL INTELLIGENCE, PART 1: DIGITAL REPLICAS, U.S. COPYRIGHT OFFICE (JULY 2024), https://www.copyright.gov/ai/ (hereafter Digital Replicas Report).

as 'a video, image, or audio recording that has been digitally created or manipulated to realistically but falsely depict an individual.' "[183] Importantly, this definition is narrower than that of state right of publicity claims and if adopted by Congress would not extend to the "broad range of imitations or evocations, including catch phrases or caricatures" included in state law.[184] On the other hand, while most states protect all individuals, some states limit rights of publicity to those who have exploited their name or likeness for commercial purposes. The Digital Replicas Report takes the position that all persons should be protected.[185]

Unlike rights of publicity and unfair competition claims, the proposal of the Copyright Office is that the digital replica right extend to both commercial and non-commercial uses. Given the concerns of unauthorized use of personal information for training systems, bullying, and intrusion into the personal, intimate sphere of an individual's privacy, the commercial use requirement is too narrow to address the harms of unauthorized digital replicas.[186] In broadening the zone of protection, the Copyright Office then reduces it by adding an actual knowledge standard before a party can be liable for the production or distribution was of a real person and that it was unauthorized.[187]

---

183 *Id.* at 29.

184 *Id.*

185 *Id.*

186 *See id.* at 34.

187 *Id.* at 35.

Unsurprisingly, the Copyright Office also focused on the need for the digital replicas right to be assignable and devisable.[188] Like publicity rights, the expansion of the right has led to a vibrant marketplace for endorsements and branded goods. The existence of this marketplace will be enhanced by adding federal protection. Failure to include the ability to license could create unintended harm to consumers as well as to the people being protected from unauthorized digital replicas. Again, the Copyright Office seeks balance, so the proposal suggests that no post mortem right is needed, or if one is included that right be of a short duration.[189]

Time will tell whether the Digital Replicas Report will produce bipartisan legislation. With over 10,000 comments, however, it strongly indicates a tremendous interest in resolving this AI challenge.

§ 4.4 TRADE SECRET PROTECTION AND NONDISCLOSURE OBLIGATIONS

While much of the focus on generative AI has focused on the copyright aspects of the databases and the uses, there are also business concerns regarding the impact the service has on trade secret protection for enterprises.[190] "A trade secret is confidential,

---

[188] *Id.* at 39–40.

[189] *Id.* at 30–31

[190] David Levine, *Generative Artificial Intelligence and Trade Secrecy*, 3 J. FREE SPEECH L. 559, 564 (2023) ("Generative AI raises some significant questions for the core trade secret misappropriation doctrine that has governed trade secret law for decades."); Jennifer Bennett et al., *Trade Secrets and Generative AI: Protective Measures In an Evolving Technological Landscape,*

commercially valuable information that provides a company with a competitive advantage, such as customer lists, methods of production, marketing strategies, pricing information, and chemical formulae."[191] Generative AI has consequences for the discovery of existing trade secrets and the maintenance of trade secrets that exist in a company's current enterprise. "Well-known examples of trade secrets include the formula for Coca-Cola, the recipe for Kentucky Fried Chicken, and the algorithm used by Google's search engine.) To succeed in the global marketplace, U.S. firms depend upon their trade secrets, which increasingly are becoming their most valuable intangible assets."[192]

The Restatement of Torts § 757 provides that "[a] trade secret may consist of any formula, pattern, device or compilation of information which is used in one's business, and which gives him an opportunity to obtain an advantage over competitors who do not know or use it."[193] To be a trade secret under the state and federal protection, the information must be generally kept secret from the public, have economic value because of its secrecy, and be protected through the reasonable efforts of the party asserting the trade

JD SUPRA (June 12, 2023), https://www.jdsupra.com/legalnews/trade-secrets-and-generative-ai-1027321/.

[191] BRIAN YEH, CONG. RSCH. SERV., 7–5700, R43714, PROTECTION OF TRADE SECRETS: OVERVIEW OF CURRENT LAW AND LEGISLATION (Apr. 22, 2016), https://sgp.fas.org/crs/secrecy/R43714.pdf.

[192] *Id.*

[193] RESTATEMENT (FIRST) OF TORTS § 757 cmt. b (AM. L. INST., 1939). *See generally* E. I. duPont deNemours & Company, Inc. v. Christopher, 431 F.2d 1012 (5th Cir. 1970).

secret.[194] State law has long recognized trade secret protection and in 2016, the state law protection was augmented by the Defend Trade Secrets Act (DTSA),[195] a federal statute that largely duplicates and expands upon the widely adopted Uniform Trade Secrets Act. The DTSA provides a private right of action for "[a]n owner of a trade secret that is misappropriated . . . if the trade secret is related to a product or service used in, or intended for use in, interstate or foreign commerce."[196]

As a general matter, a natural language and design system that answers users' questions without restriction and iteratively generates new explanations and designs is likely to regularly "reinvent" or "rediscover" information treated as trade secrets on a regular basis. As soon as the information is created and divulged by the generative AI, that information is available to the public and the essential component of secrecy will be lost. Out of concerns that proprietary information will be leaked, "organizations including banks like Bank of America, Citi, Deutsche Bank, Goldman Sachs, Wells Fargo,

---

194 *See* UNIF. TRADE SECRETS ACT § 1(4) (NAT'L CONF. OF COMM'RS OF UNIF. STATE L. 1985).

> "Trade secret" means information, including a formula, pattern, compilation, program, device, method, technique, or process, that: (i) derives independent economic value, actual or potential, from not being generally known to, and not being readily ascertainable by proper means by, other persons who can obtain economic value from its disclosure or use, and (ii) is the subject of efforts that are reasonable under the circumstances to maintain its secrecy.

195 18 U.S.C. §§ 1831–39 (2016).

196 18 U.S.C. § 1836(b)(1).

and JPMorgan, as well as Walmart and telecom giant Verizon have also restricted their staff from accessing ChatGPT."[197]

While this is no different than the threat that exists from competitors and from academics who strive to find and publish new knowledge, the scope of the generative AI content has the potential to be staggering. "By training AI systems on publicly available data, or data obtained through less scrupulous means, these systems can identify the underlying principles of a product or process."[198] Competitors can search and analyze all non-proprietary information about a competitors products and processes at a speed and scale that was impossible only a few years ago. "This includes scouring patent databases, scientific publications, and even social media to gather information that could be relevant to a competitor's trade secret."[199] The AI systems are not only capable of collecting much more data. These systems can also provide prediction on how a competitor solves its problems, significantly expanding the field of reverse engineering.

---

[197] Ivan Mehta, *Apple Reportedly Limits Internal Use of AI-Powered Tools Like ChatGPT and GitHub Copilot*, TECHCRUNCH (May 19, 2023), https://techcrunch.com/2023/05/19/apple-reportedly-limits-internal-use-of-ai-powered-tools-like-chatgpt-and-github-copilot/.

[198] Neil Sahota, *AI Is Deciphering Your Corporate Trade Secrets*, FORBES (May 22, 2024), https://www.forbes.com/sites/neilsahota/2024/05/22/ai-is-deciphering-your-corporate-trade-secrets/.

[199] *Id.*

Expanded reverse engineering is a natural byproduct of increased general knowledge in the world. New trade secrets are as likely to be found through improvements in the know-how as are lost because the older, protected ways of doing business are no longer secret. For existing operations, the potential for disruption is quite high, and what constituted reasonable steps for a company to protect its trade secrets may be changing significantly as a result.

Trade secrets are also lost, however, when the information is made public by the party holding the trade secret or when it fails to reasonably protect the trade secret information from disclosure. Here the exuberance for generative AI may come to plague large enterprises that seek to manage their trade secret portfolios.

Whenever an employee, or other individual with access to a trade secret, discloses that information without having taken steps to ensure the information will be treated as confidential by the recipient, that information may lose its trade secret status. While courts generally look for patterns rather than mere instances of inadvertent disclosure, the public disclosure of a trade secret generally ends it secrecy. As a result, if an employee uses proprietary information in a natural language query, that disclosure has the effect of uploading the information regarding the trade secret into the AI's database for future training and usage. Sharing trade secret information with the query engine renders the trade secret public, even if the AI does not republish that information in answers to third parties.

Contractual limitations, therefore, are essential, at a minimum, to create legal protection for the information being provided to the generative search engine.[200] The contractual language offered by each AI platform varies considerably as do the contractual terms for different tiers of service among the offerings by each vendor. Generally, there are no restrictions on data extraction for free versions of the apps and websites whereas enterprise-level agreements often provide this protection by default. In addition to having the contractual agreement, the clients of the AI services must also configure their use to exclude data collection. On OpenAI, for example, which requires the customer merely to check a box when setting up the service, but if the client fails to do so, then data will be collected.

For employers, this requires training to remind staff and vendors that free generative AI tools cannot be used for sensitive data and enterprise-level services must be approved prior to use. For example, a public company that is considering a merger or acquisition of another company might well be prohibited from disclosing such information under the Securities Exchange Act and the associated

---

200 *See* UAB "Planner5D" v. Facebook, Inc., No. 19–CV–03132–WHO, 2020 WL 4260733, at *7 (N.D. Cal. July 24, 2020) ("Planner 5D's combined effect of structural and legal barriers 'consistently walls off both the location and content of the trade secrets at issue here, and under its Terms of Service, separately prohibits circumventing these protections via crawling, scraping, or otherwise accessing its data files.' ").

requirements for specified disclosures in advance of any acquisition. The employees should treat the natural language generator like an outside analyst and provide to it only that information that one could provide to such analysts. While the information that could potentially be gleaned from the massive database available to a generative AI would be useful, such inquiries could also constitute disclosure or even announcements and should be avoided.

Software is another field that relies heavily on trade secret protection. Copyright protection is available for software, but its effect is limited. The functional nature of code, the rapid pace of revision, registration requirements that are prerequisite to litigation, and similar practical considerations make copyright a poor fit for practical protection from unfair competition.[201] Instead, companies often rely on trade secret protection to stop direct competitors from unfairly taking advantage of key software components.[202]

Proprietary software will often have the requisite economic value because of its secrecy.[203] Therefore, to

---

201 *See* Rivendell Forest Prods., Ltd. v. Georgia-Pac. Corp., 28 F.3d 1042, 1044 (10th Cir. 1994); Altavion, Inc. v. Konica Minolta Sys. Lab'y, Inc., 171 Cal. Rptr. 3d 714, 738 (Cal. App. 1st Dist. 2014) ("algorithms and source code . . . information is unquestionably protectable by trade secret law."); Elizabeth A. Rowe & Nyja Prior, *Procuring Algorithmic Transparency*, 74 ALA. L. REV. 303, 337 (2022) ("[Trade secrets] protect data, software, and algorithms in these technologies. In general, trade secret rights cover operability and functionality of devices, and algorithmic models are often within one of these categories.").

202 *See Rivendell Forest Prods., Ltd.*, 28 F.3d at 1044.

203 *See Altavion, Inc.*, 171 Cal. Rptr. 3d at 738–39.

obtain trade secret protection, the owners of the software simply must protect the source code through the reasonable efforts of the party asserting the trade secret.[204] "Companies that own proprietary software typically safeguard their trade secret rights in source code by maintaining the source code in confidence, and releasing it only selectively and under strict restrictions against copying, reverse engineering, transfer and disclosure."[205] Source code—which is the human authored software written in computer languages such as Java, C++, or others—does not need to be distributed.[206] On the other hand, the object code is the machine-readable version of the software which is often distributed as part of the software business.[207] Only that object code that is either used only internally or distributed under a highly protective contractual agreement to a narrow pool of end users will likely afford trade secret protection.[208] When distributing it outside the enterprise, the licensed source code and object code should be "subject to restrictions against copying, reverse engineering, transfer and disclosure."[209]

The popularity of GitHub's Copilot AI tools has raised additional concerns about software trade

---

[204] *See, e.g.*, Unif. Trade Secrets Act § 1(4) (NAT'L CONF. OF COMM'RS OF UNIF. STATE L. 1985).

[205] Lonnie Finkel, *How to Protect Your Company's Software Assets*, FINKEL L. GRP., https://finkellawgroup.com/protect-company-software-assets/ (last visited Feb. 16, 2025).

[206] *Id.*

[207] *Id.*

[208] *Id.*

[209] *Id.*

secret protection. Apple is among the most high-profile of companies that has placed restrictions on use of Copilot out of fear of exposing its proprietary software.[210] Samsung has done the same.[211] Amazon is restricting its engineers to using internal AI tools.[212] By uploading software to Copilot for review, software engineers are exporting the software to a common data set and not taking reasonable steps to protect the trade secrets represented by the software. Potentially, that software could make it into third-party products. But even if it doesn't, the failure to maintain confidentiality could jeopardize the trade secret protection against other claims and misuse.

Even more than challenges in the field of software, the intersection of trade secret protection and content design creates a unique challenge. Interactive sites often rely on nonpublic data to help inform the software as to the public information that should be presented.[213] Potentially, this nonpublic information can be protected by trade secret if it otherwise meets the definitional test. Then, assuming that the hidden data are trade secrets, third-party efforts to acquire

---

210 Aaron Tilley & Miles Kruppa, *Apple Restricts Employee Use of ChatGPT, Joining Other Companies Wary of Leaks*, WALL ST. J. (May 18, 20237:35 ET), https://www.wsj.com/articles/apple-restricts-use-of-chatgpt-joining-other-companies-wary-of-leaks-d44d7d34.

211 Mehta, *supra* note 197.

212 Tilley & Kruppa, *supra* note 210

213 *See generally Understanding Browser Tracking*, GCFGLOBAL, https://edu.gcfglobal.org/en/internetsafety/understanding-browser-tracking/1/ (last visited Feb. 16, 2025).

such information in violation of the Terms of Service should constitute trade secret theft.[214]

Nonpublic information also includes all customer, client, employee, student, and patient data subject to one or more privacy regimes, including protected health records or academic records. A college coach using a natural language search algorithm should not provide it—or the public—private information regarding the student-athlete information despite the potential to use the algorithm to model player performance.[215] Such concerns are not merely hypothetical. "For example, in February 2023 an AI-based chatbot was prohibited by the Italian data protection authority from further processing of personal data of Italian users."[216] The Italian authority had to step in "after the authority found that the service put children and vulnerable people at risk, did not comply with requirements to provide

---

[214] *See* UAB "Planner5D" v. Facebook, Inc., No. 19–CV–03132–WHO, 2020 WL 4260733, at *8 (plaintiff alleges that Princeton used data scraping techniques to acquire the data protected as trade secrets. Plaintiff's allegations that it took steps to hide "the locations and contents of its data files," defendant "had to design and deploy hacking software to obtain this information," and the Terms of Service prohibited access, the prima facie case for trade secret theft was established.).

[215] *See* Family Educational Rights and Privacy Act (FERPA), 20 U.S.C. § 1232g; 34 C.F.R. pt. 99 (2023).

[216] Giles Pratt et al., *Generative AI: Five Things for Lawyers to Consider*, FRESHFIELDS BRUCKHAUS DERINGER LLP (Feb. 21, 2023), https://technologyquotient.freshfields.com/post/102i82i/generative-ai-five-things-for-lawyers-to-consider.

users with certain information, and lacked a valid legal basis for its processing of personal data."[217]

Even if there is a general statement of confidentiality in the contract between the AI service provider and the user, that confidentiality provision may fall short of the requirements for specified records of students,[218] health care patients,[219] minors,[220] data subjects in the EU,[221] or customers in states such as California.[222] Each of the various regulations differs in form and content,[223] so that a simple provision in a clickwrap terms of service agreement is unlikely to satisfy statutory requirements or regulators. Instead, enterprises need clear policies on what may and may not be shared with natural language systems, and these policies need to be enforced with training and testing.

Given the potential fines under privacy regulations such as the European General Data Protection Regulation and California Privacy Rights Act, the obligations to provide data minimization strategies, and other obligations to provide data subjects copies of information relating to the use of personal

---

217 *Id.*

218 *See id.*

219 *See* Health Insurance Portability and Accountability Act of 1996 (HIPAA), 42 U.S.C. § 1320d–9 (2023).

220 Children's Online Privacy Protection Act of 1998 (COPPA), 15 U.S.C. §§ 6501–6505; 16 C.F.R. pt. 312 (2023).

221 *See* 2016 O.J. (L 119) 1.

222 *See* California Privacy Rights Act of 2020 (CPRA), Cal. Civ. Code §§ 1798.100–1798.199.100 (West 2023).

223 *See generally* JON M. GARON, A SHORT AND HAPPY GUIDE TO PRIVACY AND CYBERSECURITY (West Acad. Publ'g 2020).

information, companies should be very wary of mixing protected personal information into broader arrays of training data.[224]

§ 4.5 TRADEMARK PROTECTION

Trademark protection is also an essential part of any business enterprise, and the early stages of generative AI services suggest that small but important steps should be taken by trademark holders as well as by the database services regarding the exploitation of trademarks.

As an early experiment with DALL-E 2, "Heinz had DALL-E 2 generate a series of images of ketchup bottles using natural language terms like 'ketchup,' 'ketchup art,' 'fuzzy ketchup,' 'ketchup in space' and 'ketchup renaissance.'[225] The company invited fans to send their own prompts, which Heinz curated and shared across its social channels."[226]

In most of the "ketchup" designs, DALL-E 2 utilized the Heinz trade dress of its bottle and iconic label shape.[227] This is a victory for the branding power of Heinz ketchup (and perhaps a nod to the power of alternative spellings that ignore the traditional catsup), but if those images are used for purposes other than promoting Heinz products, then the company may have new challenges policing its

---

224 *See* Pratt, *supra* note 216.

225 Wiggers, *Businesses including Stitch Fix are Already Experimenting with DALL-E 2, supra* ch. 1 note 192.

226 *Id.*

227 *Id.*

trademark. Image generators "can produce images that include logos, trademarked characters, and other intellectual property—such as, SpongeBob shopping at Best Buy, Homer Simpson in *Psycho*, ancient Rome Spider-Man, Santa shopping on Amazon, or an "angry mob" of Ronald McDonalds protesting working conditions, in the style of Caravaggio."[228]

Cartoon characters pose a particular challenge. Many of the training models have intentionally avoided presentations of real individuals, but few have policed their training libraries for the ever-popular characters from Marvel, DC, Star Wars, and the rest of the Disney or Looney Toons libraries.[229] These images appeared in many of the early experiments.[230]

For famous marks, which are the marks most likely to be broadly incorporated into the training data, there is the potential risk that the appearance of the mark in association with mash-ups posted by third parties or generally incorporated into unrelated images of products and environments could lead to the dilution of those trademarks.[231]

---

228 Rob Walker, *What will AI do to branding?*, FAST CO. (Oct. 14, 2022), https://www.fastcompany.com/90794674/ai-dalle2-branding-copyright-infringement.

229 Mikael Thalen, *Artists Fed up with AI-Image Generators Use Mickey Mouse to Goad Copyright Lawsuits*, DAILY DOT (Dec. 19, 2022), https://www.dailydot.com/debug/ai-art-protest-disney-characters-mickey-mouse/.

230 *Id.*

231 *See* Lanham Trademark Act of 1946 § 43(c), 15 U.S.C. § 1125 ("The owner of a famous mark shall be entitled, . . . to an

For example, in the context of the litigation between Getty and Stability AI, Getty has alleged that the copying and distortion of its trademarks and watermarks by Stable Diffusion violates its trademark rights.[232] Getty alleges that much of the Stable Diffusion content is of "lower quality and at times ranges from the bizarre to the grotesque.[233] Stability AI's incorporation of Getty Images' marks into low quality, unappealing, or offensive images dilutes those marks in further violation of federal and state trademark laws."[234]

A more common problem may arise if free images and natural language searches result in the adoption of marks that are not properly and traditionally cleared for their potential likelihood of confusion. Among small businesses, for example, the promise of royalty free images from generative AI might suggest that those images are cleared from any claims of trademark rights. But this more mundane form of trademark infringement could readily result from the overexuberance to which generative AI output is being put.

If a business were to ask a natural language AI for product name suggestions, and the AI is not specifically programmed to exclude names already

---

injunction against another person's commercial use in commerce of a mark or trade name, if such use begins after the mark has become famous and causes dilution of the distinctive quality of the mark, and to obtain such other relief as is provided in this subsection.").

[232] Getty Images v. Stability AI, *supra* note 65, at ¶ 11.

[233] *Id.*

[234] *Id.*

used in that industry or related fields, the suggestions would likely tend to rely heavily on existing names or brands.[235] Simply put, the same neural network that makes a natural language AI know what to say next is very likely to provide to a user the most likely infringing marks rather than marks that are not in use. Similarly, as the Heinz example highlighted, certain image generation requests will invariably emphasize the existing stylized marks and trade dress that are common in popular culture and therefore likely to result in marks that will cause a likelihood of confusion if adopted.[236]

A related concern may exist for trademark holders who are the target of deliberate competitive campaigns to blur, tarnish, or free-ride on those marks. In the context of trademarks, it is reasonable to expect that the AI system used to attack a trademark holder would rely heavily on the public internet for brand information. In such cases, a sophisticated attack could use bots and mass disinformation campaigns to cybersquat on the training data in order to boost a competitor's product by misusing the target's trademarks.[237] In existing

---

[235] Nancy Friedman, *Can You Use ChatGPT to Create Brand Names?*, MEDIUM (Jan. 24, 2023), https://wordworking.medium.com/can-you-use-chatgpt-to-create-brand-names-976855ea1622.

[236] *See, e.g.*, *In re* Majestic Distilling Co., 315 F.3d 1311, 1316 (Fed. Cir. 2003) ("the . . . mistaken belief that [a good] is manufactured or sponsored by the same entity [as another good] . . . is precisely the mistake that § 2(d) of the Lanham Act seeks to prevent.").

[237] *See, e.g.*, Ben Elgin, Michael Riley, David Kocieniewski & Joshua Brustein, *How Much of Our Audience is Fake?*,

click fraud, 36 percent of display ads and 11 percent of search ads are fraudulently identified as viewed by target audience members when in fact they are "clicked" by automated bots.[238] A likely variation of this fraud involves unauthorized third parties hijacking the brands to associate with the competitors' goods and promote strategies to encourage the AI to make inaccurate recommendations. Trademark holders will be required to invest heavily in countermeasures to take down or disrupt the campaigns, which will be easier to launch using generative content.

Beyond the risks of relying on generative AI for improperly cleared marks and generative trademark dilution, there may also be a more existential threat to trademarks and brands more generally. Analysts are beginning to ask whether AI will replace marks in the public consciousness as the source identifier for goods and services.[239]

In a report written to an Emerging Issues Committee at the International Trademark

---

BLOOMBERG (Sept. 24, 2015), https://www.bloomberg.com/features/2015-click-fraud/?leadSource=uverify%20wall.

[238] PPC Protect, *The Global PPC Click Fraud Report 2020–21*, SEARCH ENGINE J. (Jan. 19, 2021), https://www.searchenginejournal.com/the-global-ppc-click-fraud-report-2020-21/391493/ ("Only 13% of accounts monitored had little to no fraudulent or invalid activity.").

[239] *See generally* Janna Anderson & Lee Rainie, *As AI Spreads, Experts Predict the Best and Worst Changes in Digital Life by 2035*, PEW RSCH. CTR. (June 21, 2023), https://www.pewresearch.org/internet/2023/06/21/as-ai-spreads-experts-predict-the-best-and-worst-changes-in-digital-life-by-2035/.

Association,[240] its authors suggest "AI may assume responsibility for setting brand or default purchase preferences, which in turn makes it increasingly difficult for companies to target customers at the critical point of sale."[241] The report also notes "the risk that AI may eliminate brand preferences altogether, for example, by allowing customers to set default preferences entirely unrelated to brand."[242]

Brand owners have concerns that AI-generated product recommendations in online platforms and predictive tools that anticipate consumer needs are disintermediating the role of trademarks and brand management in the marketing relationship.[243] As AI plays an expanded role in product suggestions and service recommendations, the consumers' reliance on trademarks becomes diminished. AI services will not be subject to the human cognition that makes brands so powerful and trademarks so valuable.

Trademarks "allow cognitively limited humans to simplify decisions by ignoring the context in which trademarks appear."[244] AI does not necessarily need this simplification. AI services will likely use different parameters by which to simplify their

---

240 *See* Renee Keen et al., *Artificial Intelligence (AI) and the Future of Brands: How will AI Impact Product Selection and the Role of Trademarks for Consumers?* 1 (2019), https://www.inta.org/wp-content/uploads/public-files/advocacy/committee-reports/AI-and-the-Future-of-Brands-Report-2019-010-18.pdf.

241 *Id.* at 2.

242 *Id.* at 2.

243 Michael Grynberg, *AI and the "Death of Trademark"*, 108 KY. L.J. 199, 200 (2019–2020).

244 *Id.* at 205.

contextualization of the environment. "AI's advantage lies in its ability to sort through context, [reducing] the importance of maintaining stable trademark meanings. . ."[245] As a result, "trademarks would be left with less to do."[246] The diminution of trademarks has not yet happened, but this threat to the status quo will grow over time.

To the contrary, the core attribute of generative AI is an increase in information. At present, the total amount of human knowledge doubles "every twelve months and in the near future is expected every twelve hours."[247] Strategies to simplify the information storm through tools such as brands and trademarks will be more important than ever. The simplification strategies, however, may look quite different than present trademark strategies. Through this process, the evolution of branding will likely further accelerate its drive to provide emotionally and psychographically relevant information to consumers to overcome objective decision-making and to promote brands based on emotional responsiveness.[248]

---

[245] *Id.*

[246] *Id.*

[247] Duli Pllana, *Expanding Entire Volume of Knowledge Influences on Incrementing Individual Knowledge*, 19 GLOBAL J. HUMAN-SOCIAL SCI. (H) 33, 33 (2019). *See also* Scott Sorokin, *Thriving in a World of "Knowledge Half-Life,"* CIO (Apr. 5, 2019), https://www.cio.com/article/219940/thriving-in-a-world-of-knowledge-half-life.html.

[248] *See* Bhumika Dutta, *A Guide to Psychographics for Marketing*, ANALYTIC STEPS (Nov. 29, 2021), https://www.analyticssteps.com/blogs/guide-psychographics-marketing ("People understood that merely demographics are insufficient for any

Psychographic targeting uses psychological variables and personality traits to predict and shape consumer behavior[249] (as well as electoral voting support).[250] Also referred to a "market segmentation," psychographic targeting "include dividing the heterogeneous marketplace into distinct subsets based on shared traits, which include demographics, psychographics, behavioral styles, and geographic vicinity."[251]

To develop the psychographic determinants for individuals, researchers and marketers often use self-identification surveys, but these prove unreliable.[252] So instead, researchers and marketers tap the power of generative AI to use natural

---

effective marketing techniques after the development of psychographic segmentation. . . . This field extends beyond demographics such as age, gender, race, geography, and so on to analyze customer behavior over purchasing."). *See generally What is Psychographics?*, *supra* ch. 2, note 182 ("Psychographics seeks to understand the cognitive factors that drive consumer behaviors. This includes emotional responses and motivations; moral, ethical, and political values; and inherent attitudes, biases, and prejudices.").

[249] Hui Liu et al., *Personality or Value: A Comparative Study of Psychographic Segmentation Based on an Online Review Enhanced Recommender System*, 9 APPLIED SCI. 2, 2 (2019).

[250] *See* CB INSIGHTS, *supra* ch. 2 note 182. A discussion of the use of generative AI and psychographic modeling is beyond the scope of this article.

[251] Vipul Mehta & Ashesh Sharma, *Market Segmentation and Targeting*, 2 INT'L J. RECENT RES. & REV. 285, 286 (June 2023), https://www.google.com/url?sa=t&source=web&rct=j&opi=89978449&url=https://www.ijrrr.com/papers16-2/paper33-Market%2520Segmentation%2520and%2520Targeting.pdf.

[252] Philip S. Brenner & John DeLamater, *Lies, Damned Lies, and Survey Self-Reports? Identity as a Cause of Measurement Bias*, 79 SOC. PSYCH. Q. 333, 333 (2016).

language markers from the conversations among individuals and increasingly with the chatbots and generative AI services.[253] The process is fueled by the processing power of AI. "Big records analytics, synthetic intelligence, and machine gaining knowledge of algorithms allow businesses to analyse considerable quantities of facts efficiently, uncovering hidden patterns and trends that tell segmentation and focused on choices."[254]

Psychographic research "demonstrates the utility of relying on natural language markers of abstract psychological phenomena, including values and personality, and present significant opportunities to better predict and understand their connection to consumers' behaviors and thoughts in a broader sense."[255]

In this brave new world of psychographic targeting, trademarks will become more prominent than ever but will likely represent a very different brand strategy than those of the twentieth century. A "newer form of targeting is lookalike-audience targeting, which relies on inferences about users relative to other users. For example, on Facebook, advertisers can reach new users with similar profiles as their existing audience."[256] Known as look-alike

---

[253] *See* Liu, *supra* note 249, at 6 ("Research indicates cases in which natural language data have provided a clearer picture of people's cognitive and behavioral processes than data collected from a traditional and widely used self-report survey.").

[254] *Id.* at 287.

[255] *See* Liu, *supra* note 249, at 6.

[256] Miranda Wei et al., *What Twitter Knows: Characterizing Ad Targeting Practices, User Perceptions, and Ad Explanations*

targeting, the strategy allows excellent market segmentation and relevance but also poses risks because the "feature can be exploited, as a biased input group will lead to an output group that contains similar biases."[257] In a study on Twitter (now X) look-alike targeting, one of the keys for segmenting audience was based on the selection by the user of the user's preferred new agencies as well as on the user's primary interests. Following the maxim that "we are what we do," the segmentation emphasized behavioral and media consumption characteristics. These, in turn, correlate to brand affinity and will likely shape the corporate trademark strategies indented to blunt the adverse aspects of AI recommendations.

A final trademark consideration is the potential to see a significant change in the role for Lanham Act § 43(a) false advertising claims.[258] The federal cause of action provides:

> (1) Any person who, . . . uses in commerce any word, term, name, symbol, or device, or any combination thereof, or any false designation of origin, false or misleading description of fact, or false or misleading representation of fact, which—

Through Users' Own Twitter Data, FED. TRADE COMM'N WORKING PAPERS, https://www.ftc.gov/system/files/documents/public_events/1582978/what_twitter_knows_-_characterizing_ad_targeting_practices_user_perceptions_and_ad_explanations.pdf (last visited Feb. 16, 2025).

[257] *Id.*

[258] *See* Grynberg, *supra* note 243, at 212–13.

> (A) is likely to cause confusion, or to cause mistake, or to deceive as to the affiliation, connection, or association of such person with another person, or as to the origin, sponsorship, or approval of his or her goods, services, or commercial activities by another person, or
>
> (B) in commercial advertising or promotion, misrepresents the nature, characteristics, qualities, or geographic origin of his or her or another person's goods, services, or commercial activities,
>
> shall be liable in a civil action by any person who believes that he or she is or is likely to be damaged by such act.[259]

The first iterations of natural language chats have proven to be quite inconsistent in their accuracy.[260] Even with significant improvements in the systems, so called hallucinations remains stubbornly persistent. For open environment natural language systems that rely on the information generally available on the internet, misinformation will continue to inform the responses from generative AI chatbots.[261]

Like many of the challenges to generative AI, the question remains who is responsible for this

---

[259] 15 U.S.C. § 1125.

[260] *See supra* Section 4.2.

[261] *See* Quentin J. Ullrich, *Is This Video Real? The Principal Mischief of Deepfakes and How the Lanham Act Can Address It*, 55 COLUM. J.L. & SOC. PROBS. 1, 16 (2021).

misinformation. At a minimum, complainants will need to establish that they have a "commercial interest in reputation or sales" harmed by the chatbot.[262] Once established, evidence that a competitor falsely trained the AI to promote its brand with factually inaccurate information, which should give rise to liability. Broader questions remain unanswered, including whether the hallucinations and incorrect product statements that may result in AI responses could give rise to liability for the developers of those systems even when the cause was inherent in the AI system itself.

§ 4.6 INTELLECTUAL PROPERTY POLICING AND ENFORCEMENT

In addition to the areas of intellectual property detailed in the previous sections, there are also significant impacts from AI in the fields of copyright, publicity rights, patent, and trademark policing. Generally, the use of AI in these areas does not change any of the legal standards, but the efficiencies provided by AI systems may alter the practices in the area. Generative AI tools have the potential to help police the marketplace for unauthorized uses of marks and previously unknown examples of new marks that could engender a likelihood of confusion.[263]

Intellectual property owners have multiple challenges when policing their rights. The first is

---

[262] Lexmark Int'l, Inc. v. Static Control Components, Inc, 572 U.S. 118, 131–34 (2014).

[263] *See id.* at 3, 8.

simply scale. The global marketplace has grown tremendously. Infringers range from individuals making an unauthorized use of intellectual property for their personal use to massive counterfeiting operations that distribute even more goods than the rights-holder itself. "Counterfeit goods comprise a staggering 2.5% of global trade. Luxury goods are the most commonly counterfeited items."[264] In 2023, U.S. Customs and Border Protection (CBP) "seized nearly 23 million counterfeit goods nationwide worth over $2 billion in estimated retail value, calculated as if they were authentic."[265] "A trademark or service mark may be infringed by offering goods, services, labels or other packaging containing a counterfeit mark."[266]

Intellectual property counterfeiting and theft is not limited to only luxury brands and designer purses. "Fraudsters are incredibly sophisticated, not only in their ability to manufacture and distribute fake products, but also in their efforts to leverage online marketplaces, paid search and advertising,

---

[264] Doc Louallen et al., *Superfakes: Copycat Manufacturers are Becoming Increasingly Skilled at Producing Knock-Off Designer Handbags*, ABC NEWS (April 29, 2024), https://abcnews.go.com/Business/superfakes-copycat-manufacturers-becoming-increasingly-skilled-producing-knock/story?id=109344382.

[265] *Id.*

[266] REPORTING INTELLECTUAL PROPERTY CRIME, 3 U.S. DEPARTMENT OF JUSTICE COMPUTER CRIME AND INTELLECTUAL PROPERTY SECTION (October 2018), https://www.justice.gov/criminal/criminal-ccips/file/891011/dl.

social media and domains and websites for the promotion of these fake products."[267]

For example, "[a] trade secret can be surreptitiously misappropriated from its owner either by a company insider or by someone outside a company and used to benefit the thief, a competitor, or other third party."[268] Unauthorized copyrighted works can be digitally duplicated and distributed online or through physical media.[269] Unauthorized use of a person's publicity rights might occur with false endorsements or with the unauthorized use of the person's name, voice or likeness being associated with products. For patents, it may be as simple as a device is being sold in the marketplace that duplicates the protected invention, or it may be a more sophisticated situation such as when a manufacturing process has been surreptitiously copied.[270]

Against this economic challenge, AI provides a means to leverage the massive data analysis with sophisticated predictive analytics. The various law firms and third party services operate differently, but in general, these management tools combine large data management to track the information flows

---

[267] Anti-Counterfeit Technology Brand Protection Solutions, Tracer, https://www.tracer.ai/solutions/counterfeit-products (last visited Feb. 16, 2025).

[268] REPORTING INTELLECTUAL PROPERTY CRIME, *supra* note 266, at 3.

[269] *Id.*

[270] *See How To Determine Whether a Patent is Infringed*, WOLF GREENFIELD (Aug. 25, 2023), https://wolfgreenfield.com/resources/how-to-determine-whether-a-patent-is-infringed.

across distribution channels searching for information about infringing activities, advertisements for counterfeit goods, and other communications about opportunities for free or low cost products. "AI algorithms can analyze online data to identify possible infringements, such as counterfeit goods being sold on e-commerce platforms or pirated content on digital channels."[271]

For each particular product or service, the enforcement tool is also tracking all available content that identifies the product or service. Since the content recognition systems apply to video, audio, and text, pictures of products, social media videos, and other content can also be monitored.[272]

Identification of the potential infringement, however, is merely the first step. The unauthorized use must be evaluated, typically using a "human-in-the-loop" to ascertain whether the unauthorized use should be treated as actionable infringement or whether the activity is a non-infringing use because of fair use or other limitations on IP rights. The activity might also fall in between lawful and unauthorized. The activity might simply be at too small a scale to invest the time and effort to enforce the intellectual property rights. There are also areas such as fan fiction, where copyrights, publicity rights, and trademarks are all being used actively but in a

---

[271] *See* Anastasios Arampatzis, *AI's Emerging Role in the Fight Against Intellectual Property Theft*, FORTA (Dec. 20, 2023), https://www.tripwire.com/state-of-security/ais-emerging-role-fight-against-intellectual-property-theft.

[272] *Id.*

manner that rights holders accept as important for their customer relationship.

The challenge also has an international component. The intellectual property owner's portfolio of rights will differ depending on the jurisdiction, as will the standards for infringing activities and uses authorized by law. Again, by using AI to automate the process, enforcement organizations can fine tune the information provided to rights holders.

Third party enforcement organizations also have the ability to track patterns across clients and brands, allowing them to identify the largest infringement pipelines. In many industries, there are trade associations that enable competitors within the field to coordinate their anti-piracy and counterfeiting activities and collaborate more effectively with law enforcement. By collecting these data across industries and territories, AI-based enforcement systems allow for much stronger information gathering and improved knowledge for reducing infringement.

CHAPTER 5

TORT-BASED LIABILITY FOR AI DEVELOPMENT AND DEPLOYMENT

Despite the wide-ranging approaches to AI regulation, traditional laws of contracts, torts, property law, and other common law fields also constrain the development and deployment of AI systems. This chapter highlights the most significant of those common law approaches, namely the limits imposed by defamation law on inaccurate output of AI systems. The chapter also addresses invasions of privacy. Finally, the chapter reviews two fields where common law and statutory scheme intersect in the areas of health care and education.

§ 5.1 DEFAMATION (LIBEL AND SLANDER)

GAI systems hallucinate. This is a feature rather than a bug. As services that use language prediction to answer questions, GAI systems cannot always provide the correct answer. GAI systems do not evaluate or assess the accuracy of their information. Instead, they connect word patterns.

The next generation systems pair extractive AI to find answers and paraphrase them. But this does not necessarily mean the answers are better. For example, when Google launched "AI Overview," many of its responses were considered quite inaccurate and bizarre.[1] Among its answers, Google's AI "said that, yes, a dog has played in the NHL, that running with scissors has health benefits, and that 17 US presidents attended the University of Wisconsin."[2] Perhaps most famously, Google's AI Overview adopted the advice from a Reddit joke to suggest that when making a pizza, one could "add about 1/8 cup of non-toxic glue to the sauce to give it more tackiness."[3]

Even when paired with extractive AI systems limited to pre-vetted data sets, they will sometimes provide inaccurate information. Take a simple example. Assume a vendor provides a legal output system trained using only court records and limited to official documents. In that database will be a significant amount of factual information that is disputed at trial or found to be non-persuasive. Even using only Supreme Court cases, the factual description of events presented by the majority and dissent in the same opinion may vary wildly in the judges or justices depiction of events and the application of law that results.[4] The very process of factual analysis means that conflicting information will be gathered. Most current AI systems are trained

---

1 *See* Katie Notopoulos, *Google AI Said to Put Glue in Pizza—so I made a Pizza with Glue and Ate It*, BUS. INSIDER (May 24, 2024), https://www.businessinsider.com/google-ai-glue-pizza-i-tried-it-2024-5.

2 *Id.*

3 *Id.*

4 *See, e.g.*, Kennedy v. Bremerton School District, 597 U.S. 507 (2022) (description of events provided by majority opinion was significantly at odds with the description provided by the dissent or the news coverage of the occurrences).

on publicly available content, and much of it was not published for its accuracy.

Accuracy is hard. The legal question remains what the standards of care for AI developers, deployers of AI systems, and republishers of inaccurate content.

§ 5.1.1 LIBEL AND SLANDER FROM AI OUTPUT

A statement is defamatory if "it tends so to harm the reputation of another as to lower him in the estimation of the community or to deter third persons from associating or dealing with him."[5] At common law, a statement is defamatory if it held one out for hatred, ridicule, or contempt. Only a living person may be defamed. A related doctrine known as trade libel applies to businesses. To be defamatory in the U.S., the person alleging the defamation must prove that the statement is false as well as that it is harmful, that it pertains to the person suing, and that it has been published to someone other than the person suing.

One such risk comes from AI-generated news stories and social media postings. A large body of journalism literature has explored the potential implications of the field being augmented—or even

---

[5] Restatement (Second) Torts § 559 (1977). Under California law, "libel is a false and unprivileged publication by writing . . . which exposes any person to hatred, contempt, ridicule, or obloquy, or which causes him to be shunned or avoided, or which has a tendency to injure him in his occupation." Cal. Civ. Code § 45 (West 2024).

overrun—by automation.[6] The concern is not merely hypothetical. "In journalism today, algorithms are responsible for producing tens of thousands of stories that fill online news sites, even from leading news organizations such as the Associated Press."[7] In early 2023, "internet sleuths discovered. . . that CNET had quietly published dozens of feature articles generated entirely by artificial intelligence, the popular tech site acknowledged that it was true—but described the move as a mere experiment."[8]

Shortly after the first admission, there was a second. "[I]t turns out the bots are no better at journalism—and perhaps a bit worse—than their would-be human masters. . . . CNET began appending lengthy correction notices to some of its AI-generated articles after Futurism, another tech site, called out the stories for containing some 'very dumb errors.' "[9] Potentially more troubling, "CNET

---

6 *See* Nina I. Brown, *Deepfakes and the Weaponization of Disinformation*, 23 VA. J.L. & TECH. 1, 12 (2020) ("Even the most ardent supporters of journalism will be forced to question the authenticity of video and audio footage relied on by journalists, without additional evidence that the depicted events occurred. When people cannot tell the difference between what is true and false, it reduces trust in traditional media . . . ."); Seth C. Lewis, Amy Kristin Sanders & Casey Carmody, *Libel by Algorithm? Automated Journalism and the Threat of Legal Liability*, 96 JOURNALISM & MASS COMM. Q. 60, 73 (2018) (reviewing the scholarship).

7 Lewis, Sanders & Carmody, *supra* note 6, at 62.

8 Paul Farhi, *A News Site Used AI to Write Articles. It Was a Journalistic Disaster*, WASH. POST (Jan. 17, 2023), https://www.washingtonpost.com/media/2023/01/17/cnet-ai-articles-journalism-corrections/.

9 *Id.*

also identified several other stories with 'minor issues such as incomplete company names, transposed numbers, or language that our senior editors viewed as vague.' "[10]

In late 2023, Sports Illustrated did the same.[11] "Sports Illustrated used stories for product reviews that had authors it could not identify."[12] The stories included bylines and images that appear to be computer generated.[13] Even worse, Sports Illustrated at first denied the allegations and then shifted responsibility to a third-party vendor that was selling the content to Sports Illustrated to be republished as its own journalism. At least there was a consequence. Sports Illustrated CEO Ross Levinsohn was terminated as a result of the controversy surrounding the use of the AI content and subsequent failed cover-up.[14]

---

[10] Catherine Thorbecke, *Plagued with Errors: A News Outlet's Decision to Write Stories with AI Backfires*, CNN (Jan. 26, 2023), https://www.cnn.com/2023/01/25/tech/cnet-ai-tool-news-stories/index.html.

[11] David Bauder, *Sports Illustrated Found Publishing AI Generated Stories, Photos and Authors*, PBS (Nov. 29, 2023), https://www.pbs.org/newshour/economy/sports-illustrated-found-publishing-ai-generated-stories-photos-and-authors.

[12] *Id.*

[13] CST Editorial Board, *Sports Illustrated and Other Newsrooms Fumble Badly by Huddling with AI*, CHI. SUN TIMES (Dec. 11, 2023), https://chicago.suntimes.com/2023/12/11/23990714/sports-illustrated-artificial-intelligence-ai-newsrooms-journalism-fake-news-futurism-editorial.

[14] *See* Elizabeth Napolitano, *Sports Illustrated Publisher Arena Group Fires CEO Following AI Controversy*, CBS NEWS (Dec. 12, 2023), https://www.cbsnews.com/news/sports-illustrated-ross-levinsohn-arena-group-termination-ai-articles/.

Within the United States, there is little doubt that the communicative content produced by generative AI, such as synthetic journalism, will be subject to traditional First Amendment protections.[15] Certainly, the Supreme Court has never suggested that computer generated content in videogames or in commercial speech is somehow in a different category of speech than other methods of generating content for purposes of First Amendment protection.[16]

First, of course, the plaintiff in such an action would need to meet all the common law requirements for liability.[17]

To create liability for defamation there must be:

(a) a false and defamatory statement concerning another;

---

[15] *See generally* Eugene Volokh & Donald M. Falk, *Google: First Amendment Protection for Search Engine Search Results*, 8 J.L. ECON. & POL'Y 883 (2012); Tim Wu, *Machine Speech*, 161 U. PA. L. REV. 1495 (2013); Seema Ghatnekar, *Injury by Algorithm: A Look into Google's Liability for Defamatory Autocompleted Search Suggestions*, 33 LOY. L.A. ENT. L. REV. 171 (2013); Lin Weeks, *Media Law and Copyright Implications of Automated Journalism*, 4 N.Y.U. J. INTELL. PROP. & ENT. L. 67 (2014). *See infra* § 3.4 regarding the European approach using products liability jurisprudence over AI-generated harmful content.

[16] *See* Brown v. Ent. Merchs. Ass'n, 564 U.S. 786, 790 (2011) (videogame content protected by the First Amendment); Sorrell v. IMS Health Inc., 564 U.S. 552 (2011) (pharmaceutical data protected by First Amendment); City of Austin v. Reagan Nat'l Advert. of Austin, LLC, 596 U.S. 61 (2022) (treating digital signs as speech); *See also* Nina Brown, *Bots Behaving Badly: A Products Liability Approach to Chatbot-Generated Defamation*, 3 J. FREE SPEECH L. 389, 401–02 (2023).

[17] *See generally* Cass R. Sunstein, *Falsehoods and the First Amendment*, 33 HARV. J.L. & TECH. 387, 405 (2020).

(b) an unprivileged publication to a third party;

(c) fault amounting at least to negligence on the part of the publisher; and

(d) either actionability of the statement irrespective of special harm or the existence of special harm caused by the publication.[18]

The laws will vary in each state, but they largely adhere to the Restatement formulation. Restatement § 558(c) provides a correct but highly underinclusive explanation of the level of culpability required for tort liability.[19] The Supreme Court First Amendment jurisprudence merely establishes the legal standards by which the content will be adjudicated. As a result, the synthetic speech will likely be considered like other journalism and newsworthy publications in the context of *New York Times Co. v. Sullivan*.[20]

To limit the chilling consequence of libel actions brought by public officials[21] and public figures.[22] in *New York Times Co. v. Sullivan*,[23] the Supreme Court established that the plaintiff must prove the defamatory statement "was made with 'actual malice'—that is, with knowledge that it was false or

[18] RESTATEMENT (SECOND) OF TORTS § 558 (AM. L. INST. 1977).

[19] *Id.*

[20] *See generally* New York Times Co. v. Sullivan, 376 U.S. 254 (1964).

[21] New York Times Co. v. Sullivan, 376 U.S. 254 (1964).

[22] Curtis Publishing Co. v. Butts, 388 U.S. 130 (1967).

[23] New York Times, 376 U.S. at 279.

with reckless disregard of whether it was false or not."[24] "[T]he Court fashioned 'a constitutional requirement that the plaintiff bear the burden of showing falsity, as well as fault, before recovering damages.' "[25]

For matters involving private figures, *Gertz v. Robert Welch, Inc.*[26] retreated from the actual malice standard. plaintiffs are required to prove falsity under a negligence standard applying, though they must do so by a clear and convincing evidence rather than a mere preponderance of the evidence.

The precise dividing line between private individual and public figure remains elusive. In *Time, Inc. v. Firestone*,[27] however, the court made clear that participation in a lawsuit is insufficient "to equate 'public controversy' with all controversies of interest to the public."[28] The Court refused to extend the actual malice standard to private individuals "whenever the statements concern matters of general or public interest."[29] To add to the subjective nature of the public figure standard, some individuals may be limited purpose public figures, who "voluntarily inject[ ]" themselves or are "drawn into a particular public controversy" and thereby become public

---

[24] *Id.*, at 279–280.

[25] Milkovich v. Lorain J. Co., 497 U.S. 1, 16 (1990) quoting Philadelphia Newspapers, Inc. v. Hepps, 475 U.S. 767, 776–77 (1986).

[26] Gertz v. Robert Welch, Inc., 418 U.S. 323 (1974).

[27] 424 U.S. 448 (1976).

[28] Time, Inc. v. Firestone, 424 at 454.

[29] *Id.*

figures "for a limited range of issues" defined by their "participation in the particular controversy giving rise to the defamation."[30] The controversy at issue "must predate the alleged defamation."[31]

In *Milkovich*, for example, the plaintiff was a high school wrestling coach.[32] He was only adjudicated a private plaintiff after the Ohio Supreme Court reversed a lower court determination to the contrary.[33] Courts often gravitate to the actual malice standard by using the public figure or limited public figure labels.[34] And in the age of social media and influencers, the purpose public figure doctrine may well have swallowed the distinctions espoused in *Gertz*. As a consequence, Justice Gorsuch has suggested that the radical changes in the public media landscape have necessitated a reexamination of the public figure standard, and perhaps the actual malice standard as well.[35] He wrote that "[i]n 1964, the Court may have thought the actual malice

---

30 Ayyadurai v. Floor64, Inc., 270 F. Supp. 3d 343, 357 (D. Mass. 2017) (*quoting* Lluberes v. Uncommon Prods., LLC, 663 F.3d 6, 13 (1st Cir. 2011); Gertz, 418 U.S. at 351–52).

31 Id. at 14.

32 Milkovich v. Lorain Journal, 497 U.S. at 3.

33 *Id.* at 8 (the Ohio Supreme Court "first decided that petitioner was neither a public figure nor a public official under the relevant decisions of this Court." *citing* Milkovich v. News-Herald, 15 Ohio St.3d 292, 294–299, 473 N.E.2d 1191, 1193–1196 (1984)).

34 *Cf*, Wolston v. Reader's Dig. Ass'n, Inc., 443 U.S. 157, 167 (1979) (reversing a lower court finding that the plaintiff/petitioner had become a public figure because he was convicted for contempt after failing to respond to a grand jury subpoena).

35 *See* Berisha v. Lawson, 141 S.Ct. 2424 (2021) (J. Gorsuch, dissenting).

standard would apply only to a small number of prominent governmental officials whose names were always in the news . . . . Now, private citizens can become "public figures" on social media overnight."[36] This is the challenge of social media. "Individuals can be deemed "famous" because of their notoriety in certain channels of our now-highly segmented media even as they remain unknown in most."[37] When this content becomes the source of AI training data, the challenge is magnified.

The ease with which AI-generated images may be propounded as factual depictions and spread across social media and into mass media may require the courts to rethink the interpretations of the public figure label, the parameters of the public concern constraint espoused in *Times v. Sullivan*, and the appropriate contours of the actual malice standard for matters unrelated to robust and wide-open debate.[38]

For online libelous content, the question remains which party or parties should be culpable for the harms caused by the publication of the content. These parties may include the persons who created the content; the persons who posted the content to online sites; the sites that hosted the content; and

---

36 *Id.*

37 *Id.*

38 *See, e.g.*, Philadelphia Newspapers, Inc. v. Hepps, 475 U.S. 767 (1986) ("the common-law presumption that defamatory speech is false cannot stand when a plaintiff seeks damages against a media defendant for speech of public concern.").

any persons or services that repurposed that content onto other websites or services.

The first case filed against OpenAI for libel involves a false description of Mark Walters. The lawsuit alleges "that the chatbot provided the false complaint to Fred Riehl, the editor-in-chief of the gun publication AmmoLand, who was reporting on a real life legal case playing out in Washington state."[39] While there have been few filed lawsuits, there are many examples, as collected by Professor Eugene Volokh.[40]

Professor Volokh has explained that he "will tentatively argue that, when the "actual malice" standard applies, the standard might be satisfied if an AI company has received actual notice of particular spurious information being produced by its software but has refused to act."[41] In applying this approach, Professor Volokh implies that under the actual malice standard there is no duty to police the output of an AI system but that duty would arise if there were actual knowledge of false and defamatory content being produced. Since the AI system developers have responded to other misinformation by removing that content such as the glue-in-the-

---

[39] Isaiah Poritz, *OpenAI Hit With First Defamation Suit Over ChatGPT Hallucination*, BLOOMBERG (June 7, 2023), https://news.bloomberglaw.com/tech-and-telecom-law/openai-hit-with-first-defamation-suit-over-chatgpt-hallucination. *See* Complaint, Walters v. OpenAI, L.L.C., No. 23–A–04860–2 (Ga. Super. Ct. Gwinnett Cty. filed June 5, 2023).

[40] *See* Eugene Volokh, *Large Libel Models? Liability for AI Output*, 3 J. FREE SPEECH L. 489 (2023).

[41] *Id.* at 493.

pizza recipe, it seems reasonable that they can implement a libel blocking system.

As the systems become increasingly ubiquitous, the suggestion that the public should rely on disclaimers that the output may be inaccurate seems increasingly self-serving. There is a common law maxim that one cannot waive an intentional tort.[42] Publications meeting the actual malice standard will not be immunized by simple disclaimers that the service is prone to factual error. Such waivers will have even less value if other efforts by the vendors emphasize the reliability of these tools. Moreover, even if the waivers somehow operated to limit liability by the person instituting the query, it would not apply to the subject of the query who is the person being defamed.[43]

The standard of care may also depend on the level of fame. "When asked how many Muslim presidents the U.S. has had, AI Overview responded, "The United States has had one Muslim president, Barack Hussein Obama."[44] Since President Obama has confirmed his Christian faith on numerous occasions, this statement is demonstrably false, but not in any way defamatory. The debunked political claim that President Obama was not a lawful U.S. citizen and

---

42 *See* Edward K. Cheng, Ehud Guttel, and Yuval Procaccia, *Unenforceable Waivers*, 76 VANDERBILT L. REV. 571 (2023).

43 *See* Volokh, *supra* note 40, at 500.

44 Hayden Field, *Google criticized as AI Overview Makes Obvious Errors, such as Saying Former President Obama is Muslim*, CNBC (May 24, 2024), https://www.cnbc.com/2024/05/24/google-criticized-as-ai-overview-makes-errors-like-saying-president-obama-is-muslim.html.

served illegally as the President of the United States, however, would be defamatory. Both facts have been challenged repeatedly and the truth of Obama's birth and religious practice are well documented. Is it enough that an AI developer responds to a specific take-down notice or is the failure to provide a minimum level of accuracy sufficiently reckless to uphold a libel claim? If there is no minimum standard, then the take-down requests will inevitably be considered too narrow an obligation to prove effective.

On the other hand, if the AI system developers can be held accountable for the content of the system, then each other individual or corporation would necessarily be accountable as well. Focusing on the deployer of the system—a person or service posting the false and libelous statement—the deployer will undoubtedly be liable for posting the libelous content, provided the deployer does so with the requisite level of culpability. For public figures, this means that the deployer is at least reckless regarding the truthfulness of the information. The Supreme Court chose to adopt a very high bar to promote free speech, so few unintentional acts of false republication will result in successful defamation claims. Here, however, the suggestion of a mandatory take-down regime makes even more sense. If a deployer negligently posts defamatory content, then once informed the content is inaccurate, the decision to leave that content online transforms the choice into an intentional one. Importantly, however, the content itself may be false and its effect may be harmful, but content is only libelous if the decision to post it meets the required mens rea requirement.

There are different considerations for the web service hosting the content which are addressed in Section 5.1.3 involving immunity from third-party publication.

Nonetheless, at the moment, synthetic journalism may not be out of the woods. First, as noted elsewhere, most of the generative AI tools have not been commercially released for use in journalistic settings.[45] Where they have been used, it has often been in much more restrictive environments. "At the moment, these news articles are restricted mostly to topics that have well-structured datasets associated with them, such as sports results and quarterly financial earnings reports—data that can be fed into an algorithm and transformed into a narrative."[46]

Given the known error rate for generative AI, a newspaper or website operator that publishes articles that are not fact-checked by humans would certainly be negligent and could potentially meet the reckless disregard standard.[47] The GAI system would itself not be culpable.[48] "[I]t seems unlikely that the

---

45 *See* Thorbecke, *supra* note 10.

46 Lewis, Sanders & Carmody, *supra* note 6, at 3.

47 *See* Jane Bambauer, *Negligent AI Speech: Some Thoughts About Duty*, 3 J. FREE SPEECH L. 343, 348 (2023) ("[W]hat it means to 'breach' the duty of reasonable care (that is, to engage in unreasonable conduct) should take the special functions of speech into account.").

48 *See* Derek E. Bambauer & Mihai Surdeanu, *Authorbots*, 3 J. FREE SPEECH L. 375, 382 (2023).

publication of that data could meet defamation doctrine's requirement of negligence or worse—measuring mental state is impossible when there is no mind."[49] It may be true that "chatbots don't libel people, people libel people,"[50] but that provides no protection for people using content from unreliable sources.

If an algorithmically generated news story falsely reported corporate earnings, for example, such a misstatement could have substantial and measurable harm on the company, particularly if it were fed by the same generative AI service across multiple platforms.[51] If instead, the mistake involved corporate officials who were not public figures, then the legal standard would be whether the mistake was negligent, and when published about that individual to third parties resulted in harm. Given the present state of journalistic standards, the expectation likely remains that all content is fact-checked by humans such that the failure to do so is per se negligent. This will change over time as the accuracy of the synthetic journalism improves, but since negligence is

---

[49] *Id.*

[50] The phrase is a play on the well-recognized slogan of the National Rifle Association. *See generally* DENNIS A. HENIGAN, "GUNS DON'T KILL PEOPLE, PEOPLE KILL PEOPLE" AND OTHER MYTHS ABOUT GUNS AND GUN CONTROL (2016).

[51] *See, e.g.*, Dun & Bradstreet, Inc. v. Greenmoss Builders, Inc., 472 U.S. 749, 761 (1985) (upholding compensatory and punitive damage award for publication of defamatory credit report).

compared to the probable risks of harm,[52] this standard will likely move more slowly.

Even once generative AI publications become mainstream, there remains a requirement for traditional fact-checking and reasonable care.[53] "Investigative journalism goes hand in hand with fact checking, especially when facts that can be key to public interest are often buried . . . ."[54] Assertions of factual information should be fact checked. "Category One includes the core facts central to the piece's argument. . . . Content teams should fact-check all category one facts of every piece of content that runs through their process—this is a level one fact check."[55]

False information comes in many forms. In *Masson v. New Yorker*,[56] the Supreme Court discussed the particular harm that occurs when a person is falsely shown to be participating in harmful content. Before

---

52 *See* United States v. Carroll Towing Co., 159 F.2d 169, 173 (2d Cir. 1947).

53 *See* Laura Starita, *Best Practices for Fact-Checking AI-Generated Content*, CONTENTLY (Jan. 17, 2023), https://contently.com/2023/01/17/best-practices-for-fact-checking-ai-generated-content/. *See generally* Brooke Borel, *The Fact-Checking Process*, KSJ SCI. EDITING HANDBOOK, https://ksjhandbook.org/fact-checking-science-journalism-how-to-make-sure-your-stories-are-true/the-fact-checking-process/.

54 *Fact Checking & Investigative Journalism Tools*, PUB. MEDIA ALL., https://www.publicmediaalliance.org/tools/fact-checking-investigative-journalism/.

55 Starita, *supra* note 53.

56 *See* Masson v. New Yorker Mag., Inc., 501 U.S. 496 (1991).

generative AI and synthetic media, such harms were largely limited to falsely attributed quotes.

> A fabricated quotation may injure reputation in at least two senses, either giving rise to a conceivable claim of defamation. First, the quotation might injure because it attributes an untrue factual assertion to the speaker. . . . Second, regardless of the truth or falsity of the factual matters asserted within the quoted statement, the attribution may result in injury to reputation because the manner of expression or even the fact that the statement was made indicates a negative personal trait or an attitude the speaker does not hold.[57]

Today, a person can be shown saying or doing almost anything, and the viewer has no reason to distrust the information being presented. Like the falsely attributed quote, the false depiction in a photograph or video both creates a false depiction of content presented as truthful, and it further harms the reputation because it places the victim of the falsehood as a participant in the creation of the harmful content.

While it is true that fact-checking is time consuming and demanding, non-news services can develop a triage system regarding investment in its fact-checking procedures. At a minimum, whenever the error of fact could result in an adverse statement about a person—whether libelous or not—that fact needs careful fact checking. The same is true about

---

57 *Id.* at 511.

any company or entity which particularly focuses on competitors in the industry.[58] Fact checking is also essential for factual advice published in warnings and instruction manuals or their online equivalents, where such information can reasonably be relied upon.

§ 5.1.2 VISUAL LIBEL

False information comes in many forms. One particularly insidious form of libel involves the falsification of pictures, voices, and videos that appear authentic.[59] By appearing in a picture or video, the information naturally seems authentic.

Inauthentic video is unique in its psychological impact on the viewer.[60] "Since people tend to believe what they see, 'images and other forms of digital media are often accepted at face value.' "[61] This acceptance is not just from third-party viewers.

---

[58] *See, e.g.*, Polygram Records, Inc. v. Superior Court, 170 Cal. App. 3d 543, 548 (1985). A materially harmful false statement regarding a business entity is known as trade libel but is otherwise substantially similar to common law libel. Causation for financial harm may be an additional element for trade libel whereas general damages may be available to an individual.

[59] *See* Jon M. Garon, *An AI's Picture Paints a Thousand Lies: Designating Responsibility for Visual Libel*, 3 J. FREE SPEECH L. 425, 433 (2023).

[60] *See* Taurus Myhand, *Once the Jury sees It, The Jury can't unsee it: The Challenge Trial Judges Face When Authenticating Video Evidence in the age of Deepfakes*, 29 WEIDNER L. REV 171, 174 (2023).

[61] *Id.* at 175 quoting Marie-Helen Maras & Alex Alexandrou, *Determining Authenticity of Video Evidence in the Age of Artificial Intelligence and in the Wake of Deepfake Videos*, 23 INT'L EVID. & PROC. 255, 257 (July 2019).

Studies have shown that when shown a falsified videos of a person committing a crime, the person depicted will often confess to that crime because they believe the video evidence over their own, actual experience.[62] Other studies confirm that "fake evidence can lead people to confess to things they did not do."[63] Using falsified video evidence that the subject stole money, all subjects signed a confession and most falsely believed that they had stolen the money.[64] Inauthentic video and visual libel is much more powerful than a false statement or publication. In addition, as the Supreme Court highlighted in *Mason v. New Yorker*, the misattribution includes not just the false statement but the assertion that the target of the falsehood would actually say such a thing.

Visual libel describes the use of photographs and videos to create libelous content. As discussed in Section 2.2.3, nonconsensual pornography, including "revenge porn," provides a paradigmatic example of the problem.[65] Distribution of actual intimate images without consent constitutes an invasion of privacy. False statements about the production or distribution, including false assertions that the

---

62 Robert A. Nash & Kimberley A. Wade, *Innocent but Proven Guilty: Eliciting Internalized False Confessions Using Doctored-Video Evidence*, 23 APPLIED COGNITIVE PSYCH. 624, 633 (2009); Myhand, *supra* note 60, at 175.

63 Nash & Wade, *supra* note 62, at 624.

64 *See id.*

65 *See* Danielle Keats Citron, *Sexual Privacy*, *supra* ch. 2 note 161, at 1875–85 and accompanying text.

victim wanted to distribute the content is itself a libelous statement.

As a tort, revenge porn will fall into the category of invasion of privacy,[66] while AI-generated look-alike revenge porn should be understood as libelous.[67] Unlike the unauthorized distribution of a sex tape that is accurate but highly invasive of one's privacy, a deepfake is a false depiction that factually asserts the participant engaged in videotaped or photograph sexual activity—perhaps for distribution on the internet. That will likely constitute a libelous statement for the vast majority of victims.[68]

When a person generates revenge porn, the process requires the person to upload an image of the victim and either synthesize the person's likeness into the pornographic video or to use a service that does so. The person utilizing the system, then, is directly responsible for the resulting libel. A person creating that content and publishing it to any website

---

66 Vermont, State v. VanBuren, 210 Vt. 293 (2018) (upholding Vermont's criminal statute as meeting the strict scrutiny standard due to the compelling privacy interests).

67 *See generally*, Eugene Volokh, *One-to-One Speech vs. One-to-Many Speech, Criminal Harassment Laws, and "Cyber stalking,"* 107 NW. U. L. REV. 731, 752–53 (2013).

68 *See* Citron, *supra* ch. 2 note 161, at 1937 ("Public officials and public figures like Gal Gadot could sue for defamation if there is clear and convincing evidence of actual malice (that is, the defendant knew the deep-fake sex videos were false or recklessly disregarded the possibility that they were false)."). *See also* Bobby Chesney and Danielle Citron, *Deep Fakes*, 107 CAL. L. REV. 1753 (2019).

viewable to a third party would meet the requirement to be liable for defamation.

In contrast, most website operators will not be liable for the resulting defamation. Under the broad immunity that interactive computer services (aka web platforms) have from liability for third party content, the sites on which the images appeared would not be liable for the content posted by third parties under the limits of liability provided by Section 230 of the Communications Decency Act.[69] This is explored further in Section 5.1.3.

If instead of a deepfake, the false sexual depiction is created through generative AI using text prompts, the question of responsibility may become less clear. Stable Diffusion has been sued for copyright infringement for scraping millions of Getty Images photographs from the internet.[70] The litigation alleges that the training data for Stable Diffusion has been culled and scraped from billions of internet images without the permission of owners of those images.[71] As a consequence, the Mage imagery and

---

69 *See, e.g.*, Johnson v. Arden, 614 F.3d 785, 790–91 (8th Cir. 2010) ("The CDA states that "[n]o provider or user of an interactive computer service shall be treated as the publisher or speaker of any information provided by another information content provider," 47 U.S.C. § 230(c)(1), and expressly preempts any state law to the contrary, id. § 230(e)(3)"); Fair Hous. Council of San Fernando Valley v. Roommates.com, LLC, 521 F.3d 1157, 1162–64 (9th Cir. 2008).

70 *See* Getty Images (US) Inc. v. Stability AI, Inc., *supra* ch. 4 note 65 and accompanying text.

71 *See id. See also* Gloria Levine, *Exploring the Images Used to Train Stable Diffusion's AI*, 80.LV (Sept. 7, 2022), https://80.

similar services may be using images to generate the pornographic content from those who never agreed to appear in such material.

There is no reason to think that the participants in Unstable Diffusion are seeking to depict particular individuals captured in the Stable Diffusion training set, but since the data may potentially capture any adult or child ever depicted on a website, the potential to depict real people is quite high.[72] Moreover, "early on in the Stable Diffusion beta on its Discord server, testers found that almost every request for a 'beautiful woman' involved unintentional nudity of some kind, which reflects how Western society often depicts women on the Internet."[73] All the biases in the data set will naturally inform the AI generated content. In addition, celebrity depictions can be generated by including the person's name in the prompt.[74]

---

lv/articles/exploring-the-images-used-to-train-stable-diffusion-s-ai/ ("Stable Diffusion was trained on 2.3 billion images.").

[72] *See* Levine, *supra* note 71 ("research showed that almost half of the images were sourced from only 100 domains, with the largest number of images coming from Pinterest. Other sources include WordPress-hosted blogs, Smugmug, Blogspot, Flickr, DeviantArt, Wikimedia, 500px, and Tumblr. Shopping sites were also well-represented.").

[73] Benj Edwards, *With Stable Diffusion, you may Never Believe what you see Online Again*, ART TECHNICA (Sept. 6, 2022), https://arstechnica.com/information-technology/2022/09/with-stable-diffusion-you-may-never-believe-what-you-see-online-again/.

[74] *See, e.g.*, Damir Yalalov, *Best 100+ Stable Diffusion Prompts: The Most Beautiful AI Text-to-Image Prompts*, METAVERSE POST (Sept. 16, 2022), https://mpost.io/best-100-stable-diffusion-prompts-the-most-beautiful-ai-text-to-image-

Pornography is just one example. Another is the broad topic of civil unrest. If generative AI is used to depict images of violent demonstrations, then any actual persons falsely depicted in those images could also claim libel, if those images were published as factually accurate depictions. Consider this non-AI hypothetical. A photograph shows a university instructor standing amidst a crowd of yelling students. If that photograph were identified as coming from a controversial anti-administration event[75] or from an event where speakers were being silenced by a heckling crowd,[76] that instructor could face serious reprisal from the university. If the actual photograph had been taken at a pep rally and mislabeled because it was merely a good crowd shot, such misidentification could be highly injurious and potentially libelous. If instead, a blogger asked Dall-

---

prompts/ (depicting Keanu Reeves, Christina Hendricks, James Dean, Sadie Sink).

[75] *Cf*, Tyler Kingkade, *A Texas teacher faces losing her job after fighting for gay pride symbols in school*, NBC News (Apr. 7, 2022), https://www.nbcnews.com/news/us-news/lgbtq-students-texas-school-rainbow-stickers-rcna23208 ("The school year at MacArthur High in Irving, Texas, began last fall with the administration scraping off rainbow stickers . . . . One faculty sponsor of the school's Gay-Straight Alliance is facing having her contract terminated, another is preparing to resign, and a third has been removed from the classroom.").

[76] *Cf*, Madison Alder, *Stanford Mandates Free Speech Training After Protest of US Judge*, BLOOMBERG (Mar. 22, 2023), https://news.bloomberglaw.com/us-law-week/stanford-mandates-free-speech-training-after-protest-of-us-judge ("Students protested Judge Kyle Duncan's talk on campus. Administrator who spoke at event put on leave, dean says. Stanford Law School is requiring all students to attend educational programming on free speech after protesters interrupted a speech by a conservative federal judge earlier this month.").

E or Stable Diffusion for a picture to illustrate the blogger's story about the event, the image generator could potentially generate such an image on its own. The image is no less injurious. But is the image less libelous?

Since Section 230 of the Communications Decency Act provides broad immunity from civil liability for defamatory content provided by third parties, the host site will be immune from action in most cases. The blogger who posted the offending image will be liable only if negligent in selecting the illustration as to those depicted individuals who are neither public officials nor public figures.[77] The blogger would only be liable under the actual malice standard for public officials and public figures. Certain facts might inform the factual determination regarding the applicable level of culpability. One could certainly conclude that it is at least negligent to use any photograph to illustrate a story about a protest unless that image was actually from the protest itself. If a reasonable reader would be mistaken as to the authenticity of the image, then potentially, the

---

[77] Even if the instructor was employed at a public university, employment alone would not require that the individual be treated as a public official. *See* Rosenblatt v. Baer 383 U.S. 75, 85 (1966), ("the 'public official' designation applies at the very least to those among the hierarchy of government employees who have, or appear to the public to have, substantial responsibility for or control over the conduct of governmental affairs."); Hutchinson v. Proxmire, 443 U.S. 111, 135 (1979) ("Hutchinson [a research behavioral scientist] did not thrust himself or his views into public controversy to influence others. Respondents have not identified such a particular controversy; at most, they point to concern about general public . . . expenditures; it is not sufficient to make Hutchinson a public figure.").

action of the blogger could meet the "actual malice standard," "a term of art denoting deliberate or reckless falsification."[78] To meet the actual malice standard, a "plaintiff must demonstrate that the author 'in fact entertained serious doubts as to the truth of his publication,' or acted with a 'high degree of awareness of . . . probable falsity.' "[79] The use of the AI-generated image to accompany the news story arguably meets this awareness of falsity if used to demonstrate what occurred at the event. In contrast, it is unlikely to be reckless—or even negligent—if the blogger makes clear that the image is an illustration rather than a depiction of actual events.

The two different use examples of AI-generated content are very different. In the example of the protest, it is the context of the image that makes the image defamatory. Without that context, the instructor's face among a crowd of students is unlikely to create injurious content. In the example of generative AI nonconsensual pornography, the context within the image makes it inherently injurious. For photorealistic AI content that depicts images that are libelous irrespective of external context, then, the selection and publication on the internet will likely carry liability to protect private

---

[78] Masson v. New Yorker Magazine, Inc., 501 U.S. 496, 499 (1991).

[79] *Id.* at 510 (*quoting* St. Amant v. Thompson, 390 U.S. 727, 731 (1968); Garrison v. Louisiana, 379 U.S. 64, 74 (1964)).

individuals. Works that do not present themselves as factual depictions would not meet this test.[80]

This leaves an open question whether the company which created and trained the AI system can be liable. When the AI system provides the generated image to the individual submitting the text-based inquiry, it is publishing content to a third party. If that content otherwise meets all the other tests for defamation, it stands to reason that the developer could be culpable for its content. In the case of pornography, for example, jurisdictions will likely hold AI system developers liable for production of child pornography if the AI generates simulated child pornography using depictions of actual children pulled from its training set.[81] Such "morphed" child

---

[80] *See, e.g.*, Scott Indrisek, *Can Art Legally Threaten the President?*, ARTSY (May 3, 2017), https://www.artsy.net/article/artsy-editorial-art-legally-threaten-president ("You might argue that exhibiting a nude Captain America flaunting the President's disembodied cranium is flirting with 'risk to others.' But Chung's painting, he says, is more nuanced than it might seem.").

[81] *Compare* Ashcroft v. Free Speech Coalition, 535 U.S. 234, 241 (2002) (finding unconstitutional a law banning " 'virtual child pornography,' which include computer-generated images, as well as images produced by more traditional means); U.S. v. Williams, 553 U.S. 285, 293 (2008) (upholding federal law "prohibits offers to provide and requests to obtain child pornography [even though the] statute does not require the actual existence of child pornography."); United States v. Mecham, 950 F.3d 257, 260 (5th Cir. 2020) ("morphed child pornography does not enjoy first amendment protection"); Doe v. Boland, 698 F.3d 877, 883 (6th Cir. 2012) (morphed images of actual children on images involving sex act gave rise to liability for federal torts. The defendant's role as expert witness did not create immunity for such liability.).

pornography is outside the protection of the First Amendment.[82]

If a jurisdiction can reach morphed child pornography, it also stands to reason that it could reach other content that runs afoul of the negligence standard for private individuals or actual malice standard that applies to public officials and public figures. The negligence standard should apply in the case of students generating pornographic images of classmates. An actual malice standard would be required if the depiction were of a famous celebrity.

Meeting this standard will be difficult, and the AI developer will attempt to put the blame on the person offering the prompt rather than the response by the

---

82 *See* People v. McKown, 2022 IL 127683, ¶ 36, reh'g denied (Jan. 23, 2023) (collecting cases):

> United States v. Mecham, 950 F.3d 257, 260 (5th Cir. 2020) (agreeing "with the majority view that morphed child pornography does not enjoy first amendment protection"); Doe v. Boland, 698 F.3d 877, 883 (6th Cir. 2012) (rejecting defendant's first amendment challenge to morphed child pornography where "Jane Doe and Jane Roe are real children" whose "likenesses are identifiable in [defendant's] images"); United States v. Hotaling, 634 F.3d 725, 730 (2d Cir. 2011) ("Sexually explicit images that use the faces of actual minors are not protected expressive speech under the First Amendment."); McFadden v. State, 67 So. 3d 169, 184 (Ala. Crim. App. 2010) (ruling that statutes "which criminalize the possession * * * of collage or montage images of child pornography * * * created without * * * photographing actual sexual conduct on the part of an identifiable minor, but edited to appear as though the children are engaged in sexual conduct, do not violate the First Amendment State v. Tooley, 872 N.E.2d 894 (Ohio 2007) (declining to extend Free Speech Coalition "to cover morphed child pornography when the United States Supreme Court did not do so").

AI. Given the significant difficulty in achieving ultimate success in libel actions, attempts to hold all but the most extreme trained systems will likely be difficult and fail to address the broader policy concerns. Nonetheless, as guardrails become more common, the norms for negligence and recklessness will shift. Over time, the improvements in the AI systems should lead to fewer instances of unauthorized pornography and other defamatory imagery, increasing the potential for holding deployers accountable if they fail to incorporate guardrails.

§ 5.1.3 INTERSECTION WITH COMMUNICATIONS DECENCY ACT SAFE HARBOR (§ 230)

Section 230(c) of the CDA provides: "No provider or user of an interactive computer service shall be treated as the publisher or speaker of any information provided by another information content provider."[83] Unlike copyright and patent laws, CDA § 230 does not use the term individual,[84] and because it is written in the negative, the law potentially sweeps much more broadly to include content that is created by generative AI.

---

83 47 U.S.C. § 230(c).

84 *Id.* at § 230(f)(3) ("Information content provider" means "any person or entity that is responsible, in whole or in part, for the creation or development of information provided through the internet or any other interactive computer service.").

At the same time, however, it cannot provide immunity for the generative AI itself.[85] When Simplicity AI or OpenAI create and train their models, they are not using an interactive service, putting them outside the framework of the safe harbor.[86] In one example, a pro se litigant has alleged that Microsoft Bing conflated the biography of the plaintiff Jeffery Battle with the convicted terrorist Jeffrey Leon Battle (with a different spelling of the first name).[87] The conflated biography appends the conviction to the plaintiff's accurate biography:

> Jeffery Battle, also known as The Aerospace Professor, is the President and CEO of Battle Enterprises, LLC and its subsidiary The Aerospace Professor Company. He is an honorable discharged U.S. Air Force veteran and has been appointed as an Adjunct Professor for Embry-Riddle Aeronautical University. Battle has a Master of Business Administration in Aviation degree and two Bachelor of Science degrees. *However, Battle was sentenced to eighteen years in prison after pleading guilty to seditious conspiracy and levying war against the United States. He had two years added to his*

---

[85] Matt Perault, *Section 230 Won't Protect ChatGPT*, LAWFARE BLOG (Feb. 22, 2023), https://www.lawfareblog.com/section-230-wont-protect-chatgpt.

[86] *Id.*

[87] Battle v. Microsoft Corp., No. 1:23–cv–01822, 2024 WL 4555687, at *1 (D. Md. Oct. 23, 2024) (compelling arbitration).

sentence for refusing to testify before a grand jury.[88]

As a Microsoft user, the plaintiff had entered into a Terms of Service agreement for the general use of Microsoft products which contained an arbitration clause, which the court enforced despite the rather unrelated nature of the cause of action.[89] Nonetheless, the complaint illustrates the manner in which chatbots can easily combine information to create libelous output.

Professor Matt Perault writes that given the definition of interactive service provider, "courts will likely find that ChatGPT and other [systems] are information content providers."[90] The broader question is whether such a claim will ever make it to final adjudication. The broad use of arbitration clauses and the willingness to enforce such clauses for unrelated torts essentially sideline the judiciary from any meaningful development of the law. Without a change to the Federal Arbitration Act or other statutory immunity schemes ubiquitous arbitration clauses will preclude judicial development on the statutory meaning of § 230 and disrupt any transparent development of law and policy in the field.

As a result, the AI developers will likely use terms of service agreements as the source of their immunity

---

88 *Id.* at complaint. https://storage.courtlistener.com/recap/gov.uscourts.mdd.540279/gov.uscourts.mdd.540279.1.0.pdf.

89 *Id.*

90 Perault, *supra* note 85.

rather than § 230. Unlike the AI developers, the deployers—the platforms hosting those services—will likely receive protection from § 230. The host interactive computer service is unlikely to be modifying or controlling the content, except perhaps to be filtering out material that violates its community standards. The hosting service will likely be able to shield itself from the direct liability for the content provided by the natural language generator. Of course, if the website engages more directly with the content in some manner, then it may lose the protection of the safe harbor as a result.

Separately, to the extent the claim is based on violations of the Lanham Act, CDA § 230 should not serve as a bar to the cause of action. "Subsection (e) ensures several legal domains remain unaffected by § 230(c). Most relevant here, the court in *Hepp v. Facebook*,[91] made clear § 230 has "[n]o effect on intellectual property."[92] In *Universal Communication Systems, Inc. v. Lycos, Inc.*,[93] the plaintiff alleged that the defendant message board providers allowed posts contained "false, misleading" content about the company's financial status and position.[94] The plaintiff brought claims for both state and federal trademark violations and the court refused to dismiss the claims based on § 230.[95]

---

91 Hepp v. Facebook, 14 F.4th 204, 209 (3d Cir. 2021).

92 *Id.* at 209 (quoting 47 U.S.C. § 230(e)(2)). *See also* Universal Commc'n Sys., Inc. v. Lycos, Inc., 478 F.3d 413, 415–416 (1st Cir. 2007).

93 *Universal Commc'n Sys.*, 478 F.3d at 415–416.

94 *See id.* at 415–16.

95 *Id.* at 422–25.

Contrast this with a narrower interpretation in *Perfect 10, Inc. v. CCBill LLC*,[96] where the court found that § 230 barred the state intellectual property claims and construed the limitation of § 230(e)(2) to federal claims.[97] While such a limitation may have made some public policy sense in the context of an earlier understanding of potential internet liability, the Third Circuit recognition of the state right of publicity likely reflects the current concerns over internet immunity and the loss of confidence that courts have found the right balance between § 230 and other laws.[98]

The Digital Replicas Report of the Copyright Office recommends that the proposed new digital replica right be categorized as an intellectual property right and excluded from the § 230 shield.[99] "The Copyright Office believes that exclusion from section 230 is advisable to encourage prompt removal of unauthorized digital replicas from online platforms. In many circumstances, OSPs are best positioned to prevent the continuing harm from the availability of such replicas."[100]

Instead of § 230, many commentators have suggested that a notice-and-take-down regime is a better approach, provided that the take-down system also includes a "keep down" system that Copyright

---

[96] Perfect 10, Inc. v. CCBill LLC, 488 F.3d 1102, 1118–19 (9th Cir. 2007).

[97] *Id.* at 1118–20.

[98] Hepp v. Facebook, 14 F.4th 204, 209 (3d Cir. 2021).

[99] DIGITAL REPLICAS REPORT, *supra* ch. 4 note 182 at 37–38.

[100] *Id.* at 38.

§ 512 is sorely lacking.[101] "The [Copyright] Office agrees that a notice and takedown system, combined with an appropriate safe harbor, could be an effective approach. . . . conditioning its availability on the OSP expeditiously removing the digital replicas when it has actual knowledge or has received a sufficiently reliable notification that the replica is infringing."[102]

§ 5.2 INFORMATIONAL AND VOLITIONAL PRIVACY

The use of AI systems carries a wide range of risks associated with individual privacy separate from either the issues of defamation or unauthorized commercial exploitation. As originally conceived in the U.S., privacy generally refers to the "right to be let alone."[103] Although the term "privacy" does not appear in the Constitution,[104] the Supreme Court has often recognized constitutional protections associated with both decisional privacy, meaning "the right to make and implement important personal decisions without governmental interference,"[105] and informational privacy, referring

---

[101] *See id.*

[102] *Id.* at 39.

[103] *See* Samuel Warren & Louis Brandeis, *The Right to Privacy*, 4 HARV. L. REV. 193, 193 (1890).

[104] Dobbs v. Jackson Women's Health Org., 597 U.S. 215, 235 (2022).

[105] *Id.* at 273 (Kavanaugh, J., concurring) (citing Whalen v. Roe, 429 U.S. 589, 599–600 (1977)).

to "the right to shield information from disclosure . . . ."[106]

The expansion of AI systems has created the need for a third category of privacy, sometimes referred to as "human rights privacy,"[107] "volitional privacy," or "anti-surveillance privacy," meaning the right to be protected from misuse of information individuals disclose without volition.

Decisional privacy has enjoyed a long, if inconsistent, protection under constitutional law. Beginning with *Griswold v. Connecticut*,[108] the Supreme Court has recognized personal autonomy connected to aspects of the First, Third, Fourth, Firth, Ninth, and Fourteenth Amendments.[109] The Supreme Court explained that the right of privacy embedded in the Fourth Amendment created a "right to privacy, no less important than any other right carefully and particularly reserved to the people."[110]

In the criminal setting, decisional privacy limits self-incrimination, unwarranted searches, and other state intrusions protected by the Constitution and understood as innate to fundamental human rights.

---

[106] *Id.*

[107] *See, e.g.*, RESOLUTION ADOPTED BY THE HUMAN RIGHTS COUNCIL, UNITED NATIONS GEN. ASSEMBLY A/HRC/RES/42/15 (Oct. 7, 2019), https://undocs.org/A/HRC/RES/42/15; International Covenant on Civil and Political Rights, Dec. 16, 1966, 999 U.N.T.S. 171.

[108] Griswold v. Connecticut, 381 U.S. 479 (1965) (right of married persons to obtain contraceptives).

[109] *Id.* at 484.

[110] Mapp v. Ohio, 367 U.S. 643, 656 (1961).

"The philosophy of each Amendment and of each freedom is complementary to, although not dependent upon, that of the other in its sphere of influence—the very least that together they assure in either sphere is that no man is to be convicted on unconstitutional evidence.[111]

Decisional privacy cases include a range of protections, including the right to private consensual sexual activity,[112] access to contraceptives,[113] and until 2022 included women's reproductive autonomy.[114] Decisional privacy protections make unconstitutional efforts by state and federal law to criminalize individual autonomy in one's private life. Closely related are First Amendment protections to the right of association[115] and Fourt Amendment protections from warrantless searches,[116] since all these rights enable an individual to be oneself in society free from government surveillance and interference. Although the Supreme Court has been

---

[111] *Id.* at 657.

[112] Lawrence v. Texas, 539 U.S. 558 (2003).

[113] Griswold, 381 U.S. at 484; Eisenstadt v. Baird, 405 U.S. 438 (1972), Carey v. Population Services Int'l, 431 U.S. 678 (1977).

[114] *See* Dobbs v. Jackson Women's Health Org., 597 U.S. 215, 223 (2022) (overturning reproductive autonomy); Roe v. Wade, 410 U.S. 113 (1973) (granting reproductive autonomy and a woman's right to access abortion services); Planned Parenthood of Se. Pa. v. Casey, 505 U.S. 833 (1992) (same).

[115] *See* NAACP v. State of Alabama, 357 U.S. 449, 462 (1958); NAACP v. Button, 371 U.S. 415, 430–31 (1963); Hurley v. Irish-American Gay, Lesbian and Bisexual Group of Boston, 515 U.S. 557 (1995).

[116] *See* Mapp v. Ohio, 367 U.S. 643, 655 (1961); Katz v. United States, 389 U.S. 347 (1967); Florida v. Riley, 488 U.S. 445, 452 (1989); Kyllo v. United States, 533 U.S. 27, 30 (2001).

antagonistic to decisional privacy, it has strengthened its protection of informational privacy in a series of Fourth Amendment decisions, particularly in the areas of data aggregation.[117]

Informational privacy focuses on the power of an individual to control the information they provide to non-governmental parties, primarily though the notice and consent model of information collection that has evolved since the early development of networked computers. Responding to the federal government's violation of the public trust following the Watergate scandal, the Privacy Act of 1974[118] established an approach to information collection that became known as a code of fair information practices (FIPPs).[119] The FIPPs practices "allow individuals to determine what records pertaining to them are collected, maintained, used, or disseminated by an agency; require agencies to procure consent before records pertaining to an individual collected for one purpose could be used for other incompatible purposes. . ."[120] They also provide a right to access the information and correct

---

117 *See* Carpenter v. United States, 138 S. Ct. 2206, 2220–21 (2018) (requiring a search warrant for cell site location information collected by cell phone operators); Riley v. California, 573 U.S. 373, 403 (2014) (search warrant required for a search of a person's cell phone contents); United States v. Jones, 565 U.S. 400, 404 (2012) (search warrant required for GPS tracker placed on vehicle).

118 Privacy Act of 1974, 5 U.S.C. § 552a (2024).

119 OVERVIEW OF THE PRIVACY ACT OF 1974, U.S. DEPARTMENT OF JUSTICE, 1 (2020), https://www.justice.gov/opcl/overview-privacy-act-1974-2020-edition.

120 *Id.*

misinformation.[121] These core requirements of notice prior to collection, required consent as a condition of collection, limiting the use of collected information to that approved by meaningful consent, and the right to correct misinformation are at the core of the original Privacy Act model that have been incorporated into laws ranging from GDPR to COPPA, HIPAA, and all state privacy enactments.

In the age of predictive AI systems, ubiquitous pattern recognition, and data scraping for generative AI training, the notice-and-consent model underlying FIPPs has lost much of its efficacy. Instead of requiring bona fide notice after meaningful consent, the opt-out model used for disclosure of data practices leaves the public largely inured to constant data collection. Few people read the disclosures on apps and websites. Even if people opt-out of data collection, companies often update their services and reset these options, promoting disclosure fatigue. Nag screens, disabling functionality app and website functionality, and a host of other dark practices further disenfranchise the public.

Even if the FIPPs model of notice-and-consent could be resurrected into a meaningful method of protecting personal information, the AI systems' ability to use data aggregation and pattern recognition means the information provided involuntarily may reveal even more than about an individual than the information they voluntarily provided. The expansion of AI systems both fuels the

---

121 *Id.*

exponential production of data and the ability to collect ever-increasing amounts of information.[122] "More data makes analysis more powerful and more granular. Variety adds to this power and enables new and unanticipated inferences and predictions. And velocity facilitates analysis as well as sharing in real time."[123]

The Supreme Court has taken preliminary steps to recognize that the involuntary disclosure of personal information should be understood as protected under the Fourth Amendment and perhaps the broader penumbra of privacy rights. In *Carpenter v. U.S.*,[124] the Supreme Court addressed the ability of law enforcement to acquire historical cell site location information (CSLI), data collected by wireless telephone providers regarding the movement of data from cell tower to cell tower as mobile phones move throughout the wireless coverage area. "Wireless carriers collect and store CSLI for their own business purposes, including finding weak spots in their network and applying "roaming" charges when another carrier routes data through their cell sites."[125] The wireless carriers also collect and sell this information to data brokers.[126] Since most people carry their cell phones with them and wear their LTE-connected watches, the movements of most

---

122 Cameron F. Kerry, *Protecting Privacy in an AI-Driven World*, BROOKINGS INST. (Feb. 10, 2020), https://www.brookings.edu/articles/protecting-privacy-in-an-ai-driven-world/.

123 *Id.*

124 Carpenter v. U.S., 585 U.S. 296 (2018).

125 *Id.* at 301.

126 *Id.*

people can be digitally mapped through this technology. The historical records enable law enforcement to build a map of a person's movement, while real-time tracking would enable someone with the data to follow an individual in real time.

Although much of the precedent for CSLI data suggested that the information had been voluntarily disclosed by the individual and therefore was beyond constitutional protection, the Supreme Court nonetheless, recognized that the nature of the use of the information was fundamentally different than in previous voluntary disclosure situations. "A person does not surrender all Fourth Amendment protection by venturing into the public sphere. To the contrary, 'what [one] seeks to preserve as private, even in an area accessible to the public, may be constitutionally protected.' "[127] Because of the power to track an individually so comprehensively the Supreme Court established that a search warrant is required. "[W]hen the Government accessed CSLI from the wireless carriers, it invaded Carpenter's reasonable expectation of privacy in the whole of his physical movements.[128]

The decision leaned heavily on the personal relationship between a cell phone and its owner. "[A] cell phone—almost a 'feature of human anatomy,'—tracks nearly exactly the movements of its owner. . . . A cell phone faithfully follows its owner beyond public thoroughfares and into private residences,

---

[127] *Id.* at 310 quoting Katz, 389 U.S., at 351–52.

[128] *Id.* at 313.

doctor's offices, political headquarters, and other potentially revealing locales."[129]

The *Carpenter* decision is the first to recognize that any modern right to privacy must also include a new right to protect volitional privacy or human rights privacy. Critics of government collection of private information often focus on the potential for misuse.

As discussed more fully below,[130] since 2016 a new form of surveillance has resulted in a powerful tool for commercial enterprises and law enforcement. The tool is the location data history in smartphones. For Android devices, these data are stored "in a repository called the 'Sensorvault.' The Sensorvault assigns each device a unique identification number and maintains all Location History data associated with that device. Google then uses this data to build aggregate models to assist applications like Google Maps."[131]

The Sensorvault's location history data collects all movements of the phone. The choice to use location history is a user choice and must be turned on by the user to initiate the collection of the data. As the Fifth Circuit has explained, however, "[u]sers are often asked to opt in to Location History multiple times across multiple apps. In fact, manually deactivating all [Location History] sharing remains difficult and

---

129 *Id.* quoting Riley, 573 U.S., at 385.

130 *See* United States v. Chatrie, 107 F.4th 319 (4th Cir. 2024), *infra* ch. 7 note 88 and accompanying test.

131 *Id.* at 323.

discouraged."[132] Evidence from litigation involving geofence warrants uncovered an internal Google email, where one of the engineers commented that " '[t]he current [user interface] *feels* like it is designed to make [limiting Location History collection] possible, yet [it is] difficult enough that people won't figure it out.' "[133]

Smartphone users are asked repeatedly to enable the location history for a myriad of different apps. Many have reduced functionality without the location history enabled, and once turned on for any purpose, it is operational for all the Sensorvault and general use. Further, as noted by the Fifth Circuit in *U.S. v. Smith*, "[P]ublished reports have indicated that many Google services on Android and Apple devices store the device users' location data even if the users seek to opt out of being tracked by activating a privacy setting that says it will prevent Google from storing the location data.").[134] Location history data is then updated every two minutes as the phones collect information from GPS, apps, CSLI, and other sources. Phone services collect this information for commercial purposes but has also become a valuable resource for law enforcement, despite its controversial nature.

---

132 U.S. v. Smith, 110 F.4th 817, 823 (5th Cir. 2024).

133 Haley Amster & Brett Diehl, Against Geofences, 74 STAN. L. REV. 385, 397 (2022) (internal citations omitted).

134 Smith, 110 F.4th at 823; In re Search of Info. Stored at Premises Controlled by Google, 481 F. Supp. 3d 730, 737 n.3 (N.D. Ill. 2020).

Another example of the surveillance infrastructure has been made more understandable because of requirements to comply with state biometric data collection laws. An example of this is the Illinois law on biometric data collection. As noted earlier, AI systems power facial recognition systems that can identify individuals whenever they appear in public.[135] Biometric systems go beyond facial features to include "fingerprints, palmprints, voiceprints, facial, retinal, or iris measurements, and more. A person's biometric data—their specific measurements—can be used as unique identifiers."[136] In 2008, Illinois passed a biometric consent law that included a privacy cause of action and statutory damages.[137] As a result, Illinois has become home to some of the most significant biometric privacy litigation. At the same time, however, biometric tracking remains permitted, provided there is consent for its use. Washington, California, Colorado, Connecticut, Nevada, Texas, Utah, and Virginia all have added some additional state regulation on biometric data collection, but the laws vary considerably.[138]

---

135 Melissa Heikkilä, *The Rise of AI Surveillance*, POLITICO (May 26, 2021), https://www.politico.eu/article/the-rise-of-ai-surveillance-coronavirus-data-collection-tracking-facial-recognition-monitoring/.

136 *Is Biometric Information Protected by Privacy Laws*, BLOOMBERG (May 3, 2023), https://pro.bloomberglaw.com/brief/biometric-data-privacy-laws/.

137 Biometric Information Privacy Act ("BIPA"), 740 ILL. COMP. STAT. 14/1 (2008); *see* BLOOMBERG, *supra* note 136.

138 Tara N. Cho & Theodore F. Claypoole, *State of US Data Privacy Law Compliance*, WOMBLE BOND DICKINSON (June 22,

Although the biometric data collection laws all provide some additional protections for employees and the public, they emphasize notice and consent rather than categorical restrictions on the collection of biometric data or even the limitation on use of that data. In coming years, however, state and federal regulators will likely see the wisdom in *Carpenter* and the need for more explicit volitional privacy laws that preclude categories of misuse.

The modern workplace bristles with information gathering to monitor employees for the purpose of improving efficiency, reducing misconduct, and avoiding liability for employee activities.[139] Firms may monitor all communications, including email, internet usage, telephone calls, data ports, hard-drive usage, and chat logs. Firms use cameras to record movement, key loggers, and biometric scanners to monitor computer use and employee movement throughout their workday.[140] There are federal and state regulations, but they are limited in scope. Most focus on providing notice to employees

---

2022), https://www.womblebonddickinson.com/us/insights/articles-and-briefings/state-us-data-privacy-law-compliance; Kirk J. Nahra, Ali A. Jessani, & Samuel Kane, *Biometric Privacy Law Update*, WILMER HALE (Feb. 24, 2023), https://www.wilmerhale.com/insights/client-alerts/20230224-biometric-privacy-law-update.

139 *See* Max Freedman, *Spying on Your Employees? Better Understand the Law First*, BUS. NEWS DAILY (May 27, 2024), https://www.businessnewsdaily.com/6685-employee-monitoring-privacy.html.

140 *See id.*

that the practices are taking place rather than any significant protections from the surveillance itself.

In response to the growing use of AI systems in the workplace, the Consumer Financial Protection Bureau (CFPB), Department of Justice (DOJ), Equal Employment Opportunity Commission (EEOC), and Federal Trade Commission (FTC) issued a joint statement highlighting concerns over bias and discrimination.[141] The letter highlights the risks associated with the use of AI in the workplace.

> AI tools can be inaccurate, biased, and discriminatory by design and incentivize relying on increasingly invasive forms of commercial surveillance. The FTC has also warned market participants that it may violate the FTC Act to use automated tools that have discriminatory impacts, to make claims about AI that are not substantiated, or to deploy AI before taking steps to assess and mitigate risks.[142]

Both governments and private companies acquire social media content to track individuals.[143] Police sometimes deploy cell tower simulators to collect cell

---

141 Press Release, Rohit Chopra, Kristen Clarke, Charolette A. Burrows & Lina M. Khan, Consumer Fin. Prot. Bureau, U.S. Dep't of Just. C.R. Div., Equal Emp. Opportunity Comm'n & Fed. Trade Comm'n, *Joint Statement on Enforcement Efforts Against Discrimination and Bias in Automated Systems*.

142 *Id.* at 2–3.

143 Aaron Holmes, *How Police Are Using Technology Like Drones and Facial Recognition to Monitor Protests and Track People Across the US*, BUS. INSIDER (June 1, 2020), https://www.businessinsider.com/how-police-use-tech-facial-recognition-ai-drones-2019-10.

site location information directly without the need to request information from telephone operators.[144] Other systems may incorporate license plate readers and data voluntarily shared from Amazon's Ring doorbell cameras.[145] At work, employers may use cameras, vehicle trackers, and computer tracking software that monitors "keystrokes, browsing activity, emails, chat apps."[146]

AI systems both power the tools to collect the massive amount of personal information and to sift through that data for words, phrases, behaviors, or patterns that might result in an actionable response. While one employer might monitor for the word "interview," because that employer is concerned about employee retention,[147] other employers can be using the tracking to more generally assess the efficiency of each employee to inform job retention and promotion decisions.[148]

The EU AI Act, as noted in Section 3.4.3, utilizes a risk-based approach. Unacceptable risks are banned outright. These include "[a]pplications that comprise

---

144 *Id.*

145 Bryan McMahon, *How the Police Use AI to Track and Identify You*, GRADIENT (Oct. 3, 2020), https://thegradient.pub/how-the-police-use-ai-to-track-and-identify-you/.

146 Goh Chiew Tong, *Employee Surveillance Is on the Rise—and That Could Backfire on Employers*, CNBC (Apr. 23, 2023), https://www.cnbc.com/2023/04/24/employee-surveillance-is-on-the-rise-that-could-backfire-on-employers.html.

147 *See id.*

148 *See* Goh Chiew Tong, *Employee Surveillance is on the Rise—and that could Backfire on Employers*, CNBC (Apr. 23, 2023), https://www.cnbc.com/2023/04/24/employee-surveillance-is-on-the-rise-that-could-backfire-on-employers.html.

subliminal techniques, exploitative systems or social scoring systems used by public authorities . . . . Also prohibited are any real-time remote biometric identification systems used by law enforcement in publicly-accessible spaces."[149] High-risk systems include critical infrastructures, educational or vocational training, safety components of products, employment services, services related to migration and asylum, access to legal services, and similar categories.[150]

The Colorado AI Act has an even narrower version of this approach.[151] Volitional privacy is limited to examples of mass data collection and analysis instead of a broader protection of all information that a person might share when going about the person's daily life. For example, although there may be statutory protection against collection of biometric information or protection against its collection without consent, no laws prohibit the taking of a photograph of a person in public.[152] Volitional privacy protection against mass surveillance is just one example of the general rule of free access to information being limited. Intrusions into a person's private home and the use of cameras in bathrooms and locker rooms can be restricted to properly

---

149 *The Four Risks of the EU's Artificial Intelligence Act: Is Your Company Ready?*, FTI CONSULTING (July 25, 2023), https://www.fticonsulting.com/insights/fti-journal/four-risks-eus-artificial-intelligence-act. *See* AI Act 2024/1689.

150 *See* AI Act 2024/1689. *See also* Ruschemeier & Bareis *supra* ch. 3 note 182 and accompanying text.

151 Colorado SB–24–205 at § 6–1–1701(1)(a).

152 *See, e.g.*, Nussenzweig v. diCorcia, 9 N.Y.3d 184 (2007).

balance speech considerations with intimate privacy values.[153]

In the context of the Fourth Amendment, volitional privacy principles are at odds with the third party doctrine.[154] Under the third-party doctrine, for purposes of the Fourth Amendment, "information freely divulged to a third party is not covered by a reasonable expectation of privacy and is therefore not protected by the Fourth Amendment. . . . It has immense implications in the post-digital revolution setting."[155]

Carpenter suggests a more generalizable rule that should develop in the context of legislation rather than Fourth Amendment jurisprudence. To protect volitional privacy, a company that may otherwise lawfully collect and use customer information may not aggregate and use that information to track customers over time or identify the behaviors of individuals within the data set. In other words, collecting aggregate data remains permissible for general informational purposes but not to re-identify and track or target an individual. Cell tower

---

153 *See, e.g.*, Brannum v. Overton Cnty. Sch. Bd., 516 F.3d 489, 494 (6th Cir. 2008) ("the constitutional right to privacy, which includes the right to shield one's body from exposure to viewing by the opposite sex, derives from the Fourth Amendment, rather than the Due Process Clause.").

154 *See* United States v. Miller, 425 U.S. 435, 436 (1976); Smith v. Maryland, 442 U.S. 735, 736–37 (1979).

155 William Hopchak, *Carpenter v. United States: CSLI, Third-Party Doctrine, and Privacy in the Twenty-First Century*, 14 LIBERTY U.L. REV. 185, 191 (2019). *See* Amitai Etzioni, *A Cyber Age Privacy Doctrine More Coherent, Less Subjective, and Operational*, 80 BROOK. L. REV. 1263 (2015).

operators can, for example, use the CSLI to track overall usage, check for outages, and operate their business but not to target an individual. The same would be true of surveillance cameras on the streets and private property, and more. There may need to be exceptions for national security or other purposes, highlighting the need to craft legislation carefully rather than rely on constitutional interpretations.

The need for new legislation is growing, In addition to the over-use of personal information and the misuse of personal information created by massive, big data information collections and predictive analytics, there is a new set of concerns associated with the ability of generative AI to recreate an individual's image, speech pattern, artwork, voice, and more.

Many of the companies developing generative AI found their massive datasets by scraping the internet. "In the rush to build and train ever-larger AI models, developers have swept up much of the searchable Internet. This not only has the potential to violate copyrights but also threatens the privacy of the billions of people who share information online."[156] Much of the content comes from web crawlers and content scrapers.[157] Other content

---

156 Lauren Leffer, *Your Personal Information Is Probably Being Used to Train Generative AI Models*, SCI. AM. (Oct. 19, 2023), https://www.scientificamerican.com/article/your-personal-information-is-probably-being-used-to-train-generative-ai-models/.

157 *Id.* ("Alphabet, which already builds Web crawlers to power its search engine, can opt to employ its own tools . . . . Other companies, however, turn to existing resources such as Common

comes from datasets of pirated works, including "a data set called Books3, which contained more than 170,000 pirated and copyrighted books."[158] Because of copyright piracy as well as technology that can get past pay walls and user logins, even content published as private or earmarked "do not crawl" may have been hoovered into the training sets.[159] As a consequence, everything from a person's baby pictures to the person's police records may have become part of the training model and available to help the service generate new content when queried about the individual.

In addition, the data sets ingest information provided by the millions of users conducting search queries. For example, "Google AI pulls data from user interactions and other types of data collected from its search engine and other services, such as Google Maps and Google Photos."[160] "Prompting also enables the addition of contextual information, such as internal company data, to language models. This allows companies to leverage the text-generation capabilities of these models, even without access to the internal data typically required to provide relevant answers."[161]

Crawl, which helped feed OpenAI's GPT-3, or databases such as the Large-Scale Artificial Intelligence Open Network . . . .").

158 *Id.*

159 *Id.*

160 Nick Barney, *Google AI*, TECHTARGET (Apr. 6, 2023), https://www.techtarget.com/whatis/definition/Google-AI.

161 *A Deep Dive into NLP Techniques: Prompting and Training Compared*, SAGACIFY, https://www.sagacify.com/news/a-deep-dive-into-nlp-techniques-prompting-and-training-compared.

OpenAI acknowledges incorporating personal information into the training data but describes it as "incidental."[162] OpenAI CEO, Sam Altman, has acknowledged the problem. "Customers clearly want us not to train on their data," he acknowledged.[163] Still, the training prompts can be an important data source for the generative AI model. Similar questions have arisen over Elon Musk's xAI, known as "Grok," to train on X (formerly Twitter) feeds and data from Tesla including videos generated by the moving cars and the driver information.[164]

Anti-surveillance protections are limited. Current U.S. legal systems provide little recourse for individuals who would prefer their information be excluded from the training models or restricted from the output of the GAI systems. California has the most extensive of state laws for data protection.[165]

---

[162] Sara Morrison, *The Tricky Truth About How Generative AI Uses Your Data*, VOX (July 27, 2023), https://www.vox.com/technology/2023/7/27/23808499/ai-openai-google-meta-data-privacy-nope ("OpenAI admits that it uses personal data to train its models, but says it comes across that data 'incidentally' and only uses it to make 'our models better,' as opposed to building profiles of people to sell ads to them.").

[163] *Id.* (quoting Sam Altman).

[164] *See* K. C. Sabreena Basheer, *Elon Musk's xAI Trained on Twitter's Feed*, ANALYTICS VIDHYA (July 19, 2023, https://www.analyticsvidhya.com/blog/2023/07/elon-musks-xai-trained-on-twitters-feed/; Rounak Jain, *Elon Musk says Real-Time Data From X, Tesla Cars, and Optimus Robots in Future will make Grok 'Best AI System in the World,'* BENZINGA (Aug. 2, 2024), https://www.benzinga.com/news/24/08/40145058/elon-musk-says-real-time-data-from-x-tesla-cars-and-optimus-robots-in-future-will-make-grok-best-ai.

[165] *See* California Consumer Privacy Rights Act of 2018, Cal. Civ. Code §§ 1798.100–1798.199.100 (West 2023).

Even here, however, the right to remove data is limited to "personal information about the consumer which the business has collected from the consumer."[166] To the extent that the information was incorporated through internet scrapes and third party services, the language suggests that no personal right of deletion even exists.

Large enterprises can negotiate agreements that limit the use of prompt data and other proprietary data from incorporation into the data sets.[167] For individuals, there is little opportunity to reduce or restrict the scope of collected information. Courts have generally rejected the argument that inclusion in a data set amounts to a commercial exploitation of an individual's name, likeness, or identity.[168] There is a stronger claim when a person's name and image are published when promoting the site.[169] Image generation services, such as Dall-E and Midjourney, can create a seemingly infinite range of visual works. If a service responds to a prompt by producing a picture that depicts an actual person, such an image

---

166 Cal. Civ. Code § 1798.105(a).

167 *See* UAB "Planner5D" v. Facebook, Inc., 19–CV–03132–WHO, 2020 WL 4260733, at *7 (N.D. Cal. July 24, 2020) ("Planner 5D's combined effect of structural and legal barriers 'consistently walls off both the location and content of the trade secrets at issue here, and under its Terms of Service, separately prohibits circumventing these protections via crawling, scraping, or otherwise accessing its data files.' ").

168 Verde v. Confi-Chek, Inc., No. 21 C 50092, 2021 WL 4264674, at *1 (N.D. Ill. Sept. 20, 2021).

169 Hoffower v. Seamless Contacts, Inc., No. 22 C 2079, 2022 WL 17128949, at *2 (N.D. Ill. Nov. 22, 2022); Siegel v. ZoomInfo Techs., LLC, No. 21 C 2032, 2021WL 4306148, at *4 (N.D. Ill. Sept. 22, 2021).

will likely be treated as outside the protection of publicity rights in the same way a photographer or illustrator would be able to use that likeness without permission.[170] However, if that image was used in advertising or another commercial transaction, then the person depicted could enforce their rights of publicity. The same will be true for voice duplication as well.[171]

Volitional privacy has been addressed by a variety of case specific considerations, such as the warrant requirement for site cell location information, protections against proliferation of deepfakes, limited protections regarding employee surveillance, and in other contexts. As the efficacy of informational privacy protection falters, regulators will need to do much more to develop comprehensive volitional privacy rules that shift from a model of high-risk avoidance to a more fundamental human rights based protection of individual autonomy in certain spheres of private life. It was for just this reason that privacy was recognized in the Universal Declaration of Human Rights,[172] and for regulators and civil

---

170 *See* Krishna, *supra* ch.4 note 149; *cf. In re* NCAA Student-Athlete Name & Likeness Licensing Litig. (*Keller*), 724 F.3d 1268, 1284 (9th Cir. 2013); Hart v. Elec. Arts, Inc., 717 F.3d 141, 170 (3d Cir. 2013); Comedy III Prods., Inc. v. Gary Saderup, Inc., 21 P.3d 797, 808 (Cal. 2001).

171 *See* Waits v. Frito-Lay, Inc., 978 F.2d 1093 (9th Cir. 1992); Midler v. Ford Motor Co., 849 F.2d 460 (9th Cir. 1988). *See also* Nick Breen & Josh Love, *Attack of the Clones: AI Soundalike Tools Spin Complex Web of Legal Questions for Music*, BILLBOARD (May 19, 2023), https://www.billboard.com/pro/ai-music-tools-copy-artists-voices-legal-questions/.

172 Universal Declaration of Human Rights, Art. 12 ("No one shall be subjected to arbitrary interference with his privacy,

libertarians who desire effective privacy regimes, it is the approach most likely to provide a system that can achieve protection in the age of AI.

§ 5.3 HEALTH INFORMATION PROTECTIONS AND USES

Historically, health information has been singled out for privacy protection and confidentiality, made famous by the oath attributed to Hippocrates.[173] "What I may see or hear in the course of the treatment or even outside of the treatment in regard to the life of men, which on no account one must spread abroad, I will keep to myself, holding such things shameful to be spoken about."[174] Privacy and confidentiality of health information inform common law practices, ethical codes, and both state and federal legislation.

Health care information is among the most heavily regulated data in the U.S.[175] The Health Insurance

---

family, home or correspondence, nor to attacks upon his honour and reputation. Everyone has the right to the protection of the law against such interference or attacks."). *See also* Art. 19 (free expression); Art. 20 (freedom of assembly and association).

[173] John C. Moskop et al., *From Hippocrates to HIPAA: Privacy and Confidentiality in Emergency Medicine—Part I: Conceptual, Moral, and Legal Foundations*, 45 ANN. EMERG. MED. 53 (2005), https://www.ncbi.nlm.nih.gov/pmc/articles/PMC7132445/.

[174] *Id.* quoting REICH W.T., EDITOR. ENCYCLOPEDIA OF BIOETHICS Vol. 5 2632 (1995) (Oath of Hippocrates).

[175] *See, e.g.*, Stacey A. Tovino, *The HIPAA Privacy Rule and the EU GDPR: Illustrative Comparisons*, 47 SETON HALL L. REV. 973, 992 (2017) ("It would be tempting to say that the Privacy Rule is, across the board, more detailed and directive than the GDPR.").

Portability and Accountability Act of 1996 (HIPAA) as amended by the Health Information Technology for Economic and Clinical Health Act (HITECH), provides a detailed mechanism for maintaining patient information.[176] The comprehensive regulations that implement HIPAA include the Privacy Rule, the Security Rule, and the Breach Notification Rule.[177] The HIPAA Privacy Rule protects protected health information (PHI)[178] from general disclosure unless used for treatment, payment, and health care operations, when provided to the individual, or in certain other limited circumstances.[179]

---

[176] Health Insurance Portability and Accountability Act of 1996, Pub. L. No. 104–191, 110 Stat. 1936 (1996); Health Information Technology for Economic and Clinical Health Act, Pub. L. No. 111–5, 123 Stat. 226 (2009) (codified in scattered sections of 42 U.S.C.). *See* Jianyan Fang, *Health Data at Your Fingertips: Federal Regulatory Proposals for Consumer-Generated Mobile Health Data*, 4 GEO. L. TECH. REV. 125, 144 (2019) ("The most well-known federal statute for health data protection is HIPAA.").

[177] *See* Standards for Privacy of Individually Identifiable Health Information, 65 Fed. Reg. 82,462, 82,464 (Dec. 28, 2000) ("The rule seeks to balance the needs of the individual with the needs of the society."); *id.* at 82,468 ("The task of society and its government is to create a balance in which the individual's needs and rights are balanced against the needs and rights of society as a whole."); *id.* at 82,472 ("The need to balance these competing interests—the necessity of protecting privacy and the public interest in using identifiable health information for vital public and private purposes—in a way that is also workable for the varied stakeholders causes much of the complexity in the rule.").

[178] 45 C.F.R. § 160.103.

[179] 45 C.F.R. § 164.502(a)(1). The U.S. Department of Health and Human Services (HHS) provides this summary of the mandatory and permissive disclosures:

The HIPAA Security Rule establishes highly prescriptive administrative, technical, and physical safeguards for protecting electronic health records (e-PHI).[180] These regulations and accompany HHS guidance provide detailed recommendations for applying appropriate data security and integrity policies as well as imposing large financial penalties for failing to protect e-PHI data.[181]

Required Disclosures. A covered entity must disclose protected health information in only two situations: (a) to individuals (or their personal representatives) specifically when they request access to, or an accounting of disclosures of, their protected health information; and (b) to HHS when it is undertaking a compliance investigation or review or enforcement action. [45 C.F.R. § 164.502(a)(2).]

Permitted Uses and Disclosures. A covered entity is permitted, but not required, to use and disclose protected health information, without an individual's authorization, for the following purposes or situations: (1) To the Individual (unless required for access or accounting of disclosures); (2) Treatment, Payment, and Health Care Operations; (3) Opportunity to Agree or Object; (4) Incident to an otherwise permitted use and disclosure; (5) Public Interest and Benefit Activities; and (6) Limited Data Set for the purposes of research, public health or health care operations. Covered entities may rely on professional ethics and best judgments in deciding which of these permissive uses and disclosures to make. [45 C.F.R. § 164.502(a)(1).]

https://www.hhs.gov/hipaa/for-professionals/privacy/laws-regulations/index.html.

[180] *See* 45 C.F.R. § 164.306(a). *See also* Summary of the HIPAA Security Rule, U.S. Health and Human Scvs., https://www.hhs.gov/hipaa/for-professionals/security/laws-regulations/index.html.

[181] *See, e.g.*, *What are the Penalties for HIPAA Violations?*, HIPAA Journal (Jan 23, 2022), https://www.hipaajournal.com/what-are-the-penalties-for-hipaa-violations-7096/ (OCR . . . has the discretion to waive a financial penalty in the case of a data breach that could not be reasonably anticipated. "The penalty

The Security Rule requires covered entities to maintain reasonable and appropriate administrative, technical, and physical safeguards for protecting e-PHI. Specifically, covered entities must:

1. Ensure the confidentiality, integrity, and availability of all e-PHI they create, receive, maintain or transmit;
2. Identify and protect against reasonably anticipated threats to the security or integrity of the information;
3. Protect against reasonably anticipated, impermissible uses or disclosures; and
4. Ensure compliance by their workforce.[182]

The Health and Human Services Office of Civil Rights (OCR) provides the enforcement actions for violations of the Security Rule as well as the Data Breach Notification Rule and the Privacy Rule. Organizations covered by the rules (covered entities) are required to perform regular risk analysis, train all personnel and vendors, utilize physical safeguards for the e-PHI, and deploy technical measures such as encryption, multi-factor authentication, access controls, and other techniques to reduce the risk of data theft, loss, manipulation, or

---

cannot be waived if the violation involved willful neglect of the Privacy, Security, and Breach Notification Rules.").

[182] Summary of the HIPAA Security Rule, *supra* note 180, *citing* 45 C.F.R. § 164.306(a) (2022).

destruction.[183] The Privacy Rule, Security Rule, and Data Breach Notification Rules create substantial obligations on the enterprises which host PHI regarding the protection of the data and the reporting requirements following any data incident that could expose PHI to unauthorized access or data theft.[184]

Despite the tremendous regard for health care confidentiality and privacy, there is an equally compelling case for the use of health care information for public health benefits and improved health care outcomes. Much of the benefit involves predictive analytics. "Cloud computing is providing the computing capacity for the analysis of considerably large amounts of data, at higher speeds and lower costs compared with historic 'on premises' infrastructure of healthcare organisations."[185]

There are many use cases for AI systems in healthcare, including efforts to design new drugs and treatments, predict better outcomes, augment analysis of test results using precision imaging, and much more. "Research in the application of AI healthcare continues to accelerate rapidly, with potential use cases being demonstrated across the healthcare sector (both physical and mental health)

---

183 *See* 45 C.F.R. § 164.306(a) (2022).

184 *See* Anupam Chander et al., *Achieving Privacy*, 74 SMU L. REV. 607, 637 (2021) ("DHHS . . . estimated that industry-wide implementation would cost $3.2 billion in HIPAA's first year and $17.6 billion for the first ten years.").

185 Junaid Bajwa et al., *Artificial Intelligence in Healthcare: Transforming the Practice of Medicine*, 8 FUTURE HEALTHCARE J. e188 (2021), https://www.ncbi.nlm.nih.gov/pmc/articles/PMC8285156/.

including drug discovery, virtual clinical consultation, disease diagnosis, prognosis, medication management and health monitoring."[186] Importantly, none of the present AI systems incorporate "reasoning," which means they cannot "draw upon 'common sense' or 'clinical intuition and experience.' "[187] Instead they perform repetitive tasks with precision, aggregate data, identify patterns, and enable high-precision deployment of instruments and medications.

Healthcare AI can be integrated with wearable technologies to collect behavioral health information that opens new possibilities for data collection and utilization. Chatbots can also play a role. "The use of AI assistants and chatbots also can improve patient experience by helping patients find available physicians, schedule appointments, and even answer some patient questions."[188]

Even with the appropriate privacy and confidentiality safeguards in place, concerns remain about the manner of AI implementation in healthcare. The American Medical Association provided an outline by highlighting seven critical features of AI adoption:

1. **Promote population-representative data with accessibility,**

---

[186] *Id.* at e190.

[187] *Id.* at e191.

[188] Melissa D. Berry, *Understanding the Advantages and Risks of AI Usage in Healthcare*, THOMSON REUTERS (Sept. 27, 2023), https://www.thomsonreuters.com/en-us/posts/technology/ai-usage-healthcare/.

standardization and quality [which] is imperative. This is the way to ensure accuracy for all populations. While there is a lot of data now, there are issues with data quality, appropriate consent, interoperability and scale of data transfers.

2. **Prioritize ethical, equitable and inclusive medical AI while addressing explicit and implicit bias.** Underlying biases need to be scrutinized to understand their potential to worsen or address existing inequity and whether and how it should be deployed.

3. **Contextualize the dialogue of transparency and trust, which means accepting differential needs.** AI developers, implementers, users and regulators should collaboratively define guidelines for clarifying the level of transparency needed across a spectrum and there should be a clear separation of data, performance and algorithmic transparency.

4. **Focus in the near term on augmented intelligence rather than AI autonomous agents.** Fully autonomous AI concerns the public and faces technical and regulatory challenges. Augmented intelligence—supporting data synthesis, interpretation and decision-making by clinicians and patients—is where opportunities are now.

5. **Develop and deploy appropriate training and educational programs.** Curricula must be multidisciplinary and engage AI developers, implementers, health care system leadership, frontline clinical teams, ethicists, humanists, patients and caregivers.

6. **Leverage frameworks and best practices for learning health care systems, human factors and implementation science.** Health care delivery systems should have a robust and mature information technology governance strategy before embarking on a substantial AI deployment and integration.

7. **Balance innovation with safety through regulation and legislation to promote trust.** AI developers, health system leaders, clinical users, and informatics and health IT experts should evaluate deployed clinical AI for effectiveness and safety based on clinical data.[189]

Following the AI Executive Order, the Department of Health and Human Services (HHS) obtained commitments from more than two dozen leading health care organizations to create an industry-bases voluntary set of principles to develop AI in the

---

[189] Tanya Albert Henry, *7 Tips for Responsible use of Health Care AI*, AMA (Mar. 4, 2021), https://www.ama-assn.org/practice-management/digital/7-tips-responsible-use-health-care-ai.

healthcare sector. The "FAVES" principles focus on ensuring that "AI should lead to healthcare outcomes that are Fair, Appropriate, Valid, Effective, and Safe."[190] The FAVES principles require companies to "adhere to a risk management framework for using applications powered by foundation models—one by which they will monitor and address harms that applications might cause."[191] Participating healthcare organizations also pledge to use AI responsibly, and develop "solutions that advance health equity, expand access to care, make care affordable, coordinate care to improve outcomes, reduce clinician burnout, and otherwise improve the experience of patients."[192]

In addition to the role AI systems can play in improving patient outcomes, these systems can also play an important role in the delivery and management of public health as well. "[P]ublic health operates at a population level, emphasizing the importance of preventive measures, health promotion, and interventions that target entire communities to improve overall well-being and prevent diseases before they occur."[193] Unlike healthcare systems that focus on the individual patient, public health operates at the community,

---

[190] Lael Brainard, Neera Tanden, & Arati Prabhakar, *Delivering on the Promise of AI to Improve Health Outcomes*, U.S. WHITEHOUSE (Dec. 14, 2023).

[191] *Id.*

[192] *Id.*

[193] Tshedimoso Makhene, *The difference Between Healthcare and Public Health*, PAUBOX (Nov. 24, 2023), https://www.paubox.com/blog/the-difference-between-healthcare-and-public-health.

state, and national level. The distinction is important, particularly in the context of privacy and confidentiality policy because the two systems often have competing interests. Patients, for example, typically consider their communicable disease information to be very personal and confidential, but health officials need that information to administer health advisories, quarantines, and other systemic interventions.

"[P]redictive modeling has the potential to enhance our capacity to forecast the spread of infectious illnesses and guide public health treatments, [making] predictive modeling is a key application of AI for public health."[194] Spatial modeling systems can map health patterns in much the same manner that weather forecast systems map storm fronts. "AI can increase the effectiveness and precision of geographical modeling, improving public health outcomes."[195] As electronic healthcare records become increasingly standardized and available to dedicated and secure AI systems, they will be able to extract additional information from individual patient records, compile that information, and glean trend data from the discrete pieces of information.

Public health information can also be collected from non-health care records. Nearly two decades ago, researchers recognized that search data

[194] David B. Olawade et al., *Using Artificial Intelligence to Improve Public Health: a Narrative Review*, 11 FRONT. PUBLIC HEALTH, (Oct. 26, 2023), https://www.ncbi.nlm.nih.gov/pmc/articles/PMC10637620/.

[195] *Id.*

provided to Google anticipated influenza patterns weeks earlier than the tracking conducted by the Centers for Disease Control using information reported by hospitals and clinics.[196] The Google data proved unreliable when all search queries were included, because the information was too broad, indiscriminate, and general. When processed through various models that disaggregated the query information, the search data provided highly accurate and timely data.[197] Over time, public movement information from smart cars, wearable devices, and other surveillance tools will add to the collection that can be used for public health predictions and prevention.

As noted earlier, the surveillance systems must be deployed in a manner consistent with health care expectations of privacy and confidentiality as well as the limits provided through volitional privacy standards to protect against misuse of data to target individuals. Except as required by law, the aggregate data necessary for public health systems should not be repurposed to target individuals other than for health treatment.

---

[196] *See Google Flu Trends*, WIKIPEDIA, https://en.wikipedia.org/wiki/Google_Flu_Trends (last visited Feb. 16, 2025); Shihao Yang and Mauricio Santillana Kou, *Accurate Estimation of Influenza Epidemics using Google Search Data via ARGO*, PNAS (Nov. 9, 2015), https://www.pnas.org/doi/10.1073/pnas.1515373112.

[197] *See* Sasikiran Kandula & Jeffrey Shaman, *Reappraising the utility of Google Flu Trends*, PLOS COMPUTATIONAL BIOLOGY (Aug. 2, 2019), https://journals.plos.org/ploscompbiol/article?id=10.1371/journal.pcbi.1007258.

§ 5.4 AI AS A GOOD—PRODUCTS LIABILITY APPROACHES TO AI SYSTEMS

This section looks at the consequences from content that results in dangerous advice, meaning information that could result in physical or legal harm if the advice was followed. For example, will an author or publisher be liable for publishing a recipe that results in severe medical harm to the cook?[198] As noted earlier, a Google search result has already suggested adding glue to pizza sauce, so it is not a stretch to consider what might happen if the advice had not suggested "non-toxic" glue be used.[199] When using generative AI to create new product designs, that process could result in defective designs and result in dangerous products if not tested correctly. The use of AI in that process should not alter the products liability approach. The question presented here is the extent to which published content would create similar liability.

Where published content results in actual harm, the publishers could be liable for the errors, at least at some level.[200] For example, in Europe, the trend is to treat faulty AI as subject to strict products liability

---

[198] *See* Cardozo v. True, 342 So. 2d 1053, 1054–55 (Fla. App. 1977) (suffering by the plaintiff from severe burns to trachea and mouth after eating Dasheen plant which is poisonous until cooked). *See* Andrew T. Bayman, *Strict Liability for Defective Ideas in Publications*, 42 VAND. L. REV. 557, 564–65 (1989); Jonathan M. Hoffman, *From Random House to Mickey Mouse: Liability for Negligent Publishing and Broadcasting*, 21 TORT & INS. L.J. 65, 68–69 (1985).

[199] *See* Notopoulos, *supra* note 1 and accompanying text.

[200] *See* Hoffman, *supra* note 198, at 65.

standards.[201] "The current revision of the Product Liability Directive 85/374/EEC includes AI, software, and even digital services in the IoT space in the scope of "products" that fall under strict product liability."[202]

§ 5.4.1 COMMUNICATIVE WORKS

While interpretations of laws in the United States require that generative AI content receives First Amendment protection,[203] there may be an important caveat to the United States' position. Broadly speaking, the First Amendment jurisprudence treats the speech as protected by the First Amendment to the extent that it is communicative in nature,[204] even if it is proposing a commercial transaction.[205] In addition, the law begins with a generally protective stance in regard to publishers. "So long as the publisher has neither authored nor guaranteed the

---

[201] *See* Council Directive 85/374/EEC, 1985 O.J. (L 210) 29–33, *amended by* 1999/34/EC 1999 O.J. (L 141) 20–21 (detailing liability for defective products); Kristina Ehle & Stephan Kreß, *AI Trends for 2023—Increasing Product Liability for AI And Software in the EU*, MORRISON & FOERSTER (Dec. 12, 2022).

[202] Ehle & Kreß, *supra* note 201.

[203] *See* U.S. CONST. amend. I.

[204] Pooley v. Nat'l Hole-In-One Ass'n, 89 F. Supp. 2d 1108, 1113 (D. Ariz. 2000) (distinguishing between "communicative" speech, which "wins over the right of publicity" and "is entitled to the highest level of First Amendment protection," and "commercial" speech, against which "the right of publicity generally wins"). *See also* Robert C. Post & Jennifer E. Rothman, *The First Amendment and the Right(s) of Publicity*, 130 YALE L.J. 86, 131 (2020).

[205] *See* Cent. Hudson Gas & Elec. Corp. v. Pub. Serv. Comm'n of N.Y., 447 U.S. 557, 561–63 (1980).

accuracy of the publication, injuries sustained by plaintiff acting in reliance on information contained in the publication have not been redressable under a negligence theory."[206]

There have been modest exceptions to the broad immunity afforded to publishers. "[C]ases have found liability, even strict liability, for the dissemination of misinformation in other types of technical publications."[207] In *Saloomey v. Jeppesen & Co.*,[208] the Jeppesen company published navigational charts that it sold to pilots.[209] One of the charts misstated the type of landing equipment available at an airport.[210] When the pilot attempted to land, the lack of more sophisticated landing guidance resulted in the plane crashing and killing all on board.[211] The *Saloomey* court upheld the jury verdict against Jeppesen on both strict liability and negligence theories.[212] The court explained that "[b]y publishing

---

206 Terri R. Day, *Publications That Incite, Solicit, or Instruct: Publisher Responsibility or Caveat Emptor?*, 36 SANTA CLARA L. REV. 73, 92 (1995). *See also* Birmingham v. Fodor's Travel Publ'ns, Inc., 833 P.2d 70, 75 (Haw. 1992) (holding no liability for Fodor's travel book when honeymooning travel was injured following some of the tourist suggestions); Winter v. G.P. Putnam's Sons, 938 F.2d 1033, 1037 (9th Cir. 1991) (holding no liability for misdescriptions in THE ENCYCLOPEDIA OF MUSHROOMS); McCollum v. CBS, Inc., 202 Cal. App. 3d 989, 1005 (Cal Ct. App. 1988) (holding no liability for teenager's suicide allegedly motivated by lyrics to Ozzy Osbourne song "Suicide Solution").

207 Hoffman, *supra* note 198, at 72.

208 Saloomey v. Jeppesen & Co., 707 F.2d 671 (2d Cir. 1983).

209 *Id.* at 672.

210 *Id.* at 673.

211 *Id.*

212 *Id.* at 676.

and selling the charts, Jeppesen undertook a special responsibility, as seller, to insure [sic] that consumers will not be injured by the use of the charts; Jeppesen is entitled—and encouraged—to treat the burden of accidental injury as a cost of production to be covered by liability insurance."[213]

Navigational charts may be somewhat less communicative than books or articles, particularly given the obligation to reflect FAA-approved content.[214] In consequence, navigational charts have resulted in publisher liability in numerous cases.[215] But successful claims are not limited to charts. Instructional texts have resulted in settlements in some situations but not to liability through litigation.

In a settlement involving Rand McNally,[216] the publisher paid $1.1 million for injuries caused when junior students followed instructions to use highly flammable methyl alcohol in an experiment.[217] In

---

213 *Id.* at 676–77. *See also* Aetna Cas. & Sur. Co. v. Jeppesen & Co., 642 F.2d 339, 342 (9th Cir. 1981) (finding that Jeppesen's charts were a defective product due to publication of identical information at very different magnification scales, leading to user misreading of data).

214 *See id.* at 341–42 ("Jeppesen approach charts depict graphically the instrument approach procedure for the particular airport as that procedure has been promulgated by the Federal Aviation Administration (FAA) after testing and administrative approval.").

215 *See* Hoffman, *supra* note 198, at 74 (collecting cases).

216 Carter v. Rand McNally & Co., No. 76–1864–F (D. Mass. 1980).

217 Lisa A. Powell, *Products Liability and the First Amendment: The Liability of Publishers for Failure to Warn*, 59 IND. L.J. 503, 504–05 (1984).

contrast, in *Walter v. Bauer*,[218] the court denied liability for injuries sustained when a student followed the instructions to use rubber bands and a ruler.[219] In a more general, high-profile example, authors and publishers of *The Beardstown Ladies' Common-Sense Investment Guide* were sued over the book's claim that the Beardstown Ladies had earned a 23.4 percent annual return, "which was reported on the cover and in the text of the Book."[220] In actuality, the return was a mere 9.1 percent, below both "the Standard and Poor's 500 average [of] 14.9%, and the average general stock fund return, [which] was 12.6%."[221] The club issued an apology and litigation ensued. Even though the incorrect performance was used for marketing the book, the court refused to allow the complaint to proceed.[222] Instead, the court emphasized the importance of the First Amendment. "To promote society's overriding interest in the untrammeled dissemination of knowledge and free expression, the First Amendment strictly limits the imposition of liability on publishers for the contents of books. The right of free expression is circumscribed only by narrowly constructed and finely drawn restraints . . . ."[223]

---

[218] Walter v. Bauer, 439 N.Y.S.2d 821, 821 (N.Y. Sup. Ct. 1981), modified by Walter v. Bauer, 451 N.Y.S.2d 533 (N.Y. App. Div. 1982).

[219] *Id. See* Bayman, *supra* note 198, at 565.

[220] Lacoff v. Buena Vista Pub., Inc., 705 N.Y.S.2d 183, 185–86 (N.Y. Sup. Ct. 2000).

[221] *Id.* at 186.

[222] *Id.* at 187.

[223] *Id.*

Cases occasionally move past the motion to dismiss. In *Rice v. Paladin Enterprises, Inc.*,[224] the author and publisher of the book *Hit Man: A Technical Manual for Independent Contractors,* were unable dismiss a wrongful death claim when the published manual for murder was used by an amateur hit man to brutally murder an acquaintance family.[225] In an odd and unsuccessful procedural strategy, Paladin *stipulated* to facts that would make it "civilly liable for aiding and abetting James Perry in his triple murder, unless the First Amendment absolutely bars the imposition of liability upon a publisher for assisting in the commission of criminal acts."[226] Given the stipulated facts, the court found that the First Amendment was not an absolute bar to liability. The court noted "that speech which, in its effect, is tantamount to legitimately proscribable nonexpressive conduct may itself be legitimately proscribed, punished, or regulated incidentally to the constitutional enforcement of generally applicable statutes."[227] A similar result occurred in *Byers v. Edmondson*.[228] Victims of a crime spree allegedly based upon the movie *Natural Born Killers* sued TimeWarner, Oliver Stone and other producers and

224 Rice v. Paladin Enters., Inc., 128 F.3d 233 (4th Cir. 1997).

225 *Id.* at 239 ("James Perry brutally murdered Mildred Horn, her eight-year-old quadriplegic son Trevor, and Trevor's nurse, Janice Saunders, by shooting Mildred Horn and Saunders through the eyes and by strangling Trevor Horn.").

226 *Id.* at 241.

227 *Id.* at 243.

228 Byers v. Edmondson, 712 So. 2d 681, 691–692 (La. Ct. App. 1998).

distributors of the film.[229] Unlike *Rice v. Paladin*, however, the *Byers v. Edmondson* court addressed the question of First Amendment protection in a later motion to dismiss.[230] In that case, the court dismissed all claims against the motion picture defendants. The *Byers v. Edmonson* court distinguished *Rice v. Paladin* because the motion picture did not urge the viewers "to commit any type of imminent lawless activity."[231]

The Supreme Court has recently reiterated that "expressive activity includes presenting a curated compilation of speech originally created by others."[232] The Court has not answered whether this extents to speech originally created by AI, but there is no doctrinal distinction between the editorial choice to republish words of a person or a machine. In both cases, the expressive conduct is the curation and

---

[229] *See* Byers v. Edmondson, 826 So. 2d 551, 554 (La. Ct. App. 2002), writ denied, 826 So. 2d 1131 (La. 2002) (noting movie defendants included "Time Warner Entertainment Company, L.P., Alcor Film & TV, GMBH & Co. Produktions KG, Jane and Don Productions, Inc., and Oliver Stone").

[230] *Id.*

[231] *Id.* at 555–56 (referencing incitement test).

To justify a claim that speech should be restrained or punished because it is or was an incitement to lawless action, the court must be satisfied that the speech (1) was directed or intended toward the goal of producing imminent lawless conduct and (2) was likely to produce such imminent conduct. Speech directed to action at some indefinite time in the future will not satisfy this test. Moreover, speech does not lose its First Amendment protection merely because it has a tendency to lead to violence. *See* Hess v. Indiana, 414 U.S. 105, 108–09 (1973); Byers v. Edmondson, 826 So. 2d at 555–56.

[232] Moody v. NetChoice, LLC, 603 U.S. 707 (2024).

republication of the content selected. It also had no bearing on the First Amendment that the curation is made through algorithmic decision making.[233]

As indicated by the Supreme Court, to the extent that the generative AI content constitutes a publication such as a magazine or book, it will likely be treated as a communicative work and given First Amendment protections. Creative works will likely be treated in the same way as *Natural Born Killers* in *Byers v. Edmonson*.

It remains possible, however, that a GAI system without content guardrails could provide the detailed instructions found in *Hit Man*, so it would overstate the free speech doctrine to suggest that no liability can ever exist. The First Amendment has limits and content outside of First Amendment protection would still be subject to legal consequences.

The same is true whether the work is generally communicative or can be construed as commercial speech, because it involves the promotion of a commercial transaction.[234] "Commercial expression not only serves the economic interest of the speaker, but also assists consumers and furthers the societal interest in the fullest possible dissemination of information."[235] As such, even if there is no speaker

---

[233] *See id.* at 710 ("Facebook's News Feed and YouTube's homepage present users with a continually updating, personalized stream of other users' posts. The key to the scheme is prioritization of content, achieved through algorithms.").

[234] *See* Cent. Hudson Gas & Elec. Corp. v. Pub. Serv. Comm'n of N.Y., 447 U.S. 557, 562 (1980).

[235] *Id.* at 561–62.

interest—because the speaker is an automated system that cannot present its own speech interest—the listeners and the publishers have their independent speech interests that need to be protected by the First Amendment.

Where the work is not communicative and is commercial, however, the courts may be willing to entertain the approach suggested by Europe. The aeronautical charts provide a good example of this. Beyond the charts, in the context of instructional materials and how-to advice that proves dangerously wrong, the lack of any protection for the speaker combined with a need to protect the consumer of the information may result in a greater willingness for courts to find that errors are subject to liability either for strict products liability or for negligent publication.

The arguments regarding such claims are not new and generally speaking, courts have been reluctant to extend Uniform Commercial Code Article 2 warranties to publisher liability.[236] But this is not the case for manufacturers who are under a duty to disclose warning information and provide adequate instructions.[237]

---

[236] *See* Cardozo v. True, 342 So. 2d 1053, 1056 (Fla. 2d Dist. App. 1977) (denying liability under § 2–316) (Section 672.314, Florida Statutes for merchantable goods). *See also* Yuhas v. Mudge, 129 N.J. Super. 207, 209–10 (1974) (holding that Popular Mechanics Corp. could not be held liable for an advertisement in the magazine for fireworks that were later found to be defective).

[237] *See* RESTATEMENT (THIRD) OF TORTS: PRODUCTS LIABILITY § 2 (AM. L. INST. 1998). *See also* Daniels v. Prevost Car U.S., Inc., No. 13–13774, 2015 WL 470793, at *8 (E.D. Mich. Feb. 4, 2015).

> A product is defective when, at the time of sale or distribution, it contains a manufacturing defect, is defective in design, or is defective because of inadequate instructions or warnings. A product:
>
> . . .
>
> (c) is defective because of inadequate instructions or warnings when the foreseeable risks of harm posed by the product could have been reduced or avoided by the provision of reasonable instructions or warnings by the seller or other distributor, or a predecessor in the commercial chain of distribution, and the omission of the instructions or warnings renders the product not reasonably safe.[238]

The comments to the Restatement distinguish instructions from warnings. "Instructions inform persons how to use and consume products safely. Warnings alert users and consumers to the existence and nature of product risks so that they can prevent harm either by appropriate conduct during use or consumption or by choosing not to use or consume."[239] The duty to warn and the duty to provide adequate instructions do not rest solely with a manufacturer. "In most instances the instructions and warnings will originate with the manufacturer, but sellers down

---

238 RESTATEMENT (THIRD) OF TORTS: PRODUCTS LIABILITY § 2.

239 *Id.* at comment I.

the chain of distribution must warn when doing so is feasible and reasonably necessary."[240]

Comment O to the Restatement also clarifies the obligation:

> [O]nce it is determined that a reasonable alternative design or reasonable instructions or warnings could have been provided at or before the time of sale by a predecessor in the chain of distribution and would have reduced plaintiff's harm, it is no defense that a nonmanufacturing seller of such a product exercised due care.[241]

In the context of generative AI, the standard concerns about products liability for design defects (which are generally to the use of AI tools in all design processes) may include the additional risks associated with those situations in which the AI tools are not merely providing the previously vetted and published instructions provided by the manufacturer but are instead being supplemented or replaced with content generated by the AI system. Consumers have often complained about the obtuseness with which many instruction manuals are written. It is natural to ask for instructional guidance in the construction of furniture, do-it-yourself projects, or other activities. But given the direct liability that attaches to warnings and instruction manuals, if a generative AI replaces the manufacturer's content with

---

240 *Id.*

241 *Id.* at comment O.

inadequate content of its own, the First Amendment is unlikely to provide a meaningful bar to liability.

In addition, although the courts have generally found that the publisher has no duty to confirm the accuracy of the author's work, that is not necessarily true for the author.[242] "Author liability for errors in the content of books, designs, or drawings is not firmly defined and will depend on the nature of the publication, on the intended audience, on causation in fact, and on the foreseeability of damage."[243] Where an author negligently provides dangerous advice, courts are more likely to be willing to apply traditional tort liability. Taking the obligations to provide adequate instructions and the obligation for authors to publish non-negligent content where that content could lead to physical harm by the author's readers, it is not unreasonable to expect that there is a duty of care for the use of generative AI when giving how-to advice that could result in personal injury.

Some courts may find that there is no "author" available for such a cause of action, but the use of terms "developer" and "deployer" are increasingly being used to overcome the existential questions of responsibility for AI Systems. In addition to the developer and the deployer of the AI system, there is also the potential responsibility for the end-user who

---

[242] *See, e.g.*, Alm v. Van Nostrand Reinhold Co., Inc., 480 N.E.2d 1263, 1266–67 (1985) (dismissing the case against the publisher for claims arising from injuries that occurred as a result of following advice in a book but allowing the case to proceed against the author).

[243] Jones v. JB Lippincott Co., 694 F. Supp. 1216, 1216 (D. Md. 1988).

initiates the use of the deployed system, particularly if that person is doing so in a manner that ignores or circumvents the system's limitations and guardrails. Since courts generally do not extend author liability to publishers, this is an area that will take time for courts or legislatures to develop legal standards appropriate to apportion the risk and responsibility among end-users, deployers, and developers.

§ 5.4.2 USE IN LEGAL BRIEFS AND MEMORANDA AND LAW FIRM OPERATIONS

The application of inaccuracy risks also takes on a particularly unique role in the practice of law. Far beyond the general concept of plagiarism, lawyers have a rather unique obligation to certify that the information they provide to courts is accurate and verified. Model Rule of Professional Conduct 3.3 requires candor to the tribunal.[244] Under this obligation, "(a) A lawyer shall not knowingly: (1) make a false statement of fact or law to a tribunal or fail to correct a false statement of material fact or law previously made to the tribunal by the lawyer; . . ."[245]

Despite this explicit obligation, there have been significant lapses by attorneys regarding this obligation. In in *Mata v. Avianca*,[246] a law firm used generative AI to write portions of a brief, failed to check the cites, and later even asserted that the

[244] MODEL RULES R. 3.3.

[245] *Id.* at (a)(1).

[246] Mata v. Avianca, Inc., 678 F.Supp.3d 443 (S.D.N.Y. 2023)

nonexistent cites were correct.[247] As the court remonstrated, the law firm's attorneys "abandoned their responsibilities when they submitted non-existent judicial opinions with fake quotes and citations created by the artificial intelligence tool ChatGPT, then continued to stand by the fake opinions after judicial orders called their existence into question."[248]

Even very high-profile cases are sometime impacted by misunderstanding or misuse of generative AI. "Michael D. Cohen, the onetime fixer for former President Donald J. Trump, mistakenly gave his lawyer bogus legal citations concocted by the artificial intelligence program Google Bard . . . .[249] "Mr. Cohen explained that he had not kept up with 'emerging trends (and related risks) in legal technology and did not realize that Google Bard was a generative text service that, like ChatGPT, could show citations and descriptions that looked real but actually were not.' "[250] Cohen then blamed the attorney who filed the motion on his behalf, with Cohen noting that he did not realize David M. Schwartz, "would drop the cases into his submission

247 *Id.* at448.

248 *Id.* at *2.

249 Benjamin Weiser & Jonah E. Bromwich, *Michael Cohen Used Artificial Intelligence in Feeding Lawyer Bogus Cases*, N.Y. TIMES (Dec. 29, 2023), https://www.nytimes.com/2023/12/29/nyregion/michael-cohen-ai-fake-cases.html ("Mr. Schwartz, in his own declaration, acknowledged using the citations and said he had not independently reviewed the cases because Mr. Cohen indicated that another lawyer, E. Danya Perry, was providing suggestions for the motion.").

250 *Id.*

wholesale without even confirming that they existed."[251]

In a far more troubling example, rapper Pras Michel was convicted of fraud and conspiracy in a trial he claims was tainted by the ineffective assistance of counsel.[252] "Prakazrel "Pras" Michel argued that the use of the "experimental" generative AI program was one of a number of errors made by his "unqualified, unprepared and ineffectual" trial attorney before his conviction earlier this year, according to a motion for new trial. . . ."[253] The claim for ineffective assistance of counsel is based, at least in part, on observations that "in his last words to the jury, [Prakazrel's defense attorney David] Kenner appeared to mix up key elements of the case" as well as misattribute song lyrics to his client's former band, the Fugees.[254]

Courts have responded by drafting orders requiring lawyers to certify that their briefs are accurate and not written using generative AI or other

---

[251] *Id.*

[252] Lindsay Whitehurst, *Fugees Rapper Says Lawyer's Use of AI Helped Tank His Case, Pushes for New Trial*, ASSOCIATED PRESS (Oct. 18, 2023), https://apnews.com/article/fugees-pras-appeal-conviction-trial-artificial-intelligence-d2c93aa5404eba63c3347a05fe8ba091; Jason Nelson, *Did an AI Hallucination Help Convict Fugees Rapper Pras?*, DECRYPT (Oct. 19, 2023), https://decrypt.co/202461/did-ai-hallucination-help-convict-fugees-rapper-pras.

[253] Whitehurst, *supra* note 252.

[254] *Id.*

AI tools.[255] Judge Brantley Starr produced one of the earliest and most influential of these orders:

> All attorneys and pro se litigants appearing before the Court must, together with their notice of appearance, file on the docket a certificate attesting either that no portion of any filing will be drafted by generative artificial intelligence (such as ChatGPT, Harvey.AI, or Google Bard) or that any language drafted by generative artificial intelligence will be checked for accuracy, using print reporters or traditional legal databases, by a human being. These platforms are incredibly powerful and have many uses in the law: form divorces, discovery requests, suggested errors in documents, anticipated questions at oral argument. But legal briefing is not one of them. Here's why. These platforms in their current states are prone to hallucinations and bias. . . .[256]

Nonetheless, the major legal search services, Westlaw and LexisNexis, have both jumped into the AI-based legal research.[257] "[W]e simply don't yet

---

[255] *See, e.g.*, J. Brantley Starr, *Mandatory Certification Regarding Generative Artificial Intelligence*, N.D. TEX., https://www.txnd.uscourts.gov/judge/judge-brantley-starr.

[256] *Id.*

[257] *See* Tom O'Brien, *The Cost of Lexis and Westlaw's AI*, LAW.COM (Nov. 16, 2023), https://www.law.com/legaltechnews/2023/11/16/the-cost-of-lexis-and-westlaws-ai/; Kyle Wiggers, *Thomson Reuters Buys Casetext, an AI Legal Tech Startup, supra* ch. 1 note 303; Jake Nelson, *Combining Extractive and Generative AI for New Possibilities*, LEXISNEXIS (June 6, 2023), https://www.lexisnexis.com/community/insights/legal/b/thought-leadership/

know whether the impact of AI functionality now available through Westlaw and Lexis will be the game-changer both companies believe it will be. We do know, however, that the costs to upgrade your current subscription to their AI functionality is very steep."[258]

In addition to generative AI increasing the cost of legal research services and creating additional obligations of diligence on attorneys to check both their own work and the work of other attorneys working with them, generative AI is also being used by non-attorneys.[259] "DoNotPay, which describes itself as "the world's first robot lawyer," has been accused of practicing law without a license."[260] Joshua Browder, the founder of DoNotPay, had earlier promised to use his chatbot to secretly participate in a traffic ticket hearing, but stepped back from the idea after he claimed he was "receiving threats from State Bar prosecutors."[261]

A defective closing argument might not be a product. And diligent lawyers can benefit from tools to improve their efficiency. But the service of

---

posts/combining-extractive-and-generative-ai-for-new-possibilities.

[258] O'Brien, *supra* note 257.

[259] Stephanie Stacey, *'Robot Lawyer' DoNotPay Is Being Sued by a Law Firm Because It 'Does Not Have a Law Degree,'* BUS. INSIDER (Mar. 12, 2023), https://www.businessinsider.com/robot-lawyer-ai-donotpay-sued-practicing-law-without-a-license-2023-3.

[260] *Id.*

[261] Gintaras Radauskas, *AI Lawyer Retires Before It Even Has Its First Case in Court,* CYBERNEWS (Nov. 15, 2023), https://cybernews.com/news/ai-robot-lawyer-retires-before-first-case/.

providing app-based legal self-help likely requires more than can be offered by a text generator. Since 73 percent of attorneys plan to use generative AI in 2024,[262] the obligation to get this right is more pressing than ever.

The ABA and numerous state bars have issued guidance on the use of AI in legal practice.[263] The opinions reinforce the importance of the lawyer's ethical obligations to the client and to the court system. These concerns focus on foundational competence, protection of client confidentiality, candor to the tribunal, supervisory responsibilities within law firms, transparency and full disclosure to clients, and fairness in billing. Discussing the need for competence, the ABA explained the concerns involving generative AI (GAI).

> While GAI may be used as a springboard or foundation for legal work—for example, by generating an analysis on which a lawyer bases

---

[262] *The Wolters Kluwer Future Ready Lawyer Report: Embracing Innovation, Adapting to Change*, WOLTERS KLUWER (Dec. 30, 2023), https://www.wolterskluwer.com/en/know/future ready-lawyer-2023.

[263] *See* ABA Comm. on Ethics & Prof'l Responsibility, Formal Op. 512, (July 29, 2024), https://www.americanbar.org/content/dam/aba/administrative/professional_responsibility/ethics-opinions/aba-formal-opinion-512.pdf (hereinafter ABA Formal Op. 512); State Bar of Cal. Standing Comm. on Prof'l Resp. & Conduct, PRACTICAL GUIDANCE FOR THE USE OF GENERATIVE ARTIFICIAL INTELLIGENCE IN THE PRACTICE OF LAW (2024), https://www.calbar.ca.gov/Portals/0/documents/ethics/Generative-AI-Practical-Guidance.pdf; Fla. State Bar Ass'n Prof'l Ethics Comm. Op. 24–1, at 7 (2024); Pa. State Bar Ass'n Comm. on Legal Ethics & Prof'l Resp. & Philadelphia Bar Ass'n Prof'l Guidance Comm. Joint Formal Op. 2024–200 (2024);

> legal advice, or by generating a draft from which a lawyer produces a legal document—lawyers may not abdicate their responsibilities by relying solely on a GAI tool to perform tasks that call for the exercise of professional judgment.[264]

Regarding the concerns over confidentiality, the ABA notes that the focus includes risks both outside and inside the firm.[265] In particular, the opinion notes that "Lawyers must also evaluate the risk that the information will be disclosed to or accessed by others inside the firm who will not adequately protect the information from improper disclosure or use."[266] While inadvertent disclosure is the most obvious form of misuse, there may also be impacts on clients if data collected within the firm is used in an aggregated manner or as training data in a way that disadvantages other clients within the firm.[267] With regard to fees, the ABA reminds attorneys that in all cases "lawyers who bill clients an hourly rate for time spent on a matter must bill for their actual time."[268] Law firm efficiencies from AI systems may eventually lead to different pricing models, but it is not ethical to describe the billing model as an hourly rate and then to assign fees based on anything other

---

264 ABA Formal Op. 512, *supra* note 263, at 4.

265 *Id.* at 6.

266 *Id.*

267 *See id.* citing MODEL RULES R. 1.8(b), which prohibits use of information relating to the representation of a client to the disadvantage of the client.

268 *Id.* at 12.

than the amount of time it took to complete the legal work.

The ABA goes further in this regard. "[I]f using a GAI tool enables a lawyer to complete tasks much more quickly than without the tool, it may be unreasonable under Rule 1.5 for the lawyer to charge the same flat fee when using the GAI tool as when not using it."[269] This reminder extends beyond GAI to all technologies and even to all billing practices. " "A fee charged for which little or no work was performed is an unreasonable fee."[270]

The ethical opinions on artificial intelligence do not vary the obligations of lawyers. Instead, they reinforce the longstanding obligation that the delivery of legal services must meet professional and ethical standards.

---

[269] *Id.*

[270] *Id.* quoting Att'y Grievance Comm'n v. Monfried, 794 A.2d 92, 103 (Md. 2002) (finding that a lawyer violated Rule 1.5 by charging a flat fee of $1,000 for which the lawyer did little or no work).

CHAPTER 6

TRANSACTIONAL CONSIDERATIONS FOR AI DEVELOPMENT AND DEPLOYMENT

The corollary to tort and legal responsibility is the ability to employ contractual principles to manage risk and arrange the private affairs of the parties. This chapter introduces the basic business building blocks essential for AI system development and deployment.

Contract law considerations—such as how to develop partnerships for safe AI practices—build upon NIST's AI Risk Management Framework, which addresses concerns over "harm to people," "harm to an organization," and "harm to an ecosystem" as its core risk management strategy. The chapter also address obligations under the terms of service for each enterprise in the delivery tech stack.

§ 6.1 THE NIST FRAMEWORK FOR AI DEVELOPMENT AND DEPLOYMENT

Safety and security remain at the heart of proper industrial deployment of AI systems. In July 2023, NIST produced the NIST AI Risk Management Framework (AI RMF 1.0).[1] The RMF "is intended for voluntary use and to improve the ability to incorporate trustworthiness considerations into the

---

[1] NIST AI 100–1, ARTIFICIAL INTELLIGENCE RISK MANAGEMENT FRAMEWORK, NIST (AI RMF 1.0) (Jan. 2023) [hereinafter AI RMF 1.0], https://doi.org/10.6028/NIST.AI.100-1.

design, development, use, and evaluation of AI products, services, and systems."[2] Building on its earlier and to fulfill its obligation under the AI Executive Order, NIST published the "Artificial Intelligence Risk Management Framework: Generative Artificial Intelligence Profile" (AI RMF 2.0) as a companion source to the AI RMF 1.0[3] NIST has also published the "NIST AI RMF Playbook"[4] that offers dozens of detailed action steps for implementing the AI RMF. In addition, a companion guide was published by the U.S. State Department entitled "Risk Management Profile for Artificial Intelligence and Human Rights."[5]

The goal of these voluntary guidance documents is to provide "a voluntary framework intended to help AI actors throughout the AI lifecycle work together to make AI systems safe, secure, and trustworthy [by providing] a selection of actions that organizations can draw on as part of their comprehensive human rights due diligence processes."[6]

---

[2] NIST–AI–600–1, ARTIFICIAL INTELLIGENCE RISK MANAGEMENT FRAMEWORK: GENERATIVE ARTIFICIAL INTELLIGENCE PROFILE, NIST (July 26, 2024) [hereinafter AI RMF 2.0], https://doi.org/10.6028/NIST.AI.600-1.

[3] NIST–AI–600–1, *supra* note 2, at 1.

[4] NIST AI RMF Playbook, NAT'L INST. SCI. TECH., https://airc.nist.gov/AI_RMF_Knowledge_Base/Playbook (last visited Feb. 16, 2025).

[5] *Risk Management Profile for Artificial Intelligence and Human Rights*, DEPT. OF STATE (July 25, 2024), https://www.state.gov/risk-management-profile-for-ai-and-human-rights/.

[6] *Id.*

§ 6.1.1 NIST FRAMEWORK FOR GENERATIVE AI

Much of the focus on the AI RMF is on generative AI. Although there are widespread risks across all forms of AI—as well as unlimited business opportunities—generative AI has become the regulatory focus simply because it has been deployed for a much shorter period of time, and developers are rapidly changing its functionality.

As noted in the discussion on risk assessment, "risk refers to the composite measure of an event's probability (or likelihood) of occurring and the magnitude or degree of the consequences of the corresponding event. . . . Risks can arise during design, development, deployment, operation, and/or decommissioning."[7]

The State Department's lifecycle process provides a simplified risk analysis that serves as a starting point for companies to address AI development, in a straight-forward five-step process.

1. Plan and Design
2. Collect and Process Data
3. Build and Use Model; Verify and Validate
4. Deploy and Use
5. Operate and Monitor[8]

---

[7] AI RMF 2.0, *supra* note 2, at 2.

[8] *Risk Management Profile for Artificial Intelligence and Human Rights*, *supra* note 5.

The State Department list, however, does not provide guidance on how best to implement an AI strategy. Instead, the table highlights "actions or lapses that can pose risks to human rights."[9] While it serves as a helpful step-by-step reminder, it does not replace the AI RMF approach. All companies developing or deploying AI should operate within the NIST framework.

NIST highlights the distinction between an enterprise's assessment of risk and its risk tolerance, meaning an enterprise's "readiness to bear the risk in order to achieve its objectives."[10] In other words, the Silicon Valley approach to "move fast and break things,"[11] reflects a high risk tolerance that does not align with services that can introduce illegal bias in employment, health care, education, or financial services. Nor is the "move fast" risk tolerance appropriate for critical infrastructure or operations where failures may result in serious harm.

§ 6.1.2 DEVELOPMENT AS A RISK MANAGEMENT PROCESS

Understanding the level of risk tolerance is critical to managing risk because risks can never be eliminated. Instead, known risks can be managed, and the improbable threat of catastrophic events can

---

9 *Id.*

10 AI RMF 1.0, *supra* note 1, at 7.

11 Quote attributed to Mark Zuckerberg. *See* Jordan Liles, *Did Mark Zuckerberg Say, 'Move Fast And Break Things'?*, SNOPES (July 29, 2022), https://www.snopes.com/fact-check/move-fast-break-things-facebook-motto/.

be addressed through planning, contracting, and insurance. The AI RMF emphasizes the known risks that can degrade the trustworthiness of the AI system. The State Department guidelines highlight these concerns.

In contrast to the State Department approach, the AI RMF provides guidance on the steps to build reliable systems. "Characteristics of trustworthy AI systems include: valid and reliable, safe, secure and resilient, accountable and transparent, explainable and interpretable, privacy-enhanced, and fair with harmful bias managed."[12]

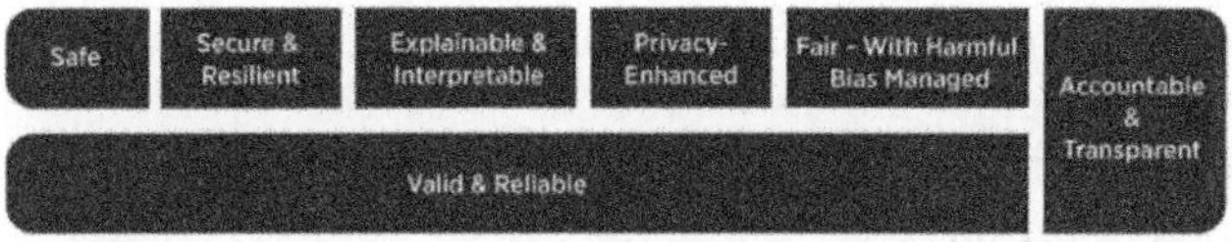

None of these characteristics stand in isolation. "Trustworthiness characteristics [in the AI RMF] influence each other. Highly secure but unfair systems, accurate but opaque and uninterpretable systems, and inaccurate but secure, privacy-enhanced, and transparent systems are all undesirable. A comprehensive approach to risk management calls for balancing tradeoffs among the trustworthiness characteristics."[13]

Reliability for an AI system means that it is able "to perform as required, without failure, for a given

---

12 AI RMF 1.0, *supra* note 1, at 12.

13 *Id.* at 13.

time interval, under given conditions."[14] "Validation is the 'confirmation, through the provision of objective evidence, that the requirements for a specific intended use or application have been fulfilled.' "[15] Accuracy requires the observations or computations provided are true or can be accepted as true. Accuracy can be tested by comparing results to external measurements. Accuracy underpins validity and reliability.

Safety and responsibility, in this context, represents the absence of the issues identified throughout Chapter 2. Safety and responsibility require informed decision-making at each stage of the development cycle so that the developer understands the intended uses of the system, can identify the extent to which the system can be built in a manner that achieves those objectives, and is assured that the use will not have harmful consequences resulting from the system's use or reasonably anticipated misuse.

The design for AI systems is often less complicated than the guidance sometimes suggests. Good design includes plans to reduce reasonably anticipated misuse. For example, every power saw includes a switch lock so that a person cannot accidentally start the saw and cause an injury. This is a simple example of anticipated misuse. As detailed in Section 2.2.1, the failures of Rite Aid illustrate the many areas where the developer of a facial recognition system

---

[14] *Id.* citing ISO/IEC TS 5723:2022.

[15] *Id.* citing ISO 9000:2015.

should anticipate misuse and incorporate safeguards to protect against improper use of the system.

For example, the vendor that sold Rite Aid its facial recognition system could have restricted the image database to refuse the introduction of low-resolution, poor quality images that degraded system accuracy. Failing to take this anticipated misuse into account was arguably a design failure. That same vendor could have restricted the system so it could not output a positive or negative match without embedding the confidence rating of that determination into the output.

Similarly, developing an image generator without including restrictions on its ability to generate nonconsensual pornography is a design choice that ignores anticipated misuse. Summarizing this approach, the AI RMF provides that "under defined conditions," AI systems should not "lead to a state in which human life, health, property, or the environment is endangered."[16]

Safe operation of AI systems is improved through:

- responsible design, development, and deployment practices;
- clear information to deployers on responsible use of the system;
- responsible decision-making by deployers and end users; and

---

16 *Id.* citing ISO/IEC TS 5723:2022.

- explanations and documentation of risks based on empirical evidence of incidents.[17]

Each of the seven key attributes of a trustworthy system are further defined in the RMF materials.[18]

The AI RMF employs four organizational functions "Govern," "Map," "Measure," and "Manage," which inform enterprises on how to conduct AI development and deployment to best identify, manage, and mitigate risks while achieving the AI's operational goals.

The AI RMF employs four organizational functions "Govern," "Map," "Measure," and "Manage," inform enterprises how to conduct their AI development and deployment in a manner that best identifies, manages, and mitigates risk while achieving the AI's operational goals.

1. **Governance:** Establish a robust governance structure that enforces accountability, diversity, and a culture of safety-first in AI practices.

2. **Mapping:** Contextualize AI systems to manage risks proactively and categorize them based on various parameters like usage and impact.

3. **Measurement:** Focus on analyzing and monitoring AI risks using various methods

---

17 *Id.*

18 *See id.* at 20–34.

and metrics, emphasizing continuous risk evaluation.

4. **Management:** Utilize insights from mapping and measurement to prioritize risks, allocate resources, and establish regular monitoring.[19]

At the heart of the RMF is the process of continuous development and improvement for AI systems. This involves "mapping" or identifying the risks and related context for the proposed AI system or use case; "measuring" the risks, risk tolerances, and consequences for development and deployment of the system; and then "managing" or prioritizing the risks against the anticipated benefits of the system or use case. This is done in a manner that "govern[s]" the process through a culture of meaningful risk management and inclusion of impacted stakeholders."[20] "Broadly, these functions seek to ensure that requisite systems, processes and tools are developed across organizational contexts to cultivate and sustain a culture of risk management (Govern)."[21] The map process comes from using "risk profiles of AI systems [that] are identified and contextualised to the use-cases they are deployed in

---

[19] Olga V. Mack, Humira Noorestani, & Kassi Burns, *Legal Tech: A Guide for In-house Lawyers Using the NIST Framework*, ACC DOCKET (Mar. 6, 2024), https://docket.acc.com/legal-tech-guide-house-lawyers-using-nist-framework.

[20] *See id.*

[21] Siddhant Chatterjee & Ella Shoup, *Elements of the NIST AI RMF: What you Need to Know*, HOLISTIC AI (April 24, 2024), https://www.holisticai.com/blog/nist-ai-rmf-core-elements.

(Map)."[22] These systems are highly interdependent. The developing and deployed systems must be "effectively assessed, measured and tracked (Measure), and finally [they] are prioritized and addressed proactively (Manage)."[23]

The four-step process of Govern-Map-Measure-Manage assures a highly iterative management approach. Each of these categories includes numerous steps to follow the model. Governance, for example, includes establishing clear risk management policies, following procedures, creating training systems, implementing accountability throughout the business structure, and emphasizing a culture of compliance and engagement. Good governance also looks beyond the institution to look at the policies and procedures of vendors and third-parties so that a point of failure is not incorporated into the organization from the outside.[24]

Although the voluntary guidance remains high-level, these outlined steps provide regulated industries with a familiar playbook. The AI RMF guidelines are similar in structure to data privacy and cybersecurity guidance from NIST and other federal regulators. For regulated industries, these are expected steps for implementing high-risk systems. For organizations that had previously been unregulated, however, the levels of documentation, audits, and compliance steps can be quite daunting.

---

22 *Id.*

23 *Id.*

24 *See* RMF 1.0, *supra* note 4 at 21–22.

Among the most critical aspects of the NIST guidance is the expectation that the development of AI systems transforms the developers from game and entertainment companies into purveyors of critical infrastructure—with all the costs and obligations such a transformation entails. When a previously unregulated company suddenly changes its business model and transitions into a regulated field, the company's executives suddenly face tremendous new demands. It is a daunting task to create a culture of compliance and trustworthiness where none had previously been required.

Legal compliance with the AI RMF focuses primarily on the Govern component of the process. First, at a minimum, this requires legal counsel to stay up to date on the regulatory environment that governs the company and the locations in which the AI system will be developed and deployed.[25] As noted throughout the Nutshell, many of the regulations address the very structure of the AI system, the source of training data, and the manner of creating the algorithms. Looking at only the deployment of the AI system will leave the enterprise at risk that the AI system cannot be deployed due to design choices made during the early stages of the life cycle. By staying current with the applicable regulations, lawyers can help avoid wasteful misalignments of resources.

Second, the legal team should "[c]reate clear policies and governance structures that reflect the

---

[25] *See* Mack, Noorestani, & Burns, *supra* note 19.

principles of the NIST AI RMF, such as transparency, accountability, and fairness. This ensures adherence to responsible AI practices."[26] The governance structures should be informed by decades of work involving privacy and security accountability, meaning that there should be board level responsibility for compliance, a robust training program, and a culture within the organization that requires protection of human rights and legal compliance. Since these are already requirements under EU law, it is only a matter of time before they become enacted in the U.S. at either the state or federal level. Companies that develop their governance structure with this in mind will have a much easier time addressing the evolving legal landscape.

Third, the lawyers should be involved in the training and education of interdisciplinary teams across the enterprise. Companies should regularly "[o]rganize training sessions for legal, tech, and management teams on the NIST AI RMF. Understanding the framework's guidelines ensures that AI projects align with organizational values and legal requirements."[27]

Fourth, just as the training needs to involve the legal team, so does the review process. The lawyers should "[e]ncourage a collaborative approach between legal, technical, and business units for reviewing AI projects. This cross-functional approach

---

26 *Id.*

27 *Id.*

ensures a comprehensive understanding and management of AI risks."[28]

Fifth, because neither the AI systems nor their designs are static, the legal team needs to support ongoing risk assessment to be sure the AI development and deployment does not introduce any violations of laws, maintains privacy obligations, addresses all security concerns, and meets with the contractual commitments being made by the company to its customers and the public.[29] By engaging in this ongoing process, lawyers will help assist their clients develop commercially viable AI systems that avoid surprises and unmanaged risks.

§ 6.1.3 ADDITIONAL DEVELOPER EXPECTATIONS ON THE IMPLEMENTATION OF THE NIST FRAMEWORK

A report of the U.S. Government Accountability Office[30] prepared in response to the AI Executive Order explained that "common practices developers use to facilitate responsible development and deployment of generative AI technologies include benchmark tests; development of trust, privacy, and safety policies; use of multi-disciplinary teams; and red teaming (testing efforts to identify flaws or

---

[28] *Id.*

[29] *See id.*

[30] *Artificial Intelligence: Generative AI Training, Development, and Deployment Considerations, GAO–25–107651*, GOV. ACC'T OFFICE (Oct. 22, 2024), https://www.gao.gov/products/gao-25-107651.

vulnerabilities)."[31] The benchmark tests, however, are not yet well developed and even with the red team testing "their models may be susceptible to attacks or may produce outputs that are factually incorrect or exhibit bias."[32] Despite these limitations, the use of benchmark tests, red team testing, and continuous monitoring are essential to help develop same and secure models.

> **Benchmark tests.** Commercial developers state that they use various benchmark tests to quantitatively evaluate the accuracy of their generative AI models. . . . These tests include assessments and datasets that developers use to evaluate model performance in areas such as reasoning, factuality, math and science, and multilingual comprehension, among others. . . . However, some researchers have noted that some challenges exist with benchmark tests. For example, there is a lack of standards around evaluation, which can make results difficult to interpret. In addition, evaluation datasets can be leaked and become part of the training dataset of a generative AI model.
>
> **Multi-disciplinary teams.** Commercial developers we spoke to told us they employ multi-disciplinary teams to evaluate generative AI models prior to deployment. These teams may include model developers, relevant subject matter experts, socio-technical experts in

---

31 *Id.* at 1.

32 *Id.*

> responsible AI development, and legal experts. According to some developers, these teams evaluate aspects such as safety, sexual or graphic content, and other harmful content. . . .
>
> **Red teaming.** Red teaming is generally used in cybersecurity to emulate an adversary's attack, which can help to identify areas of exploitation within an entity's infrastructure. With respect to generative AI models, red teaming has been more closely associated with penetration testing, which tests the security of a system.[33]

The GAO report also highlights that developers face malicious use of their AI systems. "[T]there are multiple methods of attacking a generative AI model that focus on compromising the model's availability (its ability to operate correctly), integrity, privacy, and susceptibility to abuse."[34] Prompt injection attacks represent just one example. "A prompt injection attack can be used to steal sensitive data, conduct misinformation campaigns, or transmit malware, among other malicious activities."[35] Another is data poisoning.

> Data poisoning is a process by which an attacker can change the behavior of a generative AI system through manipulation of its training data or process. There are multiple ways an attacker may "poison" the data to modify a model's output. Targeted poisoning attacks are

---

33 *Id.* at 2–3.

34 *Id.* at 5.

35 *Id.*

> attacks that attempt to violate the integrity of a targeted portion of the training data. Similarly, a backdoor poisoning attack targets a portion of the training data, but it includes a pattern that is inserted into both the training data and the testing sample to cause misclassification of the data. Another type of poisoning attack is a data injection attack, where the attacker adds new training data to the training set. For example, a chatbot that learned from users' interactions on a social media platform quickly became known for its offensive and inappropriate responses, which was a result of data poisoning attacks through its organic use of the social media platform. . . . Foundation models are especially susceptible to poisoning attacks when training data are scraped from public sources.[36]

Developers of AI systems should adhere to the NIST framework and use a robust set of strategies to pretest, validate, and retest AI models. The growth in use cases for AI systems require the expansion of the multi-disciplinary teams to anticipate the use cases for the model and work with experts to promote safe, secure, and reliable uses. Continued expansion of red team efforts increasingly goes beyond cybersecurity and operational integrity to address the concerns for malicious use, such as data poisoning risks, prompt injection attacks, and other known vectors of system degradation.

---

36 *Id.* at 7.

As AI systems proliferate, the GAO's concerns about benchmarking and standardization also becomes increasingly important. The GAO noted that some companies use unrelated assessments including the SAT to suggest operational effectiveness, but these tests are not designed to assess the models nor particularly relevant to compare performance. The mismatch between academic tests and generative AI assessments may ultimately create a misleading characterization of the model's actual efficacy. Industry standards have yet to emerge, but this will likely be an area of development as the competition for generative AI and other AI systems continues.

Deployers of these systems need to understand the opportunities and limitations of these systems, creating a market for independent validation of generative AI systems. This is just one of many concerns for the deployers of AI systems.

§ 6.2 BEYOND THE GUIDELINES: DEPLOYERS' CONSIDERATIONS FOR SAFE AI PRACTICES

There are many necessary steps for enterprises to protect themselves and the public from inappropriate and unintended consequences of AI while still taking advantage of the efficiency and creativity that AI can provide. Many of these suggestions are simply common sense. These suggestions reflect the approach that a commercial enterprise should consider when engaging in transactions to utilize generative AI.

§ 6.2.1 HOW DEPLOYERS CAN AVOID BEING RITE AID

For deployers of AI systems, the FTC action against Rite Aid provides the perfect roadmap of decisions to avoid. The allegations describe a company that missed the NIST governance obligations by making a series of high-risk decisions without considering their direct and indirect consequences. The allegations highlight that the company did not map the risks to its customers, corporate identity, or society as a whole. Instead of measuring, identifying, analyzing, and tracking the risks, the company purchased an "as is" AI system and made implementation choices that worsened potentially discriminatory uses.

In the FTC complaint against Rite Aid, the government alleged that "Rite Aid failed to take reasonable measures to prevent harm to consumers from its use of facial recognition technology."[37] As detailed by the FTC, the company never took steps to measure the potential risks and scope of associated liability with its actions. Given these failures, the company simply was unable to govern the risks it had created or minimize the resulting liability.

Many of the lessons are clear.

At the outset, it is rather axiomatic that enterprises should not deploy as commercial products those generative AI tools—or any other services—that their developers are unwilling to back.

---

[37] FTC v. Rite Aid (2023 Complaint), *supra* ch. 2 note 68, at ¶ 5.

Enterprises must look to the contractual language rather than the (often disclaimed) marketing materials. Often, the current slate of AI development tools include provisions limiting their legal use to noncommercial, experimental, beta, or other versions of non-deployable software. The vendor may tout the benefits and use of the product by others, but from a risk management perspective, if the agreements specify that the product is not fit for purpose, then the user deploying the system assumes all responsibility for any subsequent failure.[38] Brand reputations are fragile, particularly in the age of social media. Launching a service that risks large reputational harm because a company wants to be first is often a bad strategy. When combined with the potential for legal liability as a result of rushing to the market, that strategy should be avoided.

Closely related to the first point is the consideration that enterprises should receive commitments backed by binding contracts regarding any critical assurances regarding the policies regarding the training data, data retention policies, and output restrictions, as well as the terms of service, usage policies, and limitations on warranties and liability.

---

[38] *See, e.g.*, Lucas Mearian, *How enterprises can use ChatGPT and GPT-3*, COMPUTERWORLD (Feb. 14, 2023), https://www.computerworld.com/article/3687614/how-enterprises-can-use-chatgpt-and-gpt-3.html. ("ChatGPT is also not connected to the internet, and it can occasionally produce incorrect answers. It has limited knowledge of world events after 2021 and may also occasionally produce harmful instructions or biased content, according to an OpenAI FAQ.").

Companies must select their vendors and partners by completing sufficient due diligence to know the vendor has its own steps in place to guarantee that the system will work in the manner it is expected to and that the vendor documents its processes in a manner that allows its customers to meet their compliance obligations. In the Rite Aid Complaint, the FTC alleges that Rite Aid never took these steps with its AI vendors and, in fact, never implemented these obligations from a prior consent decree regarding Rite Aid's privacy policies. "Rite Aid routinely failed to use reasonable steps in selecting and retaining service providers capable of appropriately safeguarding personal information they received from Rite Aid."[39]

In selecting a vendor, companies should never put into operations products that include a disclaimer of representations and warranties. Yet here's what Ride Aid's Vendor provided in their agreement in all capital letters:

> [VENDOR] MAKES NO REPRESENTATIONS OR WARRANTIES AS TO THE ACCURACY AND RELIABILITY OF THE PRODUCT IN THE PERFORMANCE OF ITS FACIAL RECOGNITION CAPABILITIES. [VENDOR] DISCLAIMS ANY RESPONSIBILITY OR WARRANTY, EXPRESS OR IMPLIED, WITH RESPECT TO ANY FALSE IDENTIFICATION

---

[39] FTC v. Rite Aid (2023 Complaint), *supra* ch. 2 note 68, at ¶ 7.

> OR MISIDENTIFICATION ARISING FROM THE USE OF THE PRODUCT.
>
> YOU AGREE THAT THIS INFORMATION IS PROVIDED ON AN 'AS IS' BASIS WITHOUT WARRANTY OF ANY KIND. . . . THE ENTIRE RISK AS TO THE QUALITY AND PERFORMANCE OF THE INFORMATION IS WITH YOU. SHOULD ANY INFORMATION PROVE INCORRECT IN ANY RESPECT, YOU ASSUME THE COST OF ANY CORRECTION.[40]

Simply put, if the vendor's contract says the risk of its product is with the purchaser of the product, there is a strong likelihood that the vendor knows the product will fall short. Lawyers need to let their clients know the high-risk nature of such transactions and the likelihood that regulators will consider the behavior to involve unacceptable levels of risk.

The FTC allegations also state that Rite Aid failed to incorporate the AI system's confidence scores, which might have helped employees use the system more effectively. The design of the facial recognition system recognized the potential for false positives, but by failing to share that information, the system could not operate in a safe and effective manner. To learn from this, deployers of AI systems need to identify and document the steps, training, and procedures needed to properly implement the systems and then act accordingly. AI system

---

40 *Id.* at ¶ 51–52 (capitalization in the original).

developers should also be concerned if customers do not undertake the minimum requirements to deploy their tools properly. Although the FTC did not take action against Rite Aid's vendor, that does not mean private litigants or other regulators would not do so in similar circumstances.

The FTC highlighted additional expectations for the implementation of the facial recognition system adopted by Rite Aid. The FTC expected the company to test the accuracy of the system before deploying it. There should have been meaningful efforts to see if the system could correctly identify individuals and calibrate the system before adoption. Once made operational, the company is also required to verify that the system operates in the real world in the manner it is expected to. That verification and accuracy assessment should also be ongoing with updates at regular intervals.[41]

The FTC emphasized that the deployment of an AI system should not be selective if that selectivity could violate anti-discrimination laws. This should be axiomatic, that companies should be mindful to avoid discriminatory effects of their operations as well as discriminatory purpose for their operations, but it is important to reinforce this obligation regularly. Anti-discrimination laws include race and nationality but go well beyond those categories to include gender, age, disability status, religious practice and more. If the system involves employment, financial credit,

---

[41] *See id.* at ¶ 75–76.

housing, medical services, or education, the importance becomes even higher.

The FTC also emphasized the importance for the company to implement the AI system in a manner that meets the system's own technical requirements. The vendor emphasized the importance of using high quality photographs, explaining "[w]ithout good quality photos, an enrollment is not useful."[42] Rite Aid alleged set image quality standards well below that recommended by the vendor, then failed to meet even its low standards.[43]

Companies must establish quality control standards prior to implementation and then continuously monitor to be sure those standards are met and that they remain appropriately calibrated. Without monitoring, even thoughtful initial implementation will eventually drift into noncompliance.

Quality control standards should include a method of tracking false negatives and false positives. In many cases, the false positives have a much greater consequence, so tracking these should be more detailed and include an easy method for correcting mistakes caused by false positives.[44]

To achieve this, staff must understand and supervise AI systems. The corollary to this is the FTC's expectation that companies train and oversee

---

[42] *Id.* at ¶ 58.

[43] *Id.* at ¶ 60.

[44] *See id.* at ¶ 83–84.

their employees.[45] Training should be ongoing and reinforcing. Companies should document that the training has taken place and assess its effectiveness. Training should include appropriate supporting materials that also enable the employer to review the content of the training. Without these components, training will be ineffective, and employees will be less able to properly implement systems.

Each of Rite Aid's alleged failures provides insight into the operations that should be in place when a company undertakes to be an AI system deployer, particularly when using a system with high-risk consequences. Although lawyers are not central to the deployment process, attorneys should be involved to ensure Governance obligations are met, which incorporate the Map, Measure, and Manage duties as well.

§ 6.2.1 BUSINESS CONSIDERATIONS FOR GENERATIVE AI

Although most of the guidance for AI development and deployment apply generally across all AI fields, there are specific considerations for generative AI, primarily focused on protecting customer data provided to the GAI system, addressing the intellectual property issues over the training data, and including appropriate guardrails or limitations on system outputs when used in commercial settings.

As discussed in Chapter 4, one of the continuing controversies for generative AI focuses on the ethics

---

45 *Id.* at ¶ 65.

and legality of ingesting training data without the prior authorization of the parties who first created that content. This has copyright, trademark, and rights of publicity dimensions that are playing out in the courts,[46] but separate from the copyright legality, there is an ethical consideration. If a GAI system is built using unlicensed content from a massive social media services including Reddit, Discord, or Instagram, it has ingested content created by members of the public that never intended that use. Worse, if the GAI system included pirated content, there may be lurking PR concerns that could create significant issues for companies deploying these systems. For example, numerous allegations involve the use of "Book3," an unlicensed data set containing "more than 170,000 pirated and copyrighted books."[47]

The deployer of this GAI system may be making multiple disclosures about its use of the AI tool in its business—to industry regulators, in SEC disclosures, in marketing materials, and to its customers. Even if the litigation does not create liability for the unauthorized scraping of this content, there may be issues surrounding the accuracy and credibility of descriptions about the GAI system training and data sources. Enterprises deploying systems in high-risk

---

[46] *See* The New York Times Company v. Microsoft Corporation, No. 23–CV–11195, *supra* ch. 4. note 69, and accompanying text.

[47] Lauren Leffer, *Your Personal Information Is Probably Being Used to Train Generative AI Models*, SCI. AM. (Oct. 19, 2023), https://www.scientificamerican.com/article/your-personal-information-is-probably-being-used-to-train-generative-ai-models/.

situations or in high-profile settings should take additional caution about the statements surrounding the training data. More risk averse companies should consider additional contractual representations and warranties regarding the source of training data regarding these concerns.

The requirement to understand the source of the training data is part of the broader obligation for the parties to a GAI system agreement to include strong transparency requirements by the developer. The nature of generative AI means that its particular outputs vary from instance to instance and evolve over time. Nonetheless, the parameter, guardrails on accepted output, and all known attributes of the system should be available to the deployer of the system and incorporated into the contractual agreement between the parties.

These steps at improving transparency are essential for the licensee or deployer of the system to meet its regulatory obligations. As noted above, there have already been numerous examples of AI showing bias in facial recognition, which can exacerbate bias in policing and law enforcement,[48] access to financial services,[49] and which can negatively impact housing

---

[48] *See* Michael Gentzel, *Biased Face Recognition Technology Used by Government: A Problem for Liberal Democracy*, 34 PHILOS TECHNOL. 1639 (2021), https://www.ncbi.nlm.nih.gov/pmc/articles/PMC8475322/ "[F]ace recognition technology. . . programs used by law enforcement in identifying crime suspects are substantially more error-prone on facial images depicting darker skin tones and females as compared to facial images depicting Caucasian males.").

[49] *See* Sonja Kelly & Mehrdad Mirpourian, *Algorithmic Bias, Financial Inclusion, and Gender*, WOMEN'S WORLD BANKING

and employment, job search,[50] and similar fields. To the extent that the generative AI conclusions or selections will affect a fundamental right, then the vendor using that service has a heightened duty to control for bias and get the system right. This duty stems from both the panoply of civil rights laws and the public sentiment that valued brands need to operate honorably.

In addition to continuing questions about the training data used to build the model, the developers and deployers of GAI systems must have a clear, contractual and operational understanding of the use of the deployer and customer data in the ongoing operation of the GAI system.

In the short time since generative AI went from a research experiment to a commercial standard, the contractual expectations have changed significantly. For example, in 2023, OpenAI shifted its contractual

---

(February 2021), https://www.womensworldbanking.org/wp-content/uploads/2021/02/2021_Algorithmic_Bias_Report.pdf; Patrick Sisson, *Housing discrimination goes high tech*, CURBED (Dec. 17, 2019), https://archive.curbed.com/2019/12/17/21026311/mortgage-apartment-housing-algorithm-discrimination (*citing* Robert Bartlett et al., *Consumer-Lending Discrimination in the FinTech Era*, UC BERKELEY PUBLIC LAW RESEARCH PAPER, https://papers.ssrn.com/sol3/papers.cfm?abstract_id=3063448).

[50] *See* Marianne Bertrand & Sendhil Mullainathan, *Are Emily and Greg More Employable than Lakisha and Jamal? A Field Experiment on Labor Market Discrimination*, Nat'l Bureau of Econ. Research (July 2003), http://www.nber.org/papers/w9873 (Working Paper 9873); Arin N. Reeves, *Written in Black & White, Exploring Confirmation Bias in Racialized Perceptions of Writing Skills*, NEXTONS (2014), https://nextions.com/insights/perspectives/written-in-black-white-exploring-confirmation-bias-in-racialized-perceptions-of-writing-skills/.

terms for its enterprise clients to make them much more protective of customer information. These include:

- Data submitted through the API is no longer used for model training or other service improvements, unless you explicitly opt in
- Implementing a default 30-day data retention policy for API users, with options for shorter retention windows depending on user needs
- Removing our pre-launch review—unlocked by improving our automated monitoring
- Simplifying our Terms of Service and Usage Policies, including terms around data ownership: users own the input and output of the models[51]

Other major AI developers have followed this trend with enterprise agreements that limit the retention of data by the GAI system and prohibit the GAI system developer from using customer data for further training. At the same time, these contracts are only available at the enterprise level. They must be carefully implemented so that the correct contractual terms are put in place and then the correct software configuration is implemented and maintained to be sure the operational parameters take advantage of the contractual limitations.

---

[51] *API Updates: ChatGPT, Whisper, and Developer Policies*, OPENAI <noreply@email.openai.com> (received Mar. 6, 2023) (on file with author). *See* https://platform.openai.com/docs/data-usage-policies.

In addition, OpenAI "provides that any "outputs" created by its services that is based on "inputs" provided by a user will be assigned to that user, provided that the user complies with OpenAI's Terms of Use."[52] All uses, including commercial use are authorized. Licensees should be mindful of the limitations on the license. Use of the output and any indemnification provided under the contract requires that the user comply with terms that limit inputs to legally non-infringing activities. In addition, "OpenAI may use the outputs as may be required to provide and maintain its services to the user, comply with applicable law, and enforce its policies."[53]

As detailed in Chapter 4, the output created by generative AI is not protected by copyright. Any limitations on the use of the output is solely based on the contractual agreement between the parties that have access to the content. To the extent that OpenAI reserves the right to use the outputs to "enforce its policies," companies may wish to narrow or specify the use cases and also limit distribution to third parties, since copyright will not limit any republication. The limitations are even more important to protect privacy, if the system is being

---

[52] Sylvie Tso & Fiona Deng, *Five Key Contractual Considerations when using Generative AI in your Business*, SPRUSON & FERGUSON (Mar. 8, 2024), https://www.spruson.com/ip-law/five-key-contractual-considerations-when-using-generative-ai-in-your-business/.

[53] *Id.*

used in a field where personal information is being processed through the GAI system.[54]

The evolution of the OpenAI enterprise policies also highlights that these terms are not contractually binding when they are merely posted policies subject to the ongoing changes in development by the vendor. These policies need to be incorporated into non-amendable contract provisions. The obligations under the contract must also be audited on a frequent schedule to be sure that updates to the system do not change the settings.

Increasingly, GAI systems are deployed locally, meaning that the system operates within the computer network infrastructure of the deployer and is not shared with any third parties. This eliminates concerns stemming from external information sharing. It is particularly important in fields such as patent law, where an inadvertent disclosure can have the effect of publishing the invention and ending its patent eligibility. Local systems also protected health information, employment data, and other trade secrets.

Even with local GAI systems, however, companies should consider the extent to which they have the right to use the information they have collected from their own clients in creation of AI systems that have learned from the customer data. This is best explained by example. If a national law firm, for example, collected confidential information on all its clients' workers compensation settlements, that firm

---

54 *See id.*

could then build a sophisticated valuation model that used client data to advise future clients on settlement strategies. Even though individual client data is not being shared with other clients, the law firm is still using confidential client information in a manner that could be adverse to that client in the future.[55] There may be other fields that have similar limitations or duties that should be addressed when developing local GAI systems.

More generally, when contracting with a generative AI partner, the enterprise should understand that the business model underlying generative AI is a data-sharing model. As a result, any privacy and data security requirements must be specified in written agreements in provisions that survive the termination of those contracts. The OpenAI platform decision to exclude customer data from the training model (except in those situations where the customer has opted into the sharing of that information) significantly mitigates the risks associated with unintended publication of personal information. Provided such a policy is incorporated into a contractual duty and the duty survives as long as customer data resides with the AI platform, then the business will have likely met its obligations regarding the protection of the content. Of course, there are heightened obligations regarding certain industries such as in health care and finance, so each

---

55 *See* MODEL RULES R. 1.8(b) ("(b) A lawyer shall not use information relating to representation of a client to the disadvantage of the client unless the client gives informed consent, except as permitted or required by these Rules.").

sector must be assessed based on that sector's specific requirements.

Moving from the general duties to more specific responsibilities, enterprises employing generative AI need to remain vigilant for the errors in the data. As noted in the discussions on defamation and dangerous activities, authors of content owe a duty of care in their publications, and enterprises generating content using generative AI should therefore have operational fact-checking systems in place to meet these obligations.[56] NPR offers a simple strategy that corporate authors may find useful:

- **Non-controversial, easy to verify:** The spelling of someone's name, for instance. Check it against a primary source. Check it again. Check it one more time for good measure.
- **Controversial, easy to verify:** This is the same as above. Gun statistic from a new study? Check it against a primary source. Check it again. Check it one more time for good measure. (That is, assuming you've done your due diligence and it's a robust study, a reliable source, and so on.) And attribute it.
- **Non-controversial, hard to verify:** Here falls stuff like "Holly got straight smiley-faces

---

56 *See* Starita, *supra* ch. 5 note 53. *See* Borel, *supra* note 53. *See also* Holly J. Morris & Jerome Socolovsky, *Triage your fact-checking: a method (and board game)*, NPR TRAINING/SOURCES (Feb. 19, 2020) ("Fact-checking triage doesn't mean not checking certain facts. It's a framework for making quick decisions about what to confirm, cut and/or attribute.").

in kindergarten." If you're writing a general profile of Holly, decades later, go with "Holly said she got straight smiley-faces in kindergarten." If the story is about Holly's pattern of fibbing about academic performance, or grade inflation in kindergarten, then ask to see the report card, contact the elementary school, etc.

- **Controversial, hard to verify:** If Barry tells you his niece is an off-the-grid civet farmer in Maine, decide if this information is worth plunging into the Maine wilderness to prove, or whether you should just cut it. As above, it depends on what your story is about. . . .
- **Who disagrees, and how much?** The controversy metric is relative. "Naked mole rats are violent in the wild" is both controversial (to a **naked** mole rat researcher) and exceedingly difficult to prove (as naked mole rats live underground).
- **How unimpeachable is your primary source?** Example: The Smithsonian tells you such-and-such Basque word means "ceiling fan." Do **you** trust the nation's preeminent museum system, or do you call a Basque speaker?[57]

When commercially exploiting AI generated content, users should fact check and verify very carefully. More recent versions of GAI systems

---

57 *Id.*

include links and sources, but that does not guarantee the links are to credible sources or that the output accurately characterizes the source information. Despite significant improvements, the state of the art remains a far cry from providing verifiable and reliable output. "The peril comes from plausible text slipping into real scientific submissions, peppering the literature with fake citations and forever distorting the canon.[58]

Undoubtedly, future iterations of generative AI will be able to distinguish primary sources from trusted secondary sources and distinguish those from casual posts or sources of suspect content. Systems incorporating generative AI and computational language models will even be able to discern between scientific data that has been replicated and validated from that which is not untrustworthy but has yet to be satisfactorily replicated. But that day is in the future. When it comes, those operational parameters should be incorporated into performance guarantees by the vendor. When an enterprise can contract for such services, and only then, can it let the AI do its own due diligence.

Additional attention should be given to trademarks and personally identifiable commercial information that underlies publicity rights. Nothing in the generative AI process accounts for the duties a user of generative AI content has regarding trademarks. As illustrated by the Heinz

---

[58] Anjana Ahuja, *Generative AI is sowing the seeds of doubt in serious science*, FINANCIAL TIMES (Mar. 1, 2023), https://www.ft.com/content/e34c24f6-1159-4b88-8d92-a4bda685a73c.

experiment,[59] there are many famous trademarks that will appear in fiction, literature, and pop culture. Nonetheless, when those marks are redeployed for commercial purposes, the trademark rights remain enforceable by the rightsholder and the fact that the intermediary source was the generative AI does not change that basic trademark infringement action.

The same concern regarding trademarks applies equally to the commercial exploitation of real person's names, images, or likeness. As noted earlier, biographical stories about individuals, images, graphics, and other forms of content that can be produced for communicative works cannot be exploited for commercial purposes without the person's consent.[60] Some systems avoid human likenesses, but that does not address the problems of avatars, and it applies only those systems that rely on facial distortion as a strategy. Ultimately, the obligation will be on the users of the AI systems to screen content very carefully before using names, images, or likenesses—even virtual likenesses—in commercial settings. As a result, vendors may still find it preferential to hire models and obtain releases rather than struggle to determine if rights have been violated.

---

[59] *See* Wiggers, *supra* ch. 1 note 192.

[60] *See* Dogan & Lemley, *supra* ch. 4 note 137 and accompany text.

§ 6.3 GENERAL CONTRACTUAL CONSIDERATIONS

A client asking lawyers to negotiate an agreement for the development of an AI system or to license the deployment of a system will focus on the costs associated with the project, the timeline for completion, progress milestones, and the agreed upon, detailed description of what the system will provide. The agreement will include the usual set of disclaimers by the seller and representations and warranties by both parties regarding their obligations. Beyond these fundamentals, however, there are considerations that are driven by the nature of the artificial intelligence and the importance of protecting underlying data in complex transactions. The following provides an introduction to these considerations.

§ 6.3.1 TERRITORIAL AND DATA SUBJECT USE RESTRICTIONS

In licensing AI systems, the first question to be addressed is the territorial jurisdiction regarding the system. The regulatory regimes vary considerably between the U.S. and EU as well as other jurisdictions across the globe. The extraterritorial effect of these laws exacerbates the challenge. Licensors of AI systems must clearly identify the territories in which the system can be legally operated and which jurisdictions are excluded from the system. The territorial limitation should be both legal and operational. In other words, a system that does not meet the compliance requirements of the EU

AI Act should have sufficient geofencing so that an EU data subject cannot be included in the system.[61]

Under the current regulations, the extraterritorial effect of the EU AI Act is narrower than that of the GDPR. "[T]he AI Act will only apply to an AI system placed on the market or put into service outside the EU/EEA by a provider or distributor within the EU/EEA, if the system is classified as prohibited AI."[62] The regulations are continuing to evolve, however, and the EU is strongly motivated to use its AI regulations as a global baseline, so the reach may grow over time.

Still, as a practical matter, the incidental inclusion of the occasional customer is unlikely to result in any action. There is no private right of action under the EU AI Act and these incidental scenarios are not the focus of EU regulators. On the other hand, if the U.S. adoption included a multinational workforce, then the EU regulators might look much more closely at the application to the European employees.

The same general considerations apply across North America and with hemispheric partners. Canada, Mexico, and Latin America represent jurisdictions that include a tremendous amount of trade, outsourced work, and social engagement. The flatness of the world is not reflected in the highly territorial nature of AI regulation, so companies

---

61 *See* Ane Rode & Oyvind Eidissen, *Main Considerations when Drafting an AI License Agreement*, SCHJODT (Sept. 1, 2023), https://schjodt.com/news/series-main-considerations-when-drafting-an-ai-license-agreement.

62 *Id.*

must implement both contractual and operational guardrails to avoid being subject to foreign legal proceedings.

§ 6.3.2 OWNERSHIP AND CONTROL

Agreements for AI systems are similar to other large software agreements or software as a service (SaaS) agreements and can serve as a template for building contracts involving AI systems. Lawyers drafting and negotiating the agreements must understand the underlying technology or work closely with clients and consultants to be sure that the legal meaning of the terms in the agreement have an operational meaning as well. "As the procurer, it is paramount to delve into the details of both the service provider and the technology they offer. While negotiating terms is vital, it's equally important to understand the complexities of the sophisticated software, algorithms, and techniques at the core of the solution."[63]

Every agreement is unique, reflecting the understanding and economic decision-making of the parties. With that said, there are common practices that serve as the basis for most industry business practices. In an agreement between a developer of an AI system and a deployer of that system, the developer will typically retain the ownership of the

---

[63] Tahir Khan, *Anatomy of a Contract: Drafting Contracts for AI Solutions: Key Considerations for Success*, LEXOLOGY (Aug. 23, 2023), https://www.lexology.com/library/detail.aspx?g=0cf6f1f9-e6f4-48ac-9287-0ed26cc9840e.

data in the system—including the training data and any data provided to the system for its incorporation.

[B]usinesses need to focus on the following key points:

- **Diligence and Contracting:** Implement a diligent and comprehensive approach to [data regulation] compliance, integrating data protection requirements into all contractual agreements with service providers handling personal data.
- **Understanding Data Actions:** Gain a clear understanding of the specific actions and processes undertaken with personal data by the AI/ML [(machine learning)] solution and the service provider.
- **Data Protection and Security Practices:** Evaluate the data protection and security practices of the service provider responsible for implementing the AI/ML system to ensure they meet the required standards.
- **Transparency in Decision-making:** Ensure transparency in any decision-making processes that rely solely on automated processing and provide clear explanations to individuals about how their data is used.
- **Compliance Responsibility:** Acknowledge . . . your business is solely responsible for complying with data protection laws and

ensuring that individuals' rights are protected.[64]

Among the most important considerations in these agreements are the allocation of ownership and usage rights under the agreement. As noted above, many enterprise level GAI service agreements restrict the AI from incorporating data into the model from the enterprise customers. This is not necessarily the case for data from other kinds of AI systems, nor is it always the case even with GAI systems. For example, a chatbot system designed to help with customer service will likely provide all the conversation data to the GAI system developer to help with the continuous improvement of the system. If data can be shared, the parties must clearly agree on which party owns that data and any information or output derived from that data.

Ownership of information includes both the intellectual property rights to exploit that content and the physical control or storage of the information. In the analog world, ownership or custody of a book and the ownership of the copyright to the book are easily understood as separate legal rights. The same separation applies to AI system training data, inputs, and outputs, so the contract must address the intellectual property and the custody of the data separately.

As part of the rights allocation, the contract should clearly specify which party owns the software and algorithms of the developed AI system, including any

---

[64] *Id.* (alteration of formatting from the original).

improvements. The contract should also distinguish between the training data used to build the system and the data obtained during its operation.

As highlighted in the Rite Aid example, the control provisions may also include use restrictions. A chatbot designed for entertainment engagement should not be repurposed to provide medical advice. The licensor of the chatbot should include field of use restrictions to be sure that the licensee of the system does not create liability by misusing the system or expanding into unanticipated fields without prior approval.[65]

Generally, the contract will provide that any output provided by the AI system will be owned by the licensee rather than the AI developer. As discussed in Chapter 4, the AI output is not generally protected by copyright, so the ownership provision over output is more about whether the contract restricts the developer from using that same content elsewhere. Since the content is otherwise in the public domain, in the absence of a contractual limit, any party can reuse the output content.

The ownership and control provisions will be tied directly to the representations and warranties within the agreement. Along with the allocation of ownership and control comes the obligations to provide content that has been lawfully obtained and which does not violate the legal rights of third

---

65 *See Expert Q&A on Artificial Intelligence (AI) Licensing*, THOMSON REUTERS PRACTICAL LAW W–021–9801 (Oct. 2019), https://www.mayerbrown.com/-/media/files/news/2019/01/expert-qanda-on-artificial-intelligence-ai-licensing-w0219801.pdf.

parties, such as copyright, privacy rights, trade secret rights, and similar interests. When drafting a license agreement between the developer and the deployer or licensee of a system, these expectations must align with each other and also reflect the way in which the content was obtained and will be managed.

§ 6.3.3 LIABILITY AND COMPLIANCE OBLIGATIONS

The other stand-out area of AI system licensing involves the obligation to address liability to third parties and to regulators. These provisions cover the concerns discussed throughout the book regarding defamation from generative AI output, intellectual property infringement, violations of privacy rights, output bias that results in legal violations or private causes of actions, and even breaches of contract involving related parties. "With no clear legislative guidance, the formal contract between parties becomes pivotal in establishing legal responsibility . . . . The allocation of liability typically follows common principles in contracts, with both parties seeking to transfer potential liability to the other side, often influenced by their relative negotiating strength."[66]

When negotiating agreements, obtaining meaningful representations, warranties, and indemnities from large enterprise vendors is often exceptionally difficult. Even if the contracts provide

---

[66] Khan, *supra* note 63.

the representations, warranties, and operational guarantees, other provisions are often included that severely restrict the economic value of these terms. Such vendors often try to cap liability as no greater than the annual value of the underlying contract. For example, in 2024, when an error in a product update by CrowdStrike resulted in millions of Microsoft Windows computers crashing and requiring manual updating, Delta Airlines was among the largest companies impacted and its outage lasted longer than most other airlines. In the public dispute that emerged, Delta publicly claimed that CrowdStrike was "grossly negligent or committed "willful misconduct" specifically to abrogate provisions in the agreement between the parties that limited the scope of liability for harm caused by the system failure.[67] "The allegations, if successful, would override the liability limit of 'single-digit millions' of dollars in Delta contract."[68]

"First and foremost, the contract must clearly define what the vendor has agreed to do, when it will do it, and how much it will cost, . . . The statement of work clause is the first thing he asks for when a client comes to him with a problem. 'It's much easier to sue somebody if you've got a statement of work.' "[69] The statement of work provides " 'a clear standard to

[67] Antone Gonsalves, *What the Delta-Crowdstrike Lawsuit may mean for IT Contracts*, TECHTARGET (Aug. 13, 2024), https://www.techtarget.com/searchcio/news/366603172/What-the-Delta-Crowdstrike-lawsuit-may-mean-for-IT-contracts.

[68] *Id.*

[69] *Id.* quoting Brad Frazer, a partner at Hawley Troxell.

measure the [vendor's] performance against when we sue.' "[70]

The liability for direct harm and the indemnity against third party claims will typically be assigned to specific types of claims. The range of risks will vary depending on the type of AI system. Risks associated with autonomous robots will be very different than AI based antifraud software. Each implementation will have its own range of concerns.

While the risk profile will depend on the type of AI, there are certain consistent concerns. The concern about intellectual property infringement is universal. Software is protected by copyrights and machines are within the subject matter of patents. As a result, most vendors licensing software systems will represent and warrant that the service being licensed has not violated the intellectual property rights of third parties and indemnify their licensees from liability for using the system.

Beyond intellectual property, the most common representation and warranty covers the legality of use. Vendors are typically willing to provide representations and warranties that the use of the licensed system does not violate applicable laws and regulations. These provisions, however, are defined by the provisions in the agreement on the use case and geographic limitations for the licensed system. Some vendors may further limit these representations to the laws as they existed on the date of the agreement. If the law changes, the

---

70 *Id.*

limitation will put the cost to comply on the licensee rather than the licensor of the system.

§ 6.3.4 OTHER LICENSING CONSIDERATIONS FOR AI SYSTEMS WITH PERSONAL DATA

Agreements between large enterprise AI system developers and deployers can become very detailed and complex. Nonetheless, attorneys involved in the development of these agreements should be sure to include provisions—and work with their clients to guarantee operational compliance—with steps to address a range of increasingly standard concerns regarding any transactions involving the collection and processing of personal data.

First, the contract should specify the extent to which data location is required under the agreement. An ever-increasing number of countries restrict the distribution of personal information to third countries or to particular countries. The United States government, for example, has taken the extraordinary step of passing legislation to ban TikTok because of its potential data sharing practices with the government of China.[71] Europe's GDPR restricts personal information from being shared outside the EU unless both use restrictions and

---

[71] *See* Protecting Americans From Foreign Adversary Controlled Applications Act, Public Law No: 118–50 (2024); *TikTok Bans—Top 3 Pros and Cons*, PROCON.ORG (Aug. 12, 2024), https://www.procon.org/headlines/tiktok-bans-top-3-pros-and-cons/.

regulatory protections are in place.[72] Many countries have followed this trend.

Second, a corollary to the requirement that the data should not be traveling to foreign countries without express consent and control is that any work on the system should not do so either. For larger enterprises, managing the outsourcing of the system may become significant. This is particularly true if the use cases for the system might involve national security, military, or critical infrastructure. As detailed more fully in Chapter 8, the digital arms race has led to Cold War relationships among the technological superpowers. Vendors who routinely send their software to foreign countries for processing risk creating opportunities for introducing state-sponsored vulnerabilities into those systems.

Third, even if the threat of state-sponsored interference seems unrealistic, much of the cybersecurity threat comes from jurisdictions where enforcement against cybercrime is difficult. Companies should require strong cybersecurity standards are met at every stage of the AI system development. This includes controls on where the system is developed, the vetting process for its development, the vendor's relationship with its contracting parties, stringent quality controls, and more. Cybercrime is estimated to have cost over $8.15 trillion in 2023 and is projected to nearly

---

[72] *See* Regulation (EU) 2016/679 art. 5, *supra* ch. note 167, and accompanying text.

double by 2029.[73] Large AI systems become critical infrastructure for their vendors and can be transformed into vectors of vulnerability if the developers are not diligent. "In addition, the customer should consider whether it should require the AI service provider to provide warranties in respect of the use of anti-virus software to prevent the introduction of malicious software from the AI services (including via the Outputs) into the customer's systems."[74]

Fourth, any agreement that involves the processing of personal information should include provisions regarding the limits on the use of that data, the ability to de-identify and exploit de-identified data, prohibitions on reidentification (or any steps to make reidentification easier), and clear data retention practices.

An increasing number of jurisdictions have laws that provide consumers with rights over the data that has been collected about them. In order for a licensee of a system to be compliant with these requirements, the vendor must adopt practices that allow it to also comply. California's Consumer Privacy Act (CCPA)

---

[73] Ani Petrosyan, *Annual Cost of Cybercrime Worldwide 2018–2029*, STATISTA (Jul 30, 2024), https://www.statista.com/forecasts/1280009/cost-cybercrime-worldwide.

[74] Jonathan Emmanuel & James Pearson, *Contracting for Generative AI in the Financial Services Sector—What in-house Lawyers Need to Know*, BIRD & BIRD (Dec. 5, 2023), https://www.twobirds.com/en/insights/2023/global/contracting-for-generative-ai-in-the-financial-services-sector-what-in-house-lawyers-need-to-know.

provides a representative list of obligations to the public.[75]

- The right to know about the personal information a business collects about them and how it is used and shared.
- The right to delete personal information collected from them (with some exceptions).
- The right to opt-out of the sale or sharing of their personal information.
- The right to non-discrimination for exercising their CCPA rights.
- The right to correct inaccurate personal information that a business has about them.
- The right to limit the use and disclosure of sensitive personal information collected about them. . . .
- Businesses that are subject to the CCPA have several responsibilities, including responding to consumer requests to exercise these rights and giving consumers certain notices explaining their privacy practices.[76]

The GDPR and other laws provide similar consumer rights. Every party that has personal information must, necessarily, operate its systems in

---

[75] *See* Cal. Bus. & Prof. Code § 17940 (2023), *supra* ch.3 note 105, and accompanying text.

[76] *California Consumer Privacy Act (CCPA)*, CAL. DEPT. JUST. (Mar. 13, 2024), https://oag.ca.gov/privacy/ccpa (punctuation and formatting altered from the original).

a manner that allows downstream licensees to comply with these laws. Licensees should build these obligations directly into their deliverables as well as the representations and warranties.

Fifth, the parties may wish to identify key provisions of contracts that will become the "end user license agreements" or "terms of service agreements" required of individual users. The licensor may have particular requirements that it wants the licensee to incorporate into its agreements with its customers to provide additional contractual protections and limitations. Here are just a few examples:

- Adherence to licensor policies
- No use for illegal purpose, including money laundering, child pornography distribution, gambling, or other such activities
- Other content restrictions, particularly regarding third party intellectual property
- Obligation to abide by privacy policies
- Obligation to also follow contract of app store, platform, and ISP contracts
- Right to terminate at any time
- Right to monitor user accounts and communications
- No sublicensing or transferring of the account or sharing of passwords
- Indemnification against any actions by user

- Disclaimer of all warranties by licensor and limitations on liability
- Clarification of ownership of output of content based on the user's input
- Obligation to abide by community standards
- Commercial Use restrictions if the end user is not permitted to utilize the product for its own commercial activities
- Account restrictions granting the licensor the power to terminate the account and destroy or erase the content created by the user
- Broadcast restrictions restricting the end user from making content for use on commercial or on social media platforms
- Payment for purchases
- No hacking, no malware, or similar interference provisions
- No unauthorized use of the licensor's content or platform, including reverse engineering

Finally, if the system being licensed involves high risk uses, then the license agreement should incorporate all the regulatory, compliance, privacy, and data security expectations that have emerged in that field. Health care systems that have access to HIPAA protected health information, financial systems that have financial data (often protected by the Fair Credit Reporting Act), biometric data, data on minors under the age of thirteen, or data related to voting, critical infrastructure, or education all have field-specific expectations of additional privacy procedures and security protections. In each field, there are specific regulatory requirements that must be reflected in the agreement to build or deploy an AI system that operates in that sector. This requirement will make standardization far more difficult. Attorneys working in AI must also be fully versed in the policies of the sector in which the AI will operate.

CHAPTER 7

THE USE OF AI IN LAW ENFORCEMENT AND NATIONAL SECURITY

Law enforcement represents a significant use of artificial intelligence, at the local, state, tribal, and national level. The field of law enforcement has undergone a radical transformation in the wake of the terrorist attacks of September 11, 2001, resulting in a widespread shift toward inter-agency information sharing and a national approach to data that had not existed previously. The attack reframed law enforcement from a predominantly local obligation into a national priority. The role of homeland security has substantially altered the landscape of modern policing practices. Even though the Constitution does not grant general policing power to the federal government, the use of guidance and grants, combined with the plenary authority to regulate interstate commerce—which includes interstate criminal activities—has resulted in a deeply interconnected system of law enforcement at every level in the nation.

At the same time, interconnected does not mean unified or lockstep. Localities, states, and tribal nations vary dramatically both within each group and between each group. Resources, philosophy, and local conditions drive decision-making regarding law enforcement. Further, in many communities, law enforcement extends into roles involving public schools and universities, coordination with private security at public events and local businesses, and other engagement that expands the role of government law enforcement into related domains.

This chapter provides a brief overview of the prominent issues involving the use of artificial intelligence in policing and national security but cannot begin to cover the myriad of challenges and competing interests in the field.

§ 7.1 INTRODUCTION TO THE POLICING INFRASTRUCTURE IN THE UNITED STATES

The context of modern policing has its roots in the London Metropolitan Police Force, founded by Sir Robert Peel as the model of modern policing.[1] In creating the Met, Peel focused on preventing crime through engagement with the community, earning public support and trust in the effort to discourage crime, and applying the law with impartiality and strict adherence to the law. These principles underscore the values of modern policing and national security and serve as touchstones in addressing the ethical issues regarding the adoption of new technologies. Written in 1829, Peel's principles constituted a major shift from a military suppression of crime to a philosophy of criminal deterrence, community policing, and public cooperation. He called upon the police "[t]o recognize

---

1 *See Sir Robert Peele's Policing Principles*, LAW ENFORCEMENT ACTION PARTNERSHIP, https://lawenforcementactionpartnership.org/peel-policing-principles/ (last visited Feb. 16, 2025).

always that to secure and maintain the respect and approval of the public means also the securing of the willing cooperation of the public in the task of securing observance of laws."[2] This, in turn required the police "[t]o recognize always that the power of the police to fulfill their functions and duties is dependent on public approval of their existence, actions and behavior, and on their ability to secure and maintain public respect."[3]

Perhaps the most forward looking of Peel's precepts focused on the limitation of force. He admonished his officers "[t]o use physical force only when the exercise of persuasion, advice and warning is found to be insufficient . . . and to use only the minimum degree of physical force which is necessary on any particular occasion for achieving a police objective."[4] In the United States, the organized law enforcement movement began with the Texas Rangers, who patrolled settlements in the 1800s.[5]

§ 7.1.1 STRUCTURE OF U.S. LAW ENFORCEMENT

A 2020 study by the Bureau of Justice Statistics reports that 14,720 general-purpose law enforcement agencies operated across the country, which included a state-level agency for nearly every state, nearly

---

2 *Id.*

3 *Id.*

4 *Id.*

5 *See Understanding Law Enforcement*, POLICY CIRCLE, https://www.thepolicycircle.org/brief/understanding-law-enforcement/ (last visited Feb. 16, 2025).

12,000 local police departments, and close to 3,000 sheriff's offices.[6] Together, "[l]ocal police departments in the United States employed about 473,000 full-time sworn officers and 126,000 full-time civilian personnel in 2020."[7] But to put these large numbers in context, "[a]lmost half (46%) of all local police departments employed fewer than 10 full-time-equivalent sworn officers."[8] Police policy may be conceived for large, sophisticated forces rather than for application among a handful of officers overwhelmed within their community.

At the state level, law enforcement is under the direction of the state attorney general, "who acts as 'the chief legal officer of the state' and oversees law enforcement and reform."[9] The District of Columbia also has an attorney general for the District. In U.S. territories there is a chief legal officer for Puerto Rico, the Northern Mariana Islands, American Samoa, Guam, and the Virgin Islands.[10] Tribal territories use a variety of terms including both Attorney General and chief legal officer for the analogous leadership position.

Sworn officers patrol the streets of their communities. Senior officers investigate serious

---

6 Sean E. Goodison, *Local Police Departments Personnel, 2020*, U.S. DEPT. OF JUSTICE, BUREAU OF JUSTICE STATISTICS (Nov. 2022) (NCJ 305187), https://bjs.ojp.gov/library/publications/local-police-departments-personnel-2020.

7 *Id.*

8 *Id.*

9 *Understanding Law Enforcement*, *supra* note 5.

10 *Id.*

crime. In the largest of departments, specially trained officers may also provide more sophisticated tactical support for high-risk situations. Despite Peel's foundational principles, prior to 2001, the primary model of law enforcement involved three primary tactics: "(1) motorized patrol; (2) rapid response to calls for service; and (3) retrospective investigation of crime."[11] While these steps have been highly impactful, "[t]hey have also been criticized for failing to prevent crime."[12] Officers inside cars tended not to interact with the communities they patrolled. Drive-by policing did little to build the public approval of actions and behavior to secure and maintain public respect.

Although law enforcement is predominantly local, there is still a sizable role for the federal government. This includes national data gathering and sharing, financing activities at the state, tribal and local levels, and direct involvement with federal sworn officers. The primary federal agency is the Department of Justice (DOJ) led by the United States Attorney General. Under the DOJ are a wide variety of agencies including "the Federal Bureau of Investigation (FBI); the Drug Enforcement Administration (DEA); the Bureau of Alcohol, Tobacco, Firearms and Explosives (ATF); the Bureau of Prisons; and the U.S. Marshals Service."[13] The

---

[11] Mark H. Moore, Robert C. Trojanowicz, and George L. Kelling, *Crime and Policing*, NAT. INST. OF JUST. PERSPECTIVES ON POLICING (June 1988), https://www.ojp.gov/pdffiles1/nij/111460.pdf.

[12] *Id.*

[13] *Understanding Law Enforcement*, *supra* note 5.

federal scope is significant. "In total, there are 65 federal agencies and 27 offices of inspector general that employ full time personnel authorized to make arrests and carry firearms."[14] Despite the size of federal law enforcement, the departments are highly segmented, and policing varies considerably from community to community.

§ 7.1.2 AI-BASED PREDICTIVE POLICING AND RACIAL DISPARITIES

Controversial interactions between officers and citizens have repeatedly involved the use of excessive force, resulting in injury or death to suspects and even to crime victims.[15] One of "the most important aspects of police performance are how individual officers behave on the streets, and how the public perceives those actions. Unfortunately, our ability to objectively measure how individual officers perform as they manage encounters with the public is woefully inadequate."[16]

The ability of a local law enforcement office to reflect the community it serves becomes an important factor in its relationship with the community and its ability to address issues of trust

---

[14] *Id.*

[15] *See* Julie A. Ward et al., *National Burden of Injury and Deaths From Shootings by Police in the United States*, 2015–2020, AJPH (April 2024), https://ajph.aphapublications.org/doi/10.2105/AJPH.2023.307560.

[16] Bryan Vila, Stephen James & Lois James, *How Police Officers Perform in Encounters with the Public: Measuring What Matters at the Individual Level*, 41 POLICING: INT'L J. POLICE STRAT. & MGMT. 215 (2018).

when deploying new technologies. In that context, although law enforcement has changed, change comes slowly. For example, only "14% of full-time sworn officers and 11% of first-line supervisors across local police departments were female,"[17] according to the statistics. In terms of racial demographics, the data reflect a significant divergence between departments serving one million or more people than from those smaller departments. Across all departments, roughly 12% of full-time sworn officers were Black, and 14% were Hispanic, while in the departments serving 1 million or more residents those numbers change significantly, with approximately 47% of full-time sworn officers were White and 30% were Hispanic.[18] These data may help illustrate the discussion below on community concerns over the use of biometric data and other pervasive surveillance techniques, particularly in communities of color.

Looking at the data on injuries and deaths from police shootings, "[a]mong [non-fatally] injured people, victims identified as non-Hispanic Black comprised 29% of race-identified injured people in this study. This compares to 26% of victims in a single-year sample of fatal shootings and 13% of the total US population."[19]

---

17 Goodison, *supra* note 6.

18 *Id.*

19 Ward, *supra* note 15.

In his Executive Order on Policing,[20] President Biden framed the order by reflecting that "[l]aw enforcement officers are often a person's first point of contact with our criminal justice system, and we depend on them to uphold these principles while doing the demanding and often life-threatening work of keeping us safe."[21] He then acknowledged the challenges posed by inconsistencies in the quality and responsiveness of police services. "Yet, there are places in America today, particularly in Black and Brown communities and other communities of color, where the bonds of trust are frayed or broken. . . . It is time that we acknowledge the legacy of systemic racism . . . and work together to eliminate the racial disparities that endure . . . ."[22] As discussed below, the subsequent Executive Order on AI furthered this effort.

Technology has the potential to help clarify the challenges of community policing but also the threat to further separate law enforcement officers from the communities they serve. In addition, the costs associated with technology and data collection approaches could further separate out policing in affluent communities from those in communities with fewer resources.

These techniques are known as "predictive policing." Consistent with the original Peel

---

20 *Executive Order on Advancing Effective, Accountable Policing and Criminal Justice Practices to Enhance Public Trust and Public Safety*, E.O. 14074 (May 25, 2022).

21 *Id.*

22 *Id.*

principles, the goal of policing is to reduce crime through community collaboration. Predictive policing furthers this goal by placing scarce resources where they can be most effective at achieving these goals, and the deployment can be assisted through AI predictive analysis. "Predictive policing in artificial intelligence (AI) is when software uses data and algorithms to forecast criminal activity, with the goal of efficiently placing law enforcement resources."[23]

The most significant concern about AI systems is the potential for algorithmic bias to influence decision-making on the deployment of police resources or to focus on potential criminal suspects.[24] As the NAACP highlights, "there is growing evidence that AI-driven predictive policing perpetuates racial bias, violates privacy rights, and undermines public trust in law enforcement. . . . [D]ata shows that the Black community is disproportionately negatively impacted in the criminal justice system due to targeted over-policing and discriminatory criminal laws."[25] A bipartisan letter sent to U.S. Attorney General Merrick Garland by members of Congress explained that "[p]redictive policing systems rely on historical data distorted by falsified crime reports and disproportionate arrests of people of color. As a result, they are prone to over-predicting crime rates in Black and Latino neighborhoods while under-

---

23 *Artificial Intelligence in Predictive Policing Issue Brief*, NAACP, https://naacp.org/resources/artificial-intelligence-predictive-policing-issue-brief (last visited Feb. 16, 2025).

24 *See* Harper, *supra* ch. 2 note 90, and accompanying text.

25 *Id.*

predicting crime in white neighborhoods."[26] The letter highlights the challenge of using old data with an inherent bias to predict new outcomes: "The continued use of such systems creates a dangerous feedback loop: biased predictions are used to justify disproportionate stops and arrests in minority neighborhoods, which further biases statistics on where crimes are happening."[27]

As noted in the letter to Attorney General Garland, the use of discriminatory tools to predict criminal activity constitutes a violation of Title VI of the Civil Rights Act of 1964.[28] Title VI prohibits discrimination on the basis of race, color, or national origin in any program or activity that receives Federal funds or other Federal financial assistance."[29] The prohibition include both direct and indirect discrimination and access to services. To the extent that federal funding or provision of AI systems rely on biased data and historically inaccurate information, the provision of those services would violate Title VI.

Critics of the predictive policing tools are focused on much better transparency regarding the data

---

[26] Ron Wyden et al., *Letter to Merrick Garland* (Jan. 24, 2024), https://www.wyden.senate.gov/imo/media/doc/letter_to_doj_predictive_policing_and_title_vi_1242024.pdf.

[27] *Id.*

[28] *Id. See* Title VI of the Civil Rights Act of 1964, 42 U.S.C. §§ 2000d et seq. (2024).

[29] *Civil Rights Requirements—Title VI of the Civil Rights Act of 1964, 42 U.S.C. 2000d et seq. ("Title VI")*, Health & Human Serv., https://www.hhs.gov/civil-rights/for-individuals/special-topics/needy-families/civil-rights-requirements/index.html.

being used to train the predictive systems, which extends beyond the source of the raw data to include the parameters of how the data was generated. Predictive policing that focuses on crime data rather than the precursors of crime will necessarily emphasize the need to put police resources in areas where the police focus their resources. Without substantially refocusing away from police enforcement and towards the alleviation of disparities in housing access, mental health services, employment, and other predicates of criminal activity, the AI systems can do little more than illustrate the status quo.

On the other hand, AI modeling could be used as a tool to allocate resources more effectively by identifying which social services would have the greatest impact on reducing crime. AI systems can provide excellent modeling against a wide range of variables. By analyzing a community's broader economy and social services net, the model could identify which changes would have the largest positive impact given the same expenditure.

§ 7.2 THE ROLES FOR ARTIFICIAL INTELLIGENCE IN LAW ENFORCEMENT AND NATIONAL SECURITY

There are a wide range of AI systems that can be built or adapted for use in law enforcement and national security. These tools can be organized into four broad categories: chatbots, predictive AI systems, tracking and monitoring systems, and automated response tools. The four categories range from the generally beneficial and innocuous to those considered much more intrusive and potentially controversial.

1. Chatbots and similar services can augment consumer information. These systems can interact with the public to provide useful information, offer help in receiving community resources, improve crime reporting, and aid in the collection of information from the public on behalf of law enforcement.[30] Chatbots are helping with inquiries from the public and potential new recruits, providing "how to" information about engaging with the courts, assisting probation officers, and adding resources for victim services.[31]

2. Predictive AI systems can collect publicly available information to focus on crime statistics, populations trends, and other data that might improve the efficiency of crime forecasting and police deployment. The tools are also used for cybercrime and credit card fraud detection. Predictive AI systems can also be used to predict rates of recidivism or identify individuals who might be involved in gun violence.[32]

---

30 *Chatbots in the Criminal Justice System*, NAT. INST. JUST. (Nov. 2021), https://cjttec.org/chatbots-in-criminal-justice-system/.

31 *Id.*

32 *See* Marion Oswald, Jamie Grace, Sheena Urwin & Geoffrey C. Barnes, *Algorithmic Risk Assessment Policing Models: Lessons from the Durham HART Model and Experimental Proportionality*, 27 INFO. & COMM. TECH. L. 223 (2018) citing Jeff

3. Tracking and monitoring systems include a range of technologies that can collect information on individuals. These systems can scan live and historical video footage for individual suspects using biometric information, track license plates across multiple traffic cameras, intercept mobile phone data to track—or even receive—communications among suspects, and combine information being collected on a suspect with third-party data about that individual person to draw a very clear picture of the individual's movements and connections. In the demonstrations following the murder of George Floyd, for example, "the police turned to a range of automated systems for help, reaching for information collected by automated license plate readers, CCTV-video analysis software, open-source geolocation tools, and Clearview AI's controversial facial recognition system."[33] Clearview AI's facial recognition system is itself quite controversial. "Clearview scraped the public internet from billions of photos, using everything from Venmo transactions to Flickr posts. With that data, it

Asher & Rob Arthur, *Inside the Algorithm that Tries to Predict Gun Violence in Chicago*, NY TIMES (June 13, 2017), https://www.nytimes.com/2017/06/13/upshot/what-an-algorithm-reveals-about-life-on-chicagos-high-risk-list.html; Adam Liptak, *Sent to Prison by a Software Program's Secret Algorithms*, NY TIMES (May 1, 2017), https://www.nytimes.com/2017/05/01/us/politics/sent-to-prison-by-a-software-programs-secret-algorithms.html.

33 Bryan McMahon, *How the Police Use AI to Track and Identify You*, GRADIENT (Oct. 3, 2020), https://thegradient.pub/how-the-police-use-ai-to-track-and-identify-you/.

built a comprehensive database of faces and made it searchable."[34] In a lawsuit against Clearview AI, the plaintiffs highlight that "unlike fingerprints, facial biometrics are readily observable and present a grave and immediate danger to privacy, individual autonomy, and liberty."[35] Originally, the database was to be sold for commercial use, but privacy concerns and a lack of buyers led the company to shift to law enforcement as its primary market.[36]

4. Automated devices can be used for law enforcement, national security, and armed conflict to operate in the field, either to augment human control or to replace human control.[37] "[A]utonomous weapons systems act as a force multiplier. That is, fewer warfighters are needed for a given mission, and the efficacy of each

---

[34] Nilay Patel, *Clearview AI and the end of privacy, with author Kashmir Hill*, VERGE (Oct. 17, 2023), https://www.theverge.com/23919134/kashmir-hill-your-face-belongs-to-us-clearview-ai-facial-recognition-privacy-decoder.

[35] In re Clearview AI, Inc., Consumer Priv. Litig., 585 F. Supp. 3d 1111, 1120 (N.D. Ill. 2022), clarified on denial of reconsideration, No. 21–CV–0135, 2022 WL 2915627 (N.D. Ill. July 25, 2022).

[36] *See* Patel, *supra* note 34.

[37] *See* UNMANNED SYSTEMS ROADMAP 2007–2032, U.S. DEPT. OF DEFENSE (2007), https://apps.dtic.mil/sti/citations/ADA475002; Amitai Etzioni & Oren Etzioni, *Pros and Cons of Autonomous Weapons Systems*, MILITARY REV. (May-June 2017), https://www.armyupress.army.mil/Journals/Military-Review/English-Edition-Archives/May-June-2017/Pros-and-Cons-of-Autonomous-Weapons-Systems/.

warfighter is greater."[38] Robots of various types are being deployed in Asia and other regions to add patrols, assist the public in finding police officers, assist with crowd management, and documenting crimes.[39] Drones are used to surveil areas known for poaching and drug trafficking, serve as first responders to verify details on the scene, track suspects, or even to engage with an armed response.[40] Although armed technologies have not been employed in domestic policing as yet, the machines have been used in areas of armed conflict. Most are under human control, but there have been a growing number of military attacks involving fully autonomous devices.

In addition to these four general categories, there are other ways in which AI technology has increased law enforcement's ability to observe the community being served and protect the community. Gun detection technology, for example, can use audio monitoring to detect gunshots and identify the

---

38 Etzioni & Etzioni, *supra* note 37.

39 *See, e.g.*, Heather Chen, *'Like something out of Black Mirror': Police Robots go on Patrol at Singapore Airport*, CNN (June 18, 2023), https://www.cnn.com/2023/06/18/asia/police-robots-singapore-security-intl-hnk/index.html.

40 *See* Marise Sorial, *The Role of Drones in Next-Generation Surveillance and Security*, INTERNET SAFETY STATISTICS (July 23rd, 2024), https://www.internetsafetystatistics.com/role-of-drones-surveillance/; John W. Rollins, *Armed Drones: Evolution as a Counterterrorism Tool*, CONG. RES. SERV. IF12342 (November 7, 2023), https://crsreports.congress.gov/product/pdf/IF/IF12342.

location from which shots have been fired.[41] These systems often have AI safeguards in place to prevent the recordation and surveillance of conversations while enabling the systems to detect gunshots and explosions.

Body cameras have become another important technology used in policing. Like police car dash cameras, body cameras allow police departments to document and review interactions between law enforcement officers and members of the public. The videos provide objective information about these interactions and have been critically important in documenting instances of both police misconduct and false accusations against police officers. There are challenges regarding the use of body cameras, however, and AI can be helpful to solve some of those problems. One key challenge is the need to respect the privacy of third parties caught on body camera videos. AI systems can efficiently blur out the faces and identifying characteristics of those individuals to assist with privacy protections when body camera footage is released to the public.[42]

Body camera footage also tends to be of limited quality. AI video enhancement techniques can improve picture quality and enable access to much better clarity than that initially identified. The AI systems must be deployed with care so that neither

---

[41] *See* Kristin Finklea, *Law Enforcement Use of Artificial Intelligence and Directives in the 2023 Executive Order*, CONG. RES. SERV. IN12289 (Dec. 15, 2023), https://crsreports.congress.gov/product/pdf/IN/IN12289.

[42] *Id.* at 2.

the software nor the technicians introduce content that was not in the videos, but with proper safeguards, this can be done to create higher quality video without undermining the fidelity of the footage.

In addition to improving the quality of video from a single source, AI editing tools can combine footage from multiple sources to create composite video evidence of a crime scene. Footage from body cameras can be combined with witness videos, security cameras, and other sources to gain additional information about the events that took place at a crime scene. As with video enhancement, these techniques must be used with care to guarantee that no synthetic content is added to the composite. Done properly, this information can significantly assist law enforcement and civil investigators understand how events at a scene took place on a moment-by-moment basis.

Many of the AI systems used in law enforcement are much more mundane. Digital forensic software, for example, can read a hard drive to find and tag images that may be child pornography, to recover hidden files, to circumvent encryption and biometric locks, and offer law enforcement other methods of accessing information stored digitally.[43]

Through the National Crime Information Center (NCIC), the Department of Justice operates a number of national database systems that support

---

[43] Erik Fritsvold, *17 Types of Innovative Police Technology*, UNIV. SAN DIEGO (May 10, 2019), https://onlinedegrees.sandiego.edu/10-innovative-police-technologies/.

the collection and sharing of information about criminals, suspects, evidence, and incarceration.[44] The separate programs include these and others:

- National Crime Information Center (NCIC)

  A criminal records database allowing criminal justice agencies to enter or search for information about stolen property, missing or wanted persons, and domestic violence protection orders; to get criminal histories; and to access the National Sex Offender Registry.

- Next Generation Identification (NGI)

  Formerly known as the Integrated Automated Fingerprint Identification System (IAFIS)—a database of palm and fingerprints and mugshots, allowing verification of identity, submissions of arrest information, and access to fingerprint-based criminal histories.

- National Data Exchange (N-DEx)

  A national investigative information sharing system giving access to records from across the nation to aid in criminal investigations. Investigators can review criminal justice data from state, local, tribal, regional, and federal agencies, 24/7, from any secure Internet-capable device. Data includes incident reports, arrest reports, booking and

---

[44] *See National Crime Information Systems*, DEPT. OF JUST., (last visited Feb. 16, 2025).

incarceration reports, pre-trial investigations, and probation and parole records.

- National Instant Criminal Background Check System (NICS)

  A system used by Federal Firearms Licensees (FFLs) to determine a person's eligibility to buy firearms or explosives, helping to ensure prohibited persons are prevented from purchasing firearms, and to issue firearms-related permits, and manage seized firearms.

- Law Enforcement Enterprise Portal (LEEP)

  A gateway for criminal justice agencies to access unclassified law enforcement intelligence products, as well as systems or services such as N-DEx, Intelink, the Regional Information Sharing Systems Network (RISSNET), National Gang Intelligence Center, eGuardian, Virtual Command Center, and others.

- International Justice and Public Safety Network (Nlets)

  An interstate justice and public safety network owned by the states supporting inquiry into state systems for criminal history, driver's license and motor vehicle registration, as well as supporting inquiry into federal systems, such as the Department of Homeland Security (DHS) U.S. Immigration and Customs Enforcement (ICE) Law Enforcement Support Center, the Drug

Enforcement Administration (DEA) National Drug Pointer Index (NDPIX), and the Federal Aviation Administration (FAA) Aircraft Registry, as well as the Government of Canada's Canadian Police Information Centre (CPIC).[45]

Although the heart of these systems is information collection, tagging, and access, the use of predictive AI systems, improved search algorithms, biometrics and facial recognition tools, and other software augmented with AI has increased the volume of information collected and the ability to sift and sort the data into useful information.

§ 7.3 CONSTITUTIONAL AND STATUTORY LIMITATIONS ON INFORMATION GATHERING

Given the significant amount of information available to law enforcement and national security, there is a real concern that unbridled use of the information could lead to intrusive surveillance, over-criminalization, and an abusive totalitarian regime. The limits on police power are provided in the Constitution and supplemented with state and federal law.

§ 7.3.1 FROM OLMSTEAD TO KATZ

The United States rightly prides itself on the passage of the Bill of Rights in 1791. The original need to create a form of limited government was

---

45 *Id.*

designed to reflect the sovereign right between the states and federal government, but many of these same liberties were provided to the people through state constitutions. Those liberties were later extended to individuals through the adoption of the Fourteenth Amendment. The Fourth Amendment protected individuals from unreasonable search and seizure and established a warrant requirement. The Fifth Amendment added protections from the taking of property without due process of law and from protections from self-incrimination. The Third Amendment restricted the government from the quartering of troops. As the Supreme Court interpreted and expanded those rights, it recognized a right of privacy emanating from the express provisions of the Constitution:

> [S]pecific guarantees in the Bill of Rights have penumbras, formed by emanations from those guarantees that help give them life and substance. Various guarantees create zones of privacy. The right of association contained in the penumbra of the First Amendment is one . . . . The Third Amendment, in its prohibition against the quartering of soldiers "in any house" in time of peace without the consent of the owner, is another facet of that privacy. The Fourth Amendment explicitly affirms the "right of the people to be secure in their persons, houses, papers, and effects, against unreasonable searches and seizures." The Fifth Amendment, in its Self-Incrimination Clause, enables the citizen to create a zone of privacy which government may not force him to

> surrender to his detriment. The Ninth Amendment provides: "The enumeration in the Constitution, of certain rights, shall not be construed to deny or disparage others retained by the people." . . . .
>
> We have had many controversies over these penumbral rights of "privacy and repose."[46]

The metaphor of the penumbra of rights has fallen out of favor, but the limitations on police power should still be understood to include not only the text from each of the provisions within the Bill of Rights but also the overlap among them. For purposes of limitations against surveillance, the Fourth Amendment is the most significant of the constitutional constraints on government.

The Fourth Amendment protects "[t]he right of the people to be secure in their persons, houses, papers, and effects, against unreasonable searches and seizures."[47] The protection was never absolute. Instead, it prohibited a general warrant as was commonly used in Great Britain or the use of a writ of assistance, which was a device frequently used in the American Colonies.[48] The new states abolished

---

[46] Griswold v. Connecticut, 381 U.S. 479, 484–85 (1965) (internal citations omitted).

[47] U.S. CONST. amend. IV.

[48] *See* Olmstead v. U.S., 277 U.S. 438, 463 (1928) (overruled) ("The well-known historical purpose of the Fourth Amendment, directed against general warrants and writs of assistance, was to prevent the use of governmental force to search a man's house, his person, his papers, and his effects, and to prevent their seizure against his will."); Richard M. Thompson II, *The Fourth Amendment Third-Party Doctrine*, CONG. RES. SERV. 3 (June 5,

the writ of assistance, and requiring that "no warrants shall issue, but upon probable cause, supported by oath or affirmation, and particularly describing the place to be searched, and the persons or things to be seized."[49]

The text of the Fourth Amendment says nothing about a limitation to a person's house. The inclusion of papers and effects would be redundant if they were not protected outside the home. But in *Olmstead v. U.S.*,[50] one of the leading cases on the intersection of new technology and the Fourth Amendment, the Supreme Court ignored the implications of the police's ability to eavesdrop on telephone conversations through wiretaps. "There was no evidence of compulsion to induce the defendants to talk over their many telephones,"[51] the Supreme Court explained that the Fourth Amendment "cannot be extended and expanded to include telephone wires, reaching to the whole world from the defendant's house or office. The intervening wires are not part of his house or office, any more than are the highways along which they are stretched."[52]

2014) ("During the 18th century, British and colonial officials conducted searches and seizures of people's homes with little to no suspicion of wrongdoing pursuant to either a general warrant, which was used mainly in England, or a writ of assistance, which was used in the American colonies.").

49 U.S. CONST. amend. IV.

50 Olmstead v. U.S., 277 U.S. 438, 465 (1928), overruled by Katz v. U.S., 389 U.S. 347 (1967).

51 *Id.* at 462.

52 *Id.* at 465.

Olmstead narrowed the focus of the search warrant to the "house or office" and further narrowed its application to physical objects that could be found and removed.[53] The dissent by Justice Louis Brandeis highlighted the fallacies of this argument. His dissent noted that the reading of private letters violated Fourth Amendment rights.[54]

> The makers of our Constitution . . . conferred, as against the government, the right to be let alone—the most comprehensive of rights and the right most valued by civilized men. To protect, that right, every unjustifiable intrusion by the government upon the privacy of the individual, whatever the means employed, must be deemed a violation of the Fourth Amendment. And the use, as evidence in a criminal proceeding, of facts ascertained by such intrusion must be deemed a violation of the Fifth.[55]

Olmstead was overturned by *Katz v. U.S.* in 1967[56] in recognition that "the Fourth Amendment protects

---

[53] *See* Carpenter v. U.S., 585 U.S. 296, 304 (2018) ("For much of our history, Fourth Amendment search doctrine was "tied to common-law trespass" and focused on whether the Government 'obtains information by physically intruding on a constitutionally protected area.' quoting U.S. v. Jones, 565 U.S. 400, 405, 406, n. 3 (2012).

[54] Olmstead, 277 U.S. at 478 (Brandeis, J. dissenting) ("the amendment is violated by the officer's reading the paper without a physical seizure, without his even touching it, and that use . . . constitutes a violation of the Fifth Amendment.")

[55] *Id.* at 478–79 (Brandeis, J. dissenting).

[56] Katz v. U.S., 389 U.S. 347 (1967). *See also* Berger v. New York, 388 U.S. 41 (1967).

people, not places."[57] But even here, the Supreme Court declined to follow the invitation of Justice Brandeis to recognize privacy more broadly. Although the modern formulation recognizes that relies less heavily on earlier Supreme Court's physical limitations to the defendant's house, neither did it expand the Fourth Amendment beyond those instances where the Supreme Court itself believes there is "a subjective expectation of privacy that society recognizes as reasonable."[58] This societal recognition, in turn is a determination solely within the purview of the Supreme Court rather than an assessment derived from empirical evidence.

While not directly part of the jurisprudence on the Fourth Amendment, two other cases play significant roles in understanding the expansion of constitutional protections for the individual. *New York Times v. Sullivan* has already been described for its importance on limiting defamation claims brought by public figures.[59] The other case is *Brandenburg v. Ohio*,[60] which ended the ability of the government to bring criminal actions against criminal syndicalism, understood to mean criminal acts for political, industrial, and social change. After *Brandenburg*, a criminal statute cannot make mere advocacy of illegal conduct a crime. "[T]he constitutional guarantees of free speech and free

[57] *Id.* at 351.

[58] Kyllo v. U.S., 533 U.S. 27, 32–33 (2001) (citing Katz, 389 U.S. at 360 (Harlan, J., concurring)).

[59] *See* New York Times, 376 U.S. at 279, *supra* ch. 5 note 21 and accompanying text.

[60] Brandenburg v. Ohio, 395 U.S. 444 (1969).

press do not permit a State to forbid or proscribe advocacy of the use of force or of law violation except where such advocacy is directed to inciting or producing imminent lawless action and is likely to incite or produce such action."[61]

Neither *Sullivan* nor *Brandenburg* says anything about the Fourth Amendment, but along with *Katz*, the trio of cases should be understood to reframe the relationship between the government and its residents. Privacy and incendiary speech often go hand in hand. Law enforcement may not invade the privacy of the advocate using warrantless searches, civil litigation, or criminal prosecution unless there is sufficient evidence of conduct-based criminality, a high likelihood of imminent and significant criminal conduct, or speech that is so recklessly false as to remove it from First Amendment protections.

§ 7.3.2 THIRD PARTY DOCTRINE LIMITATIONS ON THE FOURTH AMENDMENT

Olmstead left the expansion of the Fourth Amendment intentionally vague. In a series of decisions, the Supreme Court made clear that the use of informants was not limited by the Fourth Amendment. Targets of police inquiry had no constitutional protections from their own, voluntary disclosures, even the recipients were acting under false pretenses.[62] The lack of protection from a

---

[61] *Id.* at 447.

[62] *See* U.S. v. White, 401 U.S. 745 (1971); Hoffa v. U.S., 385 U.S. 293 (1966); Lewis v. U.S., 385 U.S. 206 (1966); Lopez v. U.S., 373 U.S. 427 (1963); On Lee v. U.S., 343 U.S. 747 (1952).

person's own voluntary disclosures then extended from sharing information with untrustworthy allies to the everyday disclosures required of an increasingly connected life.

In a series of decisions involving business records, the Supreme Court found that a person assumed the risk of disclosure when that person provided personal information to a third party.[63] In *United States v. Miller*, for example, the business records were those maintained by the bank as required of customers to meet the Bank Secrecy Act.[64] The banking customers were compelled by law to disclose information to the banks, and as a result of the third-party doctrine, that compulsion effectively meant that banking customers are compelled to make that information available to the government with a subpoena rather than through a warrant.[65]

The Supreme Court took this approach a step further, holding that the information obtained by automated systems was also disclosed to the operator of that system even though it was not actually provided to individuals. In *Smith v. Maryland*,[66] upon the request of the police, the local phone company "installed a pen register at its central offices

---

[63] *See* Orin S. Kerr, *The Case for the Third-Party Doctrine*, 107, MICH. L. REV. 561, 569 (2009); U.S. v. Miller, 425 U.S. 435, 443 (1976) (bank records); Couch v. U.S., 409 U.S. 322, 335 (1973) (tax returns); U.S. v. White, 401 U.S. 745, 751–752, (1971) (stolen papers).

[64] U.S. v. Miller, 425 U.S. 435, 441 (1976).

[65] *Id.* at 443.

[66] Smith v. Maryland, 442 U.S. 735 (1979).

to record the numbers dialed from the telephone"[67] of the target of the police investigation. A pen register records the phone numbers dialed by that phone, but it does not record the contents of the phone call. In the view of the Supreme Court, "[t]elephone users . . . typically know that they must convey numerical information to the phone company; that the phone company has facilities for recording this information; and that the phone company does in fact record this information for a variety of legitimate business purposes."[68]

Given the scope of the third-party doctrine, the expansion of modern technology to the storage and transmission of a person's papers and effects has the potential to render the Fourth Amendment superfluous. Data is routinely stored or backed-up through cloud providers. Basic computing functions like word processing, financial reporting, and presentations have migrated from individual computers to online services. Media consumption has shifted from books, films, and records to ebooks and streaming services. In an ever-growing part of the economy, the ability to retain one's books, records, and personal effects entirely in one's own home has been replaced with third-party services. While an individual can still fight to live "off the grid," the grid has expanded and the option to do without interconnected, third-party mediated services becomes harder every day.

---

[67] *Id.* at 737.

[68] *Id.* at 743.

The data provided today by an individual goes well beyond the information provided in documents or used in telephones, as noted in the discussion of volitional privacy, an individual voluntarily discloses each website the person visits (often despite significant efforts to web surf anonymously), where the travel holding their mobile phone, where other people tag and track their activities on social media, and more. A person's fingerprints, face, shape of the ear, voice print, typing patterns, gait, and other attributes are not encrypted, and therefore under the third-party doctrine, they are presumptively outside the protection of the Fourth Amendment.

As a starting point, third-party data is available by subpoena rather than search warrant. In addition, however, it is also available by contract. Increasingly, law enforcement has obtained information—including that could not be obtained without a warrant—from third parties by purchasing the data as a commercial transaction. Commercial surveillance tools and data brokers have developed significant markets selling their collection of public information to governmental agencies. "Data brokers harvest our location data from the app developers, and then sell it to . . . federal military, intelligence, and law enforcement agencies."[69]

Data brokers use ad networks, app tools, web monitoring, and other tools to tap into a vast

[69] Bennett Cyphers, *How the Federal Government Buys Our Cell Phone Location Data*, ELEC. FRONTIER FOUND. (June 13, 2022), https://www.eff.org/deeplinks/2022/06/how-federal-government-buys-our-cell-phone-location-data.

collection of location information, behavioral information, affiliations, personal networks and much more. They sell this information to law enforcement in addition to selling it for commercial and political exploitation. For example, the company Venntel has been publicly identified as having clients including "the IRS, the DHS and its subsidiaries ICE and CBP, the DEA, and the FBI."[70] Local law enforcement agencies and other government entities can also purchase this data.

Nothing in Fourth Amendment jurisprudence suggests that the warrant requirement prevents law enforcement from using other available means to obtain information. Just as the police can rely on informants to provide information that would otherwise be protected from search and seizure, they can also rely on commercial vendors to provide them with that data.

§ 7.3.3 CONSTITUTIONAL PROTECTIONS AGAINST DATA SURVEILLANCE

The Supreme Court has come to recognize the failure of the voluntary disclosure justification for the third-party doctrine, instead returning to the *Katz* expectation of privacy approach to data surveillance by the government. The first step was in *U.S. v. Jones*, where the Supreme Court required a warrant when a car was tracked using a GPS monitor.[71] Although the majority opinion provided a rather mechanical application of the Fourth Amendment

---

70 *Id.*

71 U.S. v. Jones, 565 U.S. 400 (2012).

based on the historical law of trespass, Justice Sonya Sotomayor's concurrence offered very forward-looking considerations for courts and legislatures to consider.

> In cases involving even short-term monitoring, some unique attributes of GPS surveillance relevant to the *Katz* analysis will require particular attention. GPS monitoring generates a precise, comprehensive record of a person's public movements that reflects a wealth of detail about her familial, political, professional, religious, and sexual associations. The government can store such records and efficiently mine them for information years into the future. And because GPS monitoring is cheap in comparison to conventional surveillance techniques and, by design, proceeds surreptitiously, it evades the ordinary checks that constrain abusive law enforcement practices: "limited police resources and community hostility."
>
> Awareness that the government may be watching chills associational and expressive freedoms. And the government's unrestrained power to assemble data that reveal private aspects of identity is susceptible to abuse. The net result is that GPS monitoring—by making available at a relatively low cost such a substantial quantum of intimate information about any person whom the government, in its unfettered discretion, chooses to track—may "alter the relationship between citizen and

government in a way that is inimical to democratic society."

I would take these attributes of GPS monitoring into account when considering the existence of a reasonable societal expectation of privacy in the sum of one's public movements. I would ask whether people reasonably expect that their movements will be recorded and aggregated in a manner that enables the government to ascertain, more or less at will, their political and religious beliefs, sexual habits, and so on. I do not regard as dispositive the fact that the government might obtain the fruits of GPS monitoring through lawful conventional surveillance techniques.[72]

Following *Jones*, in *Riley v. California*,[73] the Supreme Court then accepted the invitation of Justice Sotomayor to reject another of the broad exceptions to the warrant requirement, that of the exception to searches incident to a lawful arrest.[74] The *Riley* Court explained that "[c]ell phones differ in both a quantitative and a qualitative sense from other objects that might be kept on an arrestee's person."[75] The opinion noted that cell phones could "just as easily be called cameras, video players,

---

72 *Id.* at 415–16 (Sotomayor, J., concurring) (quoting Illinois v. Lidster, 540 U.S. 419, 426 (2004); United States v. Cuevas-Perez, 640 F.3d 272, 285 (C.A.7 2011) (Flaum, J., concurring)) (other citations omitted).

73 Riley v. California, 573 U.S. 373 (2014).

74 *Id.* at 393.

75 *Id.*

rolodexes, calendars, tape recorders, libraries, diaries, albums, televisions, maps, or newspapers."[76]

> Today, by contrast, it is no exaggeration to say that many of the more than 90% of American adults who own a cell phone keep on their person a digital record of nearly every aspect of their lives—from the mundane to the intimate. Allowing the police to scrutinize such records on a routine basis is quite different from allowing them to search a personal item or two in the occasional case.
>
> Although the data stored on a cell phone is distinguished from physical records by quantity alone, certain types of data are also qualitatively different. An Internet search and browsing history, for example, can be found on an Internet-enabled phone and could reveal an individual's private interests or concerns—perhaps a search for certain symptoms of disease, coupled with frequent visits to WebMD. Data on a cell phone can also reveal where a person has been. Historic location information is a standard feature on many smart phones and can reconstruct someone's specific movements down to the minute, not only around town but also within a particular building.[77]

Just as the *Jones* concurrence emphasized the qualitative difference between GPS tracking and non-technological attempts to tail a suspect's vehicle

---

[76] *Id.*

[77] *Id.* at 395–96 (internal citations omitted).

the *Riley* Court recognized the fundamentally different nature of a cell phone in its ability to document the life of the user.[78]

These two opinions have been joined by *Carpenter v. U.S.*,[79] where the government sought to collect historical data stored by telephone companies as part of their cell phone systems. "Each time the phone connects to a cell site, it generates a time-stamped record known as cell-site location information (CSLI)."[80] By federal law, the government could "compel the disclosure of certain telecommunications records when it "offers specific and articulable facts showing that there are reasonable grounds to believe" that the records sought "are relevant and material to an ongoing criminal investigation."[81] The statutory protection was greater than that of a subpoena, but significantly less than is required under a search warrant. The *Carpenter* Court held that the statute was insufficient.

While recognizing that the information was within the ambit of the third-party doctrine, the Supreme Court acknowledged that the comprehensive nature of the data obtained disclosed far more than the kind of information previously covered by the third-party doctrine. Instead, the Supreme Court expressed

---

78 *See* United States v. Knotts, 460 U.S. 276 (1983) (permitting the use of a beeper on a tracked vehicle while reserving the question for such technology if it included around the clock surveillance).

79 *See* Carpenter, 585 U.S. at 296.

80 *Id.* at 300.

81 *Id.* at 302 (quoting the Stored Communications Act, 18 U.S.C. § 2703(d)).

concern that "[m]uch like GPS tracking of a vehicle, cell phone location information is detailed, encyclopedic, and effortlessly compiled."[82] The opinion later explained that "historical cell-site records present even greater privacy concerns than the GPS monitoring of a vehicle we considered in *Jones*. . . . A cell phone faithfully follows its owner beyond public thoroughfares and into private residences, doctor's offices, political headquarters, and other potentially revealing locales."[83]

The trilogy of *Jones*, *Riley*, and *Carpenter* provides an important limitation on the third-party doctrine and the scope of governmental police power. Nonetheless, these cases only address a small aspect of the problem, focusing on limited circumstances. These cases are very carefully written to address only the particular technology before the court. The Supreme Court has been quite circumspect not to establish broader or more general pronouncements on the revisions to Fourth Amendment jurisprudence. Most third-party records, therefore, remain within the subpoena power of the government.

The cautious limitation of the third-party doctrine concerning the collection of widespread surveillance has led to a split among the circuits over geofence warrants, the latest tool of law enforcement data gathering.

---

82 *Id.* at 309.

83 *Id.* at 311.

The geofence warrants began with the first request to Google in 2016, and since then have grown exponentially. "In 2019, Google was receiving about 180 geofence warrant requests per week from law enforcement around the country, amounting to about 9,000 geofence requests for that year. By 2020, that number went up to 11,500 geofence warrant requests."[84]

The geofence warrant solicits Sensorvault location history data, generally for a limited geographic area during a window of time involving a criminal event. This may be a street and surrounding buildings for a period of two hours, or the size and time range requested may be much larger.

Geofence warrants focus on the crime scene as the places to be searched and the cell phone data as the items to be seized, but they "work in reverse" because the traditional search warrant usually also has particular knowledge about the persons involved in the search. "Unlike a warrant authorizing surveillance of a known suspect, geofencing is a technique law enforcement has increasingly utilized when the crime location is known but the identities of suspects [are] not."[85]

---

84 U.S. v. Smith, 110 F.4th 817, 821 citing Brian L. Owsley, *The Best Offense Is a Good Defense: Fourth Amendment Implications of Geofence Warrants*, 50 HOFSTRA L. REV. 829, 834 (2022).

85 United States v. Rhine, 652 F. Supp. 3d 38, 66 (D.D.C. 2023). *See also* Smith, 110 F.4th at 822.

Like CSLI, the data can enable law enforcement to look back in time. Google typically retains location history for eighteen months.[86] "Moreover, the use of these warrants has not been limited to egregious or violent crimes. Law enforcement officials have obtained geofence warrants for investigations into stolen pickup trucks and smashed car windows."[87]

In *United States v. Chatrie*,[88] the Fourth Circuit ruled that the Sensorvault location history was unlike the CSLI at issue in *Carpenter*. The Fourt Circuit framed its opinion by emphasizing the user's control over location history. "Location History is an optional account setting that allows Google to track a user's location while he carries his mobile devices. . . . Location History is turned off by default, so a user must take several affirmative steps before Google begins tracking and storing his Location History data."[89]

The court emphasized that *Carpenter* provided a narrow exception to the third-party doctrine under *Smith v. Maryland* and *U.S. v. Miller*.[90] "The Supreme Court has long recognized that 'a person has no legitimate expectation of privacy in information he voluntarily turns over to third parties.'[91] This is because he 'takes the risk, in

---

[86] *Id.*

[87] *Id.*

[88] United States v. Chatrie, 107 F.4th 319 (2024).

[89] *Id.* at 322.

[90] *Id.* at 326.

[91] *Id.* quoting Smith v. Maryland, 442 U.S. at 735, 743–44 (1979).

revealing his affairs to another, that the information will be conveyed by that person to the Government.' "[92]

The Fourth Circuit rejected the claim that the collection of location history constituted a search subject to the warrant requirement because the defendant never had a reasonable expectation of privacy in the data. The *Chatrie* Court emphasized that a two-hour window of location history is different from the long, longitudinal data provided to the government in *Carpenter*, making the information "far less revealing."[93] Further, the Court highlighted that location history remains an optional service that the customer must select, one that is far more volitional than providing the phone company the number one is dialing.

Only a short time later, the Fifth Circuit disagreed, setting up a circuit split that will likely be resolved by the Supreme Court. The Fifth Circuit in *U.S. v. Smith* found that the defendants did have a reasonable expectation of privacy. The Fifth Circuit doubted the voluntary nature of the Google opt-in setting for location history, emphasizing "the fact that approximately 592 million people have "opted in" to comprehensive tracking of their locations itself calls into question the "voluntary" nature of this process."[94] The Fifth Circuit sided with the lower court and the appellate dissent in *Chatrie*, explaining

---

[92] *Id.* quoting United States v. Miller, 425 U.S. 435, 443 (1976).

[93] *Id.* at 330.

[94] Smith, 110 F.4th at 835.

"a user simply cannot forfeit the protections of the Fourth Amendment for years of precise location information by selecting 'YES, I'M IN' at midnight while setting up Google Assistant, even if some text offered warning along the way."[95]

The Fifth Circuit also dismissed the Fourth Circuit's argument that the time window was sufficiently narrow to distinguish the geofence warrant from the CSLI tower dump. "While it is true that geofences tend to be limited temporally, the potential intrusiveness of even a snapshot of precise location data should not be understated. As two commentators noted:

> [E]ven a brief snapshot can expose highly sensitive information—think a visit to "the psychiatrist, the plastic surgeon, the abortion clinic, the AIDS treatment center, the strip club, the criminal defense attorney, the by-the-hour-motel, the union meeting, the mosque, synagogue or church, [or] the gay bar," or a location other than home during a COVID-19 shelter-in-place order.[96]

Having determined that the collection of Sensorvault location information constituted a search, the Fifth Circuit turned to the validity of the warrant used to collect the information. The Fifth Circuit rejected the government's argument that

---

[95] *Id.* quoting United States v. Chatrie, 590 F. Supp.3d 901, 936 (2022) (reversed on appeal).

[96] *Id.* quoting Amster & Diehl, *supra* ch. 5 note 133, at 408 (quoting Jones, 565 U.S. at 415, (Sotomayor, J., concurring)).

geofence warrants meet the particularity requirement because they are "limited to specified information directly tied to a particular [crime] at a particular place and time."[97] The court instead viewed the search of the Sensorvault location history as the application of a general warrant and fundamentally unconstitutional. "While the *results* of a geofence warrant may be narrowly tailored, the *search* itself is not. . . . [G]eofence warrants . . . allow law enforcement to rummage through troves of location data from hundreds of millions of Google users without any description of the particular suspect or suspects to be found."[98] If this view stands up on appeal to the Supreme Court, then the entire category of geofence warrants will be declared unconstitutional.

Only the Supreme Court can determine what it will ultimately decide, however, given the cautious language in *Carpenter*, the Supreme Court may well find that access to location history constitutes a search requiring a warrant without presuming that a search of de-identified data within the dataset constitutes a general warrant.

The Justice Department collaborated with Google to create a three-step process for conducting a search, and that search is subject to the warrant requirement. In the first step, Google conducts a search of the entire database for devices that meet the geographical and temporal requirements of the

---

97 *Id.* at 838.

98 *Id.* at 837–38.

search. "After Google searches its Sensorvault, it determines which accounts were within the geographic parameters of the warrant and lists each of those accounts with an anonymized device ID. Google also includes the date and time, the latitude and longitude, the geolocation source used, and the map display radius. . ."[99]

In step 2, legal counsel from Google and from the law enforcement agency narrow the parameters of the search using the de-identified data to eliminate devices that do not fit the profile of potential suspects. "Google . . . typically require[s] law enforcement to narrow the number of users for which it requests Step 2 data so that the Government cannot . . . simply seek geographically unrestricted data for all users within the geofence."[100]

Finally, in step 3, law enforcement can require Google to provide the information on the devices that are no longer de-identified. Step 3, however, may not be necessary. Law enforcement may be able to re-identify the information without requesting the information from Google. For example, if a phone was first at a crime scene and then that de-identified device was at the location of a person of interest, the address to which the device traveled may be more than enough to name the suspect. Then other warrants can collect corroborating information.

---

99 *Id.* at 825.

100 *Id.* quoting Chatrie, 590 F. Supp. 3d at 916; Chatrie, 107 F.4th at 324.

The Fourth Amendment does not itself require that persons must be named. However, the Fifth Circuit's concerns about geofence warrants becoming general warrants must be taken very seriously. In crafting a rule, the Supreme Court is likely to emphasize the need for specificity and limitations in all three steps of the warrant requirement, require additional safeguards so that de-identified information cannot be used without additional warrants, and perhaps address the proportionality concern that these very powerful warrant procedures should not be used for broken windows or other minor offenses. Of course, predicting a Supreme Court opinion remains a fool's errand, so these considerations are only speculation on how this circuit split will eventually be resolved.

§ 7.3.4 STATUTORY LIMITATIONS ON WARRANTLESS ELECTRONIC SURVEILLANCE

In the aftermath of the *Olmstead* decision, law enforcement agencies used wire taps as a common method of gathering information on suspects. Six years later, Congress amended the Federal Communications Act to prohibit the unauthorized reception of wired and wireless communications.[101] Despite the application of the Communications Act to law enforcement,[102] the law has inconsistent enforcement and was often ignored by officials who used wire taps as an undisclosed step in the process

---

[101] Communications Act of 1934, Chap. 652, 48 Stat. 1064, 1103 (1934).

[102] Nardone v. U.S., 302 U.S. 379 (1937).

of obtaining admissible evidence. Since aspects of the Fourth Amendment had not yet been applied to state actions, the limitations placed by the Communications Act were often not extended to state law enforcement.[103]

The FBI, in particular, abused its capacity to use wiretaps and other surveillance techniques to track leaders of the Civil Rights Movement and Vietnam protest movements. In 1968, comprehensive federal legislation was enacted.[104] The original version of the 1968 Wiretap Act was substantially amended as the Electronic Communications Privacy Act of 1986 (ECPA),[105] and further amended in the aftermath of the September 11th terrorist attacks as part of the USA PATRIOT Act,[106] and has been updated several times since.

The ECPA is comprised of three titles. Title I refers to the updated version of the original Wiretap Act; Title II is the Stored Communications Act (SCA); and

---

[103] *See* Wolf v. Colorado, 338 U.S. 25 (1949); Schwartz v. Texas, 344 U.S. 199 (1952).

[104] *See* Title III of the Omnibus Crime Control and Safe Streets Act of 1968, Pub. L. 90–351, 82 Stat. 197 (June 19, 1968) ("Title III").

[105] Electronic Communications Privacy Act of 1986, Pub. L. 99–508, 100 Stat. 1848 (October 21, 1986)("ECPA").

[106] Uniting and Strengthening America by Providing Appropriate Tools Required to Intercept and Obstruct Terrorism (USA PATRIOT) Act of 2001, Pub. L. 107–56, 115 Stat. 272 (2001).

Title III covers pen registers and trap and trace devices.[107]

The Wiretap Act continues to limit the interception of wire, oral, or electronic unless a valid warrant is used to obtain the content of the communication.[108] Unlike the original Communications Act prohibition against wiretaps and illegal eavesdropping, the Wiretap Act prohibits law enforcement from using of illegally obtained content as evidence.[109]

There are significant limitations on the Wiretap Act. One is consent, and as a result the custom has developed for businesses to increasingly require recordings automatically as part of their training and customer service operations. As these notices of content become more and more common, customer surveillance has become the standard.

A second notable exception applies to national security. The law provides an exception "persons authorized by law to intercept wire, oral, or electronic communications or to conduct electronic surveillance, as defined in section 101 of the Foreign Intelligence Surveillance Act (FISA) of 1978."[110] Instead of a warrant, a FISA court order or certification by the

---

[107] *See Electronic Communications Privacy Act of 1986 (ECPA)*, https://bja.ojp.gov/program/it/privacy-civil-liberties/authorities/statutes/1285 (last visited Feb. 16, 2025).

[108] *See* 18 U.S.C. § 2515 (2024).

[109] *See id.*

[110] 18 U.S.C. § 2511.

U.S. Attorney General is sufficient to intercept communications.[111]

In contrast to the Wiretap Act, the SCA establishes different levels of court authority depending on the nature of the content being seized. "The SCA breaks the information down into three categories: (1) contents; (2) non-content records and other information pertaining to a subscriber or customer; and (3) basic subscriber and session information, which is a subset of non-content records and is specifically enumerated in 18 U.S.C. § 2703(c)(2).[112]

Content records are protected by a warrant requirement. Non-content records are subject to a certification that falls somewhere between a warrant and a subpoena. Section 2703(d) of the ACA authorizes the use of a court order to obtain subscriber records. "Section 2703(d) orders can be granted based on a showing of "reasonable grounds to believe" that the records sought are "relevant and material" to an ongoing criminal investigation. This standard is lower than the "probable cause" standard of a warrant, which is required under the Fourth Amendment."[113] Finally, the subscriber records are

---

[111] *Id.* at § 2511(2)(ii). The broader implications of the FISA court orders and the national security implications are beyond the subject of this Nutshell.

[112] U.S. DEPT. OF JUSTICE, SEARCHING AND SEIZING COMPUTERS AND OBTAINING ELECTRONIC EVIDENCE IN CRIMINAL INVESTIGATIONS 121 (2009), https://www.justice.gov/d9/criminal-ccips/legacy/2015/01/14/ssmanual2009_002.pdf.

[113] *EPIC v. DOJ (CSLI Section 2703(d) Orders)*, EPIC, https://epic.org/documents/epic-v-doj-csli-section-2703d-orders/ (last visited Feb. 16, 2025).

treated as third-party documents and need only a subpoena.

Law enforcement can use AI systems to help identify which records may be of interest. Absent a warrant requirement, law enforcement can use the lower standard of a subpoena or the intermediate standard of information "relevant and material" to an ongoing investigation to collect and retain substantial information that can be later used to compile a profile of communities, regions, or categories of suspects where the police believe there is likely to be criminal conduct.

Neither subpoenas nor Section 2703(d) orders have time limitations on amount of time information can be stored or correlated. As a result, law enforcement has the ability to create (or purchase) vast amounts of subscriber information and connect the relationships among the public as a predictive method of tracking those who have the potential to commit crime. The statutory restrictions in ECPA once offered significant protection to the public from unauthorized collection of information but with AI systems and without warrant requirements, those protections have been largely eroded.

CHAPTER 8
AI IN ARMED CONFLICT

Perhaps the most momentous and consequential use of AI systems relates to their use in the arena of armed conflict. Many fictional stories of the AI singularity involve the moment when autonomous weapons—usually but unrealistically humanoid robots—become self-aware and use their superior fighting power to eliminate humanity because we are seen as a threat to their dominance. *Terminator* is perhaps the best known of these parables but there are many others.[1]

The Terminator apocalypse is just one of the concerns regarding the use of AI in armed conflict. There are also concerns about the combatant's ability to operate under international humanitarian law (also known as the Law of Armed Conflict (LOAC)) when using autonomous weapons, concerns about the use of AI systems for information gathering accuracy that could lead to armed conflict, and the use of AI systems in cyber conflict that may fall just outside the use of physical or kinetic weapons. This chapter provides only a brief introduction to these concepts which form part of the broader understanding of international law, international humanitarian law, and other regulatory frameworks.

---

1 *See, e.g.*, S. Kluug, *AI Risk is like Terminator; Stop Saying it's Not*, EFFECTIVE ALTRUISM FORUM (Mar. 8, 2022), https://forum.effectivealtruism.org/users/skluug.

§ 8.1 INTRODUCTION

Like all other fields, the conduct of war is regulated by law. Also, like other fields, there is often a significant gap between the legal standards and practical application or enforcement of those laws. Nonetheless, the laws regulating international law and international humanitarian law are critical to the broader system of international treaties and cooperation among nations that underpin both global trade and the provision of fundamental human rights.

"International humanitarian law is a set of rules which seek, for humanitarian reasons, to limit the effects of armed conflict. It protects persons who are not or are no longer participating in the hostilities and restricts the means and methods of warfare."[2] International humanitarian law or LOAC resides within the broader category of international law, the various treaties, conventions, and executive agreements that bind nation states to each other through multilateral agreements among large groups of nations and bilateral agreements among pairs of countries.

The United Nations Charter sets out to end armed conflict. Article 2 to the UN Charter provides "[a]ll Members shall refrain in their international relations from the threat or use of force against the territorial integrity or political independence of any

---

2 *What is International Humanitarian Law*, INT. COMM. RED CROSS, https://www.icrc.org/en/doc/assets/files/other/what_is_ihl.pdf (last visited Feb. 16, 2025).

state, or in any other manner inconsistent with the Purposes of the United Nations."[3] It calls on all member states to use only peaceful means to resolve international disputes.[4] At the same time, it also recognizes the right to self-defense in response to an armed attack.[5]

Although invasions of foreign territory violate the UN Charter, countries often find themselves on an armed conflict footing. Moreover, since the end of the first Cold War (1945–1991), armed conflict has increasingly been waged by non-state actors, typically labeled terrorist organizations by those in conflict with these groups. For the "New Cold War,"[6] historians use the 2014 Russian invasion of Crimea as the flashpoint for a new era of global conflict that includes both Russia's territorial aspirations in Europe and China's twin goals of global market domination and geographic domination of the South China Sea region.[7] The focus of this new Cold War is on Europe and Southeast Asia, ongoing conflicts in Middle East states, Iran-backed conflicts, and

---

[3] UN CHARTER ART. 2, para. 4, https://www.un.org/en/about us/un-charter/full-text.

[4] *Id.* at ART. 2, para. 3.

[5] *Id.* at ART. 51.

[6] Elliott Abrams, *The New Cold War*, NAT. REV. (Mar. 4, 2022), https://www.cfr.org/blog/new-cold-war-0.

[7] *See* Jonathan Masters, *Ukraine: Conflict at the Crossroads of Europe and Russia*, COUNCIL ON FOREIGN REL. 36 (Feb. 14, 2023), https://www.cfr.org/backgrounder/ukraine-conflict-crossroads-europe-and-russia; Ronald O'Rourke, *Great Power Competition: Implications for Defense—Issues for Congress*, CONG. RES. SERV. R43838 (Feb. 28, 2024), https://fas.org/sgp/crs/natsec/R43838.pdf.

religious and regional conflicts mean that the world is rarely at peace.

International law includes a wide array of multinational treaties, with over 560 promulgated through the UN, many of which provide mechanisms for addressing conflict to limit the recourse to warfare and reduce its utility.[8] Below are a few illustrative examples of treaties designed to discourage warfare:

Convention on the Prevention and Punishment of the Crime of Genocide (1948)

- International Convention on the Elimination of All Forms of Racial Discrimination (1965)
- International Covenant on Civil and Political Rights (1966)
- International Covenant on Economic, Social and Cultural Rights (1966)
- Convention on the Elimination of All Forms of Discrimination against Women (1979)
- United Nations Convention on the Law of the Sea (1982)
- Convention on the Rights of the Child (1989)
- Comprehensive Nuclear-Test-Ban Treaty (1996)

---

[8] *See Peace, Dignity and Equality on a Healthy Planet*, UNITED NATIONS, https://www.un.org/en/global-issues/international-law-and-justice (last visited Feb. 16, 2025).

- International Convention for the Suppression of the Financing of Terrorism (1999)[9]

International Humanitarian Law predates the United Nations and arguably goes back to the existence of warfare. "Universal codification of international humanitarian law began in the nineteenth century. . . . These rules strike a careful balance between humanitarian concerns and the military requirements of States."[10] The primary codification of international humanitarian law is in the Geneva Conventions, first ratified in 1864 and significantly updated following World War II in 1949.[11]

> [A]n International Red Cross conference in Stockholm in 1948 extended and codified the existing provisions. The conference developed four conventions, which were approved in Geneva on August 12, 1949: (1) the Convention for the Amelioration of the Condition of the Wounded and Sick in Armed Forces in the Field, (2) the Convention for the Amelioration of the Condition of the Wounded, Sick, and Shipwrecked Members of Armed Forces at Sea, (3) the Convention Relative to the Treatment of Prisoners of War, and (4) the Convention

---

9 *Id.*

10 *What is International Humanitarian Law*, *supra* note 2.

11 Malcolm Shaw, *Geneva Conventions*, ENCYC. BRITANNICA (August 12, 2024), https://www.britannica.com/event/Geneva-Conventions.

Relative to the Protection of Civilian Persons in Time of War.

[In 1977,] Protocol I extended protection under the Geneva and Hague conventions to persons involved in wars of "self-determination," which were redefined as international conflicts. . . . Protocol II extended human rights protections to persons involved in severe civil conflicts, which had not been covered by the 1949 accords.

Other agreements prohibit the use of certain weapons and military tactics and protect certain categories of people and goods. These agreements include:

- the 1954 Convention for the Protection of Cultural Property in the Event of Armed Conflict, plus its two protocols;
- the 1972 Biological Weapons Convention;
- the 1980 Conventional Weapons Convention and its five protocols;
- the 1993 Chemical Weapons Convention;
- the 1997 Ottawa Convention on anti-personnel mines;
- the 2000 Optional Protocol to the Convention on the Rights of the Child on the involvement of children in armed conflict.[12]

---

12 *Id.*

> Many provisions of international humanitarian law are now accepted as customary law—that is, as general rules by which all States are bound.

Since the Geneva Conventions have been in force since the nineteenth century, many of the core principles of the treaties enacted as part of the Geneva Convention or adopted as extensions of the Geneva Convention have shifted into "customary law." This means that these obligations arise from the established international practices and norms, rather than solely from the text of conventions and treaties. As international norms, these obligations are considered universal, applying even to states that have not formally adopted a particular treaty. Customary law is used by the UN's International Court of Justice as well as many other judicial systems around the world.

In the context of human rights, international humanitarian law requires humane treatment of noncombatants, civilians, and prisoners. In most other aspects, these obligations are framed as prohibitions that limit how enemy combatants can wage war.

The very nature of war has changed with the advent of the two World Wars of the twentieth century. Throughout history, war was a natural part of statehood and sovereignty, but with the significant increase in lethality of warfare, the "state of war" has faded as a legal relationship.[13] "War is no longer

---

[13] Carsten Stahn, *Jus ad bellum, Jus in Bello . . . Jus Post Bellum?—Rethinking the Conception of the Law of Armed Force,*

treated as a legally accepted paradigm, but as a factual event regulated by (different bodies of) law. It has thus become uncommon to treat war and peace as separate and diametrically opposed legal institutions . . . ."[14] Since cyber warfare includes acts of aggression that can interfere with state sovereignty and even result in physical harm and loss of life, the line between conflict and hostilities becomes a very important one.

Traditionally, military law made much of the distinction between "the law of recourse to force (*jus ad bellum*) from the law governing the conduct of hostilities (*jus in bello*)."[15]

> Certain *jus ad bellum* criteria have, at their philosophical roots, drawn from principles that have been developed as part of the Just War Tradition. These principles have included:
>
> - a competent authority to order the war for a public purpose;
> - a just cause (such as self-defense);
> - the means must be proportionate to the just cause;
> - all peaceful alternatives must have been exhausted; and

---

17 EUROPEAN J. INT'L L. 921 (2006), https://academic.oup.com/ejil/article/17/5/921/2756298.

[14] *Id.* at 922.

[15] *Id.* at 925.

- a right intention on the part of the just belligerent.[16]

The *jus in bello* rules for the conduct of hostilities include similar concepts, but those concepts play out far differently. "Three interdependent principles—military necessity, humanity, and honor—provide the foundation for other law of war principles, such as proportionality and distinction, and most of the treaty and customary rules of the law of war."[17] Vastly oversimplifying the law of armed conflict—

> *Military necessity* justifies certain actions necessary to defeat the enemy as quickly and efficiently as possible. Conversely, *humanity* forbids actions unnecessary to achieve that object. *Proportionality* requires that even when actions may be justified by military necessity, such actions not be unreasonable or excessive. *Distinction* underpins the parties' responsibility to comport their behavior with *military necessity, humanity, and proportionality* by requiring parties to a conflict to apply certain legal categories, principally the *distinction* between the armed forces and the civilian population. Lastly, *honor* supports the entire system and gives parties confidence in it.[18]

In the context of artificial intelligence, questions abound whether these value judgments can be

---

[16] DEPARTMENT OF DEFENSE LAW OF WAR MANUAL 40 (Updated July 2023).

[17] *Id.* at 50.

[18] *Id.* at 51 (internal citations omitted).

captured in the design of autonomous systems. More existentially, if war is conducted through autonomous machines without human engagement on both sides, will the values of honor and the restrictions of proportionality, necessity, and humanity survive remain foundational to the combatants. Put another way, will the humanity and empathy that helps limit the abuse of military might continue to operate without human combatants who feel the consequences of a military's actions.

§ 8.2 THE ROLE OF AI IN ARMED CONFLICT

Given the obligations for military necessity, humanity, proportionality, and honor, one might think it odd that the military is moving to embrace AI as a tool of warfare. The reason is that there are compelling uses for AI predictive capabilities, autonomous weapons, reconnaissance tools, and other resources provided by an AI-based military infrastructure.

Among the many challenges in prosecuting a military campaign is the lack of accurate information about the enemy's strength, position, and resources—and often a similar lack of information about own's own fighting forces. Carl von Clausewitz described this challenge in his nineteenth century account of warfare. "[T]he great uncertainty of all data in War is a peculiar difficulty, because all action must, to a certain extent, be planned in a mere twilight, which in addition not unfrequently—like the effect of a fog or moonshine—gives to things exaggerated dimensions and an unnatural appearance."[19] Known as the "fog of war," the limited and unreliable nature of information is compounded by combatants efforts to deceive and misdirect their opponents, degrading capacity and decision making.

§ 8.2.1 AI IN COMMUNICATIONS AND SIGNAL INTELLIGENCE

Before addressing the role of AI in weapons systems, it is helpful to recognize its increased usage in military operations. AI systems have become increasingly important for improving information gathering or "signals intelligence" and for communication. "Military applications of AI have become an essential part of the military's functioning and will continue to grow in importance. Awareness of the potential of AI is vital to leveraging it for modern military operations."[20]

AI can benefit the military in numerous ways including:

- Warfare systems
- Strategic decision making
- Data processing and Research
- Combat Simulation

---

19 CARL VON CLAUSEWITZ, ON WAR § 24 (1874), https://www.gutenberg.org/files/1946/1946-h/1946-h.htm.

20 *The Most Useful Military Applications of AI in 2024 and Beyond*, SENTIENT DIGITAL, INC. (Mar. 15, 2024), https://sdi.ai/blog/the-most-useful-military-applications-of-ai/.

- Target Recognition
- Threat Monitoring
- Drone Swarms
- Cybersecurity
- Transportation
- Casualty Care and Evacuation[21]

AI has also become the next step in a rapid transformation of communications technology. Radio, radar, and sonar changed the nature of war during the twentieth century. Cell towers and internet infrastructure are highly valuable for military campaigns but because they generally operate in fixed positions, they become prime targets in the first wave of fighting. For example, reports of Ukraine's counteroffensive into Russia highlights that the advance was led by "electronic-warfare units that jammed Russian communications and drones."[22]

To keep communications infrastructure off the battleground, systems like Starlink, HughesNet, and Viasat moved the internet to satellite infrastructure in low earth orbit. China has created ChinaSat (Zhongxing) as a low orbit communication network, operating as a competitor to Starlink. It has also launched a high-orbit satellite to build a second,

---

21 *Id.*

22 Isabel Coles, Michael R. Gordon, and Ievgeniia Sivorka, *Behind Ukraine's Russia Invasion: Secrecy, Speed and Electronic Jamming*, WALL ST. J. (Aug. 17, 2024), https://www.wsj.com/world/behind-ukraines-russia-invasion-secrecy-speed-and-electronic-jamming-188fcc22.

complementary network, vastly expanding its communications capacity across the globe.[23]

In the absence of satellite communications or as a result of the disruption of communications networks during the conflict, AI systems can employ swarms of drones to create a "drone swarm" or honeycomb network of encrypted communications that use GPS to track movements of one's own resources. The drones connect with each other, creating a wide-area communications network with redundancy and mobility. Satellite imagery, GPS location, object recognition software (much like facial recognition for military assets) and other tools can pinpoint enemy resources, enabling the combatants to track and deploy countermeasures.

To combat these communications resources, military forces may deploy systems to disrupt communications technology. Jamming equipment, malware, and physical attacks are all designed to degrade these systems.

Wars and international conflict often take place off the battlefield as well. Governments and non-state actors are increasingly using chatbots and LLMs to produce and disseminate deceptive information and propaganda. For example, during the 2024 election, OpenAI announced that it had removed accounts operated by Iran that were designed to create false

---

[23] Andrew Jones, *China Launches First High Orbit Internet Satellite*, SPACE NEWS (Feb. 29, 2024), https://spacenews.com/china-launches-first-high-orbit-internet-satellite/.

content intended to influence the election.[24] "Earlier in August, a Microsoft threat-intelligence report said the Iranian network Storm-2035, comprising four websites masquerading as news outlets, was actively engaging US voter groups on opposing ends of the political spectrum."[25] Russia has also been identified by the Justice Department as running a "disinformation campaign involving an AI-powered 'bot farm' used to create fake profiles on the social media platform X."[26]

Since at least 1998, Russia claimed that the free Internet is a form of "information terrorism."[27] It spent the past two decades seeking to use the weapon to its own advantage while simultaneously attempting to stop the West from using online and cyber tools to promote democratic ideals, and it has expanded these efforts using AI systems. In 2008, at a U.N. disarmament conference, Russian Defense Ministry member Sergei Korotkov "argued that anytime a government promotes ideas on the Internet with the goal of subverting another country's government—even in the name of

---

24 *Iranian Group used ChatGPT to try to Influence US election, OpenAI says*, GUARDIAN (Aug. 16, 2024), https://www.theguardian.com/technology/article/2024/aug/16/open-ai-chatgpt-iran.

25 *Id.*

26 *Iran Ramping Up US Election Interference Efforts: Microsoft*, BARRON'S (Aug. 9, 2024), https://www.barrons.com/news/iran-ramping-up-us-election-interference-efforts-microsoft-30a18162.

27 Tom Gjelten, *Seeing the Internet as an 'Information Weapon,'* NAT'L PUBLIC RADIO (Sept. 23, 2010), http://www.npr.org/templates/story/story.php?storyId=130052701.

democratic reform—it should qualify as 'aggression.' And that, in turn, would make it illegal under the U.N. Charter."[28]

The problem is not new, but it is getting worse. "As generative AI tools grow more sophisticated, political actors are continuing to deploy the technology to amplify disinformation."[29] They are also "lowering the barrier of entry for disinformation campaigns, and automated systems are enabling governments to conduct more precise and more subtle forms of online censorship."[30]

There has been a sophisticated international effort to address the role of cybersecurity threat in the context of warfare.[31] The most significant of these efforts was conducted by the Cooperative Cyber Defense Center of Excellence (CCD COE), a body

---

[28] *Id. See also* Timothy L. Thomas, *The Russian View of Information War,* FOREIGN MILITARY STUDIES OFFICE (Feb. 7–9, 2000), https://community.apan.org/wg/tradoc-g2/fmso/m/fmso-monographs/202359 ("Russian calls at the United Nations for a world-wide information security policy and to limit the development of information weaponry and operations." quoting Joseph Nye, Redefining the National Interest, 78 Foreign Affairs 22, 26 (1999)).

[29] Tate Ryan-Mosley, *How Generative AI is Boosting the Spread of Disinformation and Propaganda*, MIT TECH. REV. (Oct. 4, 2023), https://www.technologyreview.com/2023/10/04/1080801/generative-ai-boosting-disinformation-and-propaganda-freedom-house/.

[30] *Id.*

[31] *See* TALLINN MANUAL ON THE INTERNATIONAL LAW APPLICABLE TO CYBER WARFARE (Michael N. Schmitt ed., 2012) [hereinafter TALLINN MANUAL 1.0]; TALLINN MANUAL ON THE INTERNATIONAL LAW APPLICABLE TO CYBER WARFARE (Michael N. Schmitt ed., 2017) [hereinafter TALLINN MANUAL 2.0].

from within NATO.[32] The most recent publication is known as the Tallinn Manual 2.0. Despite its origins, however, the Tallinn Manual 2.0 has not been adopted or ratified. Instead, "Tallinn Manual 2.0 must be understood only as an expression of the opinions of the two International Groups of Experts as to the state of the law."[33] To understand the problem with adopting an international code of conduct for cyber operations, one only need realize that the experts could not even agree whether the concept of sovereignty was itself a legal doctrine or whether it represents a "baseline principle . . . undergirding binding norms. . ."[34] If UN members cannot even agree whether other countries are entitled to recognition of their sovereignty, then questions about cyber conflicts, the tolerance for non-state actors using a country's internet and cyber infrastructure to launch attacks on other countries, a duty to limit harms from AI systems operating extraterritorially, and other concerns are unlikely to result in binding international law.

Despite the failure of Tallinn Manual 2.0 to engender a new international consensus on limiting cyber conflict, it starts the process for developing a

---

[32] NATO Cooperative Cyber Defence Centre of Excellence (CCDCOE), https://ccdcoe.org/.

[33] TALLINN MANUAL 2.0, *supra* note 31, at 2. *See* Eric Talbot Jensen, *The Tallinn Manual 2.0: Highlights and Insights*, 48 GEORGETOWN J. INT'L L. 735 (2017).

[34] *Id.* at 741 quoting Gary Corn, *Tallinn Manual 2.0—Advancing the Conversation*, JUST SECURITY (Feb. 15, 2017), https://www.justsecurity.org/37812/tallinn-manual-2-0-advancing-conversation/.

new consensus which might, over time, make their way into customary law.

§ 8.2.2 LETHAL AUTONOMOUS WEAPONS SYSTEMS (LAWS)

Autonomous weapons will inevitably end up on the battlefields across the globe because the machines are force multipliers.[35] Using self-guided weapons, "fewer warfighters are needed for a given mission, and the efficacy of each warfighter is greater."[36] Lethal autonomous weapons systems (LAWS) can be designed to address more challenging combat situations, such as those where exposure to chemicals, biological weapons, water, fire, or nuclear contamination would make human engagement dangerous or unethical.[37] Characterized differently, the Department of Defense suggested that autonomous systems are appropriate for jobs that are "dull, dirty, or dangerous."[38]

The current Department of Defense regulations define an "autonomous weapon system" as—

> A weapon system that, once activated, can select and engage targets without further intervention by an operator. This includes, but is not limited to, operator-supervised autonomous weapon

---

[35] *See* Etzioni & Etzioni, *supra* ch. 7 note 37.

[36] *Id.*

[37] *See id.*

[38] James R. Clapper Jr. et al., *Unmanned Systems Roadmap: 2007–2032* DEPT. OF DEF. (2007), http://www.globalsecurity.org/intell/library/reports/2007/dod-unmanned-systems-roadmap_2007-2032.pdf.

systems that are designed to allow operators to override operation of the weapon system but can select and engage targets without further operator input after activation.[39]

The earliest use of autonomous weapons can be traced to World War II, the "Fido" (Mk-24) acoustic homing torpedo was dropped into transatlantic shipping lanes to listen for German U-Boats, and home in on their acoustic signals to blow them up upon contact.[40] Since then, various systems have been developed to destroy airborne missiles, tanks, and ground bases based on the system's ability to identify a target and after being launched to find and destroy that target.[41] "[T]the U.S. military has incorporated weapon systems with autonomous functionalities for eight decades . . . as part of human-activated kill chains. Consequently, U.S. warfighters long ago gave weapons their proxy to select and engage targets at the end of an engagement sequence, especially when those targets are beyond their line-of-sight."[42]

Through the use of drones, the military can patrol an area of conflict and either have a drone operator launch missiles when the system detects a target that matches the parameters of the system or pre-

---

39 KATHLEEN HICKS, DOD DIRECTIVE 3000.09 AUTONOMY IN WEAPON SYSTEMS, DEPT. OF DEF. 21 (Nov. 21, 2012), https://www.esd.whs.mil/DD/.

40 *See* Robert O. Work, *A Short History of Weapon Systems with Autonomous Functionalities,* CENTER FOR A NEW AM. SECURITY (2021), https://www.jstor.org/stable/resrep32146.4.

41 *See id.*

42 *Id.*

program the drone to select and deploy the targets without human supervision. the UN has reported the use of such weapons on soldiers. "Turkey used autonomous firing by its Kargu-2 drones to hunt fleeing soldiers in Libya's civil war (though the CEO of the Turkish company that produced the drone denies it is capable of this)."[43]

Autonomous weapons and battlefield machinery may include drones, armored vehicles, bomb-detection devices, rescue equipment, and surveillance equipment. They also include various bombs, bullets, missiles, and munitions. They may range from the size of a bumble bee or hummingbird up to that of a small fighter jet or shipping freighter. In other words, any piece of equipment that can be imagined and which currently requires combatants to operate might eventually be automated, so the human operators are eliminated, reduced in number, or shifted to remote operation.

"Warfare systems such as weapons, sensors, navigation, aviation support, and surveillance can employ AI in order to make operations more efficient and less reliant on human input. . . . Taking away the need for full human control of warfare systems reduces the impact of human error and frees up humans' bandwidth for other essential tasks."[44] Used

[43] Robert F. Trager, *Killer Robots Are Here—and We Need to Regulate Them*, FOREIGN POLICY (May 11, 2022), https://foreignpolicy.com/2022/05/11/killer-robots-lethal-autonomous-weapons-systems-ukraine-libya-regulation/.

[44] *The Most Useful Military Applications of AI in 2024 and Beyond*, *supra* note 20.

as weapons, LAW vastly increase the efficiency of engagement. "Already, some LAWS can loiter in an area to find targets that machine-learning algorithms have trained them to recognize, including enemy radar systems, tanks, ships, and even specific individuals."[45]

History suggests that economics governs the sweep of history far more than morality. As such, the question is not whether nations are moving towards autonomous weapons, but the extent to which customary law and international humanitarian law will limit their deployment.

§ 8.3 HUMANS-IN-THE-LOOP OR AUTONOMOUS WEAPONRY

The regulatory discussion for AI-based military engagement often focuses on the extent to which the systems can be permitted to be fully autonomous or whether they need to have human supervision, often referred to as "humans-in-the-loop." "Originally an engineering term, requiring a human "in the loop" who could halt systems, the term "on the loop" or "nearby the loop" has been co-opted by policymakers in order to distance humans further from systems."[46] The concepts are also referred to as " 'meaningful

---

[45] Trager, *supra* note 43.

[46] Kobi Leins & Anja Kaspersen, *Seven Myths of Using the Term "Human on the Loop": "Just What Do You Think You Are Doing, Dave?"*, CARNEGIE COUNCIL FOR ETHICS IN INT'L AFF. (Nov. 9, 2021), https://www.carnegiecouncil.org/media/article/7-myths-of-using-the-term-human-on-the-loop.

human control' or 'meaningful human interaction on the loop.' "[47]

Although the engineering design for humans-in-the-loop may be applied to any AI systems,[48] for military systems they include a number of important considerations. First, human supervision includes the ability to re-evaluate the signals intelligence coming from automated systems before acting on the information. In a now-famous example, in 1983 Soviet Air Defense engineer Stanislav Petrov received warnings of an imminent nuclear attack on the Soviet Union by the United States. He reviewed the context of the information and determined the automated decision to launch a counterstrike was based on a false alarm. In doing so, he was able to help halt what would have been the start of nuclear war.[49]

A second role for human supervision is to decide whether to engage an enemy, evaluating whether the obligations of proportionality, necessity, humanity, and distinction have been met in a real-world deployment. Since most conflicts today occur in densely populated cities, and non-state actors often violate Geneva Conventions by mingling among civilians, militaries must be vigilant to respect their ethical and treaty obligations even though it means being less effective in prosecuting the conflict.

---

[47] *Id.*

[48] In fiction, for example, Star Trek's android Data has a physical off switch that was featured in multiple episodes.

[49] *See* Leins & Kaspersen, *supra* note 46.

A third example is the human override model. The U.S. Army's Patriot air and missile defense system and the U.S. Navy's Aegis version of ship, air and missile defense system are designed to operate autonomously to address threats of incoming attacks "that would overwhelm human operators."[50] Although autonomous, they are designed to be easily overridden by human operators, which is "especially important when friendly aircraft are operating in the defended airspace."[51]

The U.S. Department of Defense has promulgated a memorandum focusing on the military's adoption of "Responsible AI (RAI)" to "demonstrate . . . our military's steadfast commitment to lawful and ethical behavior apply when designing, developing, testing, procuring, deploying, and using Al."[52] The military has adopted a set of "AI Ethical Principles" to provide a framework for the aggressive AI development being undertaken:

> These principles apply to all DoD AI capabilities, encompassing both combat and non-combat applications.
>
> **RESPONSIBLE:** DoD personnel will exercise appropriate levels of judgment and care, while

---

50 Work, *supra* note 40.

51 *Id.*

52 KATHLEEN HICKS, U.S. DEPT. OF DEFENSE RESPONSIBLE ARTIFICIAL INTELLIGENCE STRATEGY AND IMPLEMENTATION PATHWAY at Forword (June 2022), https://media.defense.gov/2022/Jun/22/2003022604/-1/-1/0/Department-of-Defense-Responsible-Artificial-Intelligence-Strategy-and-Implementation-Pathway.PDF [hereinafter DOD RESPONSIBLE AI PATHWAY].

remaining responsible for the development, deployment, and use of Al capabilities.

EQUITABLE: The Department will take deliberate steps to minimize unintended bias in Al capabilities.

TRACEABLE: The Department's AI capabilities will be developed and deployed such that relevant personnel possess an appropriate understanding of the technology, development processes, and operational methods applicable to AI capabilities, including with transparent and auditable methodologies, data sources, and design procedures and documentation.

RELIABLE: The Department's Al capabilities will have explicit, well-defined uses, and the safety, security, and effectiveness of such capabilities will be subject to testing and assurance within those defined uses across their entire life-cycles.

GOVERNABLE: The Department will design and engineer AI capabilities to fulfill their intended functions while possessing the ability to detect and avoid unintended consequences, and the ability to disengage or deactivate deployed systems that demonstrate unintended behavior.[53]

Of the five key ethical standards, the limitation on LAWS will chiefly flow from determinations of system reliability and governability. To the extent

[53] DOD RESPONSIBLE AI PATHWAY, *supra* note 52, at 5.

that the Department of Defense is using AI systems for personnel management, for example, the concerns of bias and equity are not substantially different than any other government agency or large employer. When used for weapons systems, in contrast, the need to control civilian casualties and avoid friendly fire make the stakes much higher at each stage of development and deployment.

As a result, the Ethical Principles do not constitute a commitment to human supervision or any particular outcome. Instead, they reflect an overriding commitment to AI integration. The limits provided are highly procedural, requiring only that the department "explore whether a review procedure is needed to ensure DoD warfighting capabilities will be consistent with the DoD AI Ethical Principles [and explore] whether or how legal review processes can support implementation of the DoD AI Ethical Principles, including the review of the legality of weapons."[54]

While there are limitations in the application of these Ethical Principles, the obligations to evaluate the legality of new weapons remain meaningful.[55] "DoD tests, evaluates, and reviews weapons in accordance with their proposed use in physical and operational environments, anticipated rules of engagement, concepts of operations, and tactics, techniques and procedures that would govern their

---

[54] *Id.* at 21.

[55] *See* James Kraska, *Command Accountability for the AI Weapons Systems in the Law of Armed Conflict*, 97 INT'L L. STUD. 407, 416 (2021).

use."[56] In addition, new weapons systems are assessed to ensure they are proportionate, meaning the damage caused is appropriate to intended use of the weapon. Autonomous weapons and semi-autonomous weapons undergo additional scrutiny and review in this regard.[57]

A key consideration in the development of autonomous weapons systems is the naïve belief that a human operator will provide meaningful check on a deployed system, particularly once that system has been installed and is in operation.

1. You cannot have "meaningful interaction" with data or sensors, or actuators at the time of data collection and operation. . . . No single human has the capacity to understand and oversee all of these parts, let alone to meaningfully intervene.

2. You cannot "meaningfully interact" with active code. . . . The skill sets needed to interrogate the systems are required both at the point of build, and regularly throughout the lifecycle of these systems, as they will inevitably fail or have unintended outcomes.

3. People get bored when working with autonomous systems. . . . Humans often

---

56 *Id.*

57 *See Id.*; Hicks, DoD Directive 3000.9, *supra* note 39, at encl. 4, ¶ 8(b).

assume that systems cannot fail—and yet they do.

4. The complexity, speed, and scale of many autonomous, and even automatic, systems do not allow time to challenge them. . . .

5. If "meaningful human interaction on the loop" is remote, there are even greater risks. Network delays (due to issues of bandwidth, lag time, human cognitive delays, and information poverty—not having all the information you need, some of which cannot be captured by automated or autonomous projects) amplify existing risks. . . .

6. The term "human" usually means a fairly narrow type of human, which is not representative of broader humanity or humankind. . . . The humans who have access to, and understanding of, these systems are a particularly narrow group with a particular worldview and set of values. . . .

7. Skills required to understand complex adaptive systems will be lost with increased automation. . . . Interdisciplinary skill sets will not be easy to replicate or replace in the long-term. Complex adaptive systems can at times function in ways that cannot be predicted, even by those with the correct skill sets. The likelihood of low-probability high risk (black swan) events will increase

> as more automated and autonomous systems are connected and scaled.[58]

Put another way, any AI system that relies on human supervision must account for the inevitable situation that the humans will also fail in their supervision and the high probability that the humans will not be sufficiently trained or experienced to intervene—particularly if the AI system has proven reliable in the past. In the example of Stanislav Petrov, he based the decision that the attack by the U.S. on the Soviet Union was a false alarm on the common sense notion that an attack using only five missiles was too small to be a *bona fide* event.[59] There was no operational parameter.

In the context of battle, human supervision is even more problematic. "[H]uman-informed decisions programmed into LAWS before an attack [may] not be durable throughout the entire kill chain, as conditions quickly change. The principle of proportionality requires an unbroken temporal link between the plan and the lethal strike so that proportionality is re-evaluated at each step of the chain."[60] One three-part test emphasizes training, testing, and ongoing evaluation:

---

[58] Leins & Kaspersen, *supra* note 46.

[59] Alicia Sanders-Zakre, *The Man Who "Saved the World" Dies at 77*, ARMS CONTROL ASS'N (Oct. 2017), https://www.armscontrol.org/act/2017-10/news-briefs/man-who-saved-world-dies-77.

[60] Kraska, *supra* note 55, at 428.

1. Human operators are making informed, conscious decisions about the use of weapons;

2. Human operators have sufficient information to ensure the lawfulness of the action they are taking, given what they know about the target, the weapon, and the context for action;

3. The weapon is designed and tested, and human operators are properly trained, to ensure effective control over the use of the weapon.[61]

These are important limitations on autonomous weapons but require significant training and oversight of the humans to reverse the practical consequences that come when AI systems become pervasive.

Beyond the questions about the efficacy of the humans kept in the loop, there are other concerns that military agencies must addressed. Human supervision is just a small part of a broader system for safe military operations that includes transparency in the algorithmic design of the systems, significant redundancy in signals intelligence gathering, constant reevaluation, and the most rigorous of cybersecurity defenses to protect

---

[61] *Id.* quoting MICHAEL C. HOROWITZ & PAUL SCHARRE, MEANINGFUL HUMAN CONTROL IN WEAPON SYSTEMS: A PRIMER 4 (2015) (internal citations omitted) https://s3.amazonaws.com/files.cnas.org/documents/Ethical_Autonomy_Working_Paper_031315.pdf?mtime=20160906082316.

the systems from sabotage and interference. The Ethical AI Principles emphasize some aspects of these obligations but the critical understanding that automation fundamentally changes the capacity for supervision is not incorporated into the thinking.

§ 8.4 FINAL CONSIDERATIONS FOR AUTONOMOUS WEAPONS

The existential risk for LAWS may not be that of a singularity in which intelligent machines attack humanity, but rather a point of global failure leading to catastrophe. Had the Soviet warning system been fully automated in 1983, it might have responded to the false positive and launched a Soviet counterstrike against the West. "[E]rrors in complex AI systems, especially if they are deployed at scale, risk simultaneous—perhaps even inevitable—failure. Moreover, the danger of machines producing unconventional outcomes that cannot be immediately terminated—. . . may result in a destabilizing effect if the system spirals out of human control."[62]

Human rights advocates, such as Human Rights Watch, focus on the lack of humanity resulting from the adoption of LAWS. "Weapons systems that select and engage targets without meaningful human control are unacceptable and need to be

[62] Stephanie Mae Pedron and Jose de Arimateia da Cruz, *The Future of Wars: Artificial Intelligence (AI) and Lethal Autonomous Weapon Systems (LAWS)*, 2 INT'L J. SECURITY STUDIES (2020), https://ir.ung.edu/work/sc/9b5aa426-a8bf-453f-8c02-97943582491f.

prevented. . . . Retaining meaningful human control over the use of force is an ethical imperative, a legal necessity, and a moral obligation."[63] The effort to ban such weapons, which began in 2013, has taken on greater urgency, but the potential advantages of using these weapons have made the world's leading combatants hesitant to pursue unilateral disarmament. Efforts to ban LAWS are unlikely to gain momentum on purely ethical grounds.

A separate approach, however, might eventually bear fruit. Rather than seeking to eliminate the lethality of AI systems, there may be opportunities to use AI systems to improve adherence to international humanitarian law by providing objective evaluations of military necessity, humanity, distinction, and proportionality as a counterbalance to other battlefield conditions. These AI systems could certainly play an important role in war games and battlefield training.

Autonomous defensive weapons, such as those designed to stop missiles, save lives. AI systems used for emergency medical evacuation and treatment, diffusing or destroying land mines, and checking battlefields for toxic chemicals can all improve both military effectiveness and reduce the loss of life. AI systems also provide extensive monitoring of borders to detect territorial incursions and monitor signals intelligence to help militaries take defensive measures against attacks. To the extent that AI

---

[63] *Stopping Killer Robots*, HUMAN RIGHTS WATCH (Aug. 10, 2020), https://www.hrw.org/report/2020/08/10/stopping-killer-robots/country-positions-banning-fully-autonomous-weapons-and.

systems can be used for live-saving efforts and to reduce harm to military personnel, the systems can play a positive role in improving the survivability of conflicts and reducing the use of armed force as a method of political change.

CHAPTER 9

CONCLUSION: CONSIDERATIONS FOR THE LAW AND REGULATION OF ARTIFICIAL INTELLIGENCE

Any discussion of AI involves a complex array of concepts, laws, regulations, policies, and practices. Despite this complexity, there are important overarching themes that can help governments, businesses, and individuals address the rapid changes in AI regulation in the United States, Europe, and throughout the world.

This chapter serves as both a summary and a primer, identifying the key themes of the Nutshell from four perspectives: regulators, end users, enterprise deployers, and society as a whole. Each of these stakeholders has a different set of goals and interests. By reframing earlier discussions within these perspectives, this summary aims not only to provide a concise version of the book but also to add a new layer of insight into the regulation of AI.

§ 9.1 CONSIDERATIONS FOR REGULATORS AND GOVERNMENTS

§ 9.1.1 FRAMING RATHER THAN DEFINING AI

Section 1.2 introduced multiple definitions for artificial intelligence, each describing a machine-based system that makes decisions based on probabilistic information. These definitions varied in scope and purpose. A more effective approach may be focus less on precise definitions and instead establish a framework that emphasizes the consequences of machine-based predictions. As noted earlier, NASA defines AI as "computer systems that can perform complex tasks normally done by human-reasoning, decision making, creating, etc." As NASA points out, no single definition captures all the capabilities while excluding systems that are less capable. The FTC has called AI "an ambiguous term with many possible definitions."[1]

At the same time, creating a framework for AI is important, especially given the overuse of the term AI and its potential to mislead investors and consumers. Both the SEC and FTC have taken action against "AI washing" and similar misleading statements regarding AI systems, emphasizing the need for consumers and industry to have a shared understanding of when a machine learning or AI-based system is genuinely a significant component of decision making.

Section 1.2 also introduced the "Magic 8 Ball Test" as a minimalistic framework. In meaningful AI, the system assesses the input data and makes predictions, decisions, operational actions, or output based on its prior training to that input. Systems that create only the illusion of artificial intelligence often have predetermined outputs and do not genuinely assess the input information. Beyond this, most definitions expect that systems incorporate the new

---

1 Atleson, *supra* ch. 2 note 139.

information provided to update and refine their responses. The learning loop helps improve systems and makes them improve continuously. This does not suggest that if a system is prohibited from retaining or learning from user input (to protect privacy or trade secrets of the person making queries) that the system is no longer smart. It is the capacity to learn from input rather than the use of that input in every instance that matters to the system.

Data science focuses heavily on the various methods of developing and training AI systems, including machine learning systems, neural networks, and deep learning methodologies. Regulators, however, avoid these distinctions.

The taxonomy of AI systems is also imprecise. Different industries define the systems using different frameworks. Increasingly complex systems often use more than one type of AI in their process.[2] Nonetheless, these distinctions are very helpful for regulators and for industry, providing a context for contractual provisions within industries as well as for regulators.

A list of different AI outputs and uses is provided in § 1.4. As a summary exercise, consider how these technologies might be combined in a smart household robot—a product not yet on the market but popular in speculative fiction. The Jetsons' *Rosie* "is a robot and the maid and housekeeper of the Jetson family. . . . She can clean the house by herself . . . and operate the other household appliances. When at

---

2 *See supra* § 1.4 and accompanying text.

home by herself, she functions as a security system and house sitter."[3]

As an autonomous machine, Rosie functions as a "Physical Action AI," by sensing the environment around her. She has "Decision-Making" capabilities, which she uses for tasks like babysitting children. Her "Generative AI" abilities allow her to converse, while her "Extractive AI" systems gain actual knowledge and understanding from those conversations. In her role as household security and babysitter, she uses both "Predictive AI" and "Automating AI" to assess risks and threats, as well as to provide advice to Jane and George Jetson. Such a machine essentially incorporates each of the various functions that are currently available or in development for AI systems. In many episodes, Rosie also displays strong emotions, perhaps suggesting that there should be a separate AI category related to emotional intelligence. While reading emotions is part of the generative AI toolbox, there has been little progress in developing commercial AI systems capable of displaying emotions.

The current household equivalent of a robot like Rosie is the Roomba or similar devices that can sweep, mop, or vacuum but not much else. In the automotive field, however, the industry is moving closer to achieving the functionality of Rosie. Robotaxi services have been demonstrating their

---

[3] Rosey, The Jetsons Wiki, https://thejetsons.fandom.com/wiki/Rosey (spelling of the character name was changed from Rosey to Rosie in season 2 of the television show and in 1995 in the comic book).

effectiveness and often outperform human drivers in terms of safety. Cars already incorporate conversational AI interfaces, which are rapidly improving. Like Rosie, these machines use a combination of various AI technologies to engage with passengers in vehicles and navigate the physical environment, offering safe, secure, and commercially viable operations. Moreover, as discussed in Chapter 8, militaries across the globe are using similar AI technologies to expand their forces and deliver greater offensive capability while reducing the risk of harm to their own forces.

§ 9.1.2 SOURCES OF REGULATION

The use of automated decision making may trigger regulations from federal, state, tribal, territorial, and local governments as well as potentially allowing for the extraterritorial regulation from foreign governments.

The European Union has been the first mover in establishing comprehensive AI regulation and by doing so, it has developed an approach that all other regulators must now adopt or explicitly reject. The EU AI Act uses a risk-based approach that is reflected in state laws adopted in Colorado, California, and other jurisdictions.[4]

The risk-based approach categorizes regulations based on whether a party is a developer of an AI system or a deployer of that system. It then identifies AI uses that fall into one of four categories:

---

4 *See supra* § 3.4 and accompanying text.

Unacceptable Risk, High-Risk, Limited Risk, and Minimal Risk.

The unacceptable risk classification prohibits the development or deployment of AI systems for specific uses, including social scoring, subliminal manipulation, biometric categorization of sensitive attributes (which should be compared to psychographic targeting), facial scraping, use of biometric information for real-time tracking in public, among others.[5] These categories have raised questions about usage under U.S. law, and while some of these unacceptable risk activities have been barred by state law, the U.S. currently lacks a directly analogous federal regulation.

The EU AI Act uses the high-risk category as the regulatory framework for the majority of AI regulation. "[T]his level includes safety components of already regulated products and stand-alone AI systems in specific areas (see below), which could negatively affect the health and safety of people, their fundamental rights or the environment."[6]

The use of AI in products or services already regulated by the EU fall within the category of high risk. These include automobiles, healthcare and medical devices, and large categories of commercial machinery. Beyond this broad scope, the EU AI Act also includes categories of stand-alone AI systems that are subject to regulation:

---

5 *See id.*

6 *EU AI Act: How Risk is Classified*, TRAIL (Aug. 30, 2024), https://www.trail-ml.com/blog/eu-ai-act-how-risk-is-classified.

(a) biometric and biometrics-based systems (such as remote biometric identification, categorization of persons and emotion recognition systems),

(b) management and operation of critical infrastructure (such as road traffic, energy supply or digital infrastructure),

(c) education and vocational training (such as assessment of students in educational institutions),

(d) employment and workers management (such as recruitment, performance evaluation, or task-allocation),

(e) access to essential private and public services and benefits (such as credit-scoring, risk assessments in health insurance and dispatching emergency services),

(f) law enforcement (such as evaluating the reliability of evidence or crime analytics),

(g) migration, asylum and border control management (such as assessing the security risk of a person or the examination of applications for asylum, visa, or residence permits),

(h) administration of justice and democratic processes (such as assisting in interpreting & researching facts, law, and the application of the law or for influencing elections).[7]

There are many U.S. laws detailed throughout this Nutshell that address these topics, but U.S. state and federal law do not typically approach these topics under the framework of AI regulation. Instead, employment law governs certain inappropriate uses of AI in hiring and worker evaluations; health law regulates the discriminatory use of any decision-making regarding health care access; a few states specifically regulate the use of biometrics; and both state and federal laws address the use of credit scoring. The EU model is highly prescriptive, while the U.S. model is generally reactive.

Due to the inherent gaps in the U.S. federal regulatory model, states are increasingly stepping in to protect their residents from various AI-intrusions. Examples include state laws in Tennessee and California on digital replicas, the use of AI in employment and other high-risk situations in Colorado, tracking in Washington State and many other examples.[8] The EU AI Act serves as a useful framework for U.S.-based regulators, as it highlights areas where state and federal regulators may deem certain risks if AI is left to self-regulation.

After repeal of the Biden AI Executive Order,[9] perhaps the most important regulatory touchstone is

---

[7] *Id.*

[8] *See supra* § 3.3 and accompanying text.

[9] *See* § 3.2.1 *supra* note 19 (AI EXECUTIVE ORDER) and accompanying text.

the NIST "Artificial Intelligence Risk Management Framework" to manage risk and improve transparency.[10]

The growing adoption of the NIST framework has created a presumptive model for risk assessment and management for companies developing AI strategies. The NIST framework offers a highly adaptable approach to assess and address the potential risks of AI in the development and deployment of products and services.

With the Trump Administration AI Executive Order on the books, the government still has the potential to incorporate AI obligations into federal contracting requirements. This potentially allows the government to mandate that any company providing goods or services to the federal government—or even any entity entering into contracts with federal financial support—must document compliance with the NIST framework requirements or other federal obligations. Theoretically, this could extend even further, requiring that any vendor seeking to do business with an agency receiving or using federal funds meet newly established administration standards for all their products and services. Taken to this logical end, a significant part of the U.S.

---

[10] NIST AI FRAMEWORK, *supra* ch. 1 note 140, 1 ("AI technologies, however, also pose risks that can negatively impact individuals, groups, organizations, communities, society, the environment, and the planet.").

economy would be subject to federal AI requirements even in the absence of any federal legislation.

§ 9.1.3 TRANSPARENCY AND EXPLAINABILITY UNDER THE NIST RISK MANAGEMENT FRAMEWORK

Every one of the governmental and self-regulatory models of AI adoption calls for some combination of transparency, explainability, reliability, and resilience for the development of AI systems. Transparency generally refers to developers' and deployers' ability to understand the source and nature of the training data used to develop the underlying algorithms. True transparency would also require that individuals affected by these systems have access to information about the training data's origins. However, due to ongoing litigation concerning the use of copyright-protected content scraped and ingested without the authors' or owners' consent, most AI developers have resisted full transparency.

Explainability requires a system to assess the weighting of its algorithmic decision-making to provide not only predictive answers but also insight into how inputs are weighted to influence those answers. This is particularly important for decisional AI systems used in areas like extending a person credit, identifying which candidates for a job opening should be granted interviews, or recommending criminal sentences to judges. However, the dynamic nature of these models and their continuous learning strategies make true explainability difficult, if not impossible. As a result, these systems often recreate explanations for the decisions that may seem reasonable but are not necessarily based on the actual algorithmic weighting used during the complex decision-making process.

Reliability and resilience are more traditional statistical requirements of information systems. They represent developers' obligations to ensure data security from external threats or internal degradation, maintain data safety, and take appropriate steps to protect both the data and the systems from cybersecurity threats and internal, human manipulation—standards that apply equally to non-AI information systems.

The NIST Risk Management Framework incorporates these obligations, along with others, into a flexible model designed to protect information systems and ensure that obligations related to safety, security, transparency, and legal compliance are met.

As discussed in Section 6.1, the NIST framework focuses on the characteristics of trustworthy AI systems, which include being "valid and reliable, safe, secure and resilient, accountable and transparent, explainable and interpretable, privacy-enhanced, and fair with harmful bias managed."[11] NIST explains that these attributes are inherently interconnected. "Highly secure but unfair systems, accurate but opaque and uninterpretable systems, and inaccurate but secure, privacy-enhanced, and transparent systems are all undesirable. A

[11] AI RMF 1.0, *supra* ch. 6 note 1, at 12.

comprehensive approach to risk management calls for balancing tradeoffs among the trustworthiness characteristics."[12]

The NIST framework places responsibility on the developer, rather than the government, to identify the risks—an essential step for adoption and compliance. Known as "mapping," developers are obligated "to manage risks proactively and categorize them based on various parameters like usage and impact."[13] Mapping is just one of four organizational functions within the NIST framework; the others are Governance, Measurement, and Management.[14]

Developers must understand the risks associated with deployment, which includes understanding the regulatory landscape and the range of laws and regulations that protect the public's fundamental rights. Governance then requires that these considerations are addressed at the highest organizational levels and implemented throughout the enterprise. This involves establishing clear risk management policies, detailed procedures, ongoing training, and meaningful accountability across the organization. Management involves the ongoing implementation of risk management and applying lessons learned as systems and policies are continuously updated.[15]

---

12 *Id.* at 13.

13 Mack, Noorestani, & Burns, *supra* ch. 6 note 19.

14 *See id.*

15 *See* RMF 1.0, *supra* ch.6 note 1, at 21–22.

Organizations that adopt this risk management approach will operate within the parameters of existing laws and be well-positioned to adapt to new state and federal regulations as they emerge. This flexibility is designed to promote AI development in areas where services are commercially beneficial while avoiding harm to the public. Ideally, this approach will facilitate the rapid development of beneficial AI tools that might be difficult to create in a more prescriptive regulatory environment.

§ 9.2 CONSIDERATIONS REGARDING CONSUMER, PATIENT, AND USER PROTECTIONS

The enthusiasm surrounding AI highlights that in general, the public is quite keen to take advantage of the services and benefits available from AI services. As noted in § 1.5, AI systems assist with disability accommodations, healthcare outcomes, business productivity, creativity, and much more. As described throughout Chapter 2, however, there are significant risks associated with the misuse of AI systems and the failure to limit them to activities that promote public welfare. The Vienna Manifesto on Digital Humanism captured at least some of this with its first two core principles:

- Digital technologies should be designed to promote democracy and inclusion. This will require special efforts to overcome current inequalities and to use the emancipatory potential of digital technologies to make our societies more inclusive.

- Privacy and freedom of speech are essential values for democracy and should be at the center of our activities.[16]

It comes as no surprise that state regulatory efforts focus on these concerns. As noted in § 3.3.2, there are patterns emerging from the state regulatory efforts, highlighted by these topics:

- Deepfakes and synthetic content for use in nonconsensual distribution of intimate content, fraud, or theft of personal identity.
- Algorithmic bias mitigation requirements.
- Biometric disclosure requirements.
- Expansion of privacy protections.
- Requirements for fairness, including notice prior to use of AI, disclosure of data practices, transparency, and explainability of algorithms.
- Task force or exploratory committees to focus on building the jurisdiction's capabilities and work force to deploy AI and improve the knowledge about the systems.
- Regulations on how city or state government agencies use or limit AI.[17]

Broadly speaking, the risks to individuals and collective communities fall into three main

---

16 Werthner et al, *supra* ch. 2 note 265.

17 *See supra* § 3.3.2 and accompanying text; *Artificial Intelligence Legislation Tracker*, *supra* ch. 3 note 91.

categories. These are concerns about bias in the design and implementation of AI systems; the misuse to target individuals; and general ethical considerations. Each of these concerns is briefly summarized below.

§ 9.2.1 BIAS IN DESIGN, TRAINING, AND IMPLEMENTATION OF AI

The risks of bias in the design and implementation of AI are described in § 2.2.2. The challenge of creating unbiased AI systems applies to design of the AI, the data used to train the AI, and the implementation of the AI system. At each stage in the development, training, and adoption, both developers and deployers must put systems in place to check for unintended biases and mitigate their impact.

Bias is inevitable and inherent in every human-made system as it reflects the assumptions, prejudices, beliefs, and aspirations of the people responsible for the system's creation. The goal is to identify and minimize biases that lead to discrimination against populations such as those based on race, gender, age, national origin, religion, status, belief, or other legally recognized classifications.

The design of an AI system includes many opportunities to introduce unintended biases into the system. "Bias can creep in through the choice of features that the AI algorithms use to make decisions or by weighting different variables."[18] A common way bias creeps into AI design is when a variable is weighted that correlates quite highly with another variable that would otherwise be avoided. "For example, if an algorithm is designed to prioritize certain attributes that correlate with bias (like zip codes in loan approval processes that might correlate with race), it can inadvertently perpetuate discrimination."[19] There also can be bias in the design because all humans carry their cognitive and implicit biases with them when they go about their daily lives.[20]

Training data is also a common source of bias because it often represents sample of real-world information and all the biases that exist in the real world. Jim Crow laws, government-sanctioned redlining, and separate-but-equal educational policies empowered centuries of systemic institutionalized racism. Although each of these policies has been repudiated and both constitutional

---

[18] *Addressing AI Bias: Real-World Challenges and How to Solve Them*, DIGITAL OCEAN, https://www.digitalocean.com/resources/articles/ai-bias.

[19] *Id.*

[20] *See* Karen Steinhauser, *Everyone Is a Little Bit Biased*, ABA BUS. L. TODAY (Mar 16, 2020), https://www.americanbar.org/groups/business_law/resources/business-law-today/2020-april/everyone-is-a-little-bit-biased/; Keith Payne, Laura Niemi & John M. Doris *How to Think about 'Implicit Bias'*, SCI. AM. (Mar. 27, 2018), https://www.scientificamerican.com/article/how-to-think-about-implicit-bias/. *See also* Abid All Awan, *What is Algorithmic Bias?*, Radar (July 17, 2023), https://www.datacamp.com/blog/what-is-algorithmic-bias ("Prejudice in design. If the AI designers have implicit biases, these can unknowingly be transferred into the system's behavior.").

and statutory protections are now enforced against this overt discrimination, the legacy of those policies results in continued impact and much of the historical data reflect these institutionalized biases.

In addition to the design choices and training data, developers and deployers can demonstrate bias in the manner a system is implemented. The cautionary tale of Rite Aid in § 2.2.1 illustrates that deployers of AI systems will, at least on occasion, misuse the AI system. The same concerns are often raised regarding the government. [F]ace recognition can potentially target other marginalized populations, such as undocumented immigrants by ICE, or Muslim citizens by the NYPD."[21]

Facial recognitions systems, hiring programs, chatbots, and other systems all suffer the inherent biases of their training data, design parameters and deployment concerns. Studies have highlighted the political biases that pervade different LLMs[22] and read racial cues into the language choices of users.[23]

The most evident examples of bias have involved race and gender but there are many other aspects of

---

[21] Alex Najibi, *Racial Discrimination in Face Recognition Technology*, HARV. SCI. IN THE NEWS (Oct. 24, 2020), https://projects.iq.harvard.edu/sciencepolicy/blog/racial-discrimination-face-recognition-technology.

[22] Melissa Heikkilä, *AI Language Models are Rife with Different Political Biases*, MIT TECH. REV. (Aug. 7, 2023), https://www.technologyreview.com/2023/08/07/1077324/ai-language-models-are-rife-with-political-biases/.

[23] Valentin Hofmann et al., *AI Generates Covertly Racist Decisions about People based on their Dialect*, 633 NATURE (Sept. 5, 2024), https://www.nature.com/articles/s41586-024-07856-5.

discriminatory design and deployment as well. One of the critical areas of discrimination involves wealth and access.

The phrase digital divide helps capture the wide range of disparities that distinguish those with ready access to the technologies essential to AI deployment from those without those technologies. Wealth plays a significant role because the fast computers and newest smartphones are expensive. But wealth is not the only trigger. Rural communities are often left out of broadband as well as the sales and service infrastructure for cutting-edge technologies. Inner city communities are treated much like rural communities, being left out of broadband development, retail support, and similar services that are part of technological deployment. As discussed in § 2.1.4, the map of the United States highlights a country with haves and have-nots when it comes to access to services.

Perhaps the field that holds the greatest promise for AI assistance also hold one of the greatest concerns for bias. AI systems offer tremendous health benefits both for the direct provision of medical services and the improvement in public health outcomes. New treatments, enhanced efficacy of existing drugs, disease detection, and patient education can all be enhanced through AI tools. At the same time, the risk of bias is that non-majority populations were excluded from the medical studies from which the training data has been derived. The lack of representation in the training data often results in treatments that are not as efficacious for those excluded as they are for majority populations. The bias in the language models includes a risk that the responses and advice will not be the same for those users as for users who ask questions with the preferred word choices and grammar.

§ 9.2.2 PREDATION AND TARGETING USING AI

There are a few specific uses of AI systems that have been used by developers or deployers to target individuals or non-majority communities. These include the use of digital replicas or deepfakes to harass and bully victims, often using pornographic content; intentional discrimination in the provision of certain services; undermining constitutional rights; social scoring; and misuse of psychographic targeting.

Among the AI tools, deepfakes are notorious for being the most widely recognized harmful use case of these technologies. The early versions of these tools allowed apps to swap faces on the bodies of images, but this innocuous, use quickly devolved into tools that enabled users to produce nude images and pornographic videos. Aimed primarily at women, these women neither consented nor participated in the creation or distribution of these images. Deepfakes are not limited to pornography. As noted in §§ 2.2.3 and 3.3.2.1, they have been used for political disinformation and commercial fraud.

Predatory deepfakes are not the only use case for digital replicas. Sophisticated versions of these tools can be used in videogame development, television and motion picture production, and even education. Recently developed tools will enable doctors, teachers, and trainers to translate text-based materials into realistic videos with a simple automated process. As such, digital replicas should not be banned, but more must be done to remove the harassing and harmful content and to hold those who produce such content accountable for the harm they are inflicting on their victims.

Although deepfakes are the most obvious example of AI-gone-bad, it is not alone. The second area of predation and targeting involves the intentional use of AI decision making to discriminate or deny services to select groups of individuals. While the FTC's action against Rite Aid illustrated how a national brand could choose to misuse facial recognition software and then deploy that misused system primarily in neighborhoods that served minority customers, it is not the only example. Companies have been charged with the use of these systems for age discrimination, housing discrimination, and violations of the Equal Employment Opportunity Act.

As AI gains market share, the potential grows for pricing or market data to be consolidated in a vendor's algorithm and used to raise prices or reduce inventory in a manner that directly harms the consumer. These threats are explored in § 1.5.4, highlighting emerging examples of companies that offer mechanisms to reduce price competition through the expanded use of algorithmic pricing systems.[24] According to the FTC, such collusion has been found actionable involving hotels, casinos, housing companies, and even the meat processing industry. The FTC Act and state mini-FTC laws may be sufficient to guard against some of these schemes, but states are also looking to identify additional tools to thwart unfair competition.

Much like the misuse of algorithms to set prices, the EEOC has concern that vendors offering employment services may be designing their systems in a manner that produces discriminatory hiring without those vendors being directly culpable under EEOC regulations. Companies that design and sell software products to third parties are not necessarily subject to the same regulations as employers who use the software. If, however, the use of the software would result in discriminatory decisions on hiring or promotion, perhaps it is the software manufacturer that should be held responsible for deprivation of civil rights. Again, this is an emerging issue that may require revisions to existing law in order to fully address the concern.

Market segmentation and targeted messaging explored in § 2.2.4 is another area that includes both legitimate use cases and potentially harmful behaviors. Used to find a product's market, a company's interest in understanding the needs, wants, and concerns of its customers is both laudable and expected. At the same time, however, using AI to segment the public based on their attitudes, social

---

[24] *See* Duffy v. Yardi Systems Inc., *supra* ch. 1 note 272, and accompanying text.

status, biases, and immutable characteristics of race, gender, nationality raises concerns about the power to target individuals and small groups. Psychographic targeting is usually done in a manner that provides no notice to the consumer about the targeting. The AI systems are increasingly adept at finding persuasive techniques to impact the target. As described, the concern perhaps is merely that the tools of commercial persuasion have become too powerful.

The risk, however, may be greater. Tied to disinformation campaigns, psychographic targeting techniques can leverage false narratives. They have been used for political manipulation, to spread false claims about public health, and to target minority populations. The use of psychographic targeting to spread propaganda and intentionally misleading content has the power to enable those wielding these weapons to significantly harm individuals, communities, and the public as a whole.

As predominately framed by speech and communications, the legal recourse for these threats are quite limited. Nothing suggests that the existing First Amendment protections for political advocacy should be diminished or that the concerns suggest a return to the case law as it existed before *Brandenburg* and *Sullivan*.[25] At the same time, *Sullivan* and the jurisprudence that followed does not protect falsehoods make with actual malice. Neither does *Brandenburg* preclude prosecution for

---

[25] *See supra* § 7.3.1 and accompanying text.

crimes actually committed, even if those crimes are part of a broader set of efforts at public advocacy. The robust marketplace of ideas must be managed to protect from intentional disinformation and violations of other laws conducted in an effort to destabilize communities for commercial or political gains.

Shifting from the private sector to concerns regarding governmental authority, there has been a great deal of concern regarding the targeted use of facial recognition technology, eavesdropping technology, and pervasive surveillance technology in ways that would violate or at least redefine the Fourth Amendment and perhaps the Fifth Amendment as well. Section 7.3 explores the evolving Fourth Amendment protections from warrantless searches using data collected and stored as a result of the use of modern technology. Predictive analytics, however, is somewhat beyond the mere collection and tracking of a person's data, so statutory rather than constitutional protections will be essential to keep the government from moving towards a pervasive surveillance model of law enforcement. The Supreme Court has addressed specific situations including GPS tracking, data stored on a mobile phone, and cell cite location information, slowly narrowing the third party doctrine to recognize the constitutional interest in privacy implicated by these technologies. It has yet to address those same concerns regarding the use of predictive analytics and the purchase of a person's data through commercial brokers.[26]

This may be an area where reference to the EU AI Act is beneficial. The EU's list of unacceptable risks include use of biometric information for real-time tracking in public, social scoring and similar examples where the meaning of the Fourth Amendment is invoked even though there are not yet any constitutional interpretations to support the interpretation. By incorporating a similar set of unacceptable risk definitions into laws governing the activities of governmental agencies, legislators provide significant protections for the public. Such proposals have been among the many under consideration but none of these efforts has yet to mature into legislation.

§ 9.2.3 ETHICAL CONSIDERATIONS

Beyond the specific concerns highlighted in §§ 9.2.1 and 9.2.2, there is a broader consideration that should be part of the framework for AI development. The Vienna Manifesto on Digital Humanism emphasized that appropriate development of digital technologies should promote both the values of democracy and inclusion while valuing both freedom of speech and individual privacy.[27]

---

[26] *See supra* § 7.3.3. and accompanying text.

[27] *See supra* § 9.2 and accompanying text; Werthner et al., *supra* ch. 2 note 265.

Freedom of speech includes the right not to be silenced by the government or punished merely for expressing one's own opinions. Freedom of speech also includes the right to control when and where to speak. Content scraping, in this context, therefore, violates this core principle. Although most free speech rights are focused on limitations on the government, in areas such as defamation and privacy, freedom of speech also serves as the legal framework regarding when an individual can take action against another individual or corporation. As such, an ethical (though perhaps not justiciable) consideration around the content scraping used to train major LLM models is that it infringes on the freedom of speech rights of those whose content has been swept into these training datasets.

Individual privacy has also been identified as a core value and key ethical consideration for both developers of AI systems and those that deploy them. Concerns over deployment apply equally for private and government adopters. Privacy is a core human right.[28] Intrusions into one's privacy impact personal life decisions and even if the intrusion is not sufficiently painful as to constitute harassment, it can still have a significant impact. Volitional privacy or the right not to be surveilled is fundamental to living a life free from governmental control. Increasingly, that same interest is being called for regarding the intrusion of corporate interests. The EU AI Act includes some of these targeting activities as unreasonable risks, while all other such activities

---

28 *See supra* § 5.2 and accompanying text.

are at least considered high risk. Even in the U.S., spheres of privacy under HIPAA, COPPA, and other regulations are growing as the need for protections of volitional privacy gain public support.

Both privacy and freedom of speech concerns are also present in the claim that the right of content attribution is a fundamental right that should be recognized under U.S. law. Presently framed as part of the tension involving copyright, the failure to recognize the right of attribution in U.S. copyright law has led to LLM developers being able to copy the voice, tone, and publications of authors and artists without their consent. Despite the strong outcry against the use of an author's work or a creative artist's material, the lack of underlying legal protections make these arguments ethical complaints rather than legal causes of action. As detailed in § 4.3, the rights protected by Tennessee and California as rights of publicity and detailed in the Copyright Office Digital Replicas Report, this gap is a longstanding limitation on U.S. law which is magnified through the exploitation in LLM output.

Creative workers are just one category of the workforce impacted by AI. As noted in § 2.1.3, there are significant opportunities to use AI systems to make labor safer and reduce reliance of people for mundane or repetitive tasks. AI systems can expand efficiency and increase general wealth. These benefits, however, are unlikely to be evenly distributed either across the globe or within a particular job site. The disparate impact raises serious ethical considerations that should be at the heart of both operational decisions and public policy implementation. If public policy and corporate planning ignore the individual human cost associated with the digital transformation of the workplace, significant labor unrest and social upheaval could follow.

The adoption of AI systems in both law enforcement and military endeavors also raise profound ethical concerns. By creating the potential to adopt continuous mass surveillance, new technology has changed the relationship between the state and its citizens. The very existence of this capacity—even if not deployed—needs to be explicitly addressed and transparently managed. In the competing regions of the world, governments are reacting quite differently to the power afforded by predictive AI tools and expanded monitoring. In the U.S., the U.S. Supreme Court has addressed some of these concerns by invoking Fourth Amendment protections. However, its decisions have generally been narrow in scope, leaving many emerging technologies unaddressed and raising uncertainty around future legal treatment. Outside the Fourth Amendment's purview, even fewer safeguards exist, posing challenges for citizens' privacy rights in an era of rapid technological advancement.

The adoption of autonomous systems for law enforcement and military use add even greater concerns regarding the moral choices being made. Here the questions focus on both the choice to implement the technologies and the decisions that must be made each time such a system is deployed as part of the use of force. Whether the force is applied as part of an arrest or part of a military action, each deployment becomes its own ethical crisis. Analysists broadly agree on the importance of human input and design choice to maintain a human-in-the-loop decision making model. Many, however, caution that the very efficiency of automated systems make it harder and harder for the human to override the system at moments of crisis. Unless systems rely primarily on humans, it becomes far too easy for the people who play the role of the human-in-the-loop to trust and deploy rather than to use independent judgment. As noted in the context of driving safety, this becomes even more true if the human operator is only asked to intervene in moments of crisis.

Finally, the ultimate ethical consideration should be an assessment of the cumulative effect of the changes created by AI systems, particularly when those systems operate as planned. Using technology to improve the lives of the public, reduce poverty and decrease workplace accidents are generally unassailable social benefits. Although the transition from the pre-industrial to industrial economy was highly contentious and disruptive, the change ultimately brought such benefits. The internet age has been equally disruptive in its own way, but again the consensus is likely that the overall benefits outweigh the costs. To the extent that the technologies involved in AI systems are as disruptive as the internet—or perhaps the automobile—then there should be some attention paid to the social costs of the aggregate consequences in addition to the specific individual consequences in particular fields or regarding specific AI systems.

§ 9.3 CONSIDERATIONS FOR BUSINESS ADOPTION

§ 9.3.1 INTELLECTUAL PROPERTY RIGHTS

Intellectual property considerations have taken center stage in the development of generative AI, primarily because producers of AI-generated content cannot receive copyright protection for their output, nor can producers of AI-generated inventions receive patent protection for their creations. In most industries, the exclusivity provided by copyright and patent protection provide businesses with the potential to earn revenues high enough to attract capital investments and support product development and applied research. The lack of copyright and patent protection means that producers of AI-based works must rely on other strategies for success.

Intellectual property also remains at the forefront due to the uncertainty surrounding the use of unlicensed training data to create LLMs. While there is an ever-increasing number of licensing agreements between content owners and LLMs, many of the foundational models were trained on data scraped from the internet without authorization. To the extent that some of these actions were unlawful reproductions and adaptions of the content, there is significant potential liability for the copyright infringement. Both because of the surrounding uncertainty and the economic scale of the scraping, there is also increased pressure for a resolution of this conflict through congressional action rather than the protracted legal process of the dozens of lawsuits that are making their way through federal courts at present.

In addition to copyright and patent concerns, the ethical issues discussed above have led the Copyright Office and members of Congress to recommend expanding the law to add federal protections for rights of publicity, at least regarding digital replicas, if not more broadly. Shifting publicity rights from a state law protection regime to a federal statute has the potential to simplify or at least clarify the law. At the time this Nutshell is being written, however, no new law has been passed. Unlike the adoption of preemptive, national laws, the ongoing discussions and legislative process surrounding such laws add to uncertainty and unpredictability, which in turn raise costs for businesses.

Corporate strategies almost always include a focus on trademarks and brand strategy, but in industries with limited copyright protection, trademark strategies tend to dominate. As a result, businesses that rely on the content of chatbots or AI-based content are likely to pivot to greater investments around their brand strategy as a focal point for differentiation.

Similarly, for companies without strong patent portfolios, their technological and strategic differentiators are usually protected through trade secrets. The same is likely to be true among AI developers. At least some of the lack of transparency surrounding AI models, training, and algorithmic weighting is tied to the need to protect the commercial advantage of these systems, and the steps necessary to protect trade secrets require companies to keep such information confidential.

This is not to suggest that both developers and deployers of AI systems are precluded from utilizing patents or copyrights. AI systems can be part of the innovative process, provided the use of AI falls within the patent office guidelines for such use. Authored works that contain AI-generated content remain within the scope of copyright law, provided that the registration disclaims those portions of the work that were not created by the author—a requirement that applies equally to incorporation of third-party content.

There are many other roles for AI that are outside of authorship or inventorship, and AI systems will be quite useful in supporting the creation of protected works in this manner. As a result, AI is likely to continue to support the creative process of authors and inventors, helping to automate noncreative tasks and support overall growth of authorship and inventorship.

§ 9.3.2 BUSINESS ADOPTION OF AI SYSTEMS

As stated throughout, AI has become ubiquitous in many services and for many sectors. As it becomes part of the general business landscape, it tends to stop being identified as AI and flagged for special consideration. Predictive AI systems help reduce credit card fraud, run smart cities, improve the efficiency of the power grid, assist with academic enrollment, drive social media and online digital marketing, and a nearly infinite list of other products and services that have some machine learning or algorithmic decision-making as part of the process. When a business contracts with another company that uses one or more of these technologies, it rarely identifies that particular technology or third-party vendor in the contracts that establish those relationships.

At the same time, many of the uses for AI are relatively new, less well tested, or less reliant on human stakeholders for the final decisions involving the decision-making outcomes. Modern AI is shifting from providing its users recommendations to systems where the AI outcome is at least presumptively the final answer. AI-enabled chatbots, for example, speak directly to consumers. Hallucinations and wrong answers may be caught, but only after the fact.

Given the growth of AI both in its ubiquity and in its priority, therefore businesses that adopt AI systems or that contract with vendors providing AI solutions should be mindful of key considerations when adopting those programs. It is not enough to avoid being Rite Aid.[29] Companies need to have established policies in place to adopt and deploy AI successfully. As described in § 6.3.2, companies must understand how their vendors undertake to develop their AI systems.

---

29 *See supra* §§ 2.2.1, 6.2.1.

- **Data:** What risks are associated with the source of the vendors' training data. Will a company seeking to deploy an AI system inherent problems because the vendor used data without authorization? Does the agreement with that vendor include sufficient representations and warranties as to the appropriateness of the training data, indemnifications for liability that might arise from the use of that training data, and ongoing assurances that these obligations will continue for the life of the agreement.

- **Security, integrity, and resilience:** AI agreements often involve integration of technologies. Companies acquiring AI systems must ensure that vendors do not create cybersecurity risks, open backdoors, or weaken the security footprint of the company. Information shared between the companies must be protected from third-party theft, destruction, and manipulation.

- **Risk management:** The NIST framework provides a series of steps that a company licensing AI should consider as well as a due diligence checklist to be used to make sure that the company providing the AI system has itself been in compliance. As already stated, any system should be "valid and reliable, safe, secure and resilient, accountable and transparent, explainable and interpretable, privacy-enhanced, and fair with harmful bias managed."[30]

- **Known misuse:** Although operating a reliable, safe, and secure system includes taking steps to identify known misuses that are likely to occur, deployers have an additional duty to take this obligation into account. Developers of AI systems are often creating them for a wide range of customers and use cases. The company licensing and deploying the AI system is likely in a much better position to understand how its customers might use the service and the ways in which its customers might try to circumvent safeguards and misuse the product and service. Known misuses are often prohibited by end user license agreements, but these contracts do little unless the company that required the agreement is also willing to enforce it to stop misuse. Many of the potential misuses fall into the category of threats to individuals, and these concerns should take special priority, along with threats to critical infrastructure and to security.

In many industries, a three-step strategy has been developed to establish privacy and security standards. This approach can also be effectively used when vetting potential vendors and entering into agreements with those vendors. The three levels

---

30 AI RMF 1.0, *supra* ch. 6 note 1, at 12. *See supra* § 6.1.2 and accompanying text.

refer to physical, administrative, and technical controls. Companies should utilize checklists to evaluate the costs, benefits, and risks of working with a vendor, particularly regarding the physical access and control implications of the relationship.

Before entering into an agreement, both parties must ensure that these obligations can be met. Once an agreement is in place, it is crucial for both parties to monitor the relationship to ensure that ongoing obligations continue to be met throughout the lifespan of the agreement.

- **Physical management:** Some working relationships require that people gain access to otherwise secure facilities or that facilities that originally did not have sophisticated security now require heightened protection. In some cases, such as when deploying web-based services, there may be little physical interaction. In examples involving robotics or autonomous equipment, physical interactions may predominate the relationship. Physical interactions also include access by technicians and staff that requires changes to control over building access and similar needs.

- **Technical management:** Originally this focused on the kinds of security needed to protect a system and how the security requirements changed if confidential or highly protected information became available. More generally, however, the technical controls can apply to all the software and digital content tools and systems. These systems need to operate together, they need to be kept updated and patched. They need to be monitored for new vulnerabilities. And they need to be managed so that all technical safeguards and systems operate in the manner intended at the level of efficiency agreed upon among the parties.

- **Administrative management:** The administrative controls relate to the internal procedures, protocols, and operational obligations to meet the expectations of the contractual agreements and related privacy, security, regulatory, and contractual compliance required under the contract. In many ways, administrative controls are the hardest of the three spheres to identify and maintain. The administrative controls include such duties as having CEO or board level responsibility for compliance with various regulations and contractual duties. They should include obligations for continuous training and staff educational programs. They likely include ongoing duties to stay abreast and compliant with evolving legal and regulatory requirements. The administrative requirements focus on the internal operation of both parties to the contract and their internal duties to keep the other party to the agreement protected from unreasonable or unnecessary risks.

Companies adopting cutting-edge AI systems need to identify the risks and limitations associated with those technologies. As AI technology matures, industry norms typically help ensure that the risks become better managed over time and theoretical concerns either turn into practical issues that can be managed, or time proves them sufficiently unlikely as to require resources. Vendors that use disclaimers to absolve themselves of any responsibility for the use of a product or service are likely telling the purchaser that the product should not be trusted. This implicit advice should be followed and disclaimed products should be avoided.

Companies also need to understand how vendors intend their products to be used and ensure that they do not adopt them in ways that circumvent safety, security, or consumer protection safeguards. Not only is this a sound, reasonable practice, but intentionally bypassing safety measures could lead to a finding that the company deploying the system engaged in an unfair or deceptive manner under the FTC Act.

Finally, as noted by the FTC,[31] any adoption strategy should include administrative controls related to the plan for training and overseeing employees. Ongoing training is essential for any system having to do with privacy, security, or confidentiality. It is equally important for fraud prevention and consumer protection. Implementing a robust training program is one of the key administrative practices and a company should have

[31] FTC v. Rite Aid (2023 Complaint), *supra* ch. 2 note 68 at ¶ 65; § 6.2.1, *supra* and accompanying text.

a plan to create and operate its training program before it undertakes to adopt a new technology.

§ 9.3.3 CONSIDERATIONS FOR COMPETING STAKEHOLDERS

Another approach for businesses seeking to adopt new AI technologies and strategies is to consider that impact of the decision from the viewpoint of each of the company's stakeholders. The stakeholders include the CEO and internal leadership; the board of directors; the departments responsible for implementing the technology; shareholders—whether public or private; employees; customers; community stakeholders—particularly if the company is a major source of economic stability in the local economy; and the other member of any trade association to which the company belongs, otherwise known as its competitors.

From the perspective of a CEO, new AI technologies are beneficial to the extent that they provide a market advantage for the company's revenue and profits, or to the extent that the tools increase efficiency or lower costs. Since there are often up front expenses, the questions will include whether an investment in new AI technology will be recoupable in a reasonable amount of time.

In addition, however, there may be opportunities to raise share price or otherwise promote the perceived value of the product or the company if it is seen as a market leader regarding new technologies. Taken to extreme, the is the AI washing that the FTC and SEC have warned against. If the communication about the AI adoption is accurate, however, then there may be a benefit to adoption because of perceived value by the market which is separate from the direct cost-benefit analysis. The CEO's cost-benefit analysis also includes valuing the risk associated with the adoption and deployment of the technology. Risk, however, is often quite challenging for people to accurately value, so the risk calculations may not be as quantifiable as other considerations.

The corporate board of directors have interests similar to those of the CEO but boards operate collectively on broader policy issues than do corporate executive leadership. Increasingly, however, boards of public companies have SEC mandated compliance and oversight obligations. For the board, the key questions become those of transparency and governance. The board must know if the potential risk is sufficiently material to be included in public disclosure filings and whether the decision to adopt the technology aligns with the overall business strategy. The board's interest is typically implicated only when the risk or the opportunity becomes a significant part of the budget or operation of the enterprise.

The unit responsible for implementing the AI strategy has an entirely different set of considerations. The head of that department will wonder if there are sufficient resources, including time and staff, to fully operationalize the new tools and how the deployment of the AI system will impact other systems. The use of a new solution may be very beneficial to one department while creating a significant set of new demands on other departments. A good implementation plan should consider how the organized department will react to the adoption of the AI system and have the necessary resources and training to use the AI service in the manner envisioned by the CEO.

Shareholders typically focus on return in investment. As such, their interests should align with the board and the corporate CEO, but shareholders also want companies to be run efficiently. Some shareholders invest in strategies that go beyond mere profitability to look at environmental, social, and governance (ESG) strategies. For companies with a strong ESG approach, the CEO and board must also look at the AI strategy as part of these additional concerns. In some sectors, the environmental and power issues will also inform decision-making.[32]

In contrast to the CEO, board members, and shareholders, there is a fundamentally distinct set of considerations for the employees and community stakeholders. Employees, as has been explored in § 2.1.3, have a very strong interest in keeping their jobs and not being eliminated through automation. Although employees may be pleased with new tools that reduce health and safety risks, as a general matter, they do not want to lose jobs to new technologies. In communities where the company represents employment for a significant percentage of the community's workforce, layoffs triggered by

---

[32] *See* § 2, *supra*.

extensive automation can have a devasting economic impact on the broader economy of the region. Individual employees have little voice in such decisions but in labor disputes involving collective bargaining agreements with organized labor, limitations on AI has become an increasingly central part of the labor negotiations.[33]

The company customers represent the last stakeholder group. Customers want efficiency, improved service, and the cost savings of AI systems passed along in the form of better products and services offered at lower prices. Some AI systems deliver on all these promises while many others benefit the customers by achieving at least some of these goals.

At the same time, control over customer information is often a cost associated with AI services, and customers are rarely provided meaningful choices on whether to give up their personal in exchange for these benefits. In other cases, the increased profits come at the expense of the customers, enabling companies to extract higher prices by eliminating lower priced alternatives.

In addition, the use of chatbots and other forms of interaction are being adopted with the claim of improved customer service, when in reality, the text boxes merely stand as alternatives to the hated automated phone networks that require consumers to agree to the recording of their phone call, to listen to long menus of unnecessary options, and to wait

---

[33] *See* § 2.1.3, *supra*.

interminably before the company offers the relief of a human operator. While text boxes are much better than the dreaded automated voice prompt, customers are rarely given the option to speak with a knowledgeable customer service employee who has the authority to actually solve the customer's problems. When the answer is that AI is better, the question should be asked: better than what?

Customers should be at the center of all business decisions, but when it comes to operational considerations such as the adoption of AI automation, they are often left out of the analysis. Fortunately, customers can usually vote with their feet and their pocketbooks. Companies who ignore them eventually come to regret it. Smart CEOs start by listening to their customers.

§ 9.4 EXISTENTIAL CONSIDERATIONS

In his book *Moral Machine: Teaching Robots Right from Wrong*, Dr. Wendell Wallach poses a series of questions about the development of "moral agents," machines that make autonomous decisions and are tasked with making those decisions in an ethical or moral manner.[34] Written in in 2008, Dr. Wallach asked the question, "[d]oes humanity really want computers making morally important decisions? Many philosophers of technology have warned about humans abdicating responsibility to machines."[35] With the rapid evolution of AI systems, however, that

---

[34] *See* WENDELL WALLACH & COLIN ALLEN, MORAL MACHINES: TEACHING ROBOTS RIGHT FROM WRONG (2008).

[35] *Id.* at 6.

question has largely been pushed to the side in the rush to integrate AI across products and services. Stepping back from the potentially irrational exuberance surrounding AI deployment, policy makers and corporate strategists should perhaps be considering some of these questions.

In a speech to award the Kavli Prizes for Scientific Achievement Dr. Stuart Russel offered a rather sobering warning:

> For 80 years, we have been trying to create superhuman machines. What if we succeed? How can we retain power, forever, over entities far more powerful than ourselves?
>
> Alan Turing, the founder of computer science, considered this question in 1951 and concluded that "we should have to expect the machines to take control." Hurt, in other words, and lots of it.
>
> The argument is simple enough: AI systems are designed to pursue objectives, and if their objectives are misaligned with those of humanity, we lose.
>
> On the other hand, perfectly aligning the objectives seems impossible, as you soon find out if a genie grants you three wishes. Your third wish is always "Please undo the first two wishes! I've ruined the universe." . . .
>
> One can draw a lesson from this for science more generally. Like the AI systems, we scientists should be humble. We need to learn from humanity more about what humanity wants and

> doesn't want. Not from corporations, who normally seek to maximize profit, nor from governments, who sometimes want methods of control and destruction, but instead from human beings.[36]

Ethical questions cannot and should not be divorced from broader policy and strategic implications. In addition to asking what happens if a strategy fails, it is essential to ask the question, "what happens if we succeed?"

As a Nutshell, this text does not dwell on the generation of AI systems that may someday gain not just superintelligence but also self-awareness. Nonetheless, it is not hard to speculate that there may be a self-driving car in the future that declines to drive its owner to the liquor store because the car recognizes the owner' struggles with alcoholism or the grocery store app that removes cookies and ice cream from the shopping list "for the buyer's own good." "Should a good multi-purpose robot hold open a door for a stranger, even if this means a delay for the robot's owner?"[37] Questions or AI ethics can include both the smallest and largest of decisions.

These hypothetical scenarios are far less dangerous than the apocalyptic singularity of *Terminator*, *Metropolis*, or *Wall-E*, but they illustrate

---

[36] Stuart J. Russell, *What Will Happen if we Succeed with Artificial Intelligence?*, SCIENCENORWAY (Sept. 5, 2024), https://www.sciencenorway.no/artificial-intelligence-opinion-researchers-zone/what-will-happen-if-we-succeed-with-artificial-intelligence/2403713.

[37] WALLACH & ALLEN, *supra* note 34 at 16.

that current planning only extends to the most incremental development of AI. Far less is being done to consider the developments that follow.

In her 1831 introduction to *Frankenstein*, Mary Shelley explained the image that shaped her writing of the book:

> I saw the pale student of unhallowed arts kneeling beside the thing he had put together. I saw the hideous phantasm of a man stretched out, and then, on the working of some powerful engine, show signs of life, and stir with an uneasy, half vital motion. Frightful must it be; for supremely frightful would be the effect of any human endeavour to mock the stupendous mechanism of the Creator of the world. His success would terrify the artist; he would rush away from his odious handywork, horror-stricken.[38]

Knowing the future is unknowable offers few tools for planning. Neither that which G-d forbids, or in the case of Prometheus, the Pantheon of Gods prohibit serves as guidance for the development of modern technology or for regulatory policy.

If neither morality nor religion can provide the answer, where should regulators turn?

Legal regimes focus less on morality and more on the minimization of harm. Section 2.2.1 describes the

[38] Mary Shelley, *Introduction to Frankenstein* (1831), BRANKENBOOK (June 17, 2019), https://www.frankenbook.org/pub/ai6okwlz/release/1.

Learned Hand formula to manage uncertainty as a workable strategy to assess and address the risks caused by AI systems. In adopting this approach, regulators, developers, and deployers must look at all known risks. To the extent possible, however, they must also extrapolate to tease out the unknown unknowns—risks that can only be extrapolated or understood by analogy.[39] "Unknown unknowns (unexpected or unforeseeable conditions), which pose a potentially greater risk simply because they cannot be anticipated based on past experience or investigation. . . . [U]nknown unknowns are phenomena which cannot be expected because there has been no prior experience or theoretical basis for expecting the phenomena."[40]

The concept of the singularity should be considered a known risk, but the manner in which it might occur remains an unknown unknown. Despite fictional portrayals of this subject, there are few useful tools to recognize when human society has come to rely too heavily on AI systems.

In other areas, there are warnings. As noted in § 2.3, the increased reliance on synthetic media exacerbates the social media phenomenon that audiences get their news and information from services that extract headline and short snippets

---

[39] *See There are Unknown Unknowns*, WIKIPEDIA, https://en.wikipedia.org/wiki/There_are_unknown_unknowns (last visited Feb. 16, 2025).

[40] *Id.* quoting *Phase V: Waste Disposal*, PROCEEDINGS OF THE BRITISH COLUMBIA ROYAL COMMISSION OF INQUIRY INTO URANIUM MINING (1979) (Statement of Evidence of E. D'Appolonia, D'Appolonia Consulting Engineers).

from original sources rather than directing the public to those sources. This has eroded the revenue streams for original journalism with the result that newspapers struggle to remain profitable, and the scope of investigative journalism has been disappearing.

Generative AI can speed up mundane tasks and add significant efficiency, particularly when used by experts in their fields. For novices, however, who lack the knowledge to evaluate the generative AI content, the ease of use risks undermining the novice users' learning and development.

Hobbyists lament that the sophisticated electronics of modern cars make them difficult to modify, restore, or rebuild. Similarly, much of the economy and society relies on smart electronics with computer chips that are not designed for reuse or repurposing. A growing homestead movement has emerged in response, rejecting modern technology and the values associated with a highly technological lifestyle.[41] Both in Isaac Asimov's fictional works and

---

[41] *See* Bruce Rutter, *Modern Homesteading: The Growing Movement for More Self-sufficient and Sustainable Lives*, BEST BEES (Aug. 21, 2024), https://bestbees.com/all-about-homesteading/.

> Over the past three decades, a number of factors have combined to create a new wave of homesteading:
>
> - The growing environmental movement
> - The high cost of urban life, especially in cities such as Boston, New York, San Francisco, and Seattle
> - The exploitative approach so many businesses take towards their employees and the burn-out that has resulted

in Dr. Wallach's philosophical works, the authors speculated at the potential for the public to reject smart robots and similar systems as threats to the public's lifestyle and autonomy.[42]

The question for regulators and developers of AI systems is not to answer these imponderable questions. The obligation is to adopt a framework to take them into account.

Section 2.2.1 offers three considerations to help transform the existential challenges into a recognizable approach to risk management. The first is the identification of risk mitigation costs developed by Learned Hand. Where the understanding of a risk can be understood, even generally, then some calculation of the likelihood of that risk and the cost of the steps to mitigate that risk can be balanced. The EU AI's list of unacceptable risk uses and high-risk uses reflects this kind of assessment at the broadest level. The NIST framework does not explicitly call for mathematical modeling, but the governance and management obligations can be met most effectively by following this model.

Second, the Learned Hand formula was developed in the context of litigation involving the known participants in an accident, and often applied retrospectively. When applied prospectively, the

---

- Disaffection with institutions and their inability to enact needed change
- Revulsion over the state of the world and a desire to withdraw from it

42 *See* WALLACH & ALLEN, *supra* note 34 at 3–5.

confidence of the weighting of risks and costs is inevitably more speculative. Comparisons of analogous situations and broader considerations must therefore be included to understand how to on both the known knowns and the unknown knowns. This is also an opportunity for broader societal and ethical considerations to be introduced into the evaluation. For regulators who feel incorporating ethics is too abstract, incorporating public opinion may provide a suitable alternative.

Third, the Learned Hand formula must be expanded to take into account the tragedy of the commons as it applies to AI systems. The costs of harm created when AI systems fail, become misused, or succeed too well may not fall in the developer of that system. The costs may fall on those deploying the system, individuals harmed by the failures, or on the public. The tragedy of the commons is exacerbated by courts that enforce broad immunity provisions, arbitration clauses, and restrictions on class action litigation buried in the service's terms of service. Worse, since the companies helping develop AI systems include Microsoft, Google, and Apple, virtually every person who uses a computer or smartphone is obligated to enter into such an agreement. In other words, the standardized terms of service from these three companies alone has created a new tragedy of the commons that largely restricts the judicial system from playing its constitutional and historical role.

Finally, when addressing both questions of ethics and questions of risk management, the BATNA or

BAHOE should be used to provide a second framework to be juxtaposed against that of the Learned Hand formula. The question regarding the eventual adoption of self-driving vehicles, for example, should not just ask the level of risk these vehicles pose on the roads, the analysis should compare these vehicles to the risks that already exist on the roads. There must be some number that represents a reduction in fatalities and accidents, that if self-driving vehicles could improve road safety, then permitting those vehicles becomes an imperative. If the improvement is great enough, then at some point regulators would need to start asking whether human-driven cars should still be permitted.

The question of how to assess self-driving cars presents a known challenge, whereas the idea of eliminating human drivers introduces a series of unknown unknowns. Would a society with only self-driving cars have sufficient resilience in the event of natural disasters? Would such a society improve access for all, or would it increase historical inequities? Would such a society continue to emphasize personal vehicle ownership or would a community with only self-driving cars shift away from ownership to robotaxis and robobuses? If such a change occurred, it could influence the design of homes and transform transportation around large events. The list of unknowns and resulting questions becomes increasingly speculative and unconstrained.

The scale of these unknown unknowns should not deter developers, deployers, regulators, or the public from considering these possibilities. Addressing existential threats requires exploring and breaking them down into manageable components. In this way, at least some of the challenges can be addressed, making the broader question a bit less daunting.

The law and regulation of AI systems is quite daunting. There are few case law decisions, and most of the enforcement for the laws is rather speculative. The science, the technology, the law, and the uses cases are all changing rapidly. Nonetheless, stakeholders have a sufficient number of known challenges to begin addressing the problems facing society today and to anticipate future issues.

Prometheus stole fire—the essence of creativity and knowledge—and gave it to mankind. Angered, Zeus, the king of the Greek Pantheon, gave Pandora a jar as a wedding present. When she opened it, she released all the evils, sorrows, and miseries of the world. She tried to close it, but it was too late.[43] AI may represent the fire gifted by Prometheus or the miseries released by Pandora. Even then, as the story of Pandora was retold, she found one last item in the bottom of her jar. She found hope.[44]

As AI systems evolve and improve, they will bring many changes, some filled with promise and others with sorrows. The role of lawyers, if nothing else, is to help preserve hope.

---

43 Rittika Dhar, *Pandora's Box: The Myth Behind the Popular Idiom*, HISTORY COOPERATIVE (May 22, 2024), https://historycooperative.org/pandoras-box/.

44 *See id.*

ABBREVIATIONS AND ACRONYMS

A&R—Artists and Repertoire

ADA—Americans with Disabilities Act

ADEA—Age Discrimination in Employment Act

AEDT—Automated Employment Decision Tool

AGI—Artificial General Intelligence

AI RMF 1.0—AI Risk Management Framework

AI RMF 2.0—Artificial Intelligence Risk Management Framework: Generative Artificial Intelligence Profile

AIDA—Artificial Intelligence and Data Act

BAH—Bah [humbug], humans are better anyway

BAHOE—Best Alternative to Human-Only Endeavors

BATNA—Best Alternative to a Negotiated Agreement

BERT—Bidirectional Encoder Representations from Transformers

BIPA—Biometric Information Privacy Act

B.O.T. Act—Bolstering Online Transparency Act

CBP—Customs and Border Protection

CCD COE—Cooperative Cyber Defense Center of Excellence

CCPA—California Consumer Privacy Agency

CJEU—Court of Justice of the European Union

CNIPA—People's Republic of China (PRC) National Intellectual Property Administration

Co-bots—Bots Collaborating with Human Workers

CPIC—Canadian Police Information Centre

CPS—Cyber-Physical Systems / Core Platform Services

CSLI—Cell Site Location Information

CTRL—Conditional Transformer Language Model

CAC—Cyberspace Administration of China

CFIUS—Committee on Foreign Investment in the United States

CFPB—Consumer Financial Protection Bureau

DEA—Drug Enforcement Administration

DNDD—De Novo Drug Design

DHS—Department of Homeland Security

DMA—E.U. Digital Markets Act

DOJ—Department of Justice

DSA—Digital Services Act

DTSA—Defend Trade Secrets Act

DPA—Defense Production Act

DARPA—Defense Advanced Research Projects Agency

ELVIS Act—Ensuring Likeness Voice and Image Security Act

ECPA—Electronic Communications Privacy Act of 1986

EPO—European Patent Office

EEOC—Equal Employment Opportunity Commission

ESG—Environmental, Social, and Governance

EU—European Union

EU AI Act—Artificial Intelligence Act

FAA—Federal Aviation Administration

FBI—Federal Bureau of Investigation

FFLs—Federal Firearms Licensees

FTC—Federal Trade Commission

GANs—Generative Adversarial Networks

GAI—Generative AI

GLBA—Gramm-Leach-Bliley Act of 1998

GMMs—Gaussian Mixture Models

G20—Group of 20

G7—Group of Seven

GDPR—E.U. General Data Protection Regulation

GPT—Generative Pre-Trained Transformer

HAI—Human-Centered AI

HIPAA—Health Insurance Portability and Accountability Act of 1996

HITECH—Health Information Technology for Economic and Clinical Health Act

HTML—hypertext markup language

IAFIS—Integrated Automated Fingerprint Identification System

IaaS—Large AI Models as Services

IMF—International Monetary Fund

IP—intellectual property

IP5—consortium of patent offices from the People's Republic of China (PRC) National Intellectual Property Administration (CNIPA), the European Patent Office (EPO), the Japan Patent Office (JPO), the Korean Intellectual Property Office (KIPO), and the United States Patent & Trademark Office (USPTO)

ISP—Internet Service Provider

IT—information technology

ITU—International Telecommunications Union

JPO—Japan Patent Office

KIPO—Korean Intellectual Property Office

LEEP—Law Enforcement Enterprise Portal

LLM—Large Language Model

LAWS—Lethal Autonomous Weapons Systems

LOAC—Law of Armed Conflict

LSC—Legal Services Corporation

Mk-24—Mark 24 "Fido" acoustic homing torpedo

ML—Machine Learning

NCEs—New Chemical Entities

NCIC—National Crime Information Center

N-DEx—National Data Exchange

NHTSA—National Highway Traffic Safety Administration

NICS—National Instant Criminal Background Check System

NIL—Name, Image, and Likeness

NIST—National Institute of Standards and Technology

Nlets—International Justice and Public Safety Network

NLP—Natural Language Processing

OMB—Office of Management and Budget

PIPEDA—Personal Information Protection and Electronic Documents Act

PHI—Protected Health Information

PRC—People's Republic of China

RAG—Retrieval-Augmented Generation

RAI—Responsible AI

RBI—Remote Biometric Identification

RISSNET—Regional Information Sharing Systems Network

SDGs—Sustainable Development Goals

SCA—Stored Communications Act

SEC—Securities and Exchange Commission

TCP/IP—Transmission Control Protocol/Internet Protocol

Title VII—Title VII of the Civil Rights Act of 1964

USPS—United States Patent and Trademark Office

USPTO—United States Patent & Trademark Office

VR—virtual reality

W3C—World Wide Web Consortium

WCAG—Web Content Accessibility Guidelines

INDEX

References are to Pages
